Declarative Programming: A High-Level Approach to Simplified Logic and Readability

By Theophilus Edet

Theophilus Edet

 theo.edet@comprequestseries.com

 facebook.com/theoedet

 twitter.com/TheophilusEdet

 Instagram.com/edettheophilus

Table of Contents

Preface

In an era where software complexity is continuously increasing, programming paradigms must evolve to ensure that developers can write code that is both efficient and maintainable. Declarative programming offers an alternative to traditional imperative approaches, allowing developers to focus on describing what a program should accomplish rather than dictating how it should execute. This book, *Declarative Programming: A High-Level Approach to Simplified Logic and Readability*, explores the power of declarative paradigms and their application across multiple domains, equipping readers with the skills to write cleaner, more efficient, and more predictable software.

The Need for Declarative Programming

Over the decades, imperative programming has dominated software development, with its explicit control structures, mutable state, and step-by-step execution. While this approach is powerful, it often leads to code that is difficult to debug, maintain, and scale. Declarative programming addresses these challenges by emphasizing **clarity, expressiveness, and predictability**. Instead of focusing on the intricate details of execution, declarative paradigms shift the focus to defining rules, transformations, and relationships, leading to software that is easier to reason about and optimize.

From functional programming in Haskell and F# to rule-based logic programming in Prolog and SQL's expressive data querying, declarative programming manifests in many forms. By exploring these diverse approaches, this book aims to provide a unified perspective on how declarative programming enhances productivity, scalability, and correctness in software systems.

Structure of the Book

To provide a comprehensive understanding, this book is structured into **six well-defined parts**, each focusing on a critical aspect of declarative programming:

- **Fundamentals of Declarative Programming** establishes the core concepts, differentiating declarative from imperative approaches and laying the groundwork for understanding functional, rule-based, and constraint-driven paradigms.

- **Examples and Applications of Declarative Programming** demonstrates how declarative principles are applied in real-world scenarios, including web development, artificial intelligence, and data processing.

- **Programming Language Support for Declarative Programming** delves into how various programming languages, including Python, Haskell, JavaScript, and C#, incorporate declarative constructs.

- **Algorithm and Data Structure Support for Declarative Programming** examines how declarative techniques influence computational efficiency through SAT solvers, query optimization, and pattern matching.

- **Design Patterns and Real-World Case Studies in Declarative Programming** explores reusable design patterns and showcases industry case studies where declarative approaches excel.

- **Research Directions in Declarative Programming** looks ahead to the future of declarative paradigms, discussing emerging trends in AI, quantum computing, cybersecurity, and theoretical advancements.

Who Should Read This Book?

This book is designed for **software engineers, researchers, and students** seeking to deepen their understanding of declarative programming. Whether you are an experienced developer looking to expand your knowledge of functional and logic-based paradigms or a beginner eager to explore new ways of structuring code, this book provides a structured and practical guide to declarative approaches.

Declarative programming is not just a niche paradigm; it is a fundamental shift in how software can be written and optimized. By mastering declarative approaches, developers can **write more robust, scalable, and maintainable applications**. This book aims to equip readers with the theoretical foundations and practical tools to embrace declarative programming as a core methodology for modern software development.

Theophilus Edet

Declarative Programming: A High-Level Approach to Simplified Logic and Readability

Understanding Declarative Programming

Declarative programming represents a paradigm shift in software development, focusing on expressing logic without explicitly detailing control flow. Unlike imperative programming, where developers write step-by-step instructions, declarative programming emphasizes describing the desired outcome. This high-level approach allows for more readable, maintainable, and efficient code, making it an essential tool for modern software development. This book provides a structured, comprehensive guide to understanding declarative programming, its theoretical foundations, real-world applications, language support, and emerging trends.

Structure of the Book

This book is divided into six well-defined parts, each offering an in-depth exploration of declarative programming from foundational concepts to advanced applications. The goal is to provide both theoretical and practical knowledge, ensuring readers gain a strong command of declarative paradigms and their significance in contemporary programming.

Part 1: Fundamentals of Declarative Programming

The first part introduces the core principles of declarative programming, setting the stage for deeper exploration. It examines the historical evolution of the paradigm, contrasting it with imperative programming. By exploring readability, maintainability, and expressiveness, this section highlights the advantages of declarative programming while acknowledging its trade-offs. It delves into key concepts such as functions, rules, constraints, and side effects, explaining how declarative programming manages state without introducing unnecessary complexity. Finally, the part explores the mathematical foundations of declarative programming, including lambda calculus, predicate logic, and category theory, to provide a solid theoretical base.

Part 2: Examples and Applications of Declarative Programming

Building on foundational knowledge, this part showcases real-world applications of declarative programming. It covers functional programming principles and techniques, demonstrating their effectiveness in data transformation and error handling. The part then explores the role of declarative programming in artificial intelligence, including logic programming and automated theorem proving. Web development is another key area covered, where declarative frameworks simplify UI management and serverless computing. The book also explains declarative data querying techniques, highlighting SQL and NoSQL optimizations, and concludes with an exploration of reactive programming models that enhance scalability and responsiveness.

Part 3: Programming Language Support for Declarative Programming

This part explores declarative programming across multiple languages, demonstrating how different ecosystems support the paradigm. It covers functional constructs in C#, F#, and JavaScript, showcasing LINQ, expression trees, and state management. The discussion extends to Elixir and Go, illustrating pattern matching and concurrency models. Haskell and XSLT are examined for their pure functional and declarative data processing capabilities. Python's declarative features, such as list comprehensions and meta-programming, are analyzed alongside cross-language paradigms that highlight declarative interoperability.

Part 4: Algorithm and Data Structure Support for Declarative Programming

Declarative programming is underpinned by powerful algorithms and data structures. This part examines SAT solvers and logic resolution algorithms that enable constraint satisfaction and automated deduction. Query optimization techniques in SQL and distributed systems are explored, highlighting execution planning and indexing. The part also investigates abstract syntax trees (ASTs) and pattern-matching mechanisms that drive efficient declarative computations. Optimization strategies, such as memoization, lazy evaluation, and parallelism, further illustrate how declarative programming enhances computational efficiency.

Part 5: Design Patterns and Real-World Case Studies in Declarative Programming

This part transitions from theory to practice, demonstrating how declarative programming solves real-world problems. It covers common design patterns, including monads, functors, and streams, showing how they improve state management and composition. The discussion extends to machine learning, illustrating how declarative pipelines simplify model training and deployment. Large-scale systems benefit from declarative cloud infrastructure and event-driven architectures. Additionally, business applications leverage rule-based engines for automation. Industry case studies in web development, enterprise data processing, AI, and blockchain provide concrete examples of declarative programming in action. Finally, the part discusses challenges and best practices in debugging, performance optimization, and future-proofing declarative codebases.

Part 6: Research Directions in Declarative Programming

This final part explores the cutting edge of declarative programming research. It begins with advancements in functional and logic programming, examining innovations in parallel computing and theoretical models. The discussion extends to quantum computing, showcasing how declarative methods are shaping emerging quantum algorithms. The role of declarative programming in artificial intelligence is further explored, emphasizing explainable AI and logic-based machine learning. Security and cryptography are another focus, with discussions on policy-based security management and formal verification. The part concludes with theoretical advances, including category theory and domain-specific languages, and forecasts the future adoption of declarative programming.

Who Should Read This Book?

This book is designed for software engineers, researchers, and students seeking to deepen their understanding of declarative programming. Whether you are transitioning from imperative programming, exploring functional and logic paradigms, or looking to apply declarative techniques in your projects, this book offers valuable insights. By combining theoretical knowledge with practical applications, it equips readers with the skills needed to harness declarative programming for building robust, scalable, and maintainable software systems.

Declarative programming is revolutionizing software development by simplifying logic and enhancing readability. This book provides a structured roadmap to mastering the paradigm, from fundamental principles to cutting-edge research. By the end, readers will be well-equipped to implement declarative techniques in various domains, leveraging their advantages for modern, high-performance computing.

Part 1:

Fundamentals of Declarative Programming

Declarative programming represents a paradigm shift in software development, focusing on **describing what a program should accomplish** rather than specifying **how** it should execute. This part provides a strong conceptual foundation, differentiating declarative approaches from imperative ones while exploring their practical benefits and theoretical underpinnings. By understanding **functions, rules, constraints, and purity**, learners will be equipped with the core principles that drive declarative models. The part also delves into **mathematical logic**, which serves as the backbone of declarative languages, ensuring a rigorous basis for reasoning about computations.

Introduction to Declarative Programming

Declarative programming simplifies coding by expressing logic **without detailing control flow**. This module introduces **functional, logic, and rule-based paradigms**, demonstrating their significance in modern software development. It traces the **historical evolution** of declarative programming from **early logic systems to contemporary frameworks** like SQL, Prolog, and Haskell. A thorough comparison with imperative programming highlights **readability, maintainability, and correctness advantages**, setting the stage for deeper exploration of declarative methodologies.

Characteristics and Advantages

Declarative programming improves **code readability, maintainability, and reusability** by removing unnecessary complexity. This module emphasizes how declarative languages minimize **side effects**, enabling **predictable and deterministic execution**. It explains how **expressiveness and conciseness** lead to **more efficient development cycles** and fewer bugs. While some performance trade-offs exist, such as **potential execution overhead in functional languages**, these are often mitigated by **compiler optimizations and lazy evaluation techniques**. Learners will appreciate **how declarative models lead to more robust, scalable applications** across various domains.

Declarative vs. Imperative Paradigms

Understanding the key differences between **declarative and imperative paradigms** is crucial in software engineering. This module explores how declarative programming **abstracts control structures**, focusing on **what needs to be computed** rather than **how**. Code comparisons illustrate **the elegance of declarative syntax versus the verbosity of imperative logic**. Discussions cover **situational advantages**, guiding developers on when to **choose declarative approaches over imperative ones**. Additionally, the module introduces **hybrid programming models**, where declarative and imperative paradigms coexist, offering flexibility in solving complex problems.

Core Concepts: Functions, Rules, and Constraints

Declarative programming is built on **functions, rules, and constraints**, each defining **relationships between data elements**. This module explains **pure functions and recursion** in functional programming, showcasing their **predictability and immutability benefits**. It introduces **rule-based programming**, commonly found in **business rule engines and AI reasoning systems**. The concept of **logic constraints** is explored through constraint-solving techniques used in **optimization problems and declarative data processing**. Lastly, **constraint propagation**

mechanisms are discussed, demonstrating their application in systems requiring **automated reasoning and consistency enforcement**.

Understanding Side Effects and Purity

Side effects introduce **unpredictability in software**, making it harder to **reason about program behavior**. This module explains how declarative languages **manage state** while **preserving purity**. Learners will explore **pure and impure functions**, understanding why purity is desirable in functional programming. Concepts like **referential transparency** are introduced, showcasing how immutable state simplifies debugging. Finally, the module discusses **handling external interactions**, such as **I/O operations and database queries**, without violating the **core principles of declarative paradigms**.

Mathematical Foundations of Declarative Programming

Mathematics plays a crucial role in declarative programming, providing a **formal framework for reasoning about computations**. This module explores **lambda calculus**, the theoretical foundation of functional programming, and **predicate logic**, which underpins rule-based systems. Learners will gain insight into **category theory**, which influences modern type systems, ensuring **stronger correctness guarantees in software development**. Finally, **fixed-point theory** is introduced, explaining how recursive definitions and self-referential computations form the basis of **logic programming languages like Prolog**.

By mastering these fundamentals, learners will gain **a deep understanding of declarative principles**, enabling them to **write more expressive, maintainable, and mathematically rigorous code** across multiple programming domains.

Module 1:
Introduction to Declarative Programming

Declarative programming is a paradigm that allows developers to express *what* a program should accomplish rather than *how* to achieve it. Unlike imperative programming, which focuses on explicit control flow, declarative programming simplifies logic, enhances readability, and improves maintainability. This module introduces key declarative paradigms, their significance in modern computing, their historical evolution, and a comparative analysis with imperative programming. Understanding these foundational concepts will provide a solid grounding in declarative techniques, setting the stage for deeper explorations in subsequent modules.

Overview of Declarative Paradigms

Declarative programming encompasses various paradigms that prioritize high-level expressions of computation over step-by-step control flow. The most prominent paradigms include **functional programming**, which relies on pure functions and immutability; **logic programming**, where relationships and rules define computations; and **dataflow programming**, which models computations as the transformation of data through a network of operations. These paradigms share common traits such as abstraction, composability, and minimization of side effects. By shifting the focus from explicit commands to descriptive logic, declarative paradigms enable programmers to build scalable and predictable software systems with greater efficiency and clarity.

Importance of Declarative Programming

Declarative programming is essential in modern software development due to its ability to improve readability, maintainability, and correctness. By eliminating unnecessary state manipulation and reducing complexity, declarative techniques make code easier to understand and debug. This approach is particularly valuable in domains such as database queries, where SQL allows developers to express *what* data is needed without specifying retrieval mechanics. Similarly, in UI development, declarative frameworks like React enhance maintainability by defining component states without imperative DOM manipulation. As programming shifts towards higher abstraction levels, declarative programming continues to shape the future of software design, influencing fields such as cloud computing and AI.

Historical Development and Evolution

The roots of declarative programming trace back to mathematical logic and formal systems, with influences from **lambda calculus** (which underpins functional programming) and **predicate logic** (which forms the basis of logic programming). Early implementations emerged in the 1950s and 1960s, notably with Lisp in functional programming and Prolog in logic-based computing. Over the decades, declarative paradigms gained traction through advancements in databases, declarative UI frameworks, and parallel computing models. The evolution of modern programming languages, such as Haskell, SQL, and declarative domain-specific languages, reflects an ongoing transition towards more abstract and expressive programming methodologies.

Declarative vs. Imperative Programming

The distinction between declarative and imperative programming lies in their approach to problem-solving. **Imperative programming** dictates *how* a program should execute by explicitly defining control structures, such as loops and conditionals. In contrast, **declarative programming** describes *what* the program should achieve without specifying step-by-step execution. This difference manifests in various contexts: for example, an imperative approach to data filtering might involve iterating over a dataset, while a declarative approach simply defines a filtering condition. The shift towards declarative paradigms in modern development stems from their ability to enhance abstraction, reduce boilerplate code, and improve reasoning about program behavior.

Declarative programming represents a fundamental shift in software development, enabling more expressive, maintainable, and efficient code. By emphasizing *what* needs to be computed rather than *how*, declarative paradigms simplify logic and enhance software reliability. This module has outlined the key aspects of declarative programming, laying the foundation for deeper exploration. In subsequent sections, we will delve into specific paradigms with practical implementations.

Overview of Declarative Paradigms

Declarative programming is a paradigm that focuses on defining *what* needs to be computed rather than specifying *how* to compute it. Unlike imperative programming, which relies on explicit sequences of instructions to manipulate state, declarative programming expresses logic in a high-level, abstract manner. This approach enhances readability, maintainability, and parallelism by reducing direct control over program flow.

Several declarative paradigms exist, including **functional programming**, **logic programming**, and **dataflow programming**. **Functional programming** treats computation as the evaluation of pure functions, eliminating side effects and making code more predictable. **Logic programming** relies on rules and facts to derive conclusions, making it useful for AI and knowledge-based systems. **Dataflow programming** models computations as transformations on data streams, which is common in reactive and parallel systems.

Functional Programming Example

Functional programming avoids mutable state by relying on pure functions. Consider a simple example in Python using map and lambda, which demonstrate a declarative way to transform data:

```python
numbers = [1, 2, 3, 4, 5]
squared_numbers = list(map(lambda x: x ** 2, numbers))  # Declarative approach
print(squared_numbers)  # Output: [1, 4, 9, 16, 25]
```

Here, map applies a function to each element in the list without explicitly iterating, abstracting away control flow. An imperative approach, in contrast, would require a loop with explicit iteration and state modification.

Logic Programming Example

Logic programming defines relationships rather than execution steps. In **Prolog**, facts and rules define a knowledge base:

```prolog
parent(john, mary).
parent(mary, alice).
ancestor(X, Y) :- parent(X, Y).
ancestor(X, Y) :- parent(X, Z), ancestor(Z, Y).
```

A query like ancestor(john, alice). would return true because it infers relationships from defined rules, without requiring explicit traversal logic.

Dataflow Programming Example

Dataflow programming models execution as a sequence of data transformations. Python's pandas library provides a declarative way to filter data:

```python
import pandas as pd

df = pd.DataFrame({'Name': ['Alice', 'Bob', 'Charlie'], 'Age': [25, 30, 35]})
filtered_df = df[df['Age'] > 28]  # Declarative data filtering
print(filtered_df)
```

This filters the dataset without using loops, describing *what* should be extracted instead of iterating over rows explicitly.

Declarative paradigms are widely adopted across domains such as database management (SQL), UI development (React), and cloud infrastructure (Terraform). By shifting focus from control flow to logic specification, these paradigms enable scalable and maintainable software development. In the following sections, we will explore the significance of declarative programming, its historical development, and its advantages over imperative approaches.

Importance of Declarative Programming

Declarative programming is a transformative paradigm that enhances code readability, maintainability, and scalability by focusing on *what* should be computed rather than *how*.

By abstracting away control flow and state management, it enables developers to write cleaner, more efficient, and less error-prone code. This section explores its significance in modern software development and its practical benefits across different domains.

One of the key advantages of declarative programming is its ability to **simplify complex logic**. Traditional imperative approaches require step-by-step instructions, often leading to verbose and error-prone code. In contrast, declarative techniques allow developers to express computations concisely. This is particularly evident in **functional programming**, where transformations like map, filter, and reduce eliminate the need for explicit loops and mutable variables.

Example: Simplifying Data Processing

Consider a case where we need to filter a list of numbers and find their squares:

Imperative approach (verbose, with explicit loops and mutation):

```
numbers = [1, 2, 3, 4, 5]
squared_even = []
for num in numbers:
    if num % 2 == 0:
        squared_even.append(num ** 2)
print(squared_even)  # Output: [4, 16]
```

Declarative approach (concise, using map and filter):

```
squared_even = list(map(lambda x: x ** 2, filter(lambda x: x % 2 == 0,
        numbers)))
print(squared_even)  # Output: [4, 16]
```

This approach eliminates unnecessary state mutations and clearly expresses *what* needs to be done.

Another major benefit of declarative programming is its **enhanced maintainability**. When code is written in a declarative style, it is easier to modify and extend without introducing unintended side effects. This is especially useful in **database queries**, where **SQL (Structured Query Language)** allows users to retrieve data without specifying how it should be fetched.

Example: SQL for Database Queries

```
SELECT name, age FROM users WHERE age > 30;
```

This query simply expresses *what* data is needed. In an imperative approach, the developer would have to manually loop through records, check conditions, and build result sets, making the code more error-prone.

Declarative programming also enhances **parallelism and optimization**. Since it focuses on defining transformations rather than step-by-step execution, many declarative languages

18

and frameworks can internally optimize performance by leveraging parallel processing. For instance, **React.js** in web development efficiently updates UI components by re-rendering only what has changed, thanks to its declarative Virtual DOM approach. Similarly, **dataflow programming models**, such as Apache Spark, optimize execution by distributing computations across multiple nodes.

Lastly, declarative programming plays a crucial role in **domain-specific languages (DSLs)**, such as Terraform for infrastructure automation and CSS for web styling. These DSLs allow developers to define the desired end state without procedural scripting, improving productivity and reducing the risk of misconfigurations.

By simplifying logic, improving maintainability, and enabling performance optimizations, declarative programming continues to shape modern software development. The next section will explore its historical evolution and how it has influenced different programming paradigms over time.

Historical Development and Evolution

Declarative programming has its roots in **mathematical logic, set theory, and lambda calculus**, evolving into practical programming languages that prioritize abstraction over explicit control flow. Unlike imperative programming, which mirrors machine-level operations, declarative paradigms emphasize *what* should be computed rather than *how* it should be executed. This section explores its historical progression from theoretical foundations to modern applications, with relevant code examples.

Early Foundations: Lambda Calculus and Predicate Logic

The formal basis for declarative programming was established in the early 20th century. **Lambda calculus**, introduced by Alonzo Church in the 1930s, provided a mathematical framework for defining computation using functions. This concept directly influenced functional programming.

Lambda Calculus in Functional Programming

A simple lambda calculus expression can be represented in Python using lambda functions:

```
add = lambda x, y: x + y  # A pure function with no side effects
print(add(5, 3))  # Output: 8
```

This aligns with declarative principles by focusing on computation without explicit control structures.

Simultaneously, **predicate logic**, formalized by Gottlob Frege, laid the groundwork for **logic programming**. It led to languages like **Prolog**, which define facts and inference rules rather than explicit execution steps.

Prolog Example: Defining Relationships

```
parent(john, mary).
parent(mary, alice).
ancestor(X, Y) :- parent(X, Y).
ancestor(X, Y) :- parent(X, Z), ancestor(Z, Y).
```

Querying ancestor(john, alice). infers relationships based on the rules without requiring explicit loops or conditionals.

Development of Functional and Logic Programming Languages

By the 1950s and 1960s, declarative programming gained practical implementation. **Lisp (1958)**, developed by John McCarthy, introduced recursion and symbolic computation, both core to functional programming. This was followed by **ML (1973)** and **Haskell (1990)**, which emphasized strong type systems and immutability.

Functional Programming Example: Mapping a Function Over a List

```
numbers = [1, 2, 3, 4, 5]
squared = list(map(lambda x: x ** 2, numbers))
print(squared)  # Output: [1, 4, 9, 16, 25]
```

This functional approach eliminates explicit loops and mutable state, making the code more declarative.

Declarative Paradigms in Databases and UI Development

In the 1970s, **SQL (Structured Query Language)** became the standard for relational databases, allowing users to query data declaratively.

SQL Example: Fetching Data Without Control Flow

```
SELECT name, age FROM users WHERE age > 30;
```

Unlike imperative approaches that require iterating over data, SQL describes the desired result, allowing the database engine to optimize execution.

Declarative UI frameworks like **React.js** emerged in the 2010s, allowing developers to define *what* the user interface should look like rather than manually updating the DOM.

Declarative UI Example in React.js (JSX)

```
const Greeting = ({ name }) => <h1>Hello, {name}!</h1>;
```

React's declarative approach ensures the UI updates automatically when the state changes, abstracting away imperative DOM manipulation.

Modern Declarative Programming Trends

Today, declarative programming is widely used in cloud computing (**Terraform, Kubernetes**), big data processing (**Apache Spark**), and machine learning (**TensorFlow, PyTorch**).

TensorFlow Example: Defining a Neural Network Declaratively

```
import tensorflow as tf

model = tf.keras.Sequential([
    tf.keras.layers.Dense(64, activation='relu'),
    tf.keras.layers.Dense(10, activation='softmax')
])
```

Here, the model structure is defined declaratively, without explicitly handling the forward and backward propagation steps.

From its theoretical roots in lambda calculus and logic to its modern applications in databases, UI frameworks, and AI, declarative programming continues to shape software development. By emphasizing *what* should be computed over *how*, it enhances abstraction, maintainability, and scalability. The next section will compare declarative and imperative paradigms, highlighting their advantages and trade-offs.

Declarative vs. Imperative Programming

Declarative and imperative programming represent two fundamentally different approaches to software development. **Imperative programming** describes *how* a task should be executed by explicitly defining control flow, state changes, and step-by-step instructions. In contrast, **declarative programming** focuses on *what* the outcome should be, allowing the underlying system to determine the execution process. This section explores their differences, strengths, weaknesses, and real-world applications with Python code examples.

Key Differences Between Declarative and Imperative Programming

The primary distinction between these paradigms lies in their approach to execution. **Imperative programming** relies on explicit loops, mutable state, and detailed control structures, whereas **declarative programming** abstracts these details, often using expressions, functions, and domain-specific languages.

Example: Summing a List of Numbers

Imperative Approach (Explicit Loop and State Mutation)

```
numbers = [1, 2, 3, 4, 5]
total = 0
for num in numbers:
    total += num
print(total)  # Output: 15
```

This approach manually initializes a variable (total), iterates through the list, and updates the state in each iteration.

Declarative Approach (Using sum())

```
total = sum([1, 2, 3, 4, 5])
print(total)  # Output: 15
```

Here, the sum() function concisely expresses *what* needs to be computed without specifying the iteration details, making the code more readable and maintainable.

Advantages of Declarative Programming

1. **Readability and Maintainability** – Declarative code is often more concise and easier to understand because it focuses on the result rather than control structures.

2. **Parallelism and Optimization** – Since declarative expressions avoid explicit state changes, compilers and runtime environments can optimize execution for parallel processing.

3. **Less Prone to Errors** – Avoiding direct state manipulation reduces unintended side effects and makes debugging easier.

Example: Filtering Even Numbers from a List

Imperative Approach:

```
numbers = [1, 2, 3, 4, 5, 6]
evens = []
for num in numbers:
    if num % 2 == 0:
        evens.append(num)
print(evens)  # Output: [2, 4, 6]
```

This method requires explicit iteration and state mutation, making it more error-prone.

Declarative Approach:

```
evens = list(filter(lambda x: x % 2 == 0, [1, 2, 3, 4, 5, 6]))
print(evens)  # Output: [2, 4, 6]
```

The filter() function abstracts the iteration process, making the intent clear without modifying state.

Limitations of Declarative Programming

1. **Less Explicit Control** – In some cases, fine-grained control over execution is necessary, making imperative programming a better choice.

2. **Performance Overhead** – Some declarative approaches, such as SQL queries or functional programming constructs, may introduce performance trade-offs due to abstraction layers.

3. **Steeper Learning Curve** – Some declarative paradigms, like functional or logic programming, require a shift in mindset that can be challenging for developers accustomed to imperative coding.

Use Cases: When to Use Each Paradigm

- **Imperative programming** is useful for low-level system programming, game development, and performance-critical applications where direct control over memory and execution is necessary.

- **Declarative programming** shines in database queries (SQL), UI development (React.js, SwiftUI), cloud infrastructure (Terraform), and parallel computing (Apache Spark, TensorFlow).

Declarative and imperative programming offer distinct advantages depending on the use case. While imperative programming provides explicit control, declarative programming enhances readability, maintainability, and parallelism. Understanding both paradigms equips developers with the flexibility to choose the right approach for different problem domains.

Module 2:
Characteristics and Advantages of Declarative Programming

Declarative programming offers distinct advantages that improve code quality, maintainability, and efficiency. This module explores its defining characteristics, focusing on readability, reduced side effects, expressiveness, and performance trade-offs. By understanding these aspects, developers can better appreciate the strengths of declarative paradigms and determine their applicability to different programming tasks.

Readability and Maintainability

One of the primary benefits of declarative programming is its enhanced readability. Since declarative code emphasizes *what* should be computed rather than *how*, it often results in clearer and more concise logic. Unlike imperative programming, which requires tracking control flow and mutable state, declarative code presents a high-level abstraction that makes it easier to understand at a glance. This clarity leads to better maintainability, as developers can quickly grasp the program's intent without deciphering intricate details. Maintainable code is particularly valuable in large-scale applications, where multiple contributors must collaborate efficiently. By reducing the cognitive load, declarative programming simplifies debugging, code reviews, and long-term maintenance.

Reduction of Side Effects

Side effects occur when a function or operation alters the program's state beyond its immediate scope, often leading to unintended consequences. Declarative programming minimizes side effects by favoring **pure functions** and **immutable data structures**. Unlike imperative code, which often manipulates variables and memory directly, declarative approaches ensure that functions produce consistent outputs based solely on their inputs. This predictability makes debugging and reasoning about code significantly easier. In multi-threaded and parallel computing environments, reducing side effects is crucial, as it prevents unpredictable behavior caused by shared state modifications. Declarative programming's focus on immutability enhances software reliability by preventing unintended interactions between components.

Expressiveness and Code Conciseness

Declarative programming enables developers to write more expressive and concise code by leveraging high-level abstractions. Expressiveness refers to the ability to convey complex logic in a compact and readable manner. Many declarative paradigms, such as functional programming and SQL queries, allow developers to achieve in a single line of code what might take multiple statements in an imperative style. This conciseness leads to fewer lines of code, reducing redundancy and potential errors. More expressive syntax also allows for better domain-specific modeling, making it easier to write code that closely matches business logic or real-world scenarios. By simplifying complex operations, declarative programming enhances productivity and reduces development time.

Performance Trade-offs in Declarative Programming

While declarative programming improves code clarity and maintainability, it also introduces performance considerations. The abstraction that makes declarative code readable can sometimes lead to **overhead**, as the underlying implementation may not be as optimized as handcrafted imperative code. Additionally, declarative paradigms often rely on runtime optimizations that may not always yield the best possible performance. In some cases, the absence of direct control over execution flow can lead to inefficiencies, particularly in low-level or performance-critical applications. However, modern declarative frameworks and compilers mitigate these issues through optimization techniques such as lazy evaluation, caching, and parallel execution, ensuring that the benefits of declarative programming often outweigh its drawbacks.

Declarative programming offers significant advantages in terms of readability, reduced side effects, and expressiveness, but it also presents trade-offs in terms of performance. Understanding these characteristics allows developers to make informed decisions about when and where to apply declarative paradigms. In the following sections, we will explore these concepts in greater detail with practical implementations.

Readability and Maintainability

Declarative programming enhances **readability** by abstracting away control flow and focusing on the outcome rather than the steps to achieve it. This makes it easier for developers to understand code at a glance, reducing cognitive load. Additionally, it improves **maintainability**, ensuring that software remains manageable, scalable, and less prone to bugs. By using declarative constructs, developers can write **self-explanatory** code that remains clear and concise even as applications grow in complexity.

Imperative vs. Declarative Readability

Imperative programming requires explicit instructions for each step of computation, making it more **verbose and harder to maintain**. Consider an example of filtering even numbers from a list using an imperative approach:

```
numbers = [1, 2, 3, 4, 5, 6]
evens = []
for num in numbers:
    if num % 2 == 0:
        evens.append(num)
print(evens)  # Output: [2, 4, 6]
```

This method involves **explicit iteration** and **mutable state**, which increases complexity.

By contrast, the declarative approach expresses *what* should be done rather than *how*:

```
evens = list(filter(lambda x: x % 2 == 0, [1, 2, 3, 4, 5, 6]))
print(evens)  # Output: [2, 4, 6]
```

This version is **concise and self-explanatory**, making it **easier to read and maintain**.

Improving Maintainability Through Declarative Code

Maintainability is crucial in large projects, where complex codebases must be updated frequently. Imperative code often involves **state changes**, **loops**, and **detailed logic**, making it harder to refactor without introducing errors. Declarative paradigms eliminate unnecessary complexity, making modifications **simpler and less error-prone**.

For example, consider an imperative approach to finding the sum of squares of even numbers:

```
numbers = [1, 2, 3, 4, 5, 6]
sum_squares = 0
for num in numbers:
    if num % 2 == 0:
        sum_squares += num ** 2
print(sum_squares)  # Output: 56
```

This code explicitly tracks state (sum_squares) and uses **loops and conditionals**, making it harder to manage in larger applications.

A declarative alternative simplifies the logic:

```
sum_squares = sum(x ** 2 for x in [1, 2, 3, 4, 5, 6] if x % 2 == 0)
print(sum_squares)  # Output: 56
```

This one-liner makes the **intent clear** and reduces the chances of introducing errors during updates.

Declarative Code in Real-World Applications

Declarative paradigms are widely used in modern programming frameworks:

- **SQL for databases**: Instead of writing loops to retrieve data, SQL allows users to **declare** what data they need:

  ```
  SELECT name FROM users WHERE age > 30;
  ```

- **React.js for UI development**: Developers specify what the UI should look like, and the framework handles state updates automatically:

  ```
  const Greeting = ({ name }) => <h1>Hello, {name}!</h1>;
  ```

By focusing on **expressive, high-level constructs**, declarative programming enhances readability and maintainability. Its **concise syntax**, **elimination of side effects**, and

modular structure make it the preferred choice for modern software development. Understanding and applying declarative principles lead to cleaner, more efficient codebases.

Reduction of Side Effects

One of the key advantages of declarative programming is its ability to minimize **side effects**, which occur when functions or operations modify the program's state beyond their immediate scope. Side effects can make debugging difficult and introduce unintended behavior, especially in concurrent or large-scale systems. Declarative paradigms, particularly functional programming, encourage **pure functions** and **immutability**, reducing unpredictability and making software easier to reason about.

Understanding Side Effects in Imperative Code

In **imperative programming**, side effects commonly arise when functions modify global variables, alter mutable objects, or interact with external systems such as databases and files. These changes can lead to **unexpected behavior** if not carefully managed. Consider the following example, where a function modifies a global list:

```
numbers = [1, 2, 3, 4, 5]

def add_to_list(value):
    numbers.append(value)

add_to_list(6)
print(numbers)  # Output: [1, 2, 3, 4, 5, 6]
```

Here, add_to_list() **modifies the global numbers list**, making it difficult to track state changes across the program. This can cause unintended side effects, especially in concurrent environments where multiple parts of the program interact with the same shared state.

Pure Functions and Immutability in Declarative Programming

Declarative programming minimizes side effects by emphasizing **pure functions**, which always produce the same output given the same input and do not modify external state. This makes code more **predictable and testable**.

Rewriting the previous example in a **pure function** ensures that no external variables are modified:

```
def add_to_list_immutable(lst, value):
    return lst + [value]

new_numbers = add_to_list_immutable(numbers, 6)
print(new_numbers)  # Output: [1, 2, 3, 4, 5, 6]
print(numbers)      # Output: [1, 2, 3, 4, 5]  (Original list remains unchanged)
```

By **returning a new list instead of modifying the existing one**, this function avoids side effects and maintains **data integrity**.

Avoiding Side Effects in Functional and Declarative Programming

Declarative programming leverages **immutability** to eliminate unintended state changes. Many functional programming techniques, such as **map, filter, and reduce**, allow transformations without mutating data:

```
numbers = [1, 2, 3, 4, 5]
squared_numbers = list(map(lambda x: x ** 2, numbers))
print(squared_numbers)  # Output: [1, 4, 9, 16, 25]
```

Unlike an imperative loop that modifies an existing list, map() creates a **new list**, ensuring immutability and preventing unintended modifications.

Reducing Side Effects in Parallel and Concurrent Programming

Side effects become especially problematic in **multi-threaded** or **distributed** environments, where shared state can lead to race conditions. By minimizing state changes, declarative programming enables safe parallel execution.

For example, in **Python's multiprocessing module**, functions that **avoid modifying shared state** work more reliably:

```
from multiprocessing import Pool

def square(x):
    return x * x

numbers = [1, 2, 3, 4, 5]
with Pool(3) as p:
    result = p.map(square, numbers)

print(result)  # Output: [1, 4, 9, 16, 25]
```

Since square() is a **pure function**, it can be executed in parallel without conflicts.

By **minimizing side effects**, declarative programming makes code **predictable, testable, and scalable**. Techniques like **pure functions, immutability, and high-order functions** reduce errors and improve parallel execution. Adopting these principles leads to **more robust and maintainable** software.

Expressiveness and Code Conciseness

Declarative programming enhances **expressiveness** by allowing developers to write **concise, readable code** that clearly conveys intent. Expressiveness refers to how effectively a programming paradigm captures logic with minimal complexity, while **code conciseness** ensures that unnecessary verbosity is eliminated. By leveraging **high-level**

abstractions, declarative programming reduces boilerplate code, making software development more efficient and error-free.

Imperative vs. Declarative Expressiveness

In imperative programming, logic is often **explicitly defined**, requiring detailed steps to achieve a result. This leads to **longer, more complex code** that is harder to read and maintain. Consider the following imperative approach to filtering even numbers and squaring them:

```
numbers = [1, 2, 3, 4, 5, 6]
evens_squared = []
for num in numbers:
    if num % 2 == 0:
        evens_squared.append(num ** 2)

print(evens_squared)  # Output: [4, 16, 36]
```

This approach requires a **loop**, **conditionals**, and **explicit state modification**, making the logic **verbose**. The same operation can be achieved in a **more expressive and concise** declarative style using Python's **list comprehensions**:

```
evens_squared = [x ** 2 for x in [1, 2, 3, 4, 5, 6] if x % 2 == 0]
print(evens_squared)  # Output: [4, 16, 36]
```

This version removes unnecessary control structures, making the **intent clear** in a **single readable expression**.

Conciseness Through Functional Constructs

Declarative programming promotes **higher-order functions** like map(), filter(), and reduce() to express logic concisely. The same operation using **functional programming** looks even cleaner:

```
evens_squared = list(map(lambda x: x ** 2, filter(lambda x: x % 2 == 0, [1, 2,
        3, 4, 5, 6])))
print(evens_squared)  # Output: [4, 16, 36]
```

By composing **pure functions**, this approach avoids explicit loops, improving **clarity and reusability**.

Expressiveness in SQL and Declarative Queries

Declarative programming is also evident in **SQL queries**, where users specify *what* data they need without detailing *how* to retrieve it. Consider fetching user names older than 30 years:

```
SELECT name FROM users WHERE age > 30;
```

Instead of manually iterating over database rows, SQL **abstracts the query logic**, making it both **concise and powerful**.

Concise UI Development in Declarative Frameworks

Modern UI frameworks like **React.js** follow a declarative model, where UI components describe **what should be rendered** rather than handling **how state changes**:

```
const Greeting = ({ name }) => <h1>Hello, {name}!</h1>;
```

This component-based approach removes **manual DOM manipulation**, making UI logic **more expressive and maintainable**.

Declarative programming significantly improves **expressiveness and conciseness**, reducing verbosity while enhancing readability. By **eliminating unnecessary complexity**, it simplifies code, allowing developers to focus on **problem-solving** rather than implementation details. Adopting declarative paradigms results in **clearer, more efficient, and scalable** software development.

Performance Trade-offs in Declarative Programming

While declarative programming offers **readability, maintainability, and expressiveness**, it comes with **performance trade-offs** depending on the context. The abstraction that simplifies code can introduce **overhead**, affecting execution speed, memory usage, and optimization capabilities. Understanding these trade-offs helps developers make **informed decisions** when choosing between **declarative and imperative approaches**.

Abstraction Overhead and Performance Costs

Declarative programming **abstracts control flow**, letting the language or framework handle execution details. However, this abstraction can lead to **inefficiencies**, especially when dealing with low-level system operations. Consider the use of **list comprehensions vs. manual loops** in Python:

```
numbers = range(1, 10**6)
squared = [x ** 2 for x in numbers]  # List comprehension
```

This is concise and readable, but it **eagerly evaluates** all elements, consuming more memory. An imperative alternative using a **generator** would be more memory-efficient:

```
def square_numbers(nums):
    for num in nums:
        yield num ** 2

squared_gen = square_numbers(range(1, 10**6))  # Uses lazy evaluation
```

Here, **lazy evaluation** prevents unnecessary memory consumption, demonstrating that **declarative styles may trade efficiency for conciseness**.

Optimization by Compilers and Interpreters

Despite the abstraction overhead, modern compilers and interpreters optimize declarative code. For example, **SQL query optimizers** automatically rewrite queries for better performance:

```sql
SELECT * FROM orders WHERE customer_id = 5 AND total > 100;
```

A database engine may **reorder filters**, use **indexes**, and optimize execution plans **without developer intervention**—a benefit of declarative programming. However, in some cases, manually tuning queries in an imperative manner might yield better performance.

Parallelism and Lazy Evaluation in Declarative Languages

Declarative paradigms, particularly **functional programming**, facilitate **parallelism**. Since **pure functions** have no side effects, they can execute independently across multiple processors. The following example uses Python's multiprocessing to compute squares in parallel:

```python
from multiprocessing import Pool

def square(x):
    return x ** 2

numbers = range(1, 1000000)
with Pool(4) as p:
    result = p.map(square, numbers)
```

Here, **declarative function composition** enables easy parallel execution, improving performance.

Trade-offs in UI Frameworks and Declarative APIs

In **React.js**, a declarative UI framework, components re-render based on state changes. While this improves readability, frequent re-renders **can degrade performance**. To mitigate this, developers use optimizations like **memoization**:

```javascript
import { memo } from "react";

const Greeting = memo(({ name }) => <h1>Hello, {name}!</h1>);
```

This prevents unnecessary re-renders, balancing **declarative simplicity with performance efficiency**.

Declarative programming enhances **code quality** but may introduce **performance costs** due to abstraction overhead. While compilers, interpreters, and optimizations mitigate some inefficiencies, developers must assess trade-offs—**balancing expressiveness and efficiency** for optimal results in real-world applications..

Module 3:
Declarative vs. Imperative Paradigms

Declarative and imperative programming represent two fundamentally different ways of instructing a computer to perform tasks. While imperative programming focuses on defining explicit steps to achieve a result, declarative programming emphasizes specifying *what* needs to be achieved rather than *how* to achieve it. Understanding the distinctions between these paradigms is crucial for selecting the right approach based on problem requirements, performance considerations, and maintainability. This module explores the key differences in thought processes, compares imperative and declarative code, discusses the suitability of each paradigm for different scenarios, and examines how hybrid solutions can leverage the strengths of both approaches.

Key Differences in Thought Process

The primary distinction between declarative and imperative programming lies in their approach to problem-solving. Imperative programming follows a **step-by-step execution model**, where developers explicitly outline each operation needed to transform inputs into outputs. This approach is akin to writing out a detailed recipe, requiring precise instructions for every step. Declarative programming, on the other hand, focuses on expressing the desired result without detailing the control flow. This shift in mindset allows developers to write more abstract, high-level code, reducing complexity and making logic more intuitive.

One of the biggest advantages of the declarative paradigm is that it abstracts away low-level details, letting the underlying system optimize execution. For example, in database queries, rather than looping through data manually, declarative languages like SQL allow users to specify conditions and let the database engine handle the retrieval process. This abstraction simplifies reasoning about the program while improving maintainability. However, imperative programming remains valuable for tasks requiring fine-grained control over execution flow, such as low-level system operations or performance-critical applications.

Code Comparisons: Declarative vs. Imperative

To better understand the difference between these paradigms, it is useful to compare imperative and declarative implementations of the same logic. Imperative programming typically requires **explicit loops, conditionals, and mutable state**, while declarative programming relies on **expressive, high-level constructs** to achieve the same functionality with less verbosity. This distinction is particularly evident in functional programming, where functions like map(), filter(), and reduce() replace traditional loops.

Declarative approaches often result in **more concise and readable** code, but they may introduce performance overhead due to additional abstraction layers. Conversely, imperative programming provides **fine control over execution** but can lead to **boilerplate-heavy** and **error-prone** code. Comparing both paradigms helps developers appreciate the trade-offs and decide which approach best suits their needs.

When to Use Each Approach

The choice between declarative and imperative programming depends on factors like problem complexity, performance requirements, and readability. Declarative programming is particularly well-suited for **data transformation, UI development, query-based operations, and parallel processing**, where abstraction improves clarity and reduces errors. Imperative programming, on the other hand, is beneficial for **low-level optimizations, real-time processing, and scenarios requiring direct memory manipulation**, where precise control is necessary.

In practice, modern software development often requires a balance between both paradigms. Declarative programming enhances productivity and maintainability, while imperative techniques ensure efficiency and resource optimization. Understanding the strengths and limitations of each allows developers to make informed decisions and adapt to different programming environments effectively.

Combining Paradigms for Hybrid Solutions

Rather than choosing between declarative and imperative programming exclusively, many real-world applications benefit from **hybrid solutions** that incorporate elements of both paradigms. Functional programming, for example, introduces declarative concepts into traditionally imperative languages, while modern frameworks like React.js blend declarative UI rendering with imperative event handling. Similarly, database management systems use declarative SQL for data queries while relying on imperative constructs for procedural operations.

By combining both paradigms strategically, developers can maximize **code efficiency, readability, and performance**. Hybrid solutions provide flexibility, allowing imperative code to handle **low-level execution details** while leveraging declarative abstractions for **higher-level logic and automation**. This synergy enables the creation of scalable, maintainable, and optimized software systems.

Understanding the differences between declarative and imperative programming is essential for writing effective, maintainable, and efficient code. While declarative programming enhances readability and abstraction, imperative programming provides greater control and optimization potential. Recognizing when to use each paradigm—and how to combine them effectively—empowers developers to build more robust software solutions tailored to specific requirements.

Key Differences in Thought Process

Declarative and imperative programming differ significantly in **how** they approach problem-solving. In an imperative paradigm, the focus is on **explicit control flow**, where each step of execution is carefully defined. In contrast, declarative programming **abstracts away the control flow**, allowing developers to express *what* needs to be done rather than *how* to do it. This fundamental shift in thought process affects how code is written, structured, and understood.

Imperative Thinking: Defining Explicit Steps

Imperative programming requires breaking a task into **sequential operations**, specifying *each action* necessary to achieve the desired result. This approach mirrors **manual problem-solving**, where execution follows a defined order, often using **loops, conditionals, and mutable variables**. For instance, consider summing a list of numbers in an imperative style:

```
numbers = [1, 2, 3, 4, 5]
total = 0
for num in numbers:
    total += num

print(total)  # Output: 15
```

Here, the program explicitly **iterates through the list**, updating the total variable step by step. This requires **managing state manually**, which can introduce complexity and errors in larger programs.

Declarative Thinking: Expressing Intent

Declarative programming eliminates **step-by-step control**, allowing the system to determine the most efficient execution strategy. Instead of focusing on *how* to compute a result, declarative programming emphasizes *what* the result should be. Using Python's sum() function, the same logic can be written declaratively:

```
total = sum([1, 2, 3, 4, 5])
print(total)  # Output: 15
```

This **abstracts away iteration**, making the code **more readable and maintainable**. The programmer does not manage state directly; instead, they specify the desired computation, and the language handles execution details.

Declarative vs. Imperative in Real-World Applications

These thought process differences extend to **various domains** of software development. For example, SQL databases use declarative queries to retrieve data efficiently:

```
SELECT SUM(amount) FROM transactions;
```

Here, the query specifies *what* to retrieve, and the database engine optimizes execution automatically. An imperative equivalent would require **manual iteration** through records, significantly increasing complexity.

Similarly, in **UI development**, modern frameworks like React.js take a declarative approach:

```
const Button = () => <button>Click Me</button>;
```

This defines **what the UI should render**, rather than manually modifying the DOM. Traditional imperative methods require explicit DOM manipulation, making code more error-prone.

The key difference in thought process between **imperative and declarative programming** lies in control flow management. **Imperative programming** explicitly defines each step, while **declarative programming** abstracts execution details. By adopting a **declarative mindset**, developers can write **clearer, more maintainable, and scalable** code while leveraging built-in optimizations in modern programming paradigms.

Code Comparisons: Declarative vs. Imperative

The distinction between declarative and imperative programming is best understood through direct code comparisons. Imperative programming requires defining **explicit steps** to achieve a result, whereas declarative programming expresses the desired **outcome** and allows the underlying system to handle execution. This difference influences **code structure, readability, and maintainability** across various programming scenarios.

Example 1: Filtering a List of Numbers

Consider a scenario where we need to filter even numbers from a list. The **imperative approach** manually iterates through the list, checks conditions, and appends matching elements:

```
numbers = [1, 2, 3, 4, 5, 6, 7, 8, 9, 10]
even_numbers = []

for num in numbers:
    if num % 2 == 0:
        even_numbers.append(num)

print(even_numbers)  # Output: [2, 4, 6, 8, 10]
```

Here, the loop explicitly **manages control flow and state**, making the logic **verbose and procedural**. The **declarative approach**, using Python's filter() function, achieves the same result more concisely:

```
even_numbers = list(filter(lambda x: x % 2 == 0, numbers))
print(even_numbers)  # Output: [2, 4, 6, 8, 10]
```

This version **removes manual iteration**, making the logic more **expressive and readable**.

35

Example 2: Summing a List of Numbers

An **imperative approach** to summing a list involves explicitly iterating and maintaining a running total:

```
numbers = [1, 2, 3, 4, 5]
total = 0

for num in numbers:
    total += num

print(total)  # Output: 15
```

The **declarative approach** replaces explicit iteration with sum(), improving clarity:

```
total = sum(numbers)
print(total)  # Output: 15
```

This **shifts responsibility** to the language's built-in functions, reducing **manual control** and potential errors.

Example 3: Working with Databases

Database queries showcase the **power of declarative programming**. Instead of manually iterating over records and filtering them, SQL queries allow developers to specify what they need:

```
SELECT name FROM employees WHERE department = 'HR';
```

An **imperative approach** in Python would involve retrieving all records, iterating, and filtering manually:

```
employees = [
    {"name": "Alice", "department": "HR"},
    {"name": "Bob", "department": "IT"},
    {"name": "Charlie", "department": "HR"},
]

hr_employees = []
for emp in employees:
    if emp["department"] == "HR":
        hr_employees.append(emp["name"])

print(hr_employees)  # Output: ['Alice', 'Charlie']
```

This imperative method **requires more code and manual operations**, whereas SQL declaratively defines *what* data to retrieve.

Code comparisons illustrate that **imperative programming focuses on step-by-step execution**, while **declarative programming expresses intent** and delegates execution to the language or framework. **Declarative approaches improve readability, maintainability, and abstraction**, making them preferable in many scenarios. However, imperative programming remains useful when **fine-grained control** over execution is necessary.

When to Use Each Approach

The choice between declarative and imperative programming depends on **problem complexity, performance requirements, and maintainability**. While declarative programming enhances **readability and abstraction**, imperative programming provides **precise control over execution**. Understanding when to use each paradigm is crucial for **writing efficient, maintainable, and scalable** code.

Declarative Programming: When to Use It

Declarative programming is ideal for scenarios where **clarity and simplicity** are priorities. It works best when the focus is on **defining the logic** rather than controlling execution flow. Common use cases include:

1. **Data Queries and Processing** – SQL databases use declarative queries to retrieve, filter, and manipulate data efficiently. Instead of iterating manually, SQL abstracts away execution:

```
SELECT name FROM employees WHERE department = 'HR';
```

This simplifies database operations and allows **optimization at the system level**.

2. **Functional Transformations** – Functional programming techniques like map(), filter(), and reduce() allow for **concise and expressive** data transformations. Consider filtering a list of even numbers:

```
even_numbers = list(filter(lambda x: x % 2 == 0, [1, 2, 3, 4, 5, 6, 7, 8, 9,
           10]))
print(even_numbers)  # Output: [2, 4, 6, 8, 10]
```

This eliminates **manual loops**, making code **shorter and easier to understand**.

3. **UI Development** – Modern frameworks like React.js use a **declarative approach** to define UI components:

```
const Button = () => <button>Click Me</button>;
```

Developers specify **what** should be rendered, while the framework **handles state updates efficiently**.

4. **Parallel and Distributed Computing** – Declarative programming allows **automatic optimization** of computations across multiple cores or servers. Frameworks like Spark process **big data declaratively**, letting the system **optimize execution under the hood**.

37

Imperative Programming: When to Use It

Imperative programming is necessary when **fine-grained control** over execution is required. Use cases include:

1. **Performance-Critical Applications** – Low-level optimizations in system programming, game development, or embedded systems require **explicit control** over memory and execution. A manual loop is often more efficient than higher-level abstractions:

```
total = 0
numbers = [1, 2, 3, 4, 5]

for num in numbers:
    total += num

print(total)  # Output: 15
```

Here, manually iterating ensures **full control over execution** without hidden overhead.

2. **Complex Algorithms** – Algorithms that require intricate control over state, like sorting, pathfinding, or machine learning model training, often benefit from an imperative approach.

3. **System Programming** – Tasks involving **file handling, network sockets, or hardware interaction** require precise control. For example, reading a file imperatively:

```
with open("file.txt", "r") as file:
    content = file.read()
```

The developer **manages resources manually**, ensuring efficiency.

Choosing between **declarative and imperative programming** depends on **task complexity, maintainability, and performance needs**. Declarative programming simplifies code and improves scalability, making it ideal for **data processing, UI development, and distributed computing**. However, imperative programming is necessary for **fine-grained control over execution**, especially in **performance-critical** applications. Understanding both paradigms allows developers to select the right approach for different programming challenges.

Combining Paradigms for Hybrid Solutions

While declarative and imperative programming are often presented as opposing paradigms, modern software development frequently benefits from a **hybrid approach**. Combining these paradigms allows developers to **balance readability, maintainability, and performance**, leveraging the strengths of both styles. Many programming languages and frameworks incorporate elements of both, offering flexibility in problem-solving.

Hybrid Approach in Data Processing

One of the most common areas where declarative and imperative paradigms intersect is **data transformation and processing**. Consider a scenario where we need to process a dataset by filtering, transforming, and aggregating values.

Using **purely imperative programming**, the process requires explicit control over iteration, filtering, and aggregation:

```
numbers = [1, 2, 3, 4, 5, 6, 7, 8, 9, 10]
filtered_numbers = []
for num in numbers:
    if num % 2 == 0:
        filtered_numbers.append(num * 2)

total = 0
for num in filtered_numbers:
    total += num

print(total)  # Output: 60
```

This approach, though effective, requires **managing state manually** and handling multiple loops, which can lead to verbose and error-prone code.

By introducing **declarative elements**, the same logic can be rewritten more succinctly:

```
total = sum(map(lambda x: x * 2, filter(lambda x: x % 2 == 0, numbers)))
print(total)  # Output: 60
```

Here, the imperative iteration is replaced with **higher-order functions** like map() and filter(), allowing the language to handle execution. This hybrid approach **improves readability while maintaining efficiency**.

Declarative UI with Imperative State Management

In front-end development, frameworks like **React.js** encourage declarative UI definitions while relying on imperative code for state management. Consider a React component:

```
import { useState } from 'react';

function Counter() {
  const [count, setCount] = useState(0);

  return (
    <div>
      <p>Count: {count}</p>
      <button onClick={() => setCount(count + 1)}>Increment</button>
    </div>
  );
}
```

The UI structure is **declarative**, defining *what* should be rendered. However, the event handler (onClick) uses an **imperative update mechanism** (setCount(count + 1)). This hybrid approach simplifies UI logic while maintaining **precise state control**.

Hybrid Approach in SQL and Procedural Code

Database interactions often blend declarative SQL queries with imperative programming logic. Consider fetching data from a database in Python using SQL:

```python
import sqlite3

conn = sqlite3.connect('example.db')
cursor = conn.cursor()

# Declarative SQL query
cursor.execute("SELECT name FROM employees WHERE department = 'HR'")
hr_employees = cursor.fetchall()

# Imperative processing of results
for emp in hr_employees:
    print(emp[0])

conn.close()
```

The SQL query **declaratively** specifies what data to retrieve, while Python's imperative code handles **state management, iteration, and resource cleanup**. This hybrid model ensures efficient data retrieval while maintaining **execution control** in application logic.

A hybrid approach leverages **declarative programming for clarity and expressiveness** while using **imperative programming for control and optimization**. Modern software development frequently integrates both paradigms, allowing developers to build scalable, readable, and efficient applications. Understanding when and how to combine these paradigms is essential for writing robust and maintainable code.

Module 4:
Core Concepts: Functions, Rules, and Constraints

Declarative programming relies on core principles such as **functional constructs, rule-based logic, and constraints** to express computations in a high-level manner. Unlike imperative programming, where state and control flow are explicitly managed, declarative approaches focus on **what to compute rather than how**. This module explores **functional constructs, rule-based systems, immutability, and constraint propagation**, which collectively enable declarative programming's expressiveness, maintainability, and robustness.

4.1 Functional Constructs and Recursion

Functional programming is a **key aspect of declarative programming**, emphasizing pure functions, higher-order functions, and recursion instead of loops. Functional constructs allow developers to structure computations using expressions rather than state modifications. Recursion, a fundamental concept in functional programming, replaces explicit iteration by breaking problems into smaller instances of themselves.

Using recursion instead of loops enhances readability and reduces side effects, as functions do not modify global variables or shared state. Functional constructs like **map, filter, and reduce** provide a declarative way to manipulate data without explicit control flow. This abstraction allows developers to focus on defining transformations instead of managing execution steps, leading to cleaner, more maintainable code.

4.2 Rule-Based Programming and Logic Constraints

Rule-based programming enables developers to define logic using **declarative rules** rather than imperative conditionals and loops. This approach is particularly useful in domains such as **expert systems, decision-making algorithms, and artificial intelligence**, where rules define expected outcomes based on input conditions.

Unlike procedural logic, where conditions and actions are explicitly programmed, rule-based systems use **if-then** structures or **logical constraints** to infer results dynamically. These systems determine results based on available data and predefined logic, making them ideal for scenarios where complex relationships must be maintained without writing procedural control structures.

Logic programming languages such as **Prolog** demonstrate the power of rule-based declarative approaches, where facts and rules determine outcomes through inference mechanisms. This methodology simplifies problem-solving, enhances maintainability, and allows for dynamic knowledge representation without manually coding every decision path.

4.3 Pure Functions and Immutability

Pure functions and immutability are foundational principles in declarative programming, ensuring **predictable behavior, referential transparency, and reduced side effects**. A **pure function** is one whose output depends solely on its input values, with no reliance on external state. This property allows functions to be reasoned about in isolation, leading to easier debugging and testing.

Immutability further enforces declarative programming principles by preventing modification of existing data structures. Instead of altering variables, immutable approaches generate new data instances, ensuring that changes do not propagate unpredictably. Languages that emphasize immutability, such as **Haskell and functional Python constructs**, improve concurrency handling by eliminating shared mutable state, reducing race conditions and unexpected behaviors.

4.4 Constraint Propagation Mechanisms

Constraint propagation is a key concept in declarative programming, enabling systems to **derive solutions based on predefined constraints**. This approach is widely used in fields such as **constraint-solving, optimization problems, and declarative UI frameworks**, where constraints define relationships that must be satisfied.

Unlike imperative programming, where variables are assigned specific values and updated explicitly, constraint-based approaches establish **dependencies and rules**. The system then dynamically resolves values based on these constraints. This technique is commonly found in **constraint satisfaction problems (CSPs)**, such as scheduling algorithms, circuit design, and automated theorem proving.

Constraint-based programming simplifies problem-solving by shifting the focus from **manual computation steps** to **expressing relationships**, allowing solvers or interpreters to determine feasible solutions automatically. This methodology enhances abstraction, flexibility, and scalability in complex computational domains.

The core principles of declarative programming—**functional constructs, rule-based logic, immutability, and constraints**—enable a **high-level, maintainable, and expressive approach to software development**. By shifting the focus from **step-by-step execution** to **defining relationships and transformations**, declarative programming enhances readability, reduces errors, and simplifies complex problem-solving. This module lays the foundation for understanding how declarative paradigms optimize logic definition and computational efficiency.

Functional Constructs and Recursion

Functional constructs and recursion are fundamental principles in declarative programming, providing a way to express computations without explicit control flow or mutable state. Unlike imperative programming, which relies on loops and assignments, functional programming emphasizes **pure functions**, **higher-order functions**, and **recursion** to define operations in a concise, expressive manner. These constructs reduce side effects, improve code maintainability, and enable parallel execution by avoiding shared mutable state.

Higher-Order Functions for Declarative Computation

Higher-order functions are a key functional construct, allowing functions to take other functions as arguments or return functions as results. This abstraction removes explicit loops and conditions, promoting a declarative style of coding. For example, instead of using a for loop to double each number in a list, a declarative approach uses map():

```
numbers = [1, 2, 3, 4, 5]
doubled = list(map(lambda x: x * 2, numbers))
print(doubled)  # Output: [2, 4, 6, 8, 10]
```

This eliminates the need for a mutable variable and an explicit iteration structure, allowing the programmer to focus on **what to compute rather than how**. Similarly, filter() and reduce() enable **expressive transformations**:

```
from functools import reduce

evens = list(filter(lambda x: x % 2 == 0, numbers))
sum_of_numbers = reduce(lambda x, y: x + y, numbers)

print(evens)  # Output: [2, 4]
print(sum_of_numbers)  # Output: 15
```

These functions abstract control flow, making the code more readable and concise compared to imperative loops.

Recursion as a Replacement for Loops

Recursion is a fundamental functional programming construct that allows functions to call themselves instead of relying on iterative loops. This is particularly useful for problems that can be **broken down into smaller subproblems**, such as computing factorials, Fibonacci sequences, or tree traversals.

A classic example is calculating the factorial of a number using recursion:

```
def factorial(n):
    if n == 0:
        return 1
    return n * factorial(n - 1)

print(factorial(5))  # Output: 120
```

Here, the function calls itself with a smaller argument, gradually reducing the problem to a base case (n == 0). This **eliminates mutable state** and ensures that each function call remains independent of global variables.

Recursion is also useful in **data structure traversal**, such as navigating a tree:

```python
class Node:
    def __init__(self, value):
        self.value = value
        self.left = None
        self.right = None

def in_order_traversal(node):
    if node:
        in_order_traversal(node.left)
        print(node.value, end=" ")
        in_order_traversal(node.right)

# Constructing a simple binary tree
root = Node(5)
root.left = Node(3)
root.right = Node(8)
root.left.left = Node(1)
root.left.right = Node(4)

in_order_traversal(root)  # Output: 1 3 4 5 8
```

Here, recursion simplifies **traversing hierarchical data structures**, reducing the need for explicit stacks or loops.

Tail Recursion Optimization

One challenge with recursion is **stack overflow**, which occurs when deep recursion leads to excessive memory usage. Some languages support **tail recursion optimization (TCO)**, where the recursive call is the last operation in the function, allowing the interpreter to reuse stack frames. Python, however, does not perform TCO automatically, so converting deep recursion to an iterative approach is sometimes necessary for performance reasons.

For instance, rewriting a recursive function using **tail recursion** (though Python does not optimize it automatically):

```python
def tail_recursive_factorial(n, acc=1):
    if n == 0:
        return acc
    return tail_recursive_factorial(n - 1, acc * n)

print(tail_recursive_factorial(5))  # Output: 120
```

This avoids growing the call stack excessively, though in Python, converting it to an explicit loop is usually preferable.

Functional constructs and recursion form the backbone of **declarative programming**, enabling **clear, concise, and expressive** code. Higher-order functions like map(), filter(), and reduce() eliminate explicit loops, while recursion **replaces iterative control**

structures with self-contained function calls. These principles enhance code maintainability, reduce side effects, and facilitate parallel execution, making them essential for writing efficient and scalable declarative programs.

Rule-Based Programming and Logic Constraints

Rule-based programming and logic constraints are fundamental to declarative programming, allowing developers to express logic in terms of **rules and conditions rather than explicit control flow**. Unlike imperative programming, which requires step-by-step instructions to reach a solution, rule-based programming defines a **set of conditions** that must be satisfied. This approach is particularly useful in **artificial intelligence, expert systems, and constraint-solving applications**, where decisions and relationships must be inferred dynamically rather than explicitly coded.

Defining Rules in Declarative Programming

Rule-based programming operates on the principle of **if-then** rules, where computations are driven by **facts and logical inferences** rather than predefined execution sequences. A system determines outcomes by **matching input data against a set of rules** and deriving conclusions.

In Python, a simple rule-based system can be implemented using dictionaries and conditional checks. Consider a basic **expert system for diagnosing weather conditions**:

```
def weather_advice(conditions):
    rules = {
        "rainy": "Take an umbrella.",
        "sunny": "Wear sunglasses.",
        "snowy": "Wear a coat and gloves.",
        "windy": "Hold onto your hat!"
    }
    return rules.get(conditions, "Check the forecast.")

print(weather_advice("rainy"))  # Output: Take an umbrella.
print(weather_advice("sunny"))  # Output: Wear sunglasses.
```

This approach eliminates the need for **nested if-else statements** by directly mapping inputs to outputs. More advanced rule-based systems use **pattern matching** to infer relationships dynamically.

Logic Programming and Constraint-Based Reasoning

Logic programming extends rule-based programming by allowing a **system to infer new facts from existing rules**. A prime example is **Prolog**, a declarative language designed for logic-based computation. In Python, the sympy library provides a way to **express and solve logical constraints declaratively**.

Consider a constraint satisfaction problem where we solve a simple equation:

```
from sympy import symbols, Eq, solve
```

```
x = symbols('x')
equation = Eq(2*x + 3, 9)  # 2x + 3 = 9
solution = solve(equation, x)

print(solution)  # Output: [3]
```

Here, instead of manually computing x, we **define the equation declaratively**, allowing the solver to determine the correct value automatically. This approach scales well to **complex constraint-based problems**, such as **scheduling, optimization, and AI reasoning**.

Using Rule Engines for Inference

A more sophisticated rule-based system can be implemented using **rule engines**, such as pyknow, which allows declarative rule definitions. The following example **determines eligibility for a loan** based on predefined rules:

```
from experta import KnowledgeEngine, Rule, Fact

class LoanEligibility(KnowledgeEngine):
    @Rule(Fact(income='high'))
    def approve_loan(self):
        print("Loan approved.")

    @Rule(Fact(income='low'))
    def deny_loan(self):
        print("Loan denied.")

engine = LoanEligibility()
engine.reset()
engine.declare(Fact(income='high'))
engine.run()   # Output: Loan approved.
```

This system **declaratively defines conditions** under which a loan is approved or denied, eliminating the need for complex if-else branching.

Applying Constraints in Practical Scenarios

Constraint-based reasoning is essential in domains such as **scheduling problems, resource allocation, and validation systems**. In Python, the constraint library can be used to enforce logical constraints and find valid solutions:

```
from constraint import Problem

problem = Problem()
problem.addVariable("x", range(10))
problem.addVariable("y", range(10))
problem.addConstraint(lambda x, y: x + y == 7, ("x", "y"))

solutions = problem.getSolutions()
print(solutions)  # Output: [{'x': 0, 'y': 7}, {'x': 1, 'y': 6}, ...]
```

This example **defines a constraint ($x + y = 7$)** without specifying how to compute the solution. The solver **automatically finds valid values**, making constraint programming a powerful declarative paradigm.

Rule-based programming and logic constraints shift the focus from **procedural steps to declarative rule definitions**, making systems more adaptable, readable, and scalable. By **defining relationships rather than execution flow**, rule-based programming enables AI reasoning, expert systems, and constraint-solving applications. Whether through **if-then rules, logic programming, or constraint solvers**, declarative techniques offer powerful alternatives to imperative programming's rigid control structures.

Pure Functions and Immutability

Pure functions and immutability are core principles of declarative programming, enabling predictable, side-effect-free computations. A **pure function** is a function whose output depends solely on its input and produces no side effects, such as modifying global variables or performing I/O operations. **Immutability** ensures that data structures remain unchanged once created, improving **readability, maintainability, and concurrency safety**. These principles are fundamental in **functional programming paradigms** and are widely used in languages such as **Haskell, Lisp, and Python**.

Understanding Pure Functions

A function is considered **pure** if it satisfies the following two conditions:

1. **Deterministic Behavior** – The function always produces the same output for the same input.

2. **No Side Effects** – It does not modify external state, such as global variables, files, or databases.

For example, the following is a pure function in Python:

```
def add(a, b):
    return a + b

print(add(3, 5))   # Output: 8
print(add(3, 5))   # Output: 8 (Always the same result for the same input)
```

This function **does not modify external state**, making it easy to test, debug, and reason about.

However, a function that modifies a global variable or performs I/O is **impure**:

```
total = 0

def add_to_total(value):
    global total
    total += value   # Modifies global state (side effect)
    return total

print(add_to_total(5))   # Output: 5
print(add_to_total(5))   # Output: 10 (Not deterministic)
```

This impure function changes a global variable, making it unpredictable and harder to test.

Immutability and Data Integrity

Immutability ensures that data structures remain unchanged after creation. Instead of modifying data, immutable structures create new copies, reducing unintended side effects and improving program reliability.

For example, strings in Python are immutable:

```
s = "Hello"
s = s + " World"  # A new string is created; the original is unchanged

print(s)  # Output: "Hello World"
```

To enforce immutability in custom objects, **namedtuples and frozen dataclasses** can be used:

```
from collections import namedtuple

Person = namedtuple('Person', ['name', 'age'])
p = Person("Alice", 30)

# p.age = 31  # This would raise an error as namedtuple is immutable
```

Alternatively, using dataclasses with frozen=True makes objects immutable:

```
from dataclasses import dataclass

@dataclass(frozen=True)
class ImmutablePerson:
    name: str
    age: int

p = ImmutablePerson("Bob", 25)
# p.age = 26  # Raises an error
```

Functional Programming Benefits with Immutability

Immutability is particularly beneficial in functional programming, enabling **safe concurrency and parallelism** by preventing **race conditions and unintended modifications**. For example, rather than modifying a list in place, functional programming relies on operations that return **new transformed versions**:

```
numbers = [1, 2, 3, 4, 5]
squared = list(map(lambda x: x ** 2, numbers))

print(squared)  # Output: [1, 4, 9, 16, 25]
print(numbers)  # Output: [1, 2, 3, 4, 5] (Original list unchanged)
```

This approach eliminates unintended side effects and preserves data integrity, making functional-style programs more **robust, maintainable, and scalable**.

Pure functions and immutability are central to declarative programming, ensuring **predictable behavior, reduced side effects, and improved parallel execution**. By eliminating mutable state and side effects, programs become **easier to debug, test, and**

reason about. Adopting these principles enhances code maintainability and is particularly advantageous in multi-threaded and distributed computing environments.

Constraint Propagation Mechanisms

Constraint propagation is a powerful technique used in **constraint programming**, allowing systems to solve complex problems by reducing the possible values of variables based on predefined conditions. Instead of specifying explicit procedural steps, **declarative constraint solvers infer valid solutions** by applying rules iteratively. This method is widely used in **scheduling, optimization, logic puzzles, and artificial intelligence**. By continuously refining possible values until a solution emerges, constraint propagation efficiently narrows down the solution space, ensuring consistency across dependent variables.

Understanding Constraint Propagation

Constraint propagation is based on **eliminating inconsistent values** for variables based on the relationships between them. Consider a simple case:

- If **X must be greater than Y**, and **Y is 5**, then **X must be at least 6**.

- If **Z must be even** and **Z is between 1 and 10**, the possible values for **Z** are {2, 4, 6, 8, 10}.

A constraint solver iteratively **propagates** these constraints, reducing possibilities until a valid solution is found.

A classic example of constraint propagation is solving a **Sudoku puzzle**, where each number placement restricts the possible values for adjacent cells.

Implementing Constraint Propagation in Python

Python provides several libraries for constraint-based programming, such as **constraint** and **z3**. Below is an example using constraint to solve a simple problem:

```python
from constraint import Problem

problem = Problem()
problem.addVariable("X", range(1, 10))   # X can be 1 to 9
problem.addVariable("Y", range(1, 10))
problem.addConstraint(lambda x, y: x > y, ("X", "Y"))  # X must be greater than Y

solutions = problem.getSolutions()
print(solutions)   # Output: All valid (X, Y) pairs where X > Y
```

Here, the constraint solver **automatically enforces the rule X > Y**, eliminating invalid pairs without explicit iteration.

Real-World Applications of Constraint Propagation

1. **Sudoku Solver** – Each number placement enforces constraints on remaining cells.

2. **Timetabling and Scheduling** – Assigns meeting times based on availability and conflict rules.

3. **Route Optimization** – Finds shortest paths while satisfying road and traffic constraints.

Consider a **Sudoku solver** using z3:

```python
from z3 import Int, Solver, And

X = Int('X')
Y = Int('Y')

solver = Solver()
solver.add(X > Y, X < 10, Y > 0)

if solver.check() == "sat":
    print(solver.model())  # Output: A valid solution satisfying constraints
```

This declarative approach **defines constraints without specifying an algorithm**, allowing the solver to infer valid values.

Constraint propagation mechanisms enable **efficient problem-solving by enforcing logical rules dynamically**, reducing computational complexity. By applying declarative constraints instead of imperative loops, programmers can focus on **what conditions must be met rather than how to compute the solution**. This technique is essential in AI, optimization, and decision-making systems, ensuring correctness and efficiency in solving complex, interdependent problems.

Module 5:

Understanding Side Effects and Purity

Declarative programming emphasizes **minimizing side effects** and ensuring that computations remain **predictable and composable**. This module explores how declarative paradigms handle **state management, function purity, referential transparency, and interactions with external systems**. Understanding these concepts is crucial for writing maintainable and error-free declarative code, particularly in functional programming and constraint-based environments.

Managing State in Declarative Programming

State management in declarative programming differs significantly from imperative approaches. In imperative programming, state is frequently modified through variable assignments and mutations, making reasoning about program behavior more difficult. Declarative programming, however, **favors immutability and explicit transformations** to manage state in a controlled manner. By avoiding direct mutations, declarative code maintains **predictability and modularity**.

Functional programming offers an elegant way to manage state using **higher-order functions, recursion, and persistent data structures**. Instead of modifying variables in place, new states are derived from previous states, ensuring that earlier states remain unchanged. This approach is particularly effective in concurrent programming, where state mutation can lead to unpredictable behaviors and race conditions. Techniques such as **monads in Haskell** and **state-passing functions in Python** provide structured ways to handle state transitions without side effects.

Pure and Impure Functions

A fundamental distinction in declarative programming is between **pure and impure functions**. A **pure function** is one whose output depends solely on its input parameters and has no observable side effects. This means that for any given input, the function will always return the same result. Pure functions enhance **testability, modularity, and reasoning** in software development.

Impure functions, on the other hand, interact with external state, such as modifying global variables, performing I/O operations, or altering data structures in place. While some impurity is necessary for practical applications, declarative programming seeks to **isolate impurity** to specific parts of a program, ensuring that most of the code remains pure. This isolation makes it easier to debug and reason about behavior, as side effects are confined to well-defined locations.

Referential Transparency in Declarative Code

Referential transparency is a key property of declarative programs, ensuring that expressions can be **replaced with their corresponding values without altering program behavior**. This concept is essential in functional programming, enabling powerful optimizations like **memoization, lazy evaluation, and parallel execution**.

A function or expression is **referentially transparent** if it always evaluates to the same value for the same input. This property allows compilers and interpreters to optimize code by caching results or reordering computations safely. Conversely, referential opacity—caused by hidden dependencies or mutable state—makes reasoning about code more difficult. By enforcing referential transparency, declarative programming achieves **higher reliability and performance** in complex computations.

Handling I/O and External Interactions

Despite the emphasis on purity, real-world programs must interact with external systems such as databases, file systems, and networks. Declarative programming **encapsulates impurity** by structuring I/O operations in a way that maintains **predictability and composability**. Common strategies include **lazy evaluation, functional I/O wrappers, and explicit effect-handling constructs** like monads in Haskell or async functions in Python.

One approach is **separating pure computations from impure interactions**, ensuring that core logic remains **deterministic and testable** while external interactions are controlled. This separation is particularly beneficial in concurrent and distributed systems, where managing side effects effectively is crucial for scalability and reliability.

Understanding side effects and purity is essential for writing effective declarative programs. By managing state immutably, enforcing pure functions, maintaining referential transparency, and structuring I/O interactions thoughtfully, declarative programming enables more **robust, scalable, and maintainable** software solutions. These principles are particularly valuable in modern programming paradigms that emphasize **parallelism, reusability, and correctness**.

Managing State in Declarative Programming

State management is one of the most significant challenges in programming. In **imperative programming**, state changes frequently through variable assignments, loops, and conditionals. These mutations can lead to unintended side effects, making programs difficult to understand and debug. Declarative programming, in contrast, promotes **immutability** and **explicit transformations**, ensuring that state changes are predictable and controlled. This approach simplifies reasoning about code and enhances maintainability.

In **functional programming**, state is typically managed using **pure functions** that return new values rather than modifying existing ones. Instead of updating variables directly, functions generate **new states** derived from previous ones. This prevents **unexpected behavior due to hidden dependencies**, making code easier to test and parallelize.

Common strategies for managing state declaratively include **recursion, persistent data structures, and functional state transformations**.

Immutability and Functional State Management

A key principle of declarative programming is **immutability**—once a value is assigned, it does not change. Instead of modifying data structures, **new instances** are created with updated values. This approach avoids unintended side effects, especially in **concurrent environments** where multiple functions might access shared data.

Consider an **imperative approach** where a list is updated in place:

```
# Imperative: Modifying state directly
numbers = [1, 2, 3]
numbers.append(4)
print(numbers)  # Output: [1, 2, 3, 4]
```

In contrast, a **declarative approach** creates a new list without altering the original:

```
# Declarative: Preserving original state
numbers = [1, 2, 3]
new_numbers = numbers + [4]
print(new_numbers)  # Output: [1, 2, 3, 4]
print(numbers)  # Output: [1, 2, 3] (unchanged)
```

By ensuring **immutable state**, the declarative approach avoids unexpected modifications and makes debugging easier.

Using Functional Transformations

Functional programming provides **higher-order functions** such as map, filter, and reduce to **transform data without modifying it**. These functions allow state changes to be expressed **without explicit loops or variable assignments**.

Example: Doubling a list of numbers without modifying the original list:

```
numbers = [1, 2, 3]
doubled = list(map(lambda x: x * 2, numbers))
print(doubled)  # Output: [2, 4, 6]
print(numbers)  # Output: [1, 2, 3] (original remains unchanged)
```

This approach makes state transformations **clear, composable, and side-effect-free**, adhering to declarative programming principles.

State in Recursive Functions

Since declarative programming avoids **explicit loops and mutable variables**, **recursion** is often used to manage state changes. Recursive functions break down problems into smaller instances, passing state through function calls rather than modifying global variables.

Example: Calculating the sum of a list using recursion:

```
def recursive_sum(lst):
    if not lst:
        return 0
    return lst[0] + recursive_sum(lst[1:])

print(recursive_sum([1, 2, 3]))  # Output: 6
```

This function avoids state mutation by **passing down the remaining list** instead of modifying an index-based counter.

Declarative programming manages state by **favoring immutability, using higher-order functions, and leveraging recursion** instead of direct variable manipulation. These techniques enhance **predictability, reusability, and testability**, making declarative code more robust and easier to maintain.

Pure and Impure Functions

In declarative programming, functions are classified as **pure or impure** based on their behavior. **Pure functions** have no side effects and always return the same output for the same input. They do not modify global variables, perform I/O operations, or depend on external state. In contrast, **impure functions** interact with the outside world or modify data, making them harder to predict and test.

Pure functions are **deterministic, composable, and easier to debug**. Declarative programming encourages the use of pure functions as much as possible, isolating impurity to **specific areas** of a program. This approach enhances **modularity, concurrency, and testability** in software design.

Characteristics of Pure Functions

A function is considered pure if it satisfies two conditions:

1. **Referential Transparency** – The function always returns the same result for the same input.

2. **No Side Effects** – The function does not modify global state, perform I/O operations, or change external variables.

Example of a **pure function**:

```
# A pure function: No side effects, always returns the same output for the same
           input
def square(n):
    return n * n

print(square(4))   # Output: 16
print(square(4))   # Output: 16 (same input, same output)
```

This function meets the **criteria of purity** because it depends only on its input and does not modify any external state.

Impure Functions and Their Risks

Impure functions, while sometimes necessary, introduce **unpredictability** by modifying state, performing I/O, or depending on global variables.

Example of an **impure function**:

```
# An impure function: Modifies global state
total = 0

def add_to_total(n):
    global total
    total += n  # Modifies global variable
    return total

print(add_to_total(5))  # Output: 5
print(add_to_total(5))  # Output: 10 (same input, different output)
```

Since the function modifies a **global variable**, it loses **referential transparency**, making debugging and reasoning about state changes more difficult.

Isolating Impurity in Declarative Programming

Since real-world applications require **interactions with external systems**, declarative programming **isolates impurity** into small, controlled areas while keeping the majority of the code pure.

Example: Separating pure and impure logic in a logging function:

```
# Pure function: Generates a formatted message
def format_message(user, action):
    return f"User {user} performed {action}"

# Impure function: Performs I/O by printing to the console
def log_action(user, action):
    message = format_message(user, action)  # Delegating pure logic
    print(message)  # I/O operation (impure)

log_action("Alice", "login")  # Output: User Alice performed login
```

Here, **format_message** remains pure, while the impure function **log_action** handles I/O separately. This separation ensures that **most of the program remains pure and testable**.

Pure functions are central to declarative programming, ensuring **predictability, modularity, and maintainability**. While impure functions are sometimes necessary, they should be **isolated** to maintain code clarity and composability. This balance allows declarative programming to be both practical and efficient in real-world applications.

Referential Transparency in Declarative Code

Referential transparency is a fundamental property of declarative programming that ensures **expressions can be replaced with their corresponding values without affecting the program's behavior**. This characteristic enhances **predictability, optimization, and modularity**, making declarative code easier to reason about and refactor. By enforcing referential transparency, declarative programming enables powerful techniques such as **memoization, lazy evaluation, and parallel execution**.

A function or expression is referentially transparent if it always evaluates to the same result for the same input. In contrast, **referential opacity** occurs when an expression's result depends on external state, making the code harder to test and optimize.

Understanding Referential Transparency

To be **referentially transparent**, a function must:

1. Always return the same output for the same input.

2. Have no hidden dependencies on global state or external interactions.

Example of a **referentially transparent function**:

```
# Pure function: Referentially transparent
def add(x, y):
    return x + y

print(add(3, 4))  # Output: 7
print(add(3, 4))  # Output: 7 (always the same result)
```

This function is referentially transparent because it depends only on its inputs and has no side effects. The expression add(3, 4) can be **replaced with 7 anywhere in the code** without changing the program's behavior.

Referential Opacity and Its Challenges

Referential opacity occurs when an expression's output is affected by **external factors** such as global variables, random numbers, or user input. This makes the program less predictable and harder to optimize.

Example of a **referentially opaque function**:

```
import random

# Impure function: Returns different results for the same input
def get_random_number():
    return random.randint(1, 10)

print(get_random_number())  # Output: (varies)
print(get_random_number())  # Output: (varies)
```

Since this function **does not always return the same result**, it is **not referentially transparent**. The expression get_random_number() **cannot be safely replaced with a fixed value**, making debugging and reasoning about code more difficult.

Optimization Benefits of Referential Transparency

One of the main advantages of referential transparency is that it allows **compiler optimizations and caching techniques**. Since referentially transparent functions always produce the same result for the same input, their computations can be **cached or precomputed**.

Example: Using **memoization** to optimize a function:

```
from functools import lru_cache

# Pure function with caching
@lru_cache(maxsize=None)
def factorial(n):
    if n == 0:
        return 1
    return n * factorial(n - 1)

print(factorial(5))   # Output: 120
print(factorial(5))   # Retrieved from cache, no recomputation
```

Here, the factorial function benefits from **memoization**, as previously computed results are stored and reused, improving efficiency.

Referential transparency ensures **consistent outputs, simplifies debugging, and enables compiler optimizations**. By writing referentially transparent functions, declarative programming promotes **reliability, maintainability, and performance**, making it an essential principle for building robust software.

Handling I/O and External Interactions

Declarative programming emphasizes **pure functions and immutability**, but real-world applications require **interaction with external systems**, such as reading from files, databases, or APIs. Since these operations introduce **side effects**, they must be handled carefully to **preserve code clarity and maintainability**. The key challenge is to **isolate impurity** while keeping the majority of the program declarative.

By using **functional constructs like monads, effect tracking, and lazy evaluation**, declarative programming frameworks ensure that **I/O operations are controlled and predictable**. This approach allows programmers to build scalable systems while **maintaining the benefits of declarative paradigms**.

Why I/O is Considered Impure

I/O operations are **impure** because they interact with external state, making results unpredictable. Examples include:

- Reading from a file (content may change).

- Writing to a database (modifies external state).

- Sending a network request (dependent on server response).

Example of **impure I/O operation**:

```
# Impure function: Reads from an external file
def read_file(filename):
    with open(filename, "r") as file:
        return file.read()

print(read_file("data.txt"))  # Output depends on the file contents
```

This function is **not referentially transparent** because calling read_file("data.txt") at different times may return **different results** depending on the file's content.

Isolating I/O in Declarative Programming

A common strategy in declarative programming is **isolating impure operations** into a small, controlled part of the program while keeping the core logic pure. One approach is to **separate data processing from I/O**.

Example: **Separating Pure and Impure Logic**

```
# Pure function: Processes data without side effects
def process_data(data):
    return [line.upper() for line in data.split("\n")]

# Impure function: Handles I/O separately
def read_and_process_file(filename):
    with open(filename, "r") as file:
        data = file.read()
    return process_data(data)

print(read_and_process_file("data.txt"))  # Output depends on file contents
```

Here, **process_data** remains pure, making it **testable and reusable**, while I/O is isolated in **read_and_process_file**. This ensures **better maintainability and separation of concerns**.

Using Lazy Evaluation to Control I/O

Lazy evaluation defers computations until needed, allowing I/O to be **controlled more effectively**. Many functional languages use **lazy sequences or monads** to manage I/O while preserving declarative principles.

Example: **Lazy file reading with generators**

```python
# Generator function: Lazily reads a file line by line
def read_file_lazy(filename):
    with open(filename, "r") as file:
        for line in file:
            yield line.strip()

# Processing lines lazily
for line in read_file_lazy("data.txt"):
    print(line.upper())  # Only processes one line at a time
```

By using a generator, this function reads only one line at a time, **reducing memory usage** and **controlling side effects**.

Handling I/O in declarative programming requires **isolating impure operations**, **separating concerns**, and **using lazy evaluation** where possible. By applying these techniques, developers can maintain **code readability, modularity, and efficiency**, ensuring that declarative principles remain intact even in real-world applications.

Module 6:
Mathematical Foundations of Declarative Programming

Declarative programming is deeply rooted in mathematical concepts that define computation in terms of **expressions, rules, and transformations**, rather than sequences of instructions. Understanding its mathematical foundations provides **a theoretical basis for reasoning about programs, optimizing computations, and ensuring correctness**. This module explores four key mathematical principles: **lambda calculus, predicate logic, category theory, and fixed-point theory**. These concepts underpin declarative paradigms, shaping the way functions, logic, and types interact in computation.

Lambda Calculus and Functional Composition

Lambda calculus forms the theoretical foundation of functional programming, a core aspect of declarative paradigms. It models computation using **anonymous functions** and **function applications**, allowing expressions to be evaluated purely mathematically. Every function in lambda calculus is **first-class**, meaning it can be passed as an argument, returned from other functions, and composed to build more complex operations. Functional composition, an essential technique in declarative programming, enables the creation of **modular, reusable, and predictable** computations by chaining small, single-purpose functions. Mastering lambda calculus and functional composition helps programmers develop a **precise, structured approach to problem-solving** in declarative languages.

Predicate Logic and Logical Deduction

Predicate logic serves as the backbone of **logic programming**, a branch of declarative programming that expresses computations as a set of facts and rules. It extends propositional logic by introducing **quantifiers, predicates, and variables**, allowing for the formulation of **logical relationships** between entities. Logical deduction, a fundamental principle in logic-based programming languages like **Prolog**, enables programs to infer new facts from existing ones. This makes declarative logic-based programming particularly powerful for **knowledge representation, rule-based systems, and automated reasoning**. Understanding predicate logic allows developers to construct **robust, deterministic models** that derive solutions purely through declarative specifications.

Category Theory and Type Systems

Category theory provides a high-level abstraction for **structuring and reasoning about programs** in declarative languages. It formalizes relationships between objects and transformations, offering a **framework for type systems and functional programming concepts**. Core category-theoretic principles, such as **functors, monads, and morphisms**, facilitate **composability, data flow, and state management** in declarative programming. Type systems, influenced by category theory, ensure correctness by **constraining values and operations**, preventing errors through **static verification**. By applying category-theoretic structures, developers can design **more expressive, flexible, and mathematically sound declarative programs** that leverage **type safety and composability** for scalable architectures.

Fixed-Point Theory in Computation

Fixed-point theory plays a crucial role in understanding recursion, iteration, and **computational fixed points** in declarative programming. A **fixed point** of a function is a value that remains unchanged under that function's application. Many recursive definitions in declarative paradigms rely on fixed-point computations, allowing the definition of **self-referential functions** without explicit iteration. This principle is fundamental in defining **recursive function calls, lazy evaluation, and convergence properties** in declarative languages. Fixed-point combinators, such as the **Y combinator**, enable recursion in lambda calculus, further illustrating its relevance in **functional and logic-based programming paradigms**.

Mathematical foundations provide **rigorous, structured principles** that enhance declarative programming's expressiveness and correctness. Lambda calculus refines **functional transformations**, predicate logic enables **rule-based inference**, category theory strengthens **type abstractions**, and fixed-point theory models **recursion and convergence**. By understanding these mathematical underpinnings, developers can **design, optimize, and reason about declarative programs** with greater clarity and precision

Lambda Calculus and Functional Composition

Lambda calculus is a **formal system** in mathematical logic that expresses computation through **functions, variables, and applications**. It serves as the foundation of **functional programming**, a core paradigm in declarative programming. In lambda calculus, functions are **first-class citizens**, meaning they can be passed as arguments, returned as values, and combined to create higher-order functions. This abstraction allows developers to **build complex computations** using simple function definitions and compositions. Functional composition, an essential technique in declarative programming, enables programs to be structured in a **modular, readable, and reusable manner** by combining small, independent functions into larger operations.

Basic Lambda Calculus Notation

Lambda calculus follows a simple notation:

- $\lambda x.\ x + 2$ represents an **anonymous function** that takes x and returns x + 2.

- $(\lambda x.\ x + 2)\ 3$ applies the function to 3, yielding 5.

In Python, lambda calculus can be represented using **lambda functions**:

```
# Lambda function equivalent to λx. x + 2
add_two = lambda x: x + 2

print(add_two(3))  # Output: 5
```

This **anonymous function** does not require explicit naming, showcasing how lambda calculus **eliminates unnecessary variable assignments**.

Functional Composition in Declarative Programming

Functional composition is the **process of combining multiple functions into a single operation**, allowing complex transformations to be defined declaratively. Instead of using loops or imperative steps, functions are composed **mathematically** to define what needs to be computed.

Example: **Composing Functions**

```
# Two simple lambda functions
double = lambda x: x * 2
increment = lambda x: x + 1

# Function composition: f(g(x))
compose = lambda f, g: lambda x: f(g(x))

# Creating a new function that doubles and then increments
new_function = compose(increment, double)

print(new_function(4))  # Output: 9
```

Here, new_function(4) first **doubles** 4 (resulting in 8), then **increments** it (9). This approach promotes **code clarity** and avoids mutable state.

Higher-Order Functions and Recursion

Since functions are **first-class** in lambda calculus, they can be passed as arguments to other functions, leading to **higher-order functions**. Recursion, another key principle, allows functions to **call themselves** for iterative computations, eliminating the need for explicit loops.

Example: **Recursive Function Using Lambda**

```
# Factorial using recursion and lambda
factorial = lambda n: 1 if n == 0 else n * factorial(n - 1)

print(factorial(5))  # Output: 120
```

This **self-referential function** relies on a **mathematical definition** rather than mutable state, making it highly readable and declarative.

Lambda calculus forms the backbone of **functional programming** by expressing computations through **pure functions**. Functional composition enhances **code modularity and readability**, allowing programmers to define transformations declaratively. By leveraging **higher-order functions and recursion**, developers can build powerful, maintainable software while preserving **mathematical correctness**.

Predicate Logic and Logical Deduction

Predicate logic is the foundation of **logic programming**, enabling computations to be expressed in terms of **rules, relationships, and facts** rather than step-by-step instructions. Unlike propositional logic, which deals with simple true/false statements, predicate logic introduces **quantifiers, variables, and predicates**, making it a powerful tool for **reasoning and inference in declarative programming**. Logical deduction, a key principle in this paradigm, allows systems to derive **new facts from existing ones**, making declarative programming highly suited for applications like **expert systems, artificial intelligence, and knowledge representation**.

Basic Predicate Logic Concepts

Predicate logic consists of **predicates**, which are functions that return **true or false**, and **quantifiers** that specify the scope of variables. A simple predicate logic statement might be:

- $\forall x \ (\text{Human}(x) \rightarrow \text{Mortal}(x))$

    - "For all x, if x is a human, then x is mortal."

- $\exists x \ (\text{Bird}(x) \land \text{CanFly}(x))$

    - "There exists an x such that x is a bird and x can fly."

In Python, predicates can be represented using **Boolean functions**:

```python
# Defining predicates
def is_human(name):
    return name in ["Socrates", "Plato", "Aristotle"]

def is_mortal(name):
    return is_human(name)  # All humans are mortal

# Logical deduction
print(is_mortal("Socrates"))  # Output: True
print(is_mortal("Zeus"))  # Output: False
```

Here, is_human acts as a **predicate**, and is_mortal deduces whether a person is mortal based on logical rules.

Logical Deduction and Rule-Based Computation

Logical deduction enables programs to **infer new knowledge** by applying logical rules to given facts. This is the foundation of **logic programming languages** like **Prolog**, which use declarative rules to define relationships.

Example: **Rule-Based Deduction in Python**

```
# Knowledge base
facts = {
    "Socrates": "human",
    "Plato": "human",
    "Aristotle": "human"
}

# Rule-based deduction
def is_mortal(name):
    return facts.get(name) == "human"

print(is_mortal("Socrates"))  # Output: True
print(is_mortal("Zeus"))  # Output: False
```

This method mimics **Prolog-like logic**, where rules and facts define the computation rather than explicit instructions.

Unification and Logical Queries

Unification is the process of **matching variables** in logical statements to find solutions. In Python, this can be implemented using **pattern matching and filtering**.

Example: **Finding All Mortals from a Knowledge Base**

```
# Given a set of individuals and their properties
people = {
    "Socrates": "human",
    "Plato": "human",
    "Zeus": "god"
}

# Finding all mortals
mortals = [name for name, prop in people.items() if prop == "human"]

print(mortals)  # Output: ['Socrates', 'Plato']
```

This approach **abstracts away loops and conditions**, aligning with declarative principles by focusing on **what should be computed rather than how**.

Predicate logic enables **declarative problem-solving** by defining rules and allowing logical deduction. It eliminates explicit control flow, making it ideal for applications requiring **automated reasoning and rule-based decision-making**. By leveraging **predicate functions, logical inference, and rule-based computation**, declarative programming provides **a structured, expressive approach** to solving complex problems.

Category Theory and Type Systems

Category theory provides an **abstract mathematical framework** for understanding **structures and transformations** in programming. It is foundational to **functional programming**, influencing concepts such as **functors, monads, and type systems**. In declarative programming, category theory helps model computation in a way that **emphasizes composition, immutability, and structure** rather than explicit control flow. Type systems, another crucial aspect, enforce **correctness and predictability** in programs, ensuring functions operate on valid inputs while avoiding runtime errors. By integrating category theory principles, modern programming languages achieve **robust, scalable, and maintainable software architectures**.

Categories and Morphisms

In category theory, a **category** consists of **objects** (data types) and **morphisms** (functions) that transform one object into another. The essential idea is that computations can be viewed as a **series of transformations**, where functions compose cleanly.

Example: **Category Representation in Python**

```python
# Define category objects (data types)
class Integer:
    def __init__(self, value):
        self.value = value

# Define morphisms (functions transforming objects)
def add_one(n):
    return Integer(n.value + 1)

def multiply_two(n):
    return Integer(n.value * 2)

# Function composition: (add_one ∘ multiply_two)(x)
def compose(f, g):
    return lambda x: f(g(x))

# Create a composite function
transformation = compose(add_one, multiply_two)

# Apply transformation
result = transformation(Integer(3))
print(result.value)  # Output: 7 (3 * 2 + 1)
```

This demonstrates how **composition eliminates explicit state mutations** and enhances **code modularity**, core to declarative programming.

Functors and Monads in Declarative Computation

A **functor** is a structure that applies a function **over encapsulated data** while preserving its context. Monads extend this concept by **chaining computations** while handling side effects, such as I/O or exceptions, declaratively.

Example: **Functor Pattern in Python**

```python
class Functor:
```

```
    def __init__(self, value):
        self.value = value

    def map(self, func):
        return Functor(func(self.value))  # Apply function and wrap result

# Using Functor to transform data
box = Functor(3).map(lambda x: x * 2).map(lambda x: x + 1)
print(box.value)  # Output: 7
```

This structure ensures that transformations remain **pure, predictable, and declarative**, avoiding imperative control flow.

Type Systems and Declarative Safety

Type systems prevent errors by **enforcing rules** at compile-time or runtime. **Static type systems** (e.g., in Haskell) catch errors before execution, while **dynamic type systems** (e.g., Python) enforce rules at runtime. Strong type systems contribute to **declarative programming** by ensuring that transformations are **well-defined and error-free**.

Example: **Type Checking in Python Using Type Hints**

```
from typing import Callable

# Enforce function type signatures
def apply_function(f: Callable[[int], int], x: int) -> int:
    return f(x)

print(apply_function(lambda x: x * 2, 5))  # Output: 10
```

By incorporating type safety, declarative programming **minimizes runtime failures**, allowing for **predictable, maintainable, and scalable code**.

Category theory and type systems provide **theoretical and practical** foundations for declarative programming. By emphasizing **function composition, functors, and monads**, category theory enhances **code abstraction and reuse**. Type systems ensure that transformations remain **valid and reliable**, reducing errors. Together, these concepts reinforce **robust declarative software design**, making programs **safer, clearer, and more maintainable**.

Fixed-Point Theory in Computation

Fixed-point theory plays a crucial role in **mathematical logic, recursion, and declarative programming**, particularly in the evaluation of **recursive functions, fixpoint combinators, and self-referential computations**. In the context of programming, a **fixed point** of a function is a value that remains unchanged when the function is applied to it. This concept underlies key techniques in **functional programming, optimization, and formal verification**. By leveraging fixed-point computations, declarative languages express recursion, iterative computations, and optimization problems in a **mathematically sound and expressive manner**, eliminating the need for explicit state management.

Understanding Fixed-Point Computations

A fixed point of a function $f(x)f(x)f(x)$ is a value xxx such that:

$f(x)=x$

For example, in solving **mathematical equations like root-finding** or defining recursive structures, fixed-point computations help determine values that remain invariant under a transformation. In programming, this concept is vital for evaluating recursive functions without requiring **explicit loops or mutable state**.

Example: **Finding Fixed Points Using Iteration in Python**

```python
def fixed_point(f, x, tolerance=1e-5):
    while abs(f(x) - x) > tolerance:
        x = f(x)
    return x

# Example: Fixed point of cos(x) (converges to ~0.739)
import math
result = fixed_point(math.cos, 1.0)
print(result)  # Output: 0.739085...
```

This demonstrates an **iterative fixed-point search,** where the function repeatedly applies itself to an initial guess until convergence.

Fixed-Point Combinators and Recursive Functions

Declarative programming relies on **recursion** rather than explicit loops. The **Y combinator**, a fixed-point combinator, allows functions to refer to themselves in a **purely functional** manner. Since Python does not support anonymous recursive functions directly, we can simulate the **Y combinator** using lambda functions.

Example: **Fixed-Point Combinator for Factorial Calculation**

```python
Y = lambda f: (lambda x: f(lambda v: x(x)(v)))(lambda x: f(lambda v: x(x)(v)))

factorial = Y(lambda f: lambda n: 1 if n == 0 else n * f(n - 1))

print(factorial(5))  # Output: 120
```

This showcases how recursion can be **expressed without explicitly naming the function**, staying true to **pure declarative principles**.

Fixed-Point Applications in Optimization and Formal Methods

Fixed-point computations are widely used in **dataflow analysis, optimization algorithms, and functional language semantics**. In **constraint solving**, fixed points help find **stable solutions** that satisfy all constraints. In **optimization**, methods like **gradient descent** aim to converge to a fixed point where no further improvement is possible.

Example: **Fixed-Point Optimization Using Gradient Descent**

```
def gradient_descent(f_prime, x, lr=0.1, tolerance=1e-5):
    while abs(f_prime(x)) > tolerance:
        x = x - lr * f_prime(x)
    return x

# Example: Finding the minimum of x^2 (derivative: 2x)
min_point = gradient_descent(lambda x: 2*x, 5.0)
print(min_point)  # Output: ~0.0
```

This approach iteratively updates x until reaching a **fixed point** where further movement is minimal, effectively finding an **optimal solution**.

Fixed-point theory provides **a mathematical foundation for recursion, optimization, and constraint resolution** in declarative programming. From recursive function evaluation to numerical optimization and logic programming, fixed points allow computations to **stabilize at meaningful solutions** without requiring explicit iteration or mutable state. By integrating fixed-point principles, declarative programming achieves **elegant, scalable, and mathematically sound solutions** to complex problems.

Part 2:

Examples and Applications of Declarative Programming

Declarative programming is not merely a theoretical paradigm but a practical and highly applicable approach to solving real-world problems. This part explores how declarative principles manifest across various domains, including **functional programming, logic-based AI, web development, data querying, UI frameworks, and reactive programming models**. By examining **concrete applications**, learners will gain insight into **how declarative techniques simplify complex problem-solving, improve maintainability, and enable scalable architectures**. The modules in this section provide a well-rounded understanding of how declarative programming is actively used in modern **software development, artificial intelligence, and distributed systems**.

Functional Programming in Practice

Functional programming offers a robust paradigm where computations are expressed through **pure functions, immutability, and higher-order abstractions**. This module introduces **key functional principles**, including **first-class functions, closures, and recursion**. It explores **declarative data transformations**, such as **map-reduce pipelines and lazy evaluation**, which enhance efficiency. Functional error-handling techniques like **monads** simplify **side-effect management**, making code predictable. Finally, real-world applications in **data processing, distributed systems, and financial computations** showcase the power of functional programming.

Logic Programming in AI and Problem Solving

Logic programming is fundamental to **artificial intelligence, knowledge representation, and automated reasoning**. This module introduces **rule-based computation**, focusing on **Prolog and Datalog**, which enable declarative problem-solving. The role of **constraint logic programming (CLP)** in scheduling, optimization, and AI reasoning is explored. Learners will also discover how **automated theorem proving** leverages **first-order logic and resolution techniques** to verify formal properties. Applications in **natural language processing, expert systems, and knowledge inference** illustrate the real-world utility of logic-based approaches.

Declarative Web Developmen

Declarative programming has revolutionized web development by promoting **modular, composable, and scalable architectures**. This module examines **declarative web frameworks** like **React, Svelte, and Elm**, which simplify UI rendering through **state-driven components**. Functional reactive programming (FRP) is explored, highlighting its role in **asynchronous data streams and real-time updates**. The discussion extends to **state management techniques** such as **Redux and the Context API**, ensuring maintainability. Finally, **serverless computing and declarative deployment models** demonstrate how cloud applications can be efficiently orchestrated.

Declarative Data Querying

Data querying is inherently declarative, with languages like **SQL and NoSQL** providing **high-level abstractions** over data storage and retrieval. This module examines how **query optimization strategies** improve performance, ensuring efficient data access. Learners will explore **declarative data manipulation techniques**, including **functional joins, aggregations, and transformations**, which streamline data workflows. The growing field of **streaming and real-time data querying** is also covered, showcasing how declarative paradigms enable event-driven architectures. Applications in **business intelligence, big data analytics, and data warehousing** illustrate practical implementations.

Declarative UI Frameworks

Modern UI development embraces declarative paradigms, focusing on **component-based design and virtual DOM reconciliation**. This module introduces **JSX and functional components**, which simplify UI composition. The importance of **state synchronization techniques**, such as **React's state management and reactivity patterns**, is examined. Styling and theming using **declarative CSS-in-JS and utility-based styling approaches** is also discussed. By understanding these principles, learners can build **scalable, maintainable, and responsive web applications**, leveraging the advantages of **unidirectional data flow and component reusability**.

Reactive Programming Models

Reactive programming extends declarative principles to event-driven systems, allowing applications to **respond dynamically to changing data streams**. This module explores **event-driven and dataflow paradigms**, explaining how **Functional Reactive Programming (FRP)** models real-time computations. Learners will understand the role of **Reactive Extensions (RxJS, ReactiveX) and Observables**, which simplify asynchronous programming. Finally, the module examines how **reactive systems scale across distributed environments**, enabling robust architectures for **real-time data processing, live dashboards, and microservices-based applications**.

By exploring these applications, learners gain **practical experience in declarative programming**, enabling them to build **efficient, scalable, and maintainable systems** in functional, logic-based, and event-driven paradigms.

Module 7:

Functional Programming in Practice

Functional programming is a core paradigm within declarative programming, emphasizing **pure functions, immutability, and higher-order functions**. This module explores the **fundamental principles** of functional programming, techniques for **transforming data declaratively**, strategies for **handling errors using monads**, and practical real-world applications. Understanding functional programming helps programmers write **concise, predictable, and scalable** code by eliminating side effects and relying on **function composition**. This module provides an in-depth look at the **real-world advantages of functional programming**, making it accessible for developers looking to adopt declarative techniques in modern software development.

Core Principles of Functional Programming

Functional programming is based on a set of well-defined principles that differentiate it from imperative paradigms. One of the **most fundamental** principles is **pure functions**, which ensure that function outputs depend solely on inputs, without modifying external states. This principle leads to **predictable behavior and easier debugging**. Another key concept is **immutability**, where variables are not modified after creation, reducing unintended side effects. **Higher-order functions** allow functions to accept other functions as arguments or return them as values, enabling **modular and reusable** code structures. By adhering to these principles, functional programming facilitates **easier testing, parallel execution, and scalability** in software development.

Declarative Data Transformation Techniques

Functional programming provides **powerful abstractions** for manipulating and transforming data declaratively. Instead of relying on **explicit loops or mutable state**, functions such as **map, filter, and reduce** allow developers to process data **expressively and concisely**. These transformations ensure that operations remain **stateless** and are applied consistently across collections. This technique is especially valuable in **big data processing, functional reactive programming, and data pipeline management**. By structuring transformations using functional techniques, developers can write **clear, efficient, and composable** code that is **independent of specific data structures**, improving maintainability and readability.

Functional Error Handling and Monads

Error handling is a critical aspect of functional programming, often managed using **monads**— mathematical constructs that encapsulate computations while handling side effects. Unlike traditional **try-catch** mechanisms that introduce control flow complexity, functional approaches provide **composable error-handling techniques**. **Option (Maybe) monads** ensure functions gracefully handle missing values, while **Either monads** enable functions to represent success or failure without **throwing exceptions**. These functional constructs **eliminate unnecessary branching** in code and promote **safe, predictable computation pipelines**. Understanding how monads work allows developers to manage errors without breaking the declarative flow of their programs, making functional code more robust and maintainable.

Real-World Functional Programming Examples

Functional programming is widely applied in **modern web development, data science, and distributed computing**. Popular functional languages such as **Haskell, Scala, and Clojure** leverage these principles extensively. Even in multi-paradigm languages like **Python and JavaScript**, functional techniques are used to build **scalable microservices, data processing pipelines, and event-driven architectures**. Functional programming is particularly useful in **concurrent and parallel computing**, where immutability and pure functions help prevent **race conditions and unexpected side effects**. This section explores real-world examples where declarative and functional programming principles are leveraged to improve **code maintainability, performance, and scalability**.

Functional programming is a **powerful paradigm** that enhances **readability, composability, and robustness** in software development. By understanding **core principles, data transformation techniques, functional error handling, and real-world applications**, developers can leverage functional programming to **write scalable and efficient code**. This module provides the foundation for applying **declarative programming techniques** effectively, enabling programmers to **build complex systems with simplicity and elegance**.

Core Principles of Functional Programming

Functional programming is centered around **pure functions, immutability, and higher-order functions**, which create a foundation for building predictable and maintainable software. A **pure function** is one where the output is determined solely by its input values, without modifying any external state. This ensures that calling the function multiple times with the same input always produces the same result, leading to **referential transparency**.

In functional programming, **immutability** is another key principle, meaning data structures cannot be modified after creation. Instead of changing existing values, functional programs create new ones when transformations are required. This prevents unintended side effects and makes concurrent programming easier since data is never shared between processes in a mutable state.

Another crucial aspect of functional programming is **higher-order functions**, which treat functions as first-class citizens. This means that functions can be assigned to variables, passed as arguments, and returned from other functions. This enables **function composition**, where complex operations are built from smaller reusable functions. For example, instead of using explicit loops to process data, developers can use **map**, **filter**, and **reduce** to express transformations declaratively.

Example: Pure Functions in Python

Below is an example of a **pure function** that calculates the square of a number:

```
def square(x):
    return x * x

print(square(5))  # Output: 25
```

Since square(5) will always return 25 without modifying any external variables, it is **pure**.

Example: Immutability in Python

Using immutable data structures ensures data integrity in functional programming. Consider using tuples instead of lists:

```
def add_to_tuple(tup, value):
    return tup + (value,)

numbers = (1, 2, 3)
new_numbers = add_to_tuple(numbers, 4)

print(numbers)       # Output: (1, 2, 3)
print(new_numbers)   # Output: (1, 2, 3, 4)
```

Here, numbers remains unchanged, and new_numbers holds the new tuple.

Example: Higher-Order Functions

Higher-order functions allow passing functions as arguments to achieve code reusability. Below is an example using Python's map:

```
def double(x):
    return x * 2

numbers = [1, 2, 3, 4]
doubled = map(double, numbers)

print(list(doubled))  # Output: [2, 4, 6, 8]
```

The map function applies double to each element, demonstrating a functional approach to transformations.

The core principles of functional programming—**pure functions, immutability, and higher-order functions**—lead to more readable, predictable, and modular code. By eliminating side effects and embracing **function composition**, developers can write **maintainable and scalable** programs. These principles form the foundation of declarative programming, helping programmers **reason about code with greater clarity and confidence**.

Declarative Data Transformation Techniques

One of the key strengths of functional programming is its ability to transform data **declaratively**. Instead of using explicit loops and mutable variables, functional programming relies on **higher-order functions** such as map, filter, and reduce to express transformations in a concise and readable manner. These techniques allow developers to write **clean, modular, and efficient** code while avoiding unnecessary state mutations.

Declarative data transformations provide several advantages. They promote **immutability**, making it easier to debug programs since data is not modified in place. They also **enhance composability**, allowing different transformation functions to be combined seamlessly. This is particularly beneficial when working with large datasets, functional pipelines, and parallel processing, where explicit loops would introduce unnecessary complexity.

Using map for Element-Wise Transformations

The map function applies a given function to every element in a sequence and returns a new transformed sequence. This is a powerful alternative to traditional loops for data transformation.

```
def square(x):
    return x * x

numbers = [1, 2, 3, 4, 5]
squared_numbers = list(map(square, numbers))

print(squared_numbers)  # Output: [1, 4, 9, 16, 25]
```

Instead of modifying the original list, map creates a **new transformed list**, maintaining immutability and readability.

Filtering Data with filter

The filter function is used to select elements from a sequence that satisfy a given condition. This enables declarative selection without modifying the original dataset.

```
def is_even(x):
    return x % 2 == 0

numbers = [1, 2, 3, 4, 5, 6]
even_numbers = list(filter(is_even, numbers))

print(even_numbers)  # Output: [2, 4, 6]
```

Using filter, the code remains expressive and concise without relying on **explicit conditional loops**.

Reducing Data with reduce

The reduce function is used to **accumulate a result** from a sequence. It repeatedly applies a function to elements in the sequence, reducing them to a single value.

```
from functools import reduce

def add(x, y):
    return x + y

numbers = [1, 2, 3, 4, 5]
sum_of_numbers = reduce(add, numbers)

print(sum_of_numbers)  # Output: 15
```

Instead of looping over the list manually, reduce expresses the accumulation operation **declaratively**.

Chaining Transformations for Declarative Pipelines

A major advantage of functional programming is that transformations can be **chained together** to create a clear, declarative data pipeline.

```
numbers = [1, 2, 3, 4, 5, 6]

result = list(map(lambda x: x * 2, filter(lambda x: x % 2 == 0, numbers)))

print(result)  # Output: [4, 8, 12]
```

Here, the filter function selects even numbers, and map doubles them, demonstrating **composable functional programming**.

Declarative data transformation techniques allow developers to **express intent clearly** without relying on **mutable state or explicit loops**. Functions like map, filter, and reduce provide an elegant way to **process data efficiently and immutably**. By leveraging these techniques, developers can create **modular, scalable, and readable** functional code.

Functional Error Handling and Monads

Error handling in functional programming follows a **declarative** approach, where computations are structured to gracefully handle failures without disrupting program flow. Unlike imperative programming, which often relies on exceptions and control structures like try-except, functional error handling emphasizes **immutability, explicit return types, and composition**. This makes programs more predictable and easier to test.

A key concept in functional error handling is the use of **monads**, such as Maybe or Either, which encapsulate computations that might fail. Monads provide a structured way to **propagate errors without breaking composition**, ensuring that functions remain **pure** and side effects are minimized.

Handling Errors Functionally Without Exceptions

Instead of throwing exceptions, functional programming prefers returning special **error-aware values**, which can be processed declaratively. Python's None can be used to simulate functional approaches, but a more structured way is using **custom error-handling types**.

75

```python
def safe_divide(a, b):
    return a / b if b != 0 else None

result = safe_divide(10, 2)
print(result)  # Output: 5.0

error_result = safe_divide(10, 0)
print(error_result)  # Output: None
```

Here, safe_divide avoids exceptions and returns None for invalid operations, making error handling explicit.

Using Either Monad for Better Error Handling

A more advanced way to handle errors in a functional style is by implementing an **Either monad**, which represents computations that might fail. This ensures that failures are carried along without causing abrupt program termination.

```python
class Either:
    def __init__(self, value, is_error=False):
        self.value = value
        self.is_error = is_error

    def bind(self, func):
        return self if self.is_error else func(self.value)

    def __repr__(self):
        return f"Error({self.value})" if self.is_error else
            f"Success({self.value})"

def safe_divide(a, b):
    return Either("Division by zero", True) if b == 0 else Either(a / b)

result = safe_divide(10, 2).bind(lambda x: Either(x * 2))
print(result)  # Output: Success(10.0)

error_result = safe_divide(10, 0).bind(lambda x: Either(x * 2))
print(error_result)  # Output: Error(Division by zero)
```

Here, computations are **chained declaratively** using bind, allowing error propagation **without explicit conditionals**.

Using Python's Optional Type with map for Error Handling

The map function can be used to **apply transformations only if a value is valid**, preventing unnecessary operations on None values.

```python
def double(x):
    return x * 2 if x is not None else None

result = double(safe_divide(10, 2))
print(result)  # Output: 10.0

error_result = double(safe_divide(10, 0))
print(error_result)  # Output: None
```

This approach eliminates **nested conditionals**, keeping error handling clean and declarative.

Functional error handling ensures **predictability and composability** by encapsulating failures within specialized constructs. Monads like Either allow for **explicit and structured error propagation**, reducing reliance on exceptions. By embracing functional techniques, developers can write **robust, maintainable, and failure-resistant** declarative programs.

Real-World Functional Programming Examples

Functional programming is widely used in modern software development for tasks such as **data processing, concurrency, and web development**. Many programming languages, including Python, JavaScript, and Scala, incorporate functional programming concepts to improve code readability and maintainability. This section explores practical applications of functional programming, demonstrating its advantages in real-world scenarios such as data transformation, parallel processing, and functional API design.

By structuring code declaratively, functional programming allows developers to write **predictable, reusable, and scalable** solutions. Whether handling **large datasets, implementing event-driven architectures, or optimizing computations**, functional paradigms provide an effective way to **simplify complex logic** while maintaining robustness.

Data Processing with Functional Pipelines

One of the most common uses of functional programming is in **data transformation pipelines**. By using **higher-order functions** like map, filter, and reduce, data can be processed in a clean, declarative manner.

```
orders = [
    {"id": 1, "amount": 250, "status": "completed"},
    {"id": 2, "amount": 450, "status": "pending"},
    {"id": 3, "amount": 300, "status": "completed"},
    {"id": 4, "amount": 150, "status": "failed"},
]

# Get the total amount of completed orders
from functools import reduce

completed_orders = filter(lambda o: o["status"] == "completed", orders)
total_revenue = reduce(lambda acc, o: acc + o["amount"], completed_orders, 0)

print(total_revenue)  # Output: 550
```

This pipeline extracts and aggregates completed orders **without explicit loops**, making it highly readable and modular.

Parallel Processing with Functional Programming

Functional programming works well with **concurrent and parallel processing** because of its emphasis on **immutability and pure functions**. This prevents race conditions and side effects, making functional code more suitable for multi-threaded applications.

77

```
from multiprocessing import Pool

def square(n):
    return n * n

numbers = [1, 2, 3, 4, 5, 6]
with Pool(3) as p:
    results = p.map(square, numbers)

print(results)  # Output: [1, 4, 9, 16, 25, 36]
```

Here, multiple processes compute square values concurrently, **optimizing performance** for large datasets.

Declarative Functional API Design

Web frameworks often benefit from functional programming concepts to **simplify request handling**. A declarative approach ensures **clean, modular, and composable** API endpoints.

```
from flask import Flask, jsonify

app = Flask(__name__)

users = [{"id": 1, "name": "Alice"}, {"id": 2, "name": "Bob"}]

@app.route("/users")
def get_users():
    return jsonify(list(map(lambda u: {"id": u["id"], "name":
        u["name"].upper()}, users)))

if __name__ == "__main__":
    app.run(debug=True)
```

This approach **transforms data declaratively** while keeping API logic modular and functional.

Functional programming is widely applied in **data transformation, concurrency, and web development**, enhancing **code maintainability and scalability**. Its declarative nature enables developers to write **clear, efficient, and composable** programs, reducing complexity in large-scale applications. By leveraging functional paradigms, developers can **create robust and adaptable software solutions** across various domains.

Module 8:

Logic Programming in AI and Problem Solving

Logic programming is a powerful paradigm within declarative programming, particularly useful in artificial intelligence (AI) and automated problem-solving. This module explores how logic programming defines computations through formal logic, rather than step-by-step instructions. The emphasis is on symbolic reasoning, knowledge representation, and constraint solving, making logic programming ideal for AI, decision-making systems, and complex problem domains. By understanding these principles, developers can leverage declarative techniques to create intelligent systems capable of inference, planning, and automated reasoning, making problem-solving more efficient and adaptable across diverse applications.

Introduction to Logic Programming

Logic programming is a declarative paradigm where computations are expressed as logical statements, and the system derives solutions by applying inference rules. Unlike imperative programming, which requires explicit control flow, logic programming focuses on **what needs to be achieved** rather than **how to achieve it**. A fundamental component of logic programming is **predicate logic**, where facts and rules are defined declaratively. This paradigm is particularly effective in areas requiring rule-based reasoning, such as **expert systems, natural language processing, and knowledge representation**. Prolog, one of the most well-known logic programming languages, is widely used for defining and querying logical relationships.

Declarative Approaches in Artificial Intelligence

Artificial intelligence relies heavily on declarative paradigms for knowledge representation and automated reasoning. Logic programming provides a structured approach to AI by enabling systems to **derive conclusions based on predefined rules and facts**. For example, AI applications in **automated planning, chatbots, and decision support systems** utilize logic programming to process vast knowledge bases efficiently. Unlike machine learning, which often requires large datasets and training, logic programming enables AI to **reason symbolically**, making it highly effective for structured domains such as **medical diagnosis, legal reasoning, and fraud detection**. Declarative AI approaches lead to interpretable and transparent decision-making models.

Constraint Logic Programming (CLP)

Constraint Logic Programming (CLP) extends traditional logic programming by incorporating constraints, allowing efficient problem-solving in domains like **scheduling, optimization, and**

resource allocation. Instead of defining explicit procedural steps, CLP enables the specification of constraints that **must be satisfied**, and the system searches for feasible solutions. This technique is widely applied in **supply chain logistics, workforce scheduling, and automated verification**. By leveraging **constraint solvers**, developers can declaratively model complex real-world problems, reducing computational complexity while maintaining flexibility. The efficiency of CLP stems from its ability to prune infeasible solutions early, optimizing search space exploration.

Automated Theorem Proving

Automated theorem proving is a core application of logic programming, used to validate mathematical proofs and verify software correctness. Theorem provers rely on logical inference rules to determine whether a given proposition is true based on a set of axioms. This approach is crucial in **formal methods, cybersecurity, and algorithm verification**, where correctness and reliability are paramount. Automated reasoning engines use declarative logic to generate proofs systematically, ensuring rigor and reducing human error in critical applications. By leveraging logic programming, theorem provers contribute to advancements in artificial intelligence, enabling self-learning systems capable of deriving new knowledge autonomously.

Logic programming provides a powerful declarative framework for AI and problem-solving, emphasizing reasoning and constraint-based decision-making. From **expert systems and knowledge representation to constraint logic and theorem proving**, this paradigm enables the development of robust, intelligent solutions. By understanding logic programming concepts, developers can harness declarative techniques to build AI systems that are **efficient, interpretable, and scalable** across various domains.

Introduction to Logic Programming

Logic programming is a declarative paradigm where programs consist of logical statements, and computations are performed by inference engines. Unlike imperative programming, where developers specify *how* to perform a task, logic programming focuses on *what* needs to be satisfied. This approach is particularly useful in artificial intelligence, natural language processing, and knowledge representation, as it allows for automatic reasoning and symbolic computation.

A logic program consists of **facts, rules, and queries**. Facts represent known truths, rules define relationships between facts, and queries allow users to retrieve information by leveraging inference mechanisms. The inference engine applies logical reasoning to determine valid conclusions.

One of the most widely used logic programming languages is **Prolog (Programming in Logic)**, which follows a **Horn clause representation**—a form of first-order logic that enables efficient pattern matching and rule evaluation. In Prolog, facts and rules define relationships, while queries are executed to retrieve solutions.

Basic Example in Prolog

```
% Facts
parent(john, mary).
parent(mary, alice).

% Rule
grandparent(X, Y) :- parent(X, Z), parent(Z, Y).

% Query
?- grandparent(john, alice).
% Output: true
```

Here, the grandparent/2 rule deduces a grandparent relationship by chaining parent/2 facts. The Prolog engine automatically searches for solutions based on the given rules, demonstrating the declarative nature of logic programming.

Logical Inference and Backtracking

Logic programming employs **backtracking** as a search mechanism to explore possible solutions systematically. When a query is posed, the inference engine attempts to match it with available facts and rules. If multiple solutions exist, the engine explores different branches using **depth-first search** until a valid solution is found or all possibilities are exhausted.

Consider the following Prolog program:

```
likes(alice, pizza).
likes(alice, pasta).
likes(bob, pizza).

% Query to find what Alice likes
?- likes(alice, X).
% Output: X = pizza; X = pasta.
```

The query returns multiple results due to backtracking, demonstrating how logic programming enables exploration of multiple possibilities without requiring explicit loops or conditionals.

Pattern Matching and Unification

Logic programming relies on **unification**, a process that binds variables to values that make logical statements true. When a query is executed, the inference engine attempts to unify terms by finding substitutions that satisfy logical relationships.

Example:

```
sibling(X, Y) :- parent(Z, X), parent(Z, Y), X \= Y.

% Query
?- sibling(mary, alice).
```

The Prolog engine searches for individuals who share the same parent, excluding self-matches. Unification simplifies complex queries by leveraging predefined logical structures, making programs concise and expressive.

Logic programming offers a powerful declarative paradigm for knowledge representation, inference, and automated reasoning. By leveraging **facts, rules, and queries**, developers can model complex relationships naturally. Features like **backtracking, unification, and pattern matching** make logic programming well-suited for AI, database querying, and automated problem-solving. Prolog remains one of the most effective languages for logic-based applications, enabling concise and highly expressive programming solutions.

Declarative Approaches in Artificial Intelligence

Declarative programming plays a crucial role in artificial intelligence (AI) by allowing developers to define problems using logic rather than explicitly coding procedural steps. This approach is particularly beneficial in AI applications such as **expert systems, knowledge representation, natural language processing (NLP), and decision-making systems**. By specifying **what conditions must be satisfied** rather than dictating the **how**, declarative programming enables AI models to infer and deduce solutions automatically.

Logic programming languages like **Prolog** and functional paradigms like **Haskell** provide powerful tools for AI by leveraging **rule-based reasoning, pattern matching, and constraint solving**. These languages help in developing AI applications that require knowledge inference, search algorithms, and complex decision-making. Unlike imperative AI programming, which involves step-by-step execution, declarative AI programming focuses on high-level descriptions of problems, leaving the underlying logic engine to handle computations.

Rule-Based AI and Expert Systems

One of the most common declarative approaches in AI is **rule-based systems**, where knowledge is encoded in the form of rules and facts. These systems use **inference engines** to derive conclusions based on logical relationships. Expert systems, which simulate human decision-making, rely heavily on declarative programming to define **if-then** rules.

In Prolog, an expert system can be built using **fact and rule-based inference**:

```
% Knowledge Base
disease(flu) :- symptom(fever), symptom(cough), symptom(body_ache).
disease(cold) :- symptom(runny_nose), symptom(sneeze).

% Query
?- symptom(fever), symptom(cough), symptom(body_ache), disease(X).
% Output: X = flu.
```

The Prolog engine automatically evaluates whether the symptoms provided match any known diseases, mimicking human reasoning in medical diagnostics.

Search Algorithms in Declarative AI

Declarative programming is particularly effective in implementing **search algorithms**, which are fundamental to AI applications such as **pathfinding, game AI, and automated reasoning**. Logic programming languages allow developers to define **search spaces and constraints**, letting the inference engine determine optimal solutions.

A common example is **graph traversal** in AI, where declarative programming can be used to model connections between entities:

```
% Graph representation
connected(a, b).
connected(b, c).
connected(c, d).

% Pathfinding rule
path(X, Y) :- connected(X, Y).
path(X, Y) :- connected(X, Z), path(Z, Y).

% Query to find a path from A to D
?- path(a, d).
% Output: true
```

This **recursive rule-based approach** allows the Prolog engine to determine whether a path exists between nodes without explicitly specifying the search procedure.

Declarative AI in Natural Language Processing (NLP)

Declarative programming is also widely used in **NLP applications** such as **syntax analysis, semantic parsing, and text classification**. In Prolog, sentences can be analyzed using logical grammar rules:

```
% Simple sentence structure
sentence(S) :- noun_phrase(NP), verb_phrase(VP).

% Defining noun and verb phrases
noun_phrase(NP) :- noun(N).
verb_phrase(VP) :- verb(V).

% Lexical rules
noun(cat).
verb(runs).

% Query
?- sentence(X).
% Output: true (if a valid structure exists)
```

By leveraging declarative techniques, AI models can perform **syntactic parsing, entity recognition, and sentiment analysis** efficiently, making declarative programming an essential tool in NLP development.

Declarative approaches in AI enable **automated reasoning, efficient search, and robust pattern matching**, making them ideal for knowledge-based systems, expert systems, and NLP applications. By defining **rules and constraints**, developers can build AI systems that infer solutions dynamically, reducing the complexity of manually coding procedural steps. Logic programming remains a foundational paradigm in AI research and development, offering a concise and expressive way to solve complex problems.

Constraint Logic Programming (CLP)

Constraint Logic Programming (CLP) is a declarative paradigm that extends traditional logic programming by incorporating **constraint solving** into the inference process. Unlike standard logic programming, where solutions are derived purely through pattern matching and rule-based inference, CLP introduces constraints—mathematical or logical conditions—that must be satisfied for a solution to be valid. This makes CLP particularly powerful for solving problems in domains such as **scheduling, optimization, resource allocation, and combinatorial puzzles**.

CLP is built upon **three key principles**: **logic programming, constraint solving, and domain-specific solvers**. It allows developers to declare constraints over different domains, such as integers (CLP(FD) for finite domains), real numbers (CLP(R) for real arithmetic), and Boolean values (CLP(B) for Boolean logic). The solver then efficiently searches for valid assignments that satisfy the given constraints.

Applying CLP to Scheduling Problems

One of the most common applications of CLP is **constraint-based scheduling**, where tasks must be assigned to specific time slots while satisfying given constraints. For example, in a school timetable, subjects must be scheduled in a way that ensures no teacher or student has overlapping classes.

Using Prolog's **CLP(FD) library**, we can model this problem:

```
:- use_module(library(clpfd)).

schedule([Math, Science, English]) :-
    Math in 8..10,        % Math can be scheduled between 8 and 10 AM
    Science in 9..11,     % Science can be between 9 and 11 AM
    English in 10..12,    % English can be between 10 and 12 PM
    all_different([Math, Science, English]).  % No overlapping classes

% Query
?- schedule(Times).
% Output: Times = [8, 9, 10]; [8, 10, 11]; ...
```

Here, the **all_different/1 constraint** ensures that no two subjects overlap, and the solver efficiently finds valid schedules. This approach eliminates the need for manual loops and conditionals, making the solution both **concise and scalable**.

Solving Combinatorial Puzzles with CLP

CLP is widely used in solving **combinatorial optimization problems**, such as Sudoku, N-Queens, and cryptarithms. In Sudoku, constraints are placed on numbers in a grid such that each row, column, and subgrid contains distinct values.

Using CLP(FD), a simplified version of the **N-Queens problem**, where queens must be placed on a chessboard such that no two attack each other, can be implemented as:

```
:- use_module(library(clpfd)).

n_queens(N, Queens) :-
    length(Queens, N),
    Queens ins 1..N,
    all_different(Queens),  % No queens in the same column
    safe(Queens).

safe([]).
safe([Q|Rest]) :-
    no_attack(Q, Rest, 1),
    safe(Rest).

no_attack(_, [], _).
no_attack(Q, [Q1|Rest], D) :-
    Q #\= Q1 + D,  % Diagonal constraint
    Q #\= Q1 - D,
    D1 #= D + 1,
    no_attack(Q, Rest, D1).

% Query
?- n_queens(4, Q).
% Output: Q = [2, 4, 1, 3]; [3, 1, 4, 2]; ...
```

This declarative approach defines **only the problem constraints** and lets the **CLP solver** determine the correct queen placements without explicit iteration.

Real-World Applications of CLP

Beyond puzzles, CLP is used in **real-world optimization problems** like:

- **Vehicle Routing:** Finding the optimal route for delivery trucks while minimizing travel time and cost.

- **Workforce Scheduling:** Assigning employees to shifts based on availability and skill constraints.

- **Finance and Budgeting:** Optimizing investment allocations while adhering to budget constraints.

For example, in airline crew scheduling, constraints such as **maximum working hours, required rest periods, and route compatibility** can be encoded declaratively, letting the solver generate optimal schedules.

Constraint Logic Programming is a powerful extension of logic programming that integrates **constraint-solving capabilities** to tackle complex **combinatorial, scheduling,**

and optimization problems. By defining rules and constraints, developers can focus on **what needs to be solved** rather than implementing **how to solve it**, leading to more efficient, readable, and scalable solutions.

Automated Theorem Proving

Automated Theorem Proving (ATP) is a key application of **logic programming** that aims to mechanize the process of proving mathematical theorems. It leverages **formal logic, inference rules, and search algorithms** to determine whether a given proposition logically follows from a set of axioms. ATP is widely used in **formal verification, artificial intelligence, and symbolic computation**, where correctness and rigor are essential.

In declarative programming, theorem proving is expressed through **logical rules and constraints** rather than imperative control structures. This allows the solver to infer proofs systematically rather than manually constructing them step by step. **Prolog, Coq, and Isabelle** are examples of systems used for ATP, each supporting different levels of formal reasoning.

Prolog and Resolution-Based Theorem Proving

One of the simplest implementations of ATP is through **resolution-based theorem proving** in **Prolog**, where logical statements are expressed as **Horn clauses**. Prolog's built-in **backtracking and unification mechanisms** enable it to derive conclusions based on given facts and rules.

Consider a classic example of proving logical entailments:

```
% Facts
mortal(socrates).
mortal(plato).
human(socrates).
human(plato).

% Rule: All humans are mortal
mortal(X) :- human(X).

% Query: Is Socrates mortal?
?- mortal(socrates).
% Output: true.
```

Here, the **mortal/1 predicate** is derived from both explicit facts and an inference rule. When queried, Prolog automatically applies logical inference to determine that **Socrates is mortal** based on the given rules.

First-Order Logic in Theorem Proving

Automated theorem provers often work with **first-order logic (FOL)**, which extends propositional logic by allowing quantifiers ($\forall$ for "for all", $\exists$ for "there exists") and predicates with variables. Systems like **Prover9 and E theorem prover** employ

unification, resolution, and rewriting techniques to simplify logical expressions and find proofs.

For instance, proving that if **all men are mortal and Socrates is a man, then Socrates is mortal** can be formally written as:

$$\forall x(man(x) \rightarrow mortal(x)), man(Socrates) \Rightarrow mortal(Socrates)$$

Automated systems transform these statements into a form suitable for **resolution refutation**, where they assume the negation of the conclusion and attempt to derive a contradiction, thereby proving the theorem.

Formal Verification with Coq

For higher rigor, tools like **Coq** provide a **proof assistant** for verifying properties of software, algorithms, and mathematical theorems. Coq allows users to define mathematical objects, state theorems, and interactively construct proofs using **tactics**.

A simple proof of a logical proposition in Coq might look like this:

```
Theorem modus_ponens: forall P Q: Prop, (P -> Q) -> P -> Q.
Proof.
  intros P Q H1 H2.
  apply H1.
  assumption.
Qed.
```

This theorem states that if **P implies Q and P is true, then Q must be true**, following the classic **modus ponens rule**. The proof is interactive, ensuring correctness through **formal verification techniques**.

Applications of Automated Theorem Proving

ATP has numerous real-world applications, particularly in areas requiring **high assurance and correctness**:

- **Software Verification**: Ensuring that critical software systems (e.g., avionics, medical devices) meet safety specifications.

- **Cryptographic Protocol Analysis**: Validating the correctness and security of cryptographic algorithms.

- **Artificial Intelligence**: Enhancing AI reasoning capabilities in **expert systems and decision-making models**.

- **Mathematical Proof Checking**: Verifying large, complex mathematical theorems that are infeasible for manual proof, such as the **Four-Color Theorem** and **Kepler's Conjecture**.

Automated Theorem Proving represents the power of **declarative logic and formal reasoning** in solving complex logical problems. By leveraging **resolution-based inference, first-order logic, and proof assistants**, ATP enables **rigorous verification, software correctness, and AI reasoning**. As theorem provers become more sophisticated, their integration with **machine learning and symbolic AI** will further expand their capabilities in the future.

Module 9:
Declarative Web Development

Declarative web development shifts the focus from writing step-by-step instructions to defining the desired outcome of a web application. This approach improves **readability, maintainability, and scalability**, making web development more intuitive and efficient. Declarative frameworks, functional reactive programming, state management, and serverless computing embody this paradigm, enabling developers to build responsive, efficient, and scalable web applications.

Declarative Frameworks for Web Applications

Declarative frameworks such as **React, Vue.js, and Svelte** enable developers to define UI structures and behaviors without manually manipulating the DOM. Unlike imperative approaches, where developers must specify how elements are updated, declarative frameworks allow them to describe the UI state and let the framework handle the updates efficiently. This results in cleaner, more readable code, where the focus is on **what the interface should look like rather than how to render it**. These frameworks employ virtual DOM diffing, component-based architecture, and declarative data binding to achieve seamless and efficient UI rendering, making modern web development more intuitive and modular.

Functional Reactive Programming in UI Development

Functional Reactive Programming (FRP) extends the declarative paradigm by treating UI elements as **reactive data streams**. In contrast to traditional event-driven programming, FRP allows developers to express user interactions as a series of transformations on immutable data. Frameworks such as **RxJS and Elm** provide abstractions for handling asynchronous data flow, ensuring that UI updates are managed in a declarative and predictable manner. By leveraging concepts like **observables, event streams, and pure functions**, FRP minimizes side effects and enhances the composability of UI components. This results in applications that are easier to test, debug, and maintain.

State Management in Declarative Web Applications

State management in declarative applications ensures that UI components remain in sync with the underlying data model. Traditional imperative approaches require manual updates, leading to complex and error-prone logic. Declarative state management libraries such as **Redux, Recoil, and MobX** allow developers to manage application state in a predictable and centralized manner. By structuring state as an immutable tree and utilizing **unidirectional data flow**, these libraries prevent inconsistencies and facilitate efficient state transitions. State updates are triggered through **pure functions (reducers)**, ensuring that application behavior remains deterministic and easy to debug while scaling efficiently.

Serverless Computing and Declarative Deployment

Serverless computing aligns well with the declarative paradigm by abstracting away infrastructure management. Cloud providers like **AWS Lambda, Azure Functions, and Google Cloud Functions** allow developers to deploy applications by defining high-level execution rules rather than provisioning and maintaining servers. **Infrastructure-as-Code (IaC)** tools like **Terraform and AWS CloudFormation** further enhance declarative deployment by enabling developers to define infrastructure configurations in a descriptive format. This approach ensures **scalability, cost efficiency, and reduced operational overhead**, allowing developers to focus on building features instead of managing servers.

Declarative web development enables modern applications to be more **modular, scalable, and maintainable**. By leveraging declarative frameworks, functional reactive programming, state management techniques, and serverless computing, developers can build robust applications with minimal complexity. The declarative paradigm continues to shape the future of web development, offering greater efficiency, predictability, and ease of use in software engineering.

Declarative Frameworks for Web Applications

Declarative frameworks in web development provide an abstraction layer that allows developers to define **what the UI should look like**, rather than specifying step-by-step instructions for rendering elements. This contrasts with imperative approaches, where developers manually manipulate the DOM. Popular declarative frameworks such as **React, Vue.js, and Svelte** rely on component-based architectures to improve reusability and maintainability. These frameworks enable **automatic UI updates**, where changes to application state trigger efficient re-rendering without requiring direct DOM manipulation. This section explores how declarative frameworks function and how they simplify modern web development.

In a declarative framework like **React**, components describe the expected output of the UI based on the application's state. When the state changes, React automatically determines the minimal changes required to update the UI, rather than executing direct DOM operations. Consider the following example of a simple **React component** that renders a counter:

```
import React, { useState } from 'react';

function Counter() {
    const [count, setCount] = useState(0);

    return (
        <div>
            <p>Count: {count}</p>
            <button onClick={() => setCount(count + 1)}>Increment</button>
        </div>
    );
}

export default Counter;
```

In this example, the UI **reacts to state changes** automatically. The developer **only specifies what should be displayed**, while React manages the underlying DOM operations. This declarative approach eliminates manual event handling and directly modifying HTML elements, making the code **more readable and maintainable**.

Similarly, **Vue.js** offers a declarative syntax for binding data to the UI. Vue templates use directives like v-bind and v-model to connect state variables to HTML elements.

```
<template>
  <div>
    <p>Count: {{ count }}</p>
    <button @click="count++">Increment</button>
  </div>
</template>

<script>
export default {
  data() {
    return { count: 0 };
  }
};
</script>
```

This declarative binding allows Vue to update the UI whenever the count variable changes, **without requiring direct DOM manipulation**. The framework efficiently tracks dependencies and ensures updates happen only when necessary.

One of the **core benefits** of declarative frameworks is their use of a **virtual DOM**, an in-memory representation of the UI that optimizes rendering. When changes occur, the framework calculates the **smallest set of updates** needed, improving performance. **Svelte**, in contrast, compiles components into highly optimized JavaScript at build time, removing the need for a virtual DOM and enhancing runtime performance.

Declarative frameworks **enhance productivity** by allowing developers to build UI components without handling low-level DOM operations. Their component-based structures promote **code reusability**, while features like **state-driven rendering, reactivity, and virtual DOM diffing** optimize efficiency. By abstracting away imperative logic, declarative frameworks empower developers to focus on building user experiences rather than handling UI state manually.

Functional Reactive Programming in UI Development

Functional Reactive Programming (FRP) is a declarative approach to handling dynamic data flows in UI development. It allows developers to **model user interactions, animations, and asynchronous updates as streams of data**, making it easier to manage complex state changes. FRP-based frameworks, such as **RxJS (Reactive Extensions for JavaScript)** and **Elm**, treat events as sequences that can be composed, transformed, and combined declaratively. Unlike traditional imperative event handling, where developers manually track state changes, FRP provides a **clear and predictable structure for managing UI reactivity**.

A core concept of FRP is the **observable stream**, which represents a sequence of values that change over time. These streams can be manipulated using functional transformations like **map, filter, and reduce**, ensuring **concise and expressive UI logic**. Consider an example using **RxJS** in a React application to handle real-time user input:

```
import { useState, useEffect } from "react";
import { fromEvent } from "rxjs";
import { map, debounceTime } from "rxjs/operators";

function SearchBox() {
    const [query, setQuery] = useState("");

    useEffect(() => {
        const input = document.getElementById("search");
        const stream$ = fromEvent(input, "input").pipe(
            debounceTime(300),
            map(event => event.target.value)
        );

        const subscription = stream$.subscribe(setQuery);
        return () => subscription.unsubscribe();
    }, []);

    return (
        <div>
            <input id="search" type="text" placeholder="Search..." />
            <p>Searching for: {query}</p>
        </div>
    );
}

export default SearchBox;
```

In this example, **RxJS** is used to create a **reactive stream** from the input field. The debounceTime(300) operator prevents unnecessary updates by delaying execution until the user stops typing for 300ms. The map operator extracts the value from the input event, and the stream updates the state without requiring explicit event listeners.

Reactive State Management in Functional UI

Many modern UI libraries, such as **React, Vue, and Svelte**, adopt a functional reactive approach to state management. Instead of imperatively updating the DOM, these frameworks **automatically update the UI when state changes**. Consider a **Svelte** example, where reactivity is built into the language:

```
<script>
  let count = 0;
</script>

<button on:click="{() => count++}">
  Clicked {count} times
</button>
```

Here, **Svelte automatically updates the UI whenever count changes**, eliminating the need for a manual setState call. This declarative approach aligns with **FRP principles**, where the UI is a **function of state**, updating reactively based on changes.

Benefits of Functional Reactive Programming in UI Development

FRP simplifies **asynchronous programming, event handling, and state management** by treating UI updates as **pure functions of state**. It reduces complexity by replacing **manual event listeners and callbacks** with **composable data streams**. This leads to cleaner, more maintainable code, making FRP a powerful paradigm for building responsive and scalable web applications.

State Management in Declarative Web Applications

State management is a crucial aspect of web applications, ensuring that user interactions, UI updates, and data flows remain synchronized. In declarative web development, state management follows a **functional and immutable approach**, eliminating the need for manually tracking changes. **React, Redux, MobX, and Recoil** are some popular libraries that facilitate declarative state management. The key principle is that the **UI is derived from the application state**, meaning changes to state automatically reflect in the UI without direct DOM manipulation.

Unlike imperative programming, where developers manually update variables and DOM elements, declarative state management abstracts away these details. **State is typically immutable and updated through pure functions**, ensuring predictable behavior. A common approach involves using **reducers and actions**, where state transitions occur through predefined operations.

Managing State with React and Hooks

React's state management is built on functional principles, where the useState and useReducer hooks allow managing state in a declarative manner. Consider a simple counter component:

```
import { useState } from "react";

function Counter() {
    const [count, setCount] = useState(0);

    return (
        <div>
            <p>Count: {count}</p>
            <button onClick={() => setCount(count + 1)}>Increment</button>
        </div>
    );
}

export default Counter;
```

Here, useState provides an immutable state, and setCount updates it declaratively. The UI **automatically re-renders** whenever the state changes, removing the need for imperative DOM updates.

Global State Management with Redux

93

For complex applications requiring **global state management**, Redux provides a structured approach using a **central store**. State changes occur through **actions and reducers**, enforcing a predictable state transition model.

```javascript
import { createStore } from "redux";

const initialState = { count: 0 };

function counterReducer(state = initialState, action) {
    switch (action.type) {
        case "INCREMENT":
            return { count: state.count + 1 };
        default:
            return state;
    }
}

const store = createStore(counterReducer);

store.dispatch({ type: "INCREMENT" });
console.log(store.getState()); // { count: 1 }
```

Here, the counterReducer ensures that state transitions occur **immutably**, making state changes more predictable and easier to debug.

Immutable State and Performance Optimization

Immutable state ensures that updates **do not mutate existing objects**, which improves performance in frameworks like React, where reconciliation algorithms can efficiently detect changes. Libraries like **Immutable.js** help enforce immutable data structures, reducing unnecessary re-renders.

Declarative state management eliminates complexity by ensuring the UI is always **in sync with state changes** without manual intervention. By leveraging **functional principles, immutability, and predictable state transitions**, developers can build scalable, maintainable applications. This approach significantly enhances **code readability, maintainability, and debugging**, making declarative state management a preferred paradigm in modern web development.

Serverless Computing and Declarative Deployment

Serverless computing is a cloud-based execution model that abstracts infrastructure management, allowing developers to **focus on writing declarative code rather than managing servers**. In a serverless architecture, cloud providers handle provisioning, scaling, and maintenance, enabling applications to run dynamically as needed. Declarative deployment complements serverless computing by defining infrastructure and resources through **Infrastructure as Code (IaC)** rather than manually configuring environments.

With declarative deployment, developers specify **what the desired system state should be**, and cloud platforms automatically handle provisioning. Tools like **Terraform, AWS**

CloudFormation, and Kubernetes allow defining infrastructure in a **high-level configuration format**, making deployments more predictable and repeatable.

Declarative Deployment with Terraform

Terraform is an **Infrastructure as Code (IaC)** tool that enables defining cloud resources using a declarative approach. Instead of executing manual commands, developers specify resources in a configuration file, and Terraform ensures the infrastructure is provisioned accordingly. Below is an example Terraform script to create an **AWS Lambda function** in a serverless architecture:

```
provider "aws" {
  region = "us-east-1"
}

resource "aws_lambda_function" "example" {
  function_name = "MyLambdaFunction"
  role          = aws_iam_role.lambda_exec.arn
  handler       = "index.handler"
  runtime       = "python3.8"

  source_code_hash = filebase64sha256("lambda.zip")

  environment {
    variables = {
      STAGE = "production"
    }
  }
}
```

Here, the script **defines what the infrastructure should look like** rather than imperatively managing deployments. Terraform ensures the Lambda function is deployed with the specified configurations, abstracting the complexities of cloud infrastructure.

Serverless Function Deployment with AWS Lambda

Serverless functions execute code on demand without provisioning a dedicated server. Using the **AWS Serverless Application Model (SAM)** or **Serverless Framework**, developers can **declare functions, API endpoints, and permissions** in a configuration file. Below is an example using AWS SAM to deploy a serverless function:

```
Resources:
  MyFunction:
    Type: AWS::Serverless::Function
    Properties:
      Handler: app.lambda_handler
      Runtime: python3.8
      Events:
        Api:
          Type: Api
          Properties:
            Path: /hello
            Method: get
```

This YAML configuration **declares a Lambda function** that is automatically deployed and exposed via an API Gateway. The declarative nature ensures consistency and eliminates the need for manual deployment steps.

Scaling and Event-Driven Execution

Serverless platforms, such as AWS Lambda and Google Cloud Functions, **dynamically scale** applications based on demand. Developers do not need to manage load balancing or provisioning since **execution scales automatically**. Event-driven execution models further align with declarative principles, where functions respond to events such as HTTP requests, database changes, or message queue triggers.

Declarative deployment and serverless computing remove the complexity of infrastructure management, allowing developers to **focus on business logic**. By leveraging **Infrastructure as Code, event-driven execution, and auto-scaling**, declarative paradigms enhance application maintainability, scalability, and cost efficiency. This approach simplifies cloud deployments, making it ideal for modern, distributed applications.

Module 10:
Declarative Data Querying

Declarative data querying is a fundamental aspect of modern database management, enabling efficient and readable data retrieval without explicitly defining the procedural steps. Unlike imperative querying, which focuses on how to retrieve data, declarative querying allows users to specify what data they need, letting the database engine determine the best way to execute the query. This module explores various aspects of declarative querying, from SQL and NoSQL query languages to optimization strategies, data manipulation techniques, and real-time data querying approaches. Understanding these principles ensures efficient database interaction, improving system performance and maintainability.

SQL and NoSQL Query Languages

Structured Query Language (SQL) is the most widely used declarative query language, allowing users to retrieve and manipulate data using a high-level syntax. SQL queries specify what data is needed rather than how to retrieve it, making operations intuitive and consistent. Relational databases like **PostgreSQL, MySQL, and SQL Server** use SQL to enforce schema constraints and manage structured data.

In contrast, NoSQL databases such as **MongoDB, Cassandra, and Firebase** adopt a flexible schema, offering declarative querying approaches suited for unstructured and semi-structured data. NoSQL queries often use JSON-like formats and provide optimized indexing and aggregation methods, making them efficient for large-scale applications. While SQL queries use **SELECT, WHERE, and JOIN** clauses, NoSQL databases often rely on **find() and aggregate()** functions.

Query Optimization Strategies

Query optimization is essential in declarative data querying, ensuring that database operations execute efficiently. The optimization process involves techniques such as **indexing, query rewriting, and execution plan analysis** to enhance performance. Database engines, including **PostgreSQL, MySQL, and MongoDB**, automatically optimize declarative queries by choosing the most efficient execution plan based on cost estimation.

Indexes significantly improve query performance by reducing the need for full-table scans. The use of **B-trees, hash indexes, and bitmap indexes** allows databases to retrieve data more efficiently. Additionally, query planners optimize **JOIN operations** by selecting the best join strategy, whether **nested loops, hash joins, or merge joins**. Understanding how a query planner executes queries helps in writing efficient declarative statements that minimize execution time.

Declarative Data Manipulation Techniques

Declarative data manipulation involves inserting, updating, and deleting records using high-level statements. SQL databases use **INSERT, UPDATE, DELETE, and MERGE**, ensuring atomicity and consistency in transactions. NoSQL databases, on the other hand, provide declarative functions such as **updateMany() in MongoDB** to modify documents without explicit iteration.

Techniques such as **bulk updates, transactional consistency, and materialized views** enhance the efficiency of declarative data manipulation. While **triggers and stored procedures** automate certain operations, declarative batch processing enables large-scale data modifications with minimal performance overhead. Declarative transformations using **SQL views and NoSQL aggregation pipelines** further improve data consistency and retrieval efficiency.

Streaming and Real-Time Data Querying

Real-time data querying is essential for applications requiring instantaneous insights, such as financial transactions, monitoring systems, and recommendation engines. Declarative stream processing frameworks, such as **Apache Kafka, Apache Flink, and Spark Streaming**, allow continuous querying of live data streams.

SQL-based streaming engines, including **KSQL for Kafka and Apache Flink SQL**, extend the declarative paradigm by enabling real-time query execution over incoming data. NoSQL databases like **Firebase Realtime Database** and **DynamoDB Streams** provide event-driven querying capabilities, ensuring seamless integration with real-time applications. The combination of declarative querying with streaming engines optimizes real-time analytics and event-driven architectures.

Declarative data querying simplifies database interactions by allowing users to focus on **what data is needed rather than how to retrieve it**. SQL and NoSQL languages provide structured and flexible querying capabilities, while optimization strategies ensure efficient execution. Declarative data manipulation enhances consistency, and real-time streaming frameworks enable instantaneous data processing. Mastering these techniques leads to efficient and scalable data-driven applications.

SQL and NoSQL Query Languages

Declarative data querying is a foundational concept in database management, with SQL and NoSQL representing two major paradigms. SQL (Structured Query Language) is the dominant language for relational databases, enabling users to interact with structured data using a high-level, declarative syntax. NoSQL databases, on the other hand, cater to diverse data models, such as document-oriented, key-value, column-family, and graph databases, offering more flexibility for handling unstructured or semi-structured data. Understanding how declarative queries function in both SQL and NoSQL environments helps developers optimize data retrieval while maintaining readability and performance.

In SQL databases, such as **PostgreSQL, MySQL, and SQL Server**, queries follow a declarative approach where users specify what they need rather than defining the procedural steps to retrieve data. A basic SQL query to fetch data from a relational database might look like this:

```
import sqlite3

conn = sqlite3.connect("example.db")
cursor = conn.cursor()

cursor.execute("SELECT name, age FROM users WHERE age > 25;")
results = cursor.fetchall()

for row in results:
    print(row)

conn.close()
```

In this example, SQL's declarative nature allows the database engine to determine the most efficient way to retrieve the data, optimizing performance under the hood.

NoSQL databases, such as **MongoDB, Cassandra, and DynamoDB**, adopt a different approach, often using document-based or key-value storage instead of strict table relationships. A similar query in MongoDB would look like this:

```
from pymongo import MongoClient

client = MongoClient("mongodb://localhost:27017/")
db = client["example_db"]
collection = db["users"]

results = collection.find({"age": {"$gt": 25}}, {"name": 1, "age": 1, "_id": 0})

for doc in results:
    print(doc)
```

While NoSQL databases maintain the declarative nature of querying, they offer greater flexibility by allowing nested structures and dynamic schema evolution, making them suitable for applications with complex, evolving data needs.

Comparing SQL and NoSQL

The key distinction between SQL and NoSQL lies in their **data modeling approach**. SQL databases enforce **strict schemas and relationships**, making them ideal for transactional applications where **ACID compliance (Atomicity, Consistency, Isolation, Durability)** is crucial. NoSQL databases, in contrast, provide **schema-less flexibility**, supporting **eventual consistency** and horizontal scalability, which is beneficial for **big data applications, real-time analytics, and distributed computing**.

Another difference is in query execution. SQL databases use **JOINs** to link multiple tables, whereas NoSQL databases rely on **denormalized documents or key-value lookups,** reducing the need for computationally expensive operations. For example, in SQL, a JOIN operation might look like this:

```
cursor.execute("""
    SELECT users.name, orders.total
    FROM users
    JOIN orders ON users.id = orders.user_id
    WHERE orders.total > 100;
""")
```

Whereas, in a NoSQL document store, the order information might be embedded directly within the user document, eliminating the need for a join:

```
results = collection.find({"orders.total": {"$gt": 100}}, {"name": 1,
        "orders.total": 1, "_id": 0})
```

While SQL's relational approach ensures **data consistency**, NoSQL's flexibility enhances **scalability and performance for high-volume workloads**.

Declarative data querying, whether through SQL or NoSQL, allows developers to efficiently interact with databases without explicitly defining the execution steps. SQL databases excel in **structured, transactional** applications, while NoSQL databases cater to **scalable, flexible data storage** needs. Understanding the strengths and trade-offs of each paradigm ensures effective data modeling and optimized query performance in various application scenarios.

Query Optimization Strategies

Query optimization is a crucial aspect of database performance, ensuring that queries execute efficiently with minimal resource consumption. In declarative query languages like SQL and NoSQL, optimization strategies differ but share common goals: reducing execution time, minimizing memory and CPU usage, and improving response times for complex queries. Optimization is especially vital in large-scale applications, where inefficient queries can lead to significant performance bottlenecks.

SQL databases rely on **query execution plans**, **indexes**, and **normalization** techniques to improve efficiency. The query planner analyzes different execution strategies and selects the optimal one based on factors such as indexing, table relationships, and data distribution. NoSQL databases, in contrast, optimize queries through **denormalization**, **sharding**, and **caching** mechanisms, which enhance performance in distributed environments. Understanding these techniques is essential for writing efficient declarative queries that scale well in production systems.

Indexing for Faster Queries

Indexes are one of the most effective ways to optimize queries in relational databases. They act as lookup tables that speed up search operations by reducing the number of rows scanned. Consider an unoptimized SQL query:

100

```
cursor.execute("SELECT * FROM users WHERE email = 'john.doe@example.com';")
```

If the users table contains millions of records, scanning each row for a matching email would be inefficient. Creating an index on the email column significantly improves query performance:

```
cursor.execute("CREATE INDEX idx_email ON users(email);")
```

With an index, the database engine can quickly locate the requested record instead of scanning the entire table. In NoSQL databases like MongoDB, indexes function similarly:

```
collection.create_index([("email", 1)])
```

Indexes improve **read performance**, but they also introduce write overhead, as each insertion or update must maintain the index structure. Therefore, indexes should be carefully chosen based on query patterns.

Using Query Execution Plans

SQL databases provide execution plans that reveal how a query will be processed. Running the EXPLAIN or EXPLAIN ANALYZE command in PostgreSQL or MySQL shows details such as index usage, join strategies, and estimated costs.

```
cursor.execute("EXPLAIN ANALYZE SELECT * FROM users WHERE age > 30;")
```

By analyzing execution plans, developers can identify inefficiencies and refine queries using techniques such as **index hints**, **query restructuring**, or **partitioning**.

Denormalization and Query Optimization in NoSQL

NoSQL databases optimize performance by reducing the need for complex joins. Instead of normalizing data into multiple related collections, denormalization involves embedding frequently accessed data within documents. This approach reduces the number of queries needed to fetch related information.

For example, a relational database might store user and order information in separate tables, requiring a JOIN to fetch data. In MongoDB, this could be optimized by embedding order details directly in the user document:

```
{
    "name": "John Doe",
    "email": "john.doe@example.com",
    "orders": [
        {"order_id": 1, "total": 150.0},
        {"order_id": 2, "total": 200.0}
    ]
}
```

By structuring data this way, queries become faster since they avoid expensive join operations. However, denormalization increases **storage redundancy**, so it should be used strategically.

Sharding and Partitioning for Scalability

In distributed database systems, **sharding** (horizontal partitioning) splits data across multiple servers to handle high query loads. For example, a large dataset in MongoDB can be divided across shards:

```
db.adminCommand({
    "shardCollection": "example_db.users",
    "key": {"email": "hashed"}
})
```

Partitioning in SQL databases follows a similar approach, dividing large tables into smaller, more manageable pieces to enhance query performance.

Query optimization is essential for maintaining high performance in declarative data querying. Techniques such as **indexing, execution plans, denormalization, and sharding** enable databases to efficiently process queries at scale. A well-optimized query structure ensures fast response times, reduces resource consumption, and improves application scalability.

Declarative Data Manipulation Techniques

Declarative data manipulation techniques allow developers to interact with databases at a high level without specifying explicit step-by-step instructions. Unlike imperative programming, where data is manipulated through explicit loops and conditionals, declarative approaches focus on describing the desired outcome. SQL, functional transformations in Pandas, and NoSQL aggregation pipelines are key techniques that enhance readability, maintainability, and efficiency. By leveraging declarative operations, developers can perform complex data transformations, filtering, and aggregations in a concise and optimized manner.

In SQL-based databases, **INSERT, UPDATE, DELETE, and MERGE** commands provide powerful ways to manipulate data efficiently. In contrast, NoSQL databases offer **document updates, bulk operations, and map-reduce** for handling large datasets. Functional programming constructs like **map, filter, and reduce** in Python's Pandas and NumPy libraries also enable efficient declarative data processing. Understanding these approaches allows developers to write scalable and performant data manipulation queries.

Inserting and Updating Data Declaratively

SQL provides a structured way to insert and update records without requiring procedural code. Instead of iterating over data manually, declarative statements efficiently apply changes at the database level. Consider a bulk insert operation in SQL:

```
cursor.execute("""
    INSERT INTO employees (name, department, salary)
    VALUES
    ('Alice', 'HR', 60000),
    ('Bob', 'Engineering', 75000),
    ('Charlie', 'Marketing', 50000);
""")
```

This approach is more efficient than looping over individual records in an imperative fashion. Similarly, updates can be applied declaratively:

```
cursor.execute("""
    UPDATE employees
    SET salary = salary * 1.1
    WHERE department = 'Engineering';
""")
```

This command increases salaries for all employees in the engineering department in a single operation, eliminating the need for row-by-row updates.

Filtering and Transforming Data in Functional Style

Functional programming techniques provide another declarative approach to data manipulation. In Python, the **map()**, **filter()**, and **reduce()** functions allow for efficient transformations without explicit loops. Using Pandas, filtering data declaratively is straightforward:

```
import pandas as pd

df = pd.DataFrame([
    {'name': 'Alice', 'department': 'HR', 'salary': 60000},
    {'name': 'Bob', 'department': 'Engineering', 'salary': 75000},
    {'name': 'Charlie', 'department': 'Marketing', 'salary': 50000}
])

# Declaratively filtering employees with salaries above 60,000
high_earners = df[df['salary'] > 60000]
print(high_earners)
```

This concise approach eliminates the need for explicit loops, making the code easier to read and maintain.

Aggregation and Summarization with SQL and NoSQL

Aggregation is a powerful declarative technique for summarizing large datasets. In SQL, the **GROUP BY** clause simplifies complex data analysis:

```
cursor.execute("""
    SELECT department, AVG(salary) AS avg_salary
    FROM employees
    GROUP BY department;
""")
```

Similarly, NoSQL databases like MongoDB provide aggregation pipelines:

```
pipeline = [
```

```
        {"$group": {"_id": "$department", "avg_salary": {"$avg": "$salary"}}}
    ]
    result = collection.aggregate(pipeline)
```

Both approaches enable efficient data summarization without requiring imperative iteration.

Combining Declarative Techniques for Efficient Data Processing

By combining SQL bulk operations, functional programming constructs, and NoSQL aggregation pipelines, developers can manipulate data efficiently and concisely. Declarative techniques ensure that operations scale well, reducing execution time and resource consumption. Whether working with relational or NoSQL databases, adopting a declarative mindset simplifies data transformations and enhances application performance.

Streaming and Real-Time Data Querying

Streaming and real-time data querying are essential for modern applications that require immediate insights from continuously generated data. Unlike traditional batch processing, which processes large datasets periodically, real-time querying focuses on handling data as it arrives, enabling applications such as financial analytics, IoT monitoring, and live dashboards. Declarative approaches to real-time data querying involve using structured query languages, stream processing frameworks, and reactive programming paradigms to define how data should be processed rather than specifying step-by-step operations.

Technologies such as Apache Kafka, Apache Flink, and Spark Streaming allow developers to define declarative data transformations that process events in real-time. SQL-based solutions like **Materialized Views** in PostgreSQL and **Streaming SQL** in Apache Flink enable continuous queries that update results dynamically as new data flows in. By adopting declarative paradigms, organizations can efficiently query, filter, and aggregate real-time data with minimal complexity.

Declarative Streaming Queries with SQL

SQL extensions for stream processing allow users to define continuous queries that react to incoming data without requiring imperative loops. In a real-time analytics scenario, a streaming query might track incoming sales transactions and compute rolling averages dynamically.

```
cursor.execute("""
    CREATE MATERIALIZED VIEW live_sales AS
    SELECT product_id, COUNT(*) AS sales_count, AVG(price) AS avg_price
    FROM sales_stream
    GROUP BY product_id;
""")
```

This declarative SQL query continuously updates the **live_sales** view as new transactions are recorded, eliminating the need for polling or manual updates.

Reactive Stream Processing with Pandas and Kafka

For applications handling real-time logs or sensor data, a declarative approach using Pandas and Apache Kafka simplifies stream processing. Consider a Python-based consumer that processes real-time IoT temperature readings:

```python
from kafka import KafkaConsumer
import pandas as pd
import json

consumer = KafkaConsumer('temperature_readings',
        bootstrap_servers='localhost:9092')

def process_stream():
    data = []
    for message in consumer:
        record = json.loads(message.value)
        data.append(record)

        df = pd.DataFrame(data)
        avg_temp = df['temperature'].mean()
        print(f"Updated Average Temperature: {avg_temp}")

process_stream()
```

This reactive processing approach declaratively transforms incoming temperature data without explicitly managing loops and buffers.

Event-Driven Aggregation in NoSQL Databases

NoSQL databases, such as MongoDB, provide aggregation pipelines for real-time analytics. Consider tracking website visitor counts by processing logs in real-time:

```python
pipeline = [
    {"$match": {"event": "page_view"}},
    {"$group": {"_id": "$page", "views": {"$sum": 1}}}
]

result = collection.aggregate(pipeline)
```

This declarative query continuously updates view counts, making it ideal for live dashboards.

Scalability and Performance Considerations

Declarative streaming queries optimize performance by leveraging built-in indexing, partitioning, and distributed computing. Unlike imperative approaches that require explicit iteration and state management, declarative stream processing frameworks handle data efficiently with built-in optimizations. Whether using SQL materialized views, Kafka-based reactive consumers, or NoSQL aggregation pipelines, adopting a declarative approach ensures scalable, real-time data querying while maintaining code simplicity and clarity.

Module 11:
Declarative UI Frameworks

Declarative UI frameworks simplify user interface development by enabling developers to define what the UI should look like rather than describing how to build it step by step. This approach enhances maintainability, readability, and consistency across applications. By focusing on state-driven rendering and abstraction, declarative UI frameworks allow developers to build dynamic interfaces efficiently. This module explores key principles of declarative UI development, including Virtual DOM mechanisms, JSX and functional components, and styling using declarative methods. Understanding these concepts empowers developers to create scalable and reactive applications with minimal effort, leveraging the strengths of declarative paradigms.

Principles of Declarative UI Development

Declarative UI development is centered on the concept of describing the desired state of the interface, and allowing the framework to handle updates and rendering accordingly. This contrasts with imperative UI programming, where developers must manually manipulate the DOM and handle state changes explicitly. Declarative UI frameworks such as React, SwiftUI, and Jetpack Compose provide high-level abstractions that simplify UI creation by allowing developers to focus on structure rather than implementation details. These frameworks embrace unidirectional data flow, state-driven rendering, and composability, ensuring that UI updates remain predictable and efficient. The declarative approach makes it easier to develop complex interfaces while reducing errors associated with direct DOM manipulation.

Virtual DOM and State Synchronization

The Virtual DOM is a key optimization strategy used in declarative UI frameworks to enhance performance. Instead of updating the actual DOM directly, a lightweight in-memory representation of the DOM is maintained. When changes occur, the Virtual DOM computes the difference between the new and previous states, updating only the necessary parts of the UI. This approach minimizes costly DOM operations, leading to smoother user experiences. State synchronization further ensures that UI components remain in sync with the underlying application state. By leveraging declarative state management techniques such as React's hooks or Vue's reactivity model, developers can efficiently update the UI without manually handling the DOM, reducing complexity and improving maintainability.

JSX and Functional Components in UI Development

JSX (JavaScript XML) is a syntax extension that enables developers to write UI components in a way that resembles HTML while maintaining the power of JavaScript. JSX allows for the seamless integration of logic and presentation, making it a popular choice in declarative UI

106

frameworks like React. Functional components further streamline UI development by encapsulating logic within reusable functions. By utilizing state and props, functional components enable the dynamic composition of UI elements while promoting modularity and code reuse. This paradigm shift from class-based components to functional components with hooks has simplified UI development, making it more intuitive and less error-prone.

Styling and Theming Using Declarative Methods

Styling in declarative UI frameworks follows a structured approach, ensuring that design consistency is maintained across applications. Techniques such as CSS-in-JS, scoped styles, and theme providers allow developers to apply styles in a modular and reusable manner. By defining styles as objects or using declarative syntax, frameworks like Styled Components or Tailwind CSS enable dynamic styling based on application state. Theming mechanisms further enhance flexibility, allowing developers to define global styles and easily switch between themes without modifying component structures. This declarative approach to styling simplifies UI customization, improves maintainability, and ensures that applications remain visually cohesive across different screens and user preferences.

Declarative UI frameworks revolutionize front-end development by prioritizing simplicity, maintainability, and efficiency. By leveraging principles such as Virtual DOM, state-driven rendering, JSX, and functional components, developers can build robust and scalable interfaces with minimal effort. Additionally, declarative styling techniques streamline design implementation, ensuring consistent and flexible UI experiences. Mastering these concepts is essential for modern UI development, enabling the creation of highly responsive applications.

Principles of Declarative UI Development

Declarative UI development focuses on defining the desired UI state rather than dictating the step-by-step process of updating the interface. This high-level approach improves readability, maintainability, and scalability while reducing complexity. Unlike imperative programming, where developers manually manipulate the DOM, declarative UI frameworks such as React, SwiftUI, and Jetpack Compose allow developers to describe the structure of the UI using a component-based model. These components automatically update in response to state changes, ensuring consistency without requiring explicit control over rendering.

A key feature of declarative UI development is its reliance on unidirectional data flow. This model ensures that data moves in a predictable manner, reducing potential side effects and making debugging easier. State management is handled through frameworks or libraries, allowing developers to focus on defining components and their relationships rather than worrying about how changes propagate through the system. Additionally, declarative UI frameworks often embrace immutability, ensuring that components do not alter their state directly but instead rely on updates propagated through controlled state changes.

Consider the following example of a declarative UI in React. Here, the interface is defined in terms of its state, and any changes in the application state automatically update the UI without explicit manipulation of the DOM:

```
import React, { useState } from 'react';

function Counter() {
    const [count, setCount] = useState(0);

    return (
        <div>
            <h1>Counter: {count}</h1>
            <button onClick={() => setCount(count + 1)}>Increment</button>
        </div>
    );
}

export default Counter;
```

In this example, the component Counter renders based on its count state. The button click event updates the state, causing the component to re-render automatically. Unlike imperative approaches that would require direct DOM manipulation, React handles rendering efficiently through its internal Virtual DOM diffing algorithm.

Another essential principle in declarative UI development is **composition over inheritance**. Instead of using complex class-based hierarchies, modern frameworks encourage breaking down UIs into smaller, reusable components. This modularity enhances maintainability and allows teams to collaborate more effectively by focusing on individual components that can be reused throughout the application.

Declarative UI development also improves cross-platform consistency. Frameworks such as React Native, SwiftUI, and Jetpack Compose allow developers to use the same declarative principles across web and mobile platforms. This reduces duplication and ensures that UI behavior remains predictable across different environments.

By shifting focus from "how" the UI updates to "what" the UI should look like at any given moment, declarative UI development leads to more intuitive, scalable, and bug-resistant applications. The principles of state-driven rendering, unidirectional data flow, and component-based architecture define modern UI development, making it easier to build and maintain complex user interfaces.

Virtual DOM and State Synchronization

The Virtual DOM (VDOM) is a key optimization in declarative UI frameworks that enhances performance by minimizing direct manipulation of the real DOM. In traditional imperative programming, every UI change triggers a direct DOM update, which is computationally expensive. In contrast, the Virtual DOM serves as a lightweight in-memory representation of the actual DOM, allowing changes to be computed efficiently before applying the minimal necessary updates to the real DOM. This approach drastically reduces rendering overhead and improves application responsiveness.

State synchronization in declarative UI frameworks ensures that the UI remains consistent with the underlying application data. Instead of manually updating the UI in response to state changes, developers define the UI structure based on the state, and the framework automatically updates the UI when the state changes. This eliminates the risk of UI inconsistencies and race conditions common in imperative programming.

Consider the following example in React, which demonstrates Virtual DOM updates and state synchronization:

```
import React, { useState } from 'react';

function TaskList() {
    const [tasks, setTasks] = useState(["Learn React", "Build an App", "Refactor
        Code"]);

    const addTask = () => {
        setTasks([...tasks, `Task ${tasks.length + 1}`]);
    };

    return (
        <div>
            <h1>Task List</h1>
            <ul>
                {tasks.map((task, index) => (
                    <li key={index}>{task}</li>
                ))}
            </ul>
            <button onClick={addTask}>Add Task</button>
        </div>
    );
}

export default TaskList;
```

In this example, the tasks state determines the content of the list. When the addTask function is triggered, React updates the state using setTasks, which causes the Virtual DOM to re-calculate the necessary UI changes. React then efficiently updates only the modified elements in the real DOM rather than re-rendering the entire UI, optimizing performance.

The Virtual DOM follows a three-step process:

1. A new Virtual DOM tree is created whenever state changes.

2. React compares this new Virtual DOM tree with the previous one using a process called **reconciliation**, determining the minimal changes required.

3. Only the necessary updates are applied to the real DOM, minimizing expensive re-render operations.

State synchronization ensures that every component automatically updates when its dependent data changes. This contrasts with imperative approaches, where developers must track and manually update every DOM element affected by a state change, leading to complex and error-prone code.

Beyond React, similar concepts apply in other declarative frameworks like Vue.js and Svelte. Vue uses a reactive system to track dependencies and re-render only the affected parts, while Svelte compiles declarative components into optimized imperative code, bypassing the Virtual DOM for even greater performance.

By leveraging the Virtual DOM and state synchronization, declarative UI frameworks significantly improve performance and developer productivity. These techniques abstract away low-level DOM manipulation, allowing developers to focus on defining the UI structure while the framework optimizes updates behind the scenes.

JSX and Functional Components in UI Development

JSX (JavaScript XML) is a syntax extension used in declarative UI frameworks like React to describe UI structures in a format that resembles HTML but is embedded within JavaScript. JSX enables developers to define component structures in an intuitive and readable way, seamlessly integrating JavaScript logic within the UI definition. Instead of manually constructing DOM elements using JavaScript functions, JSX allows developers to declaratively specify UI components, improving maintainability and expressiveness.

Functional components in UI development follow a declarative approach by representing UI elements as pure functions. These components receive props as input and return a UI structure without directly modifying the DOM. Unlike class-based components, functional components simplify state management and encourage the use of hooks such as useState and useEffect for managing side effects. This approach aligns with the core principles of declarative programming, where UI logic is described in terms of "what to render" rather than "how to render."

Consider the following example of JSX and a functional component in React:

```
import React, { useState } from 'react';

function Counter() {
    const [count, setCount] = useState(0);

    return (
        <div>
            <h1>Counter: {count}</h1>
            <button onClick={() => setCount(count + 1)}>Increment</button>
        </div>
    );
}

export default Counter;
```

In this example, the Counter component is a pure function that accepts no external props and manages its state using the useState hook. The JSX syntax within the return statement allows HTML-like structure to be embedded directly within JavaScript. When the button is clicked, the state updates declaratively, triggering a re-render of the component without directly manipulating the DOM.

JSX compiles into standard JavaScript function calls using React.createElement(). The following JSX:

```
<h1>Hello, World!</h1>
```

Compiles to:

```
React.createElement('h1', null, 'Hello, World!');
```

This transformation ensures that JSX remains declarative while leveraging JavaScript's flexibility. Functional components are particularly beneficial because they simplify component logic and facilitate reusability. Unlike class-based components, they do not require lifecycle methods like componentDidMount or componentDidUpdate. Instead, hooks manage side effects efficiently within functional components.

Another advantage of JSX and functional components is their composability. Developers can break complex UIs into smaller, reusable components, leading to more modular and maintainable codebases. For example, a Button component can be reused across multiple UI elements:

```
function Button({ label, onClick }) {
    return <button onClick={onClick}>{label}</button>;
}
```

This approach promotes the declarative nature of UI programming, ensuring that components focus solely on rendering based on state and props.

By combining JSX with functional components, declarative UI frameworks like React offer a clean, efficient, and expressive way to build user interfaces. These concepts abstract imperative UI manipulation and align with modern best practices in UI development.

Styling and Theming Using Declarative Methods

Styling and theming are essential aspects of UI development, and declarative methods provide a structured, maintainable approach to defining styles. Unlike traditional imperative styling techniques that involve directly modifying the DOM or CSS properties using JavaScript, declarative methods enable developers to define styles in a structured and reusable manner. Modern UI frameworks such as React, Vue, and Angular promote styling techniques that align with declarative programming principles, including CSS-in-JS, theme providers, and scoped styles.

One of the most commonly used declarative styling techniques is CSS-in-JS, where styles are defined as JavaScript objects and applied within components. This approach ensures that styles are encapsulated and dynamically adjustable based on application state. Consider the following example using the styled-components library in React:

111

```
import styled from 'styled-components';

const Button = styled.button`
    background-color: ${(props) => (props.primary ? 'blue' : 'gray')};
    color: white;
    padding: 10px 20px;
    border: none;
    border-radius: 5px;
    cursor: pointer;
`;

function App() {
    return <Button primary>Click Me</Button>;
}

export default App;
```

Here, the Button component dynamically adjusts its background color based on the primary prop, making it easy to manage themes declaratively. This ensures consistency across the application while allowing flexibility in UI customization.

Another declarative styling method involves theme providers, which allow global themes to be defined and applied consistently across an application. The ThemeProvider component from styled-components enables developers to centralize style definitions:

```
import { ThemeProvider } from 'styled-components';

const theme = {
    primaryColor: 'blue',
    secondaryColor: 'gray',
};

const Button = styled.button`
    background-color: ${(props) => props.theme.primaryColor};
    color: white;
    padding: 10px 20px;
    border: none;
    border-radius: 5px;
    cursor: pointer;
`;

function App() {
    return (
        <ThemeProvider theme={theme}>
            <Button>Click Me</Button>
        </ThemeProvider>
    );
}

export default App;
```

This approach ensures a consistent color scheme across multiple components while allowing easy customization by modifying the theme object.

Scoped styles, such as CSS Modules, provide another declarative styling method by ensuring that styles are component-specific and do not affect other parts of the application. A CSS Module file (Button.module.css) might look like this:

```
button {
```

```css
    background-color: blue;
    color: white;
    padding: 10px 20px;
    border: none;
    border-radius: 5px;
    cursor: pointer;
}
```

The styles are then imported and applied within a React component:

```javascript
import styles from './Button.module.css';

function Button() {
    return <button className={styles.button}>Click Me</button>;
}

export default Button;
```

This method enhances maintainability and prevents global style conflicts.

Declarative theming approaches simplify UI styling by centralizing design decisions, reducing redundancy, and ensuring consistency. Whether through CSS-in-JS, theme providers, or scoped styles, these methods promote reusability, flexibility, and clarity in UI development.

Module 12:
Reactive Programming Models

Reactive programming is a declarative approach to handling asynchronous data streams, enabling efficient, event-driven, and scalable applications. Unlike imperative programming, where state changes are explicitly controlled, reactive programming models focus on data flows and propagate changes automatically. This module explores the core paradigms of event-driven and dataflow programming, the principles of Functional Reactive Programming (FRP), the role of reactive extensions and observables, and strategies for building scalable reactive systems. Understanding these concepts helps developers design resilient applications capable of handling complex event interactions while maintaining clarity and readability in code.

Event-Driven and Dataflow Paradigms

At the core of reactive programming are event-driven and dataflow paradigms, which emphasize responding to changes rather than explicitly controlling program execution. In an event-driven model, components react to external stimuli, such as user interactions, system messages, or network responses. This paradigm is fundamental to user interface frameworks, real-time processing, and distributed systems where asynchronous events trigger state transitions.

Dataflow programming extends event-driven principles by treating computation as a series of transformations applied to data streams. Instead of focusing on how to achieve a result step by step, developers specify relationships between inputs and outputs, allowing automatic updates when inputs change. This approach minimizes state management complexity and ensures that system behavior remains predictable even as data dependencies evolve dynamically.

Functional Reactive Programming (FRP)

Functional Reactive Programming (FRP) combines functional programming principles with reactive programming concepts to model time-varying values as continuous data streams. Unlike traditional imperative event-handling mechanisms, FRP abstracts over time-dependent computations, enabling developers to express complex dependencies concisely.

FRP frameworks provide tools to work with signals, streams, and behaviors, which represent evolving values over time. These abstractions simplify reactive state management, making applications more modular and composable. For example, instead of handling UI updates with explicit event listeners, FRP enables declarative expressions that define how user actions propagate through a system. The result is cleaner, more predictable, and maintainable code, particularly in applications that require real-time responsiveness.

Reactive Extensions and Observables

114

Reactive Extensions (Rx) provide a standardized way to handle event streams in a declarative manner. Observables, a core concept in Rx, represent sequences of data that can be processed asynchronously. By applying operators such as map, filter, and merge, developers can transform, combine, and manage asynchronous events with ease.

The key advantage of observables lies in their ability to abstract away low-level asynchronous handling, such as callbacks and promises. Instead of manually managing subscriptions and state transitions, developers can compose pipelines that automatically react to changes. This is particularly useful in applications involving real-time data processing, event-driven architectures, and concurrent workflows where managing dependencies imperatively would introduce unnecessary complexity.

Building Scalable and Reactive Systems

Scalability is a critical consideration in modern software systems, and reactive programming offers powerful mechanisms for handling high-throughput, distributed applications. By leveraging non-blocking data streams, reactive architectures minimize performance bottlenecks and enhance system responsiveness. Reactive systems embrace concepts such as backpressure, which prevents overwhelming consumers with excessive data, and event sourcing, where state transitions are captured as immutable sequences of events.

These techniques enable applications to remain resilient under load, efficiently process concurrent requests, and dynamically adjust to varying operational conditions. Whether used in cloud computing, microservices, or real-time analytics, reactive programming provides a robust foundation for building scalable and maintainable software solutions.

Reactive programming simplifies handling asynchronous data by embracing event-driven, dataflow-based, and functional paradigms. This module introduces core principles such as Functional Reactive Programming, reactive extensions, and observables, providing a structured approach to developing scalable applications. Mastering these concepts allows developers to create responsive, efficient, and resilient systems while maintaining the readability and declarative clarity essential to modern software development.

Event-Driven and Dataflow Paradigms

Event-driven programming is a fundamental paradigm in reactive systems where components react to external inputs instead of executing instructions in a predefined sequence. Events can originate from user interactions, sensor inputs, or system notifications, triggering specific responses in an application. This approach is prevalent in UI development, microservices, and distributed systems, where applications must remain responsive to changing conditions.

Dataflow programming extends event-driven principles by structuring programs as networks of data transformations. In this paradigm, computation is expressed as a series of connected operations where the output of one function serves as the input to another.

Unlike imperative approaches that require explicit state management, dataflow programming automatically propagates changes through the system, reducing complexity.

Example: Event-Driven vs. Dataflow in Python

Consider an event-driven model where a function is executed when a button is clicked:

```python
import tkinter as tk

def on_button_click():
    print("Button clicked!")

root = tk.Tk()
button = tk.Button(root, text="Click Me", command=on_button_click)
button.pack()
root.mainloop()
```

Here, the event-driven paradigm listens for an event (button click) and responds with a function execution.

Now, consider a dataflow-based approach using reactive programming with the RxPy library:

```python
from rx import create

def temperature_observable(observer, _):
    temperatures = [20, 22, 24, 26, 28]
    for temp in temperatures:
        observer.on_next(temp)
    observer.on_completed()

observable = create(temperature_observable)
observable.subscribe(lambda temp: print(f"Temperature: {temp}°C"))
```

This example processes a stream of temperature values, demonstrating dataflow execution where values propagate automatically.

Key Differences and Benefits

Event-driven programming is ideal for handling discrete interactions where specific user actions trigger responses. It provides a natural way to model GUI applications, network protocols, and microservices. However, managing event dependencies can become complex in large applications.

Dataflow programming, by contrast, emphasizes automatic updates and declarative data transformations. It minimizes state management and ensures that changes propagate consistently throughout the system. This makes it highly useful for spreadsheet-like applications, functional reactive UIs, and parallel computing.

Event-driven and dataflow paradigms both support responsive, reactive systems but differ in execution models. Event-driven programming responds to external inputs with defined handlers, while dataflow programming structures execution around data transformations.

Understanding these paradigms enables developers to design scalable and maintainable reactive applications.

Functional Reactive Programming (FRP)

Functional Reactive Programming (FRP) is a programming paradigm that combines functional programming principles with reactive event handling. It provides a high-level abstraction for managing asynchronous data streams and time-varying values. Unlike traditional event-driven programming, where events trigger imperative callbacks, FRP treats events as composable, declarative data streams. This simplifies the management of complex asynchronous workflows while improving readability and maintainability.

FRP is widely used in real-time systems, GUI applications, game development, and distributed computing. By leveraging pure functions and immutable data, FRP avoids many pitfalls of callback hell and shared mutable state, resulting in cleaner and more predictable code.

Declarative Event Handling with FRP in Python

A core concept in FRP is the ability to process continuous event streams in a functional manner. Consider a simple implementation using RxPy, a Python library for reactive programming:

```python
from rx import from_iterable
from rx.operators import map, filter

# Simulated event stream: user input values
event_stream = from_iterable([10, 15, 20, 25, 30])

# Transforming and filtering event data
processed_stream = event_stream.pipe(
    filter(lambda x: x > 15),   # Only values greater than 15
    map(lambda x: x * 2)        # Double the remaining values
)

processed_stream.subscribe(lambda x: print(f"Processed Value: {x}"))
```

Here, events flow through a series of transformations without modifying external state. The event stream is declaratively filtered and mapped, showcasing FRP's ability to manage reactive transformations.

Continuous Signals vs. Discrete Events

FRP distinguishes between discrete events (e.g., user clicks, network responses) and continuous signals (e.g., temperature readings, stock prices). Traditional event-driven programming handles these using imperative callbacks, whereas FRP models them as first-class objects. This approach allows developers to compose event pipelines more naturally, reducing side effects and boilerplate code.

Consider a real-time temperature monitoring system:

117

```python
import rx
from rx.subject import Subject

temperature_sensor = Subject()

temperature_sensor.pipe(
    filter(lambda temp: temp > 25),
    map(lambda temp: f"Warning: High Temperature {temp}°C")
).subscribe(print)

# Simulating incoming temperature readings
temperature_sensor.on_next(22)
temperature_sensor.on_next(26)
temperature_sensor.on_next(30)
```

This system continuously processes temperature readings, applying transformations and conditions to emit warnings dynamically.

Advantages of FRP

1. **Declarative Composition** – FRP provides higher-order functions for composing event-driven logic concisely.

2. **Predictable State Management** – By avoiding shared mutable state, FRP reduces side effects and unexpected behavior.

3. **Simplified Asynchronous Programming** – FRP abstracts away complex callback chains, improving readability and maintainability.

FRP offers a powerful alternative to traditional event-driven programming by modeling event streams as composable data flows. Its declarative nature improves maintainability and scalability, making it a valuable paradigm for handling real-time interactions, UIs, and concurrent data processing.

Reactive Extensions and Observables

Reactive Extensions (Rx) is a library that provides tools for composing asynchronous and event-driven programs using observable sequences. Observables are a core abstraction in reactive programming, representing data streams that can be transformed, filtered, and combined declaratively. Unlike traditional event-driven programming, where callback functions handle events imperatively, observables allow data flows to be managed functionally, leading to cleaner and more predictable code.

Observables support various types of event sources, such as user inputs, network responses, or system events. They also enable operators like map, filter, merge, and combineLatest, allowing developers to compose complex event-driven logic with ease. This makes reactive extensions a powerful tool for managing asynchronous behavior in applications.

Creating and Subscribing to Observables

In Python, the RxPy library provides an implementation of Reactive Extensions. Below is an example of creating an observable and subscribing to it:

```python
from rx import create

def data_observable(observer, _):
    observer.on_next("Event 1")
    observer.on_next("Event 2")
    observer.on_next("Event 3")
    observer.on_completed()

observable = create(data_observable)
observable.subscribe(lambda x: print(f"Received: {x}"))
```

In this example, an observable emits three events before signaling completion. The subscriber listens to these events and prints them as they arrive. This demonstrates the declarative nature of reactive programming—data flows from the producer to the consumer without imperative state manipulation.

Transforming Data Streams with Operators

Reactive Extensions provide a rich set of operators for transforming event streams. Below, we demonstrate filtering and mapping events:

```python
from rx import from_iterable
from rx.operators import filter, map

event_stream = from_iterable([5, 10, 15, 20, 25])

processed_stream = event_stream.pipe(
    filter(lambda x: x > 10),  # Keep values greater than 10
    map(lambda x: x * 2)       # Double each remaining value
)

processed_stream.subscribe(lambda x: print(f"Processed Event: {x}"))
```

Here, events are declaratively transformed using filter and map. This approach eliminates the need for imperative loops and conditional statements, resulting in cleaner and more maintainable code.

Combining Multiple Event Streams

One of the strengths of Reactive Extensions is the ability to merge and combine multiple event streams. Consider a scenario where user input and network requests need to be synchronized:

```python
from rx import merge, of

input_stream = of("User Click 1", "User Click 2")
api_response_stream = of("API Response 1", "API Response 2")

merged_stream = merge(input_stream, api_response_stream)
merged_stream.subscribe(lambda x: print(f"Event: {x}"))
```

Here, multiple event sources are combined into a single observable, making it easier to coordinate asynchronous data flows. This is particularly useful in UI development, where user interactions and backend responses must be handled together.

Reactive Extensions and observables provide a powerful abstraction for handling asynchronous data streams in a declarative manner. By enabling functional transformations and composition, they simplify event-driven programming, improve maintainability, and enhance scalability. These concepts are fundamental in modern applications, particularly in real-time data processing and UI development.

Building Scalable and Reactive Systems

Scalability and responsiveness are critical aspects of modern software systems, particularly those that handle large-scale data processing and real-time interactions. Reactive programming provides a framework for building scalable systems by modeling data flows as declarative event streams. Unlike traditional imperative architectures that rely on explicit control structures, reactive systems react to changes asynchronously, making them highly responsive and efficient under varying workloads.

Reactive systems achieve scalability by leveraging event-driven architectures, non-blocking I/O, and backpressure mechanisms. These principles ensure that resources are efficiently utilized, preventing bottlenecks that could degrade performance. Reactive programming is widely used in distributed systems, real-time analytics, and web applications that require high concurrency and responsiveness.

Non-Blocking Asynchronous Processing

A core advantage of reactive systems is their non-blocking nature, which ensures that a process does not halt execution while waiting for an operation to complete. In traditional synchronous programming, blocking I/O operations can cause significant performance bottlenecks. Reactive programming mitigates this issue by using observables to handle asynchronous streams efficiently.

Below is an example demonstrating a non-blocking API request in Python using RxPy:

```
import time
from rx import interval
from rx.operators import take

def process_event(x):
    print(f"Processing event {x} at {time.time()}")

observable = interval(1).pipe(take(5))  # Emits values every second
observable.subscribe(process_event)

print("Non-blocking execution continues...")
time.sleep(6)  # Keep the program alive to observe event emissions
```

In this example, the interval observable emits values every second without blocking execution. The program remains responsive while handling events asynchronously, making it well-suited for scalable architectures.

Backpressure and Load Management

In high-throughput systems, controlling data flow is essential to prevent resource exhaustion. Reactive programming provides backpressure mechanisms to regulate the rate at which data is processed. When an observable emits values faster than they can be handled, backpressure strategies such as buffering, throttling, and dropping events ensure system stability.

Here's an example implementing throttling using RxPy:

```
from rx import interval
from rx.operators import throttle_first

observable = interval(0.1).pipe(throttle_first(1))  # Emit one event per second
observable.subscribe(lambda x: print(f"Processed event {x}"))

import time
time.sleep(5)  # Allow time for throttled events to process
```

By applying throttle_first, the system ensures that only one event per second is processed, preventing overload when dealing with high-frequency data streams. This is crucial in distributed systems where excessive event rates could overwhelm components.

Event-Driven Microservices and Distributed Systems

Reactive programming seamlessly integrates with microservice architectures, where independent services communicate asynchronously. By using event-driven messaging, services can scale dynamically without being tightly coupled. A common pattern involves using message brokers like Kafka or RabbitMQ to handle inter-service communication.

For example, a producer service could publish user activity events to a message queue, while multiple consumer services process these events asynchronously:

```
from rx import from_iterable
from rx.operators import delay

events = from_iterable(["User Logged In", "User Clicked", "User Logged
          Out"]).pipe(delay(2))

events.subscribe(lambda x: print(f"Processed Event: {x}"))
```

This pattern ensures that services process events independently, enhancing scalability and fault tolerance.

Reactive programming is a powerful paradigm for building scalable and resilient systems. By leveraging non-blocking execution, backpressure management, and event-driven architectures, reactive systems can handle high loads while remaining responsive. These principles are widely applied in microservices, real-time analytics, and cloud-based applications to ensure performance at scale.

Part 3:

Programming Language Support for Declarative Programming

Declarative programming is supported across multiple programming languages, each offering unique constructs that enable developers to express computation more concisely. This part explores how **functional, logic, and declarative paradigms are implemented in languages such as C#, F#, JavaScript, Elixir, Go, Haskell, XSLT, Python, and MathCAD**. The modules in this section delve into **functional features, concurrency models, symbolic computation, and declarative data processing**, highlighting how different languages incorporate declarative principles. By examining real-world implementations, learners will gain insights into **language-specific declarative capabilities and cross-language interoperability**.

Functional and Logic Constructs in C#, F#, and JavaScript

C#, F#, and JavaScript each provide **declarative constructs** that simplify complex programming tasks. This module explores **LINQ and expression trees in C#**, demonstrating how queries can be written declaratively. The discussion extends to **F#'s functional features**, including **currying, immutability, and computation expressions**. In JavaScript, **functional paradigms enable declarative DOM manipulation**, while **Redux state management** provides a structured way to manage state changes in web applications using a declarative approach.

Pattern Matching and Concurrency in Elixir and Go

Elixir and Go offer powerful declarative constructs for **pattern matching and concurrent execution**. This module explores **functional composition in Elixir**, which enables concise and modular code. **Pattern matching and recursion**, fundamental to declarative computation, simplify control flow in functional programs. Go's **goroutines and dataflow mechanisms** provide declarative concurrency models that efficiently manage parallel computations. Additionally, the module covers **domain-specific languages (DSLs) in Go**, showcasing how declarative computation can be embedded into system-level applications.

Pure Functional Programming in Haskell and XSLT

Haskell is a **purely functional language**, emphasizing **lazy evaluation, purity, and type safety**. This module explores **monadic computation, type inference, and proof-assisted programming**, which enable developers to reason formally about program correctness. The discussion extends to **declarative XML processing with XSLT**, highlighting how transformations are expressed as **purely declarative rules**. XPath and XQuery further illustrate **data extraction and manipulation using functional paradigms**, providing a powerful alternative to imperative XML processing techniques.

Symbolic and Computational Mathematics with MathCAD

MathCAD provides a **declarative approach to mathematical computation**, allowing engineers and scientists to define symbolic expressions without procedural logic. This module explores **constraint solving techniques** in engineering applications, demonstrating how **automated symbolic manipulation** streamlines problem-solving. **Formula automation and functional dependencies** are examined, showing how MathCAD's environment facilitates **declarative dataflow modeling**. The discussion also covers **symbolic computation for scientific research**, emphasizing how declarative paradigms simplify complex mathematical formulations.

Declarative Features in Python

Python supports declarative paradigms through **list comprehensions, functional iterators, and higher-order functions**. This module explores **declarative machine learning pipelines**, demonstrating how frameworks like **TensorFlow and Scikit-learn** enable high-level data transformations. **Functional programming constructs in pandas and NumPy** provide expressive means to manipulate large datasets declaratively. The module also examines **meta-programming techniques,** such as decorators and lambda functions, showcasing how Python enables **abstraction and code reusability** while adhering to declarative principles.

Cross-Language Declarative Paradigms

Understanding declarative programming across multiple languages enhances a developer's ability to build **scalable, maintainable, and interoperable systems**. This module compares **functional constructs across languages**, demonstrating how **immutability, higher-order functions, and type inference** manifest in different ecosystems. **Logic programming support in multi-paradigm languages**, such as Prolog integration with Python and Java, is explored. The module also covers **interoperability mechanisms** for declarative paradigms, showing how systems can leverage **functional, logic, and constraint-based programming models**. Future trends in **declarative language development** offer insights into emerging paradigms.

This part provides **deep insights into declarative programming across multiple languages**, equipping learners with the skills to **apply declarative principles effectively in various programming environments**.

Module 13:

Functional and Logic Constructs in C#, F#, and JavaScript

Declarative programming is supported across multiple languages, each offering unique functional and logic-based constructs. This module explores how declarative paradigms are implemented in C#, F#, and JavaScript. The discussion begins with Language Integrated Query (LINQ) and expression trees in C#, demonstrating how functional and declarative programming simplifies data manipulation. The module then explores F#, a functional-first language, highlighting its strong support for immutability, higher-order functions, and pattern matching. JavaScript's declarative programming capabilities are examined through DOM manipulation, followed by an exploration of Redux, a predictable state management library that follows declarative principles for maintaining application state.

LINQ and Expression Trees in C#

C# provides powerful declarative constructs through Language Integrated Query (LINQ), enabling seamless data manipulation without explicit loops or control structures. LINQ allows developers to filter, transform, and aggregate data using a high-level syntax, making queries more readable and expressive. The declarative nature of LINQ abstracts away iteration logic, making code more maintainable. Expression trees complement LINQ by representing code in a structured format that enables dynamic execution and analysis. This section examines how LINQ and expression trees simplify data processing and how they contribute to more declarative programming in C#. Their application extends beyond databases, supporting collections, XML, and other data structures.

Functional Features in F#

F# is a functional-first programming language in the .NET ecosystem that encourages immutability, pattern matching, and higher-order functions. Unlike imperative languages, F# promotes function composition, allowing developers to build robust and reusable logic with minimal side effects. Type inference and concise syntax enable declarative programming without excessive boilerplate code. One of the strongest aspects of F# is its built-in support for asynchronous workflows, making it ideal for concurrent programming. Pattern matching allows complex data structures to be processed declaratively, reducing the need for verbose control flow statements. This section explores how F#'s functional features simplify problem-solving while maintaining code clarity and correctness.

Declarative DOM Manipulation with JavaScript

In traditional imperative programming, DOM manipulation requires explicit commands to alter page elements, leading to complex and error-prone code. Modern JavaScript frameworks embrace a declarative approach, allowing developers to define UI changes without direct DOM manipulation. Virtual DOM concepts, popularized by libraries like React, abstract away low-level operations by enabling state-driven rendering. This approach improves performance by updating only the necessary elements, reducing redundant computations. By leveraging functional programming techniques, JavaScript frameworks streamline UI updates, ensuring consistency across components. This section examines how declarative DOM manipulation enhances maintainability and improves responsiveness in modern web applications.

State Management with Redux

State management in large-scale applications is often a complex challenge, requiring careful synchronization across components. Redux provides a declarative state management solution based on functional principles. By enforcing unidirectional data flow and immutability, Redux ensures predictability and testability. State transitions are expressed through pure functions known as reducers, making logic explicit and easier to debug. Actions and middleware further enhance Redux's capabilities, allowing asynchronous data handling in a structured manner. This section explores how Redux integrates declarative programming into state management, offering a robust framework for handling application state while maintaining scalability and performance.

This module highlights the application of declarative programming across C#, F#, and JavaScript, demonstrating how functional and logic-based constructs improve readability, maintainability, and scalability. LINQ and expression trees simplify data manipulation in C#, while F#'s functional features enable expressive programming. Declarative DOM manipulation in JavaScript enhances UI rendering, and Redux provides structured state management, reinforcing declarative paradigms in modern development.

LINQ and Expression Trees in C#

C# offers a declarative way to manipulate data using **Language Integrated Query (LINQ)**, a feature that enables developers to interact with collections, databases, and XML using high-level, SQL-like syntax. Instead of writing verbose loops and conditionals, LINQ provides concise expressions that enhance readability, maintainability, and expressiveness in C# programming.

LINQ operates on **IEnumerable<T>** collections and provides a rich set of standard query operators like Where, Select, OrderBy, and GroupBy. These methods allow developers to filter, transform, and aggregate data concisely. Consider an imperative approach using loops and conditionals to filter even numbers from a list:

```
List<int> numbers = new List<int> { 1, 2, 3, 4, 5, 6 };
List<int> evenNumbers = new List<int>();

foreach (int num in numbers)
{
    if (num % 2 == 0)
```

```
    {
        evenNumbers.Add(num);
    }
}
```

This imperative approach explicitly iterates over the collection and modifies the list. A declarative alternative using LINQ eliminates the loop boilerplate:

```
var evenNumbers = numbers.Where(n => n % 2 == 0).ToList();
```

Here, Where(n => n % 2 == 0) filters the collection, and ToList() materializes the result. This approach is more readable and expressive.

Expression Trees in C#

Expression trees in C# provide a way to represent code as data, enabling dynamic query generation and manipulation. They are particularly useful in LINQ to SQL and Entity Framework, where queries must be translated into SQL expressions.

Consider a scenario where a function dynamically generates a filtering expression:

```
using System;
using System.Linq.Expressions;

Expression<Func<int, bool>> isEven = num => num % 2 == 0;

Console.WriteLine(isEven); // Output: num => (num % 2 == 0)
```

Here, the lambda expression is represented as an **Expression<Func<T, bool>>**, allowing it to be analyzed, modified, or compiled at runtime. This feature is fundamental in building dynamic queries where filtering conditions are not known at compile time.

Combining LINQ and Expression Trees

A major advantage of expression trees is their use in LINQ-to-Entities and LINQ-to-SQL, where they allow deferred query execution. A LINQ query that retrieves users with an age greater than 25 can be dynamically created:

```
Expression<Func<User, bool>> ageFilter = user => user.Age > 25;
var filteredUsers = dbContext.Users.Where(ageFilter);
```

Since ageFilter is an expression tree, it is parsed and translated into an equivalent SQL query, avoiding unnecessary object loading and improving performance.

LINQ and expression trees enhance C# by enabling declarative programming, making code more concise, readable, and maintainable. LINQ simplifies data querying, while expression trees enable dynamic query generation and runtime manipulation of code structures. Mastering these features is essential for developers working with C# in data-driven applications and complex query systems.

Functional Features in F#

F# is a functional-first programming language that provides a declarative approach to problem-solving. Unlike imperative languages that rely on state mutation and explicit control flow, F# emphasizes **immutability, first-class functions, pattern matching, and type inference**. These features make F# an excellent choice for writing clean, concise, and maintainable code, particularly in domains like data science, financial modeling, and distributed computing.

Immutability and First-Class Functions

In F#, immutability is the default, meaning variables cannot be reassigned once defined. This eliminates side effects and makes reasoning about code easier. Consider defining an immutable value:

```
let x = 10
// x <- 20 // This would cause an error
```

Functions in F# are **first-class citizens**, meaning they can be passed as arguments, returned from other functions, and assigned to variables. A simple function to square a number can be written concisely:

```
let square x = x * x
```

Functions can also be **higher-order**, taking other functions as arguments:

```
let applyTwice f x = f (f x)
applyTwice square 2   // Output: 16
```

This ability to pass and compose functions dynamically is fundamental in functional programming.

Pattern Matching and Discriminated Unions

Pattern matching is one of the most powerful features of F#. It allows concise handling of complex data structures and control flow without explicit conditionals. Consider a function that matches different shapes:

```
type Shape =
    | Circle of float
    | Rectangle of float * float

let area shape =
    match shape with
    | Circle r -> Math.PI * r * r
    | Rectangle (w, h) -> w * h

let myCircle = Circle 5.0
let myRectangle = Rectangle (4.0, 6.0)

area myCircle      // Output: 78.54
area myRectangle   // Output: 24.0
```

Discriminated unions allow defining complex data structures declaratively. Here, Shape can be either a Circle or a Rectangle, and pattern matching elegantly extracts values for computation.

Pipelining and Composition

One of F#'s strengths is **function composition and pipelining**, which enhance code readability by reducing nesting. Instead of writing deeply nested function calls, F# provides the |> operator to pipe values through functions:

```
let addOne x = x + 1
let double x = x * 2

let result = 5 |> addOne |> double  // Output: 12
```

This reads as: **take 5, add 1, then double the result**, making code flow naturally from left to right.

F# embraces functional programming by enforcing immutability, leveraging pattern matching, and promoting function composition. These features enable developers to write declarative, expressive, and maintainable code, making F# a powerful tool for functional-first development in .NET environments.

Declarative DOM Manipulation with JavaScript

JavaScript, traditionally an imperative language, has embraced a more declarative style with the rise of frameworks like React and modern browser APIs. Declarative DOM manipulation shifts the focus from manually modifying elements using document.querySelector() and innerHTML to defining what the UI should look like and letting the framework handle rendering. This approach improves readability, maintainability, and reusability.

Imperative vs. Declarative DOM Manipulation

In traditional JavaScript, updating the DOM requires explicit instructions for selecting and modifying elements. Consider an imperative approach:

```
const button = document.createElement("button");
button.textContent = "Click Me";
button.addEventListener("click", () => {
    document.getElementById("message").textContent = "Button Clicked!";
});
document.body.appendChild(button);
```

Here, each step must be manually coded: creating the element, setting attributes, and attaching event listeners. As the application scales, managing state changes becomes complex and error-prone.

By contrast, a declarative approach describes the desired state, and the framework ensures the DOM matches it. With React, the same functionality can be written as:

```
function App() {
  const [message, setMessage] = React.useState("");

  return (
    <div>
      <button onClick={() => setMessage("Button Clicked!")}>Click Me</button>
      <p>{message}</p>
    </div>
  );
}
```

Here, React automatically updates the UI when the state changes, eliminating the need for direct DOM manipulation.

Declarative Rendering with JSX

JSX (JavaScript XML) allows writing UI components in a declarative manner, closely resembling HTML. Consider rendering a dynamic list:

```
const items = ["Apple", "Banana", "Cherry"];

function ItemList() {
  return (
    <ul>
      {items.map((item, index) => (
        <li key={index}>{item}</li>
      ))}
    </ul>
  );
}
```

Rather than iterating over elements and appending them manually, JSX declaratively maps items to <li> elements, making the code more intuitive.

Virtual DOM and Efficient Updates

One advantage of declarative manipulation is the **Virtual DOM**. In frameworks like React, instead of updating the actual DOM directly, changes are first applied to a virtual representation. This allows React to efficiently determine what has changed and update only the necessary parts, improving performance.

For example, if a single item in a list updates, the entire list isn't re-rendered—only the affected item is updated. This prevents unnecessary reflows and repaints in the browser, enhancing efficiency.

Declarative DOM manipulation simplifies UI development by allowing developers to define the desired UI state while the framework handles updates efficiently. Through JSX, Virtual DOM, and state-driven rendering, JavaScript frameworks like React enable a cleaner, more maintainable approach to building web applications.

State Management with Redux

State management is a crucial aspect of web application development, ensuring consistency across UI components and enabling predictable data flow. Redux, a widely adopted state management library, enforces a declarative and centralized approach to managing state in JavaScript applications. It follows a unidirectional data flow, making debugging and testing more efficient.

The Core Principles of Redux

Redux is based on three key principles:

1. **Single Source of Truth** – The application state is stored in a single JavaScript object, known as the **store**, making state predictable and easily manageable.

2. **State is Read-Only** – The only way to modify state is by dispatching **actions**, ensuring state updates follow a controlled and trackable process.

3. **Changes are Made with Pure Functions** – Reducers, which specify how state changes, must be **pure functions**, meaning they return a new state object without modifying the existing one.

These principles ensure applications remain maintainable, scalable, and easier to debug.

Defining the Redux Store

In a Redux-based application, the store holds the global state. To define a store, a **reducer** function is required. A reducer takes the current state and an action, returning a new state based on the action type. Consider a simple counter example:

```
import { createStore } from "redux";

// Initial state
const initialState = { count: 0 };

// Reducer function
function counterReducer(state = initialState, action) {
  switch (action.type) {
    case "INCREMENT":
      return { count: state.count + 1 };
    case "DECREMENT":
      return { count: state.count - 1 };
    default:
      return state;
  }
}

// Create store
const store = createStore(counterReducer);
```

The counterReducer ensures that state changes are **immutable**, returning a new object each time instead of modifying the existing state.

Dispatching Actions

Actions are simple JavaScript objects describing what should happen. The Redux store listens for these actions to update state.

```
store.dispatch({ type: "INCREMENT" });
console.log(store.getState()); // { count: 1 }

store.dispatch({ type: "DECREMENT" });
console.log(store.getState()); // { count: 0 }
```

Since actions follow a declarative approach, they describe "what happened" rather than explicitly modifying state. This improves maintainability and allows features like time-travel debugging.

Connecting Redux with a UI

Redux integrates seamlessly with frameworks like React. The **React-Redux** library provides hooks such as useSelector to access state and useDispatch to send actions.

```
import { useSelector, useDispatch } from "react-redux";

function Counter() {
  const count = useSelector((state) => state.count);
  const dispatch = useDispatch();

  return (
    <div>
      <p>Count: {count}</p>
      <button onClick={() => dispatch({ type: "INCREMENT" })}>+</button>
      <button onClick={() => dispatch({ type: "DECREMENT" })}>-</button>
    </div>
  );
}
```

This declarative approach ensures the UI always reflects the current state, with Redux handling updates efficiently.

Redux enforces a structured, declarative method for managing state, ensuring consistency across applications. By defining actions, reducers, and a global store, developers can build scalable and maintainable applications while minimizing state-related bugs.

Module 14:

Pattern Matching and Concurrency in Elixir and Go

Declarative programming extends beyond syntax and structure to include paradigms that simplify logic, enhance concurrency, and optimize computation. Elixir and Go are two modern languages that incorporate declarative principles for functional composition, pattern matching, and efficient concurrency handling. This module explores functional composition in Elixir, the power of pattern matching and recursion, the lightweight concurrency model of Go through Goroutines, and the use of domain-specific languages (DSLs) for declarative computation in Go. These concepts collectively demonstrate how declarative approaches improve performance, readability, and maintainability in concurrent and high-performance applications.

Functional Composition in Elixir

Elixir is a functional programming language that excels at handling concurrent, distributed systems. One of its key strengths lies in **functional composition**, which allows developers to build complex operations by combining smaller, reusable functions. Unlike imperative programming, where step-by-step instructions dictate execution, functional composition in Elixir enables declarative programming by expressing logic as a series of transformations on data.

By leveraging **pure functions** and **pipe operators**, Elixir simplifies function chaining, making code more readable and maintainable. Functional composition promotes modularity, reducing redundancy and ensuring that functions remain independent and reusable. This results in predictable execution flows, improved testability, and minimal side effects. The ability to declaratively compose functions enables seamless data transformations and process flow control, making Elixir an ideal language for building scalable applications, particularly in distributed systems such as real-time communication platforms and web services.

Pattern Matching and Recursion

Pattern matching is one of Elixir's most powerful declarative features, allowing developers to concisely destructure and transform data structures. Unlike traditional conditional logic, which relies on explicit comparisons, pattern matching enables a more expressive and declarative approach to handling diverse input structures. This is particularly useful when working with lists, tuples, and maps, as it facilitates clear and intuitive data extraction.

Recursion, another fundamental concept in functional programming, pairs seamlessly with pattern matching to handle iterative processes without mutable state. Instead of using loops, recursive functions break problems into smaller subproblems, naturally expressing solutions in a declarative manner. When combined, pattern matching and recursion create an elegant means of handling tasks such as processing lists, parsing nested data, and implementing stateful computations in a purely functional way. This declarative approach minimizes complexity, eliminates unnecessary control flow statements, and ensures predictable function behavior.

Goroutines and Dataflow in Go

Go is designed for efficiency, and one of its standout features is **Goroutines**, which provide lightweight concurrency management. Unlike traditional threading models, Goroutines offer an efficient, declarative way to manage concurrent operations without manual thread creation or synchronization overhead. They enable developers to express concurrent workflows in a clear and scalable manner, making Go particularly well-suited for building high-performance applications, including distributed systems, microservices, and network services.

In addition to Goroutines, Go's **channel-based concurrency model** ensures safe data sharing between concurrent processes. Channels provide a declarative means of synchronizing data exchange, eliminating the complexities of manual locking mechanisms. By structuring concurrent execution using Goroutines and channels, Go achieves a model where computation flows naturally, avoiding race conditions and ensuring efficient resource utilization. This approach aligns with the principles of declarative programming, where emphasis is placed on describing *what* should happen rather than *how* it is achieved.

DSLs for Declarative Computation in Go

Domain-Specific Languages (DSLs) allow developers to create specialized declarative syntax tailored for specific computational tasks. In Go, DSLs provide a structured way to define computations, workflows, and configurations without the need for imperative code structures. By abstracting complex logic into high-level expressions, DSLs improve readability and make domain-specific operations more intuitive.

Go's support for DSLs is evident in frameworks designed for infrastructure automation, testing, and data processing. Libraries enable declarative definitions for state management, workflow execution, and constraint-based computations. By utilizing DSLs, Go programmers can model problems in an intuitive, structured manner while ensuring scalability and maintainability. This further enhances the declarative nature of Go's programming paradigm, allowing developers to define computation in a way that closely aligns with problem-domain logic.

Elixir and Go exemplify declarative programming principles through functional composition, pattern matching, lightweight concurrency, and DSL-based computation. By leveraging Elixir's expressive function chaining and recursion and Go's Goroutines and declarative dataflow mechanisms, developers can build scalable, efficient, and maintainable applications. This module highlights how both languages reinforce declarative thinking, enabling clear, predictable, and high-performance software development.

Functional Composition in Elixir

Functional composition in Elixir enables developers to create modular, declarative, and reusable code by combining simple functions into more complex behaviors. Unlike imperative programming, which relies on explicit loops and state management, functional composition emphasizes **what** should be done rather than **how** it should be implemented. Through **pure functions**, **higher-order functions**, and **the pipe operator (|>)**, Elixir facilitates an expressive and readable programming style.

Using the Pipe Operator (|>)

The pipe operator (|>) in Elixir allows function calls to be chained together in a linear, readable manner. Instead of nesting function calls inside each other, the pipe operator enables output from one function to be passed as input to the next.

```
defmodule MathOps do
  def square(x), do: x * x
  def increment(x), do: x + 1
  def double(x), do: x * 2
end

IO.puts MathOps.double(MathOps.increment(MathOps.square(3)))  # Nested Calls

# Using the pipe operator for readability
IO.puts 3 |> MathOps.square() |> MathOps.increment() |> MathOps.double()
```

By using |>, the function sequence becomes more declarative, making the transformation steps explicit and easy to understand.

Composing Functions for Data Processing

Functional composition is particularly useful in data transformations. Elixir's Enum module provides higher-order functions that work seamlessly with the pipe operator to process lists declaratively.

```
defmodule DataProcessing do
  def process_numbers(numbers) do
    numbers
    |> Enum.filter(&(&1 > 0))  # Keep only positive numbers
    |> Enum.map(&(&1 * 2))     # Double each number
    |> Enum.sum()              # Sum the values
  end
end

IO.puts DataProcessing.process_numbers([-2, 3, -1, 4, 5])  # Output: 24
```

Each step in the transformation is applied sequentially, eliminating the need for explicit loops or intermediate variables.

Higher-Order Functions for Flexibility

Higher-order functions in Elixir allow behavior to be passed as arguments, making function composition more dynamic and reusable.

135

```
defmodule Transformer do
  def apply_transform(numbers, transform_fn) do
    numbers |> Enum.map(transform_fn)
  end
end

double_fn = fn x -> x * 2 end
IO.inspect Transformer.apply_transform([1, 2, 3], double_fn)  # Output: [2, 4,
       6]
```

Here, apply_transform/2 applies a transformation function (double_fn) to each element in the list, demonstrating how functions can be treated as first-class citizens.

Anonymous Functions for Inline Composition

Elixir supports inline function composition using anonymous functions (fn -> end). This allows quick modifications without defining named functions.

```
composed_fn = fn x -> x |> (&(&1 * &1)).() |> (&(&1 + 3)).() end
IO.puts composed_fn.(4)  # Output: 19
```

By structuring programs with functional composition, Elixir code remains concise, expressive, and scalable, making it ideal for concurrent and distributed applications.

Pattern Matching and Recursion in Elixir

Elixir leverages **pattern matching** and **recursion** as fundamental constructs for structuring declarative programs. Pattern matching allows data to be deconstructed concisely, eliminating the need for explicit conditionals. Recursion, in turn, replaces loops, providing an elegant mechanism for iterating over data. Together, these features enhance code readability and expressiveness.

Pattern Matching in Function Definitions

Elixir enables function overloading using pattern matching. Instead of using if or switch statements, different function clauses are defined for varying inputs.

```
defmodule Greeting do
  def hello("Alice"), do: "Hello, Alice!"
  def hello("Bob"), do: "Hey Bob, how's it going?"
  def hello(_name), do: "Hello, stranger!"
end

IO.puts Greeting.hello("Alice")   # Output: Hello, Alice!
IO.puts Greeting.hello("Charlie") # Output: Hello, stranger!
```

The _name wildcard ensures that any unmatched input receives a default response, preventing errors and keeping code concise.

Pattern Matching with Tuples and Lists

Pattern matching also simplifies tuple and list operations by allowing direct data extraction.

136

```
defmodule TupleMatcher do
  def status({:ok, result}), do: "Success: #{result}"
  def status({:error, reason}), do: "Error: #{reason}"
end

IO.puts TupleMatcher.status({:ok, "File uploaded"})     # Output: Success: File
          uploaded
IO.puts TupleMatcher.status({:error, "Network issue"}) # Output: Error: Network
          issue
```

Matching ensures data structures are safely unpacked without manual indexing.

Recursion for Iteration

Elixir avoids traditional loops by relying on **recursion**. A function calls itself with updated parameters until a base case is reached.

```
defmodule Factorial do
  def compute(0), do: 1
  def compute(n), do: n * compute(n - 1)
end

IO.puts Factorial.compute(5)  # Output: 120
```

Each recursive call reduces n until 0 is reached, where the base case terminates execution.

Tail-Recursive Optimization

For large computations, Elixir optimizes recursive functions using **tail recursion**, preventing stack overflow by ensuring the last operation is a function call.

```
defmodule TailRecFactorial do
  def compute(n), do: compute(n, 1)

  defp compute(0, acc), do: acc
  defp compute(n, acc), do: compute(n - 1, n * acc)
end

IO.puts TailRecFactorial.compute(5)  # Output: 120
```

Using an accumulator (acc), the function avoids excessive memory consumption, improving efficiency.

By integrating pattern matching and recursion, Elixir promotes declarative, expressive, and performant programming, eliminating imperative constructs and making code more maintainable.

Goroutines and Dataflow in Go

Go is designed for **concurrent programming**, allowing lightweight threads called **goroutines** to execute independently. Goroutines simplify concurrent execution by handling multiple tasks in parallel without complex thread management. In addition, Go's **channels** facilitate safe communication between goroutines, ensuring synchronized dataflow. These features enable scalable, efficient, and declarative concurrency patterns.

Creating and Running Goroutines

A **goroutine** is launched using the go keyword before a function call. It executes independently without blocking the main execution thread.

```
package main

import (
        "fmt"
        "time"
)

func greet() {
        fmt.Println("Hello from a goroutine!")
}

func main() {
        go greet() // Runs asynchronously
        fmt.Println("Main function execution")
        time.Sleep(time.Second) // Prevents program from exiting before
        goroutine executes
}
```

Since greet() runs in a separate goroutine, main() continues executing, printing its message first. The time.Sleep() ensures the goroutine gets a chance to execute before the program exits.

Communicating with Channels

Goroutines use **channels** to exchange data safely without race conditions. Channels are created using make(chan Type), allowing goroutines to send and receive values.

```
package main

import "fmt"

func sendMessage(ch chan string) {
        ch <- "Hello from Goroutine!"
}

func main() {
        message := make(chan string) // Create a channel
        go sendMessage(message)      // Start goroutine
        fmt.Println(<-message)       // Receive message from channel
}
```

Here, the goroutine sendMessage sends a string to the channel ch. The main() function waits to receive this message before continuing, ensuring safe synchronization.

Buffered Channels for Dataflow Management

Buffered channels allow multiple values to be sent without immediate synchronization, improving performance when sending multiple items.

```
package main
```

```
import "fmt"
func main() {
        ch := make(chan int, 3) // Buffered channel with capacity 3

        ch <- 1
        ch <- 2
        ch <- 3

        fmt.Println(<-ch) // Output: 1
        fmt.Println(<-ch) // Output: 2
        fmt.Println(<-ch) // Output: 3
}
```

By buffering values, the sender does not wait for an immediate receiver, allowing efficient **dataflow processing**.

Using select for Multiple Channels

Go's select statement waits on multiple channel operations, allowing dynamic message handling.

```
package main

import (
        "fmt"
        "time"
)

func main() {
        ch1 := make(chan string)
        ch2 := make(chan string)

        go func() {
           time.Sleep(2 * time.Second)
           ch1 <- "Message from channel 1"
        }()

        go func() {
           time.Sleep(1 * time.Second)
           ch2 <- "Message from channel 2"
        }()

        select {
        case msg := <-ch1:
           fmt.Println(msg)
        case msg := <-ch2:
           fmt.Println(msg)
        }
}
```

Since ch2 receives data first, its message is printed first. This non-blocking approach makes Go highly suitable for declarative **concurrent programming**.

DSLs for Declarative Computation in Go

A **Domain-Specific Language (DSL)** is a specialized language designed for a specific task, improving readability and maintainability. In Go, DSLs can be embedded as **fluent APIs**, **configuration-driven scripting**, or **domain-specific expression parsing**. These approaches enable declarative computation by defining logic in a high-level, domain-relevant syntax rather than imperative code.

Fluent APIs as Embedded DSLs

A **fluent API** enables declarative programming by chaining method calls in a readable way. Go supports this using struct methods.

```go
package main

import "fmt"

type Query struct {
        filter string
        limit  int
}

func NewQuery() *Query {
        return &Query{}
}

func (q *Query) Filter(condition string) *Query {
        q.filter = condition
        return q
}

func (q *Query) Limit(n int) *Query {
        q.limit = n
        return q
}

func (q *Query) Execute() {
        fmt.Printf("Executing Query: WHERE %s LIMIT %d\n", q.filter, q.limit)
}

func main() {
        NewQuery().Filter("age > 30").Limit(10).Execute()
}
```

Here, the Query struct forms a **DSL-like syntax** by chaining calls to Filter() and Limit(), making it **declarative** rather than imperative.

Configuration-Driven DSLs

A common approach to declarative computation is defining **configurations in JSON or YAML** and processing them in Go.

Config file (config.json):

```json
{
    "operation": "sum",
    "values": [10, 20, 30]
}
```

Go implementation:

```go
package main
```

```go
import (
        "encoding/json"
        "fmt"
        "os"
)

type Config struct {
        Operation string `json:"operation"`
        Values    []int  `json:"values"`
}

func compute(config Config) int {
        sum := 0
        for _, v := range config.Values {
            sum += v
        }
        return sum
}

func main() {
        file, _ := os.ReadFile("config.json")
        var config Config
        json.Unmarshal(file, &config)

        result := compute(config)
        fmt.Println("Computed Result:", result)
}
```

This approach separates computation logic from control flow, **allowing users to define operations declaratively** through JSON rather than hardcoded Go logic.

Expression Parsing for Custom DSLs

For advanced DSLs, Go can parse **custom expressions** using a tokenizer or an expression evaluation library like govaluate.

```go
package main

import (
        "fmt"
        "github.com/Knetic/govaluate"
)

func main() {
        expression, _ := govaluate.NewEvaluableExpression("10 + 5 * 2")
        result, _ := expression.Evaluate(nil)
        fmt.Println("Evaluated Result:", result)
}
```

This enables declarative mathematical computations dynamically, making Go suitable for **dataflow DSLs** and **computational logic**.

By leveraging fluent APIs, configuration-driven logic, and expression evaluation, Go can support **declarative computation via embedded DSLs**, enhancing readability and maintainability in domain-specific applications.

Module 15:

Pure Functional Programming in Haskell and XSLT

Pure functional programming is a paradigm that eliminates side effects, ensuring that functions always produce the same output for the same input. Haskell exemplifies this approach through lazy evaluation and a strong type system, while XSLT provides a declarative method for transforming XML data. This module explores these concepts, illustrating how functional purity and declarative computation contribute to robust, maintainable software.

Lazy Evaluation and Purity in Haskell

Haskell enforces purity, meaning functions cannot modify state or interact with external systems unless explicitly managed. This property ensures **referential transparency**, where an expression can be replaced by its evaluated result without affecting program behavior. **Lazy evaluation** further enhances efficiency by computing values only when required. This approach enables infinite data structures and optimized performance, as computations are deferred until needed. While this provides flexibility, it also demands careful handling to prevent memory leaks due to unevaluated expressions. Understanding how laziness and purity interact is essential for writing efficient and correct functional programs in Haskell.

Type Systems and Proof-Assisted Programming

Haskell's **strong and static type system** prevents many runtime errors by enforcing correctness at compile time. The **Hindley-Milner type inference** mechanism allows type safety without explicit annotations, making code both concise and reliable. Advanced type system features such as **algebraic data types, type classes, and higher-kinded types** enable powerful abstractions. Proof-assisted programming is an extension of this concept, where types act as a form of formal verification. Dependent types and theorem-proving tools like **Agda and Coq** allow programmers to prove properties about their code, ensuring correctness beyond traditional testing methods. These features make Haskell a prime language for mathematically verified software.

Declarative XML Processing with XSLT

XSLT (Extensible Stylesheet Language Transformations) is a **rule-based declarative language** designed for transforming XML documents into other formats such as HTML, plain text, or different XML structures. Unlike imperative approaches, where transformation logic is explicitly programmed step by step, XSLT defines **templates and pattern-matching rules** that specify how elements should be processed. The declarative nature of XSLT makes it highly adaptable to **complex hierarchical data transformations**, ensuring that XML transformations remain

modular, maintainable, and scalable. By using **XPath expressions**, XSLT enables fine-grained selection of elements, streamlining complex XML modifications without requiring imperative code.

XPath and XQuery for Data Extraction

XPath and XQuery are **declarative query languages** optimized for extracting and transforming structured data from XML documents. XPath provides a concise syntax for navigating XML trees, allowing precise element selection through expressions that resemble filesystem paths. XQuery extends XPath by adding **functional programming constructs**, enabling filtering, aggregation, and transformation of XML datasets. These tools are indispensable in XML-heavy applications such as **data integration, document processing, and web services**. By leveraging XPath and XQuery, developers can perform sophisticated queries and transformations with minimal effort, reinforcing the **power of declarative programming** in structured data manipulation.

This module underscores the significance of **pure functional programming and declarative XML processing**. Haskell's **lazy evaluation and strong type system** promote correctness and efficiency, while XSLT, XPath, and XQuery offer **expressive, rule-based** methods for transforming structured data. Understanding these concepts equips developers with the tools to write **maintainable, verifiable, and scalable** software in purely declarative paradigms.

Lazy Evaluation and Purity in Haskell

Haskell is a **purely functional language**, meaning functions cannot have side effects—ensuring that they always return the same output for the same input. This property, known as **referential transparency**, allows for greater predictability and easier reasoning about code. Another key feature of Haskell is **lazy evaluation**, which delays computations until their results are actually needed. This technique allows infinite data structures, reduces redundant calculations, and enhances efficiency by avoiding unnecessary computations. However, it also introduces potential pitfalls, such as space leaks when unevaluated expressions accumulate in memory.

Lazy evaluation is best understood through infinite data structures. In an eagerly evaluated language, an infinite list would cause an immediate runtime error, as the program would attempt to allocate infinite memory. However, in Haskell, computations proceed incrementally, evaluating only what is necessary. Consider the following example of an infinite list in Haskell:

```
naturals :: [Integer]
naturals = [1..]  -- An infinite list of natural numbers

takeTen :: [Integer]
takeTen = take 10 naturals  -- Extracts the first 10 numbers lazily
```

Here, naturals is an infinite list, but Haskell does not attempt to evaluate it fully. Instead, when take 10 is applied, only the first 10 elements are computed, avoiding unnecessary evaluations.

Another advantage of lazy evaluation is performance optimization through **function composition**. Suppose we have a function that squares each number in a list and another that filters even numbers:

```
squares :: [Integer] -> [Integer]
squares = map (^2)

evens :: [Integer] -> [Integer]
evens = filter even
```

Instead of generating an intermediate list of squared values before filtering, Haskell defers execution, only computing values that meet the filtering condition. This avoids unnecessary computations and improves efficiency.

However, lazy evaluation can also lead to space leaks. If unevaluated expressions (thunks) accumulate in memory without being used, performance degrades. Consider the following function:

```
sumList :: [Integer] -> Integer
sumList [] = 0
sumList (x:xs) = x + sumList xs
```

In a strict (eagerly evaluated) language, sumList would accumulate values as it iterates. In Haskell, however, it builds up a chain of unevaluated expressions $(x + (y + (z + ...)))$, leading to high memory consumption. Using **strict evaluation** in key areas can mitigate this:

```
sumList' :: [Integer] -> Integer
sumList' = foldl' (+) 0
```

Here, foldl' (from Data.List) forces evaluation at each step, preventing excessive memory buildup.

Lazy evaluation in Haskell enables efficient computation by delaying evaluations until necessary, supporting infinite data structures and optimizing performance. However, improper use can lead to space leaks. Understanding **when to leverage laziness** and **when to enforce strictness** is crucial for writing performant Haskell programs.

Type Systems and Proof-Assisted Programming

Haskell's type system is one of its defining features, providing strong static typing that ensures program correctness before execution. The language uses **parametric polymorphism**, **type inference**, and **higher-kinded types**, making it both expressive and safe. Moreover, Haskell's type system can be leveraged for **proof-assisted programming**, where the compiler helps guarantee properties about programs, reducing errors and enhancing reliability.

The **Hindley-Milner type system** in Haskell allows for powerful type inference, meaning explicit type annotations are often unnecessary. For example, the compiler can deduce the type of a function like:

```
add :: Num a => a -> a -> a
add x y = x + y
```

Here, Num a => is a **type class constraint**, indicating that a must be a numeric type. This allows add to work with integers, floating-point numbers, or any other numeric type without requiring separate implementations.

Haskell also supports **algebraic data types (ADTs)**, which provide a robust way to model complex data. Consider a simple example of a custom Shape type:

```
data Shape = Circle Float | Rectangle Float Float
    deriving (Show)
```

Here, Shape is a **sum type**, meaning it can be either a Circle (with a radius) or a Rectangle (with width and height). This kind of structured type definition eliminates many potential runtime errors by ensuring exhaustive pattern matching at compile time.

Proof-Assisted Programming with Types

Haskell's strong type system allows for **proofs through types**, enforcing program correctness by preventing invalid states. Consider a function that ensures division by zero is impossible:

```
safeDiv :: Double -> Double -> Maybe Double
safeDiv _ 0 = Nothing
safeDiv x y = Just (x / y)
```

Here, safeDiv returns a Maybe Double, explicitly handling division by zero without causing runtime errors. This ensures safe execution through the type system itself.

For more advanced proof-based programming, Haskell supports **dependent types** and **refinement types** through extensions like **LiquidHaskell**. Refinement types allow specifying additional properties within type signatures, enabling more precise guarantees about program behavior.

For example, LiquidHaskell can enforce that a function always returns a positive number:

```
{-@ positiveAdd :: x:Int -> y:Int -> {v:Int | v > 0} @-}
positiveAdd :: Int -> Int -> Int
positiveAdd x y = x + y
```

The type annotation guarantees that positiveAdd never produces a negative result, acting as a form of **formal verification**.

Haskell's type system is not just for catching errors but also for enforcing correctness through **proof-assisted programming**. By leveraging **type inference, algebraic data types, and refinement types**, developers can write safer, more predictable programs with built-in guarantees about correctness—effectively reducing runtime failures while improving code quality.

Declarative XML Processing with XSLT

XSLT (Extensible Stylesheet Language Transformations) is a declarative language designed for transforming XML documents. Unlike imperative programming, where step-by-step instructions dictate how to manipulate data, XSLT follows a **rule-based approach** that declaratively describes how elements should be transformed. This makes it particularly useful in scenarios where XML data needs to be reformatted, extracted, or combined dynamically.

XSLT operates using **templates** that match elements in an XML document and specify how they should be processed. For example, an XSLT template might transform an XML document representing a book catalog into an HTML table. The power of XSLT comes from its ability to apply transformations recursively and use pattern matching to manipulate data efficiently.

XSLT Transformation Example

Consider an XML document containing book information:

```
<books>
    <book>
        <title>Declarative Programming</title>
        <author>Jane Doe</author>
        <year>2025</year>
    </book>
    <book>
        <title>Functional Paradigms</title>
        <author>John Smith</author>
        <year>2023</year>
    </book>
</books>
```

An XSLT script to transform this XML into an HTML table could look like this:

```
<xsl:stylesheet version="1.0"
    xmlns:xsl="http://www.w3.org/1999/XSL/Transform">

    <xsl:template match="/">
        <html>
            <body>
                <h2>Book Catalog</h2>
                <table border="1">
                    <tr>
                        <th>Title</th>
                        <th>Author</th>
                        <th>Year</th>
                    </tr>
                    <xsl:apply-templates select="books/book"/>
                </table>
```

146

```
        </body>
      </html>
    </xsl:template>

    <xsl:template match="book">
        <tr>
            <td><xsl:value-of select="title"/></td>
            <td><xsl:value-of select="author"/></td>
            <td><xsl:value-of select="year"/></td>
        </tr>
    </xsl:template>

</xsl:stylesheet>
```

Understanding the Declarative Approach

1. **Pattern Matching:** XSLT applies transformations based on templates that match elements in the XML document. Here, <xsl:template match="/"> matches the root node and starts processing.

2. **Recursive Application:** The <xsl:apply-templates select="books/book"/> directive tells XSLT to process each <book> element using the corresponding template.

3. **Data Extraction:** The <xsl:value-of select="title"/> extracts the content of the <title> element for each book.

When applied to the XML, this XSLT transformation produces the following HTML output:

```
<html>
    <body>
        <h2>Book Catalog</h2>
        <table border="1">
            <tr>
                <th>Title</th>
                <th>Author</th>
                <th>Year</th>
            </tr>
            <tr>
                <td>Declarative Programming</td>
                <td>Jane Doe</td>
                <td>2025</td>
            </tr>
            <tr>
                <td>Functional Paradigms</td>
                <td>John Smith</td>
                <td>2023</td>
            </tr>
        </table>
    </body>
</html>
```

XSLT provides a powerful declarative mechanism for XML transformations, relying on **pattern matching, templates, and recursive processing** to modify structured data. Its rule-based execution ensures that transformations remain **concise, maintainable, and reusable**, making it a valuable tool in web development, data conversion, and content syndication.

147

XPath and XQuery for Data Extraction

XPath and XQuery are powerful declarative languages designed for querying and extracting data from XML documents. XPath is primarily used for **navigating XML structures**, selecting nodes, and applying functions, while XQuery extends this capability by providing **querying, filtering, and transformation functionalities** similar to SQL but for XML data. Both are widely used in applications where structured data retrieval is necessary, such as in web services, configuration management, and document storage systems.

XPath expressions work by specifying **paths to elements or attributes** within an XML document. XQuery, on the other hand, is a **functional language** built on top of XPath, enabling advanced filtering, sorting, and transformations. Together, they allow efficient data retrieval and manipulation without imperative loops or conditions, following a declarative approach.

Using XPath for Data Selection

Consider an XML document representing a collection of books:

```
<library>
    <book>
        <title>Declarative Programming</title>
        <author>Jane Doe</author>
        <year>2025</year>
    </book>
    <book>
        <title>Functional Paradigms</title>
        <author>John Smith</author>
        <year>2023</year>
    </book>
</library>
```

With XPath, we can extract specific elements using path expressions. Below are some common XPath queries:

- Select all book titles:

  ```
  /library/book/title
  ```

- Select the title of the first book:

  ```
  /library/book[1]/title
  ```

- Select books written after 2024:

  ```
  /library/book[year > 2024]/title
  ```

Using XQuery for Data Extraction

XQuery extends XPath with additional filtering and transformation capabilities. Below is an XQuery example that retrieves books published after 2024:

```
for $b in /library/book
where $b/year > 2024
return <result>{$b/title/text()}</result>
```

The result would be:

```
<result>Declarative Programming</result>
```

XQuery can also transform XML into different formats, such as JSON, making it useful for **API development** and **data interchange**.

Applying XPath and XQuery in Real Applications

1. **Web Scraping and Content Extraction:** XPath is used in web automation tools like Selenium to extract structured content from HTML pages.

2. **Database Queries:** XQuery is used in XML databases to retrieve structured data efficiently.

3. **Configuration Management:** Many enterprise applications store settings in XML, where XPath allows precise querying and updates.

XPath and XQuery provide **concise, expressive, and efficient** ways to extract and manipulate XML data declaratively. By eliminating the need for imperative loops and conditions, they enhance readability and maintainability, making them essential tools in XML-based data processing.

Module 16:

Symbolic and Computational Mathematics with MathCAD

Mathematical computation plays a crucial role in engineering, science, and data analysis, and **declarative mathematical approaches** allow for solving complex problems efficiently. This module explores **MathCAD**, a powerful symbolic and computational mathematics tool that facilitates **declarative problem-solving** through **symbolic computation, formula automation, constraint solving, and functional dependencies**. Unlike imperative programming languages that require step-by-step execution, MathCAD allows users to define mathematical relationships and derive results through **declarative expressions**. This module delves into declarative mathematical modeling, its applications in engineering, automation of formulas, and dependencies in dataflow computations.

Declarative Mathematics and Computation

Declarative mathematics involves **expressing mathematical concepts in a high-level symbolic form** rather than specifying computation steps explicitly. MathCAD provides a **symbolic computation engine** that enables users to **define variables, equations, and constraints** while allowing the system to solve them automatically. This approach enhances readability, reduces complexity, and ensures **reusability of formulas**.

A key feature of MathCAD is its **live symbolic evaluation**, meaning mathematical expressions remain dynamic and update as variables change. Unlike procedural programming, where values must be manually updated, **MathCAD maintains dependencies automatically**. This is particularly useful for modeling **physical phenomena, solving differential equations, and optimizing mathematical models** in engineering and physics.

Constraint Solving in Engineering Applications

Constraint solving is an essential technique in **engineering, physics, and optimization problems**, allowing declarative systems to derive valid solutions while adhering to predefined constraints. MathCAD supports **solving nonlinear equations, structural analysis, and simulation problems** without requiring explicit iteration. Users can define **boundary conditions, algebraic constraints, and differential equations**, and MathCAD intelligently determines feasible solutions.

For instance, in mechanical engineering, constraint-based modeling helps optimize designs by **imposing physical limitations, such as load distribution or stress tolerances**. Similarly, in electrical engineering, it assists in circuit analysis by ensuring **Kirchhoff's laws and Ohm's law**

are satisfied without the need for procedural simulation. By leveraging declarative constraint solving, engineers can focus on defining **relationships rather than execution details**, streamlining problem-solving.

Symbolic Computation and Formula Automation

MathCAD's symbolic computation engine allows for **automatic formula derivation, simplification, and algebraic transformations**. Unlike numerical computation, symbolic methods preserve **variables and exact values**, ensuring precision. This is particularly beneficial in **calculus, differential equations, and algebraic manipulations**, where closed-form solutions are required.

Formula automation further enhances declarative programming by **eliminating redundant recalculations** and maintaining functional consistency across equations. Users can define general **formula templates** that automatically adjust based on input values, reducing manual effort and improving efficiency. This is especially valuable in **scientific research, financial modeling, and statistical analysis**, where symbolic representation is required for **theoretical derivations and proof verification**.

Dataflow and Functional Dependencies

Dataflow programming in MathCAD enables **automatic updates of dependent variables** when input values change, following a declarative paradigm. Instead of explicitly specifying the computation order, users define **mathematical dependencies**, and MathCAD manages the updates dynamically.

This concept is critical in **simulation modeling, financial forecasting, and real-time computational systems**, where changes in one parameter influence a network of related variables. Functional dependencies ensure **consistent, error-free calculations** without requiring imperative control structures, making declarative dataflow models **scalable and modular**.

MathCAD exemplifies **declarative mathematics** by enabling symbolic computation, constraint solving, and automated formula derivation without requiring explicit procedural programming. By focusing on **mathematical relationships rather than computational steps**, users can efficiently model **engineering, scientific, and financial problems**. This declarative approach enhances clarity, reusability, and correctness, making MathCAD a powerful tool for symbolic and computational mathematics.

Declarative Mathematics and Computation

Declarative mathematics enables users to **define mathematical relationships** without specifying the step-by-step procedures needed to solve them. Unlike imperative programming, where operations must be executed sequentially, declarative approaches like **MathCAD** focus on defining equations and constraints, allowing the system to compute results automatically. This abstraction is particularly beneficial in **symbolic mathematics,**

engineering simulations, and scientific analysis, where precision and automation are crucial.

MathCAD provides **live symbolic evaluation**, meaning that equations update automatically when variables change. This eliminates the need for manual recalculations, ensuring that all expressions remain **consistent and interconnected**. By treating **mathematical expressions as declarative statements**, MathCAD enables users to focus on **modeling the problem** rather than the mechanics of computation.

For example, in MathCAD, defining a quadratic equation is straightforward:

```
f(x) := ax^2 + bx + c
```

Once defined, MathCAD can solve for x when f(x) = 0, without requiring an explicit solution algorithm. The software applies symbolic computation techniques such as **algebraic factorization, differentiation, and simplification** to derive results automatically.

This approach enhances **mathematical clarity, reduces the risk of computational errors, and improves reusability**. It allows researchers and engineers to manipulate equations symbolically, **transforming and optimizing mathematical models** without needing to write complex algorithms.

Symbolic Computation in MathCAD

One of MathCAD's most powerful features is its **symbolic computation engine**, which enables algebraic manipulation and equation-solving without numerical approximation. Traditional programming languages rely on **numeric approximations** and iterative calculations, which can introduce **rounding errors**. In contrast, **symbolic computation retains exact representations** of expressions, preserving accuracy in **calculus, linear algebra, and differential equations**.

For example, differentiating a function symbolically in MathCAD is as simple as:

```
diff(f(x), x)
```

This allows **automatic differentiation**, which is essential in **optimization problems, physics simulations, and machine learning applications**. Similarly, MathCAD supports **symbolic integration**, enabling users to compute **definite and indefinite integrals** without numerical approximation:

```
∫ f(x) dx
```

By maintaining symbolic representations, MathCAD ensures that **computations remain precise** and allows for **algebraic simplifications** that are often lost in numerical approaches.

Defining Functional Dependencies

Declarative mathematics in MathCAD is inherently **functional**, meaning that variables and expressions maintain **dependencies** without requiring explicit state management. A simple example of functional dependency is defining an equation that automatically updates based on input changes:

```
y := 2x + 5
```

Whenever x changes, y is recalculated without the need for procedural logic. This concept extends to **multi-variable equations, system modeling, and real-time data calculations**, ensuring that updates propagate **automatically and consistently**.

Declarative mathematics in MathCAD simplifies **problem-solving by eliminating procedural complexity** and focusing on mathematical relationships. Through **symbolic computation, live evaluation, and functional dependencies**, MathCAD enhances mathematical clarity and precision. This declarative approach is particularly useful in **scientific research, engineering applications, and data analysis**, where accuracy and automation are paramount.

Constraint Solving in Engineering Applications

Constraint solving is a fundamental technique in engineering applications, where multiple variables are interdependent, and solutions must satisfy predefined conditions. Unlike imperative approaches that require iterative adjustments, **declarative constraint solvers** allow engineers to define relationships among variables and let the system compute the best possible solutions. **MathCAD** excels in this domain by enabling engineers to express **equations, inequalities, and constraints** without prescribing a step-by-step algorithm for solving them.

For example, in structural engineering, constraints like **load-bearing limits, material properties, and geometric tolerances** need to be enforced while designing components. Instead of manually computing possible configurations, engineers can **define the constraints declaratively**, and MathCAD will derive a feasible solution automatically.

A simple system of constraints in MathCAD might look like this:

```
F1 + F2 = 1000  // Total force balance
F1 * L1 = F2 * L2  // Torque equilibrium
```

Given values for L1 and L2, MathCAD can solve for F1 and F2 to satisfy both conditions. This declarative approach ensures **error-free calculations, automatic updates, and optimal parameter selection**.

Nonlinear and Multi-Variable Constraint Solving

Many real-world engineering problems involve **nonlinear relationships** where variables interact in complex ways. Traditional numerical methods, such as Newton-Raphson or finite difference approaches, require iterative tuning, making them time-consuming and prone to approximation errors. MathCAD's symbolic constraint solver, however, **handles nonlinear systems algebraically**, preserving accuracy and efficiency.

Consider an electrical circuit where voltage, resistance, and current must adhere to Ohm's Law and Kirchhoff's Current Law:

```
V1 = I1 * R1
V2 = I2 * R2
I1 + I2 = I3
```

Instead of solving this system manually, MathCAD can **automatically determine the unknowns** given certain initial conditions. This ability is crucial in **electronics, fluid dynamics, and thermodynamics**, where multiple interdependent equations govern system behavior.

Optimization and Feasibility Analysis

Beyond solving equations, engineers often need to **optimize designs** while satisfying constraints. MathCAD allows users to define **objective functions** and apply constraint-solving techniques to find optimal solutions.

For example, in **aerospace engineering**, minimizing aircraft weight while maintaining structural integrity involves optimizing parameters like **material thickness, aerodynamic shape, and load distribution**. Engineers can define:

```
minimize(weight)
subject to:
    stress < allowable_limit
    deflection < maximum_tolerance
```

MathCAD will compute the best combination of parameters that satisfies these constraints, leading to **efficient and cost-effective designs**.

Constraint solving in MathCAD allows engineers to define **complex relationships without procedural complexity**, making it ideal for **structural analysis, electrical circuits, and mechanical system design**. By leveraging **symbolic computation, nonlinear equation solving, and optimization techniques**, MathCAD provides a robust declarative framework for tackling **real-world engineering challenges** efficiently and accurately.

Symbolic Computation and Formula Automation

Symbolic computation is a key feature of MathCAD that enables engineers and scientists to perform algebraic manipulations, calculus operations, and equation simplifications without numerical approximation errors. Unlike numerical methods, which provide only approximate solutions, symbolic computation retains exact expressions, making it invaluable for **formula derivation, theorem proving, and automated algebraic transformations**.

One of the primary advantages of symbolic computation in MathCAD is its ability to **manipulate equations and expressions algebraically** before substituting numerical values. This is useful in scenarios like **physics, engineering, and financial modeling**, where formulas must be derived and validated before actual computations take place.

For example, consider an equation representing motion under gravity:

```
s = ut + (1/2)gt²
```

MathCAD can differentiate this equation symbolically to find velocity (v) and acceleration (a):

```
v = d(s)/dt = u + gt
a = d(v)/dt = g
```

This symbolic differentiation process ensures precise analytical results, avoiding the approximation errors introduced by finite difference methods in numerical computation.

Automated Formula Simplification and Transformation

MathCAD's symbolic engine allows **automatic simplification** of complex mathematical expressions, making equations more readable and computationally efficient. Engineers working with **fluid dynamics, circuit analysis, or structural mechanics** frequently encounter expressions that are cumbersome to evaluate directly.

For instance, a complex algebraic fraction can be automatically simplified:

$$(x^2 - 4) / (x - 2) \rightarrow x + 2$$

By using **symbolic factorization, expansion, and rationalization**, MathCAD simplifies equations into their most compact forms, making further computations easier and more efficient.

Another powerful feature is **automatic unit conversion**, where equations involving different unit systems can be **symbolically adjusted** to ensure consistency. If an engineer accidentally mixes **imperial and metric units**, MathCAD can automatically convert all expressions to a standard unit system, preventing calculation errors.

Symbolic Integration and Differential Equations

Symbolic computation in MathCAD extends beyond algebraic manipulation to **integration and differential equation solving**. Engineers and scientists often deal with **integrals that**

have no simple closed-form solutions, requiring symbolic techniques to **transform them into solvable expressions**.

Consider the integral of a function:

∫ (x³ + 2x² - 5) dx

MathCAD will return the symbolic result:

(x⁴/4) + (2x³/3) - 5x

For differential equations, MathCAD can symbolically solve problems such as:

dy/dx + 3y = e^x

By using **symbolic solvers**, MathCAD derives an exact solution, eliminating the need for **numerical approximations** commonly found in iterative solvers.

MathCAD's symbolic computation capabilities make it an essential tool for **formula automation, equation simplification, and differential equation solving**. By providing **exact algebraic transformations, automatic differentiation, and integral evaluation**, MathCAD enables engineers and scientists to **develop, analyze, and optimize formulas with precision**, ensuring correctness before numerical computation.

Dataflow and Functional Dependencies

Dataflow modeling is a key feature of MathCAD that enables users to construct complex mathematical and engineering models using a declarative approach. Unlike procedural programming, where the focus is on step-by-step execution, **dataflow programming emphasizes relationships between variables**, allowing automatic recalculations when inputs change. This model is particularly useful for **engineering simulations, real-time data processing, and dependency-driven calculations**.

In MathCAD, variables and expressions are **interconnected through functional dependencies** rather than explicit sequencing. This means that **when one variable is updated, all dependent expressions automatically recalculate**. This feature simplifies **iterative design processes** in areas such as **mechanical design, circuit analysis, and structural engineering**, where parameter changes must propagate consistently through an entire system.

For example, consider a **stress-strain model in material science**, where stress (σ) is computed as:

$\sigma = F / A$

If the force (F) or area (A) changes, MathCAD automatically updates the calculated stress without requiring manual re-evaluation. This **functional dependency ensures correctness and reduces human error** in complex models.

Automatic Propagation of Changes in Dataflow Systems

One of the major advantages of dataflow modeling in MathCAD is its ability to **automatically propagate changes through dependent calculations**. In traditional procedural programming, a change in an initial parameter might require re-execution of multiple steps manually. However, in MathCAD, **the system tracks dependencies and dynamically updates all affected expressions**.

Consider an **engineering heat transfer problem** where the temperature (T) of a component is dependent on heat energy (Q), specific heat capacity (c), and mass (m):

$$T = Q / (m * c)$$

If Q is modified due to changing energy input, MathCAD will automatically recalculate T without the need for manual intervention. This functionality is particularly **beneficial in parametric modeling**, where different scenarios can be evaluated by modifying input variables.

Dataflow Applications in Real-Time Systems

MathCAD's dataflow approach is well-suited for **real-time monitoring and control systems** that rely on continuous data updates. In **signal processing, process automation, and control engineering**, dataflow modeling ensures that outputs always reflect the most recent inputs without requiring explicit reprogramming.

For instance, in an **electrical circuit analysis**, Ohm's Law states that voltage (V) depends on current (I) and resistance (R):

$$V = I * R$$

If the resistance changes due to **temperature variations**, MathCAD dynamically updates the computed voltage, allowing engineers to analyze circuit behavior under varying conditions in real-time.

Functional Dependencies and Model Optimization

In addition to automatic updates, MathCAD allows users to **define functional dependencies explicitly**, ensuring that large models remain modular and maintainable. By structuring equations in a **dependency-driven format**, users can build **hierarchical models** where **subsystems interact seamlessly**.

For example, a **mechanical vibration analysis** may involve equations for displacement (x), velocity (v), and acceleration (a), where:

```
v = dx/dt
a = dv/dt
```

MathCAD ensures that **a change in displacement automatically affects velocity and acceleration**, preserving the integrity of the physical model.

The **dataflow paradigm** in MathCAD enables **automatic dependency tracking, real-time updates, and optimized model structuring**. By eliminating the need for manual recalculations and ensuring **consistent propagation of changes**, MathCAD enhances productivity and reliability in **scientific, engineering, and computational mathematics applications**, making it a powerful tool for **declarative computation**.

Module 17:
Declarative Features in Python

Python is a versatile programming language that supports both imperative and declarative paradigms. In this module, we explore how Python's declarative features simplify data processing, functional programming, and machine learning pipelines. By leveraging **list comprehensions, functional iterators, higher-order functions, and meta-programming**, Python enables a more concise, readable, and maintainable approach to programming. These declarative techniques allow developers to express logic without explicitly defining control flow, leading to more efficient and expressive code.

List Comprehensions and Functional Iterators

List comprehensions in Python provide a declarative way to generate and manipulate lists, reducing the need for verbose loops. This feature allows for **concise, readable transformations** of data structures. Functional iterators, such as map, filter, and zip, provide **lazy evaluation**, ensuring that computations are **performed efficiently without excessive memory consumption**. These declarative constructs simplify operations like filtering, transformation, and aggregation in data processing workflows. By using **iterators and generators**, Python enables developers to express computations in a high-level, declarative manner, avoiding the complexities of traditional loops and mutable state.

Declarative Machine Learning Pipelines

Machine learning workflows often involve multiple stages, such as **data preprocessing, feature extraction, model training, and evaluation**. Python's declarative libraries, such as **Scikit-learn and TensorFlow**, offer **pipeline abstractions** that simplify the process of building complex ML models. By structuring machine learning steps declaratively, developers can **define data transformations and model configurations concisely**, leading to cleaner and more maintainable code. **Pipeline-based models ensure reproducibility and modularity**, allowing different components to be reused and easily adjusted without affecting the overall workflow. This declarative approach enhances efficiency in **data science and artificial intelligence applications**.

Functional Programming with Libraries (e.g., pandas, NumPy)

Python's ecosystem includes libraries such as **pandas and NumPy**, which embrace **functional programming principles** to enable declarative data manipulation. Instead of writing **explicit loops to iterate over data**, these libraries provide **vectorized operations** that allow users to **express computations at a higher level. Declarative data transformations**, such as filtering, grouping, and aggregating data, improve both readability and performance. By utilizing **pure**

functions and immutable data structures, Python's declarative capabilities in data science workflows **reduce side effects and enhance code reliability**, making large-scale data processing more efficient.

Meta-Programming and Higher-Order Functions

Meta-programming and higher-order functions provide Python with a **dynamic and flexible programming paradigm**. By defining **functions that operate on other functions**, Python enables **abstraction and code reuse**. Decorators, a key declarative feature in Python, allow for **behavioral modifications without altering function definitions**. Meta-programming techniques, such as using **introspection and code generation**, facilitate **automated transformations** of code structures, reducing redundancy. These declarative constructs enhance **flexibility, maintainability, and modularity**, making them useful in **framework design, automated code generation, and aspect-oriented programming**.

Python's declarative features provide a powerful mechanism for **expressing complex logic concisely and efficiently**. Through **list comprehensions, machine learning pipelines, functional programming libraries, and meta-programming**, developers can write **high-level, readable, and maintainable code**. By adopting these declarative techniques, Python programmers can **enhance productivity and simplify problem-solving across multiple domains, from data science to functional programming and beyond**.

List Comprehensions and Functional Iterators

Python's list comprehensions and functional iterators provide a powerful way to express transformations on collections **declaratively**. Instead of using traditional loops, list comprehensions allow developers to generate new lists by specifying **what** they want rather than **how** to achieve it. Similarly, functional iterators such as map, filter, and zip help process sequences efficiently by applying transformations in a concise, readable manner. These constructs enhance Python's expressiveness while improving performance and reducing unnecessary boilerplate code. In this section, we explore **list comprehensions, generator expressions, and functional iterators** to demonstrate how Python facilitates declarative data processing.

List Comprehensions

List comprehensions provide an elegant way to create lists by specifying **output expressions and conditions** in a single line. Instead of iterating over an existing list using a for loop and appending elements manually, we can define the transformation in a compact, declarative manner.

```python
# Traditional loop-based approach
numbers = [1, 2, 3, 4, 5]
squared = []
for num in numbers:
    squared.append(num ** 2)
```

```
# List comprehension (declarative approach)
squared = [num ** 2 for num in numbers]

print(squared)  # Output: [1, 4, 9, 16, 25]
```

We can also apply **filtering conditions** directly within the list comprehension, reducing the need for additional conditionals in loops.

```
# Filtering even numbers declaratively
even_numbers = [num for num in numbers if num % 2 == 0]
print(even_numbers)  # Output: [2, 4]
```

Generator Expressions for Lazy Evaluation

While list comprehensions generate a full list in memory, **generator expressions** allow lazy evaluation, **improving memory efficiency** when dealing with large datasets.

```
# Using a generator expression for efficiency
squared_gen = (num ** 2 for num in numbers)

# Converting generator to a list (on-demand evaluation)
print(list(squared_gen))  # Output: [1, 4, 9, 16, 25]
```

Generators avoid storing the entire list in memory, making them ideal for large-scale data processing.

Functional Iterators: map(), filter(), and zip()

Python provides built-in functional iterators that allow declarative transformations without explicit loops.

- **map(func, iterable)** applies a function to each element.

- **filter(func, iterable)** selects elements that satisfy a condition.

- **zip(iter1, iter2, ...)** combines multiple sequences element-wise.

```
# Using map() to apply transformations
squared = list(map(lambda x: x ** 2, numbers))

# Using filter() to retain only even numbers
even_numbers = list(filter(lambda x: x % 2 == 0, numbers))

# Using zip() to combine sequences
names = ["Alice", "Bob", "Charlie"]
scores = [85, 90, 78]
paired = list(zip(names, scores))

print(squared)        # Output: [1, 4, 9, 16, 25]
print(even_numbers)   # Output: [2, 4]
print(paired)         # Output: [('Alice', 85), ('Bob', 90), ('Charlie', 78)]
```

Python's list comprehensions and functional iterators offer a **concise, expressive, and memory-efficient way** to manipulate collections declaratively. By using these constructs, developers can **avoid unnecessary loops, enhance readability, and improve**

performance. The combination of **list comprehensions, generator expressions, and functional iterators** allows Python programmers to work with collections more effectively while adhering to a declarative programming style.

Declarative Machine Learning Pipelines

In machine learning, declarative programming allows developers to focus on defining **what needs to be done** rather than explicitly coding every step of the process. **Machine learning pipelines** encapsulate data preprocessing, feature selection, model training, and evaluation in a structured, high-level manner. Frameworks such as **scikit-learn and TensorFlow** provide declarative APIs that enable the seamless composition of steps without requiring imperative loops or manual data handling. This section explores how declarative pipelines in Python streamline machine learning workflows, making them more **modular, reusable, and scalable**.

Defining a Machine Learning Pipeline

In **scikit-learn**, a machine learning pipeline is constructed using the Pipeline class, which allows data transformations and model training steps to be chained declaratively. Consider a classification task where we preprocess text data, convert it into numerical features, and apply a machine learning model.

```
from sklearn.pipeline import Pipeline
from sklearn.feature_extraction.text import TfidfVectorizer
from sklearn.svm import SVC

# Define a pipeline with text vectorization and SVM classification
pipeline = Pipeline([
    ("vectorizer", TfidfVectorizer()),  # Convert text to numerical features
    ("classifier", SVC(kernel="linear"))  # Train a support vector machine
])

# Sample data
texts = ["Machine learning is powerful", "Declarative pipelines simplify
         workflows"]
labels = [1, 0]  # Example binary labels

# Train the pipeline
pipeline.fit(texts, labels)

# Make predictions
predictions = pipeline.predict(["Declarative programming enhances readability"])
print(predictions)  # Output: [0] (Example prediction)
```

This pipeline abstracts feature extraction and model training into a **single high-level definition**, reducing boilerplate code and improving readability.

Data Preprocessing as a Declarative Step

Declarative machine learning pipelines also integrate **data preprocessing** seamlessly. Instead of writing separate scripts for handling missing values, scaling data, or encoding categorical features, pipelines encapsulate these steps declaratively.

```python
from sklearn.impute import SimpleImputer
from sklearn.preprocessing import StandardScaler
from sklearn.compose import ColumnTransformer

# Define preprocessing steps
preprocessor = ColumnTransformer([
    ("impute", SimpleImputer(strategy="mean"), [0]),  # Handle missing values
    ("scale", StandardScaler(), [1])  # Normalize numerical features
])

# Integrate into a full pipeline
full_pipeline = Pipeline([
    ("preprocess", preprocessor),
    ("model", SVC(kernel="rbf"))
])
```

By defining transformations declaratively, we ensure that **data preprocessing is consistently applied** during training and inference.

TensorFlow's Declarative Keras API

Deep learning frameworks like **TensorFlow and Keras** provide declarative APIs for defining and training neural networks. Instead of manually managing weight updates, gradient calculations, and backpropagation, we define a model structure and let the framework handle execution.

```python
from tensorflow import keras
from tensorflow.keras.layers import Dense

# Define a simple feedforward neural network declaratively
model = keras.Sequential([
    Dense(64, activation="relu", input_shape=(10,)),
    Dense(32, activation="relu"),
    Dense(1, activation="sigmoid")  # Binary classification output
])

# Compile and train the model
model.compile(optimizer="adam", loss="binary_crossentropy",
              metrics=["accuracy"])
```

This approach ensures **separation of concerns** by letting developers focus on model architecture without manually handling lower-level computations.

Declarative machine learning pipelines **simplify the model development lifecycle** by abstracting preprocessing, feature extraction, and training into high-level constructs. Frameworks like **scikit-learn and TensorFlow** allow developers to define machine learning workflows in a **structured, readable, and reusable manner**, enhancing scalability and reducing implementation complexity.

Functional Programming with Libraries (e.g., pandas, NumPy)

Python supports **functional programming paradigms**, enabling **declarative data processing** using high-level libraries such as **pandas** and **NumPy**. These libraries provide **vectorized operations, functional transformations, and lazy evaluation**, allowing developers to manipulate data concisely without explicit loops. This section explores how

163

functional programming constructs streamline numerical computations and data analysis using **map-reduce patterns, lambda functions, and functional transformations**.

Vectorized Computations with NumPy

NumPy is optimized for numerical operations using **vectorized functions**, which apply transformations to entire arrays at once. Unlike imperative programming, where computations iterate over individual elements, NumPy operates on entire data structures, resulting in **concise, efficient, and readable** code.

```
import numpy as np

# Define an array of numbers
data = np.array([1, 2, 3, 4, 5])

# Apply a transformation declaratively
squared = np.square(data)  # Element-wise squaring

print(squared)  # Output: [ 1  4  9 16 25 ]
```

Here, np.square() applies an element-wise operation without requiring explicit loops, leveraging **NumPy's optimized backend** for performance gains.

Functional Transformations with Pandas

Pandas enables **functional transformations** on tabular data using methods such as apply(), map(), and transform(). These methods allow column-wise operations without explicit iteration, making data transformations **declarative and readable**.

```
import pandas as pd

# Create a DataFrame
df = pd.DataFrame({"Name": ["Alice", "Bob", "Charlie"], "Score": [85, 92, 78]})

# Apply a functional transformation
df["Grade"] = df["Score"].apply(lambda x: "A" if x >= 90 else "B" if x >= 80
            else "C")

print(df)
```

This transformation uses **lambda functions** to process column values declaratively, eliminating the need for for loops.

Lazy Evaluation with Generators and Functional Iterators

Functional programming in Python promotes **lazy evaluation**, where computations are performed only when required. This is particularly useful for handling large datasets efficiently.

```
# Generator function for lazy evaluation
def square_numbers(numbers):
    for num in numbers:
        yield num ** 2  # Computation occurs only when accessed
```

```
# Using the generator
squares = square_numbers(range(1, 6))
print(list(squares))  # Output: [1, 4, 9, 16, 25]
```

Here, the square_numbers() function **yields** values instead of returning a list, preventing unnecessary memory consumption.

Map-Reduce Functional Style in Python

Python's built-in map() and reduce() functions allow declarative transformations without explicitly managing iteration.

```
from functools import reduce

# Mapping values to their squares
squares = list(map(lambda x: x ** 2, range(1, 6)))

# Reducing a list to compute the sum
sum_of_squares = reduce(lambda a, b: a + b, squares)

print(sum_of_squares)  # Output: 55
```

This **map-reduce paradigm** ensures data transformations remain functional and declarative.

Functional programming in Python simplifies **data processing and numerical computations** by utilizing declarative transformations, lazy evaluation, and vectorized operations. Libraries like **pandas and NumPy** provide high-level APIs that reduce boilerplate code and improve efficiency, enabling Python developers to adopt **concise and expressive** programming paradigms.

Meta-Programming and Higher-Order Functions

Meta-programming allows Python programs to modify or generate code dynamically, enhancing **flexibility and abstraction**. Combined with **higher-order functions**, which accept functions as arguments or return them as results, meta-programming enables a more **declarative approach** to structuring Python applications. This section explores **decorators, function factories, and dynamic code generation** for building expressive and extensible programs.

Higher-Order Functions for Declarative Abstraction

Higher-order functions enable **function composition**, improving code modularity and reducing repetition. Python's built-in functions like map(), filter(), and reduce() exemplify declarative constructs using higher-order functions.

```
def apply_operation(operation, numbers):
    return [operation(n) for n in numbers]

# Define two different operations
square = lambda x: x ** 2
```

```
double = lambda x: x * 2

# Apply transformations declaratively
numbers = [1, 2, 3, 4, 5]
print(apply_operation(square, numbers))   # Output: [1, 4, 9, 16, 25]
print(apply_operation(double, numbers))   # Output: [2, 4, 6, 8, 10]
```

Here, apply_operation() abstracts the transformation logic, allowing dynamic behavior modification based on the function passed as an argument.

Decorators for Code Reusability and Abstraction

Decorators modify function behavior **without altering the original implementation**, making them a powerful meta-programming tool. They wrap functions to **add cross-cutting concerns** like logging, caching, or access control.

```
def log_execution(func):
    def wrapper(*args, **kwargs):
        print(f"Executing {func.__name__}...")
        result = func(*args, **kwargs)
        print(f"Execution completed.")
        return result
    return wrapper

@log_execution
def compute_sum(a, b):
    return a + b

print(compute_sum(3, 7))
```

The @log_execution decorator **wraps** compute_sum(), adding logging behavior **without modifying** its core logic.

Dynamic Code Generation with exec() and eval()

Python's exec() and eval() functions enable **runtime code execution**, supporting dynamic meta-programming. These functions are useful in **interpreters, compilers, and dynamic configurations**.

```
code = """
def generated_function(x):
    return x * 2
"""

exec(code)  # Dynamically defines the function
print(generated_function(10))  # Output: 20
```

Here, exec() dynamically injects a function into the program, showcasing Python's **self-modifying capabilities**.

Metaclasses for Declarative Class Customization

Metaclasses define the behavior of classes, enabling declarative constraints and validations.

166

```
class MetaEnforcer(type):
    def __new__(cls, name, bases, dct):
        if "process" not in dct:
            raise TypeError("Classes must define a 'process' method.")
        return super().__new__(cls, name, bases, dct)

class ValidClass(metaclass=MetaEnforcer):
    def process(self):
        print("Processing data...")

valid_instance = ValidClass()
valid_instance.process()
```

If a class **fails to implement** the required process() method, the metaclass prevents its instantiation, enforcing **declarative constraints**.

Meta-programming and higher-order functions **enhance Python's declarative capabilities** by enabling **code abstraction, dynamic execution, and function composition**. These techniques help developers **reduce redundancy, enforce constraints, and extend behavior dynamically**, making Python a powerful language for **expressive and scalable programming paradigms**.

Cross-Language Declarative Paradigms

Declarative programming is not confined to a single language but extends across various programming paradigms. This module explores how different languages implement declarative constructs, how logic programming integrates into multi-paradigm environments, and how declarative interoperability enhances cross-system development. Finally, it examines emerging trends shaping the future of declarative programming, emphasizing the evolution of functional, logic-based, and domain-specific languages.

Comparing Functional Constructs Across Languages

Functional programming offers a declarative approach by treating computation as the evaluation of mathematical functions, minimizing side effects. While languages like Haskell strictly enforce purity, others like Python, JavaScript, and C# provide functional constructs within an otherwise imperative structure. Understanding how functional features manifest in different languages allows developers to leverage declarative techniques effectively in their chosen environments.

Higher-order functions, immutability, and lazy evaluation are core functional features present in varying degrees across languages. Haskell's purity enforces strict immutability, whereas JavaScript allows higher-order functions but maintains a more flexible approach. Python, through libraries like functools, facilitates functional techniques, whereas C# incorporates LINQ for declarative data transformations. A comparative analysis of these constructs helps developers appreciate the strengths and trade-offs of functional programming in different ecosystems.

Logic Programming Support in Multi-Paradigm Languages

Logic programming, typically associated with languages like Prolog, provides a declarative approach to problem-solving based on formal logic. However, multi-paradigm languages such as Python, Java, and C# have incorporated logic programming elements through constraint solvers and symbolic computation libraries. This integration allows developers to solve problems declaratively without fully adopting a logic programming language.

For instance, Python's sympy enables symbolic mathematics, allowing declarative equation solving without imperative constructs. Similarly, Prolog-style reasoning can be implemented in languages like JavaScript using constraint-based approaches. Understanding how multi-paradigm languages embed logic programming helps developers apply declarative techniques within familiar environments while benefiting from logic-based reasoning and automated inference.

Declarative Interoperability Across Systems

With the rise of distributed and cloud computing, declarative interoperability has become essential for system integration. Different languages and frameworks often need to communicate declaratively, leveraging domain-specific languages (DSLs), APIs, and functional interfaces. Technologies like GraphQL, SQL, and JSON Schema enable declarative interoperability, allowing seamless data exchange while preserving declarative principles.

Declarative configuration management tools, such as Terraform and Ansible, exemplify cross-system declarative interoperability. These tools use declarative syntax to define infrastructure and automate deployments, ensuring consistency across heterogeneous environments. Additionally, WebAssembly (WASM) enables declarative execution of functions across different languages, allowing polyglot programming where declarative constructs can be applied efficiently.

Future Trends in Declarative Language Development

The evolution of declarative programming is driven by advancements in functional, logic-based, and DSL innovations. Languages like Rust and Kotlin are integrating functional constructs, making declarative programming more accessible in performance-critical and mobile environments. Meanwhile, AI-driven programming assistance is enabling declarative specifications to be automatically translated into optimized imperative implementations.

Quantum computing introduces new declarative paradigms, where quantum logic gates and probabilistic programming rely on declarative principles. Additionally, AI and machine learning advancements are promoting declarative techniques in model development, making declarative machine learning a critical area of research. As programming languages evolve, declarative paradigms will continue shaping the way developers structure and reason about complex systems.

Cross-language declarative paradigms allow developers to leverage functional and logic programming techniques across different environments. From functional constructs in multi-paradigm languages to declarative interoperability and emerging trends, understanding how declarative programming extends beyond a single language enables more scalable, maintainable, and expressive software development. This module provides a comprehensive perspective on declarative techniques and their role in modern computing.

Comparing Functional Constructs Across Languages

Functional programming is a cornerstone of declarative paradigms, allowing developers to focus on what should be computed rather than how. Many programming languages incorporate functional constructs, but they vary in their approach and strictness. Haskell, for instance, enforces purity, ensuring that functions produce the same output for the same input without side effects. In contrast, Python and JavaScript provide functional features but allow imperative programming as well. Understanding these differences helps developers leverage the best declarative tools across different environments.

One of the fundamental features of functional programming is **higher-order functions**, which treat functions as first-class citizens. In Python, this is evident in built-in functions like map, filter, and reduce.

```
numbers = [1, 2, 3, 4, 5]
squared = list(map(lambda x: x ** 2, numbers))
print(squared)  # Output: [1, 4, 9, 16, 25]
```

JavaScript follows a similar pattern, allowing functions to be passed as arguments to other functions, making declarative transformations more intuitive.

```
const numbers = [1, 2, 3, 4, 5];
const squared = numbers.map(x => x ** 2);
console.log(squared); // Output: [1, 4, 9, 16, 25]
```

Another essential functional construct is **immutability**, which prevents modification of existing data, encouraging a declarative approach. Haskell enforces immutability by default, whereas Python provides the frozenset and namedtuple to support immutable structures.

```
from collections import namedtuple

Point = namedtuple('Point', ['x', 'y'])
p1 = Point(2, 3)
# p1.x = 5  # This would raise an AttributeError since namedtuples are
            immutable.
```

Languages like JavaScript and C# offer immutable operations through libraries like **Immutable.js** and **LINQ**, respectively. In C#, LINQ (Language Integrated Query) allows declarative data transformations, minimizing side effects.

```
var numbers = new List<int> {1, 2, 3, 4, 5};
var squared = numbers.Select(x => x * x);
Console.WriteLine(string.Join(", ", squared)); // Output: 1, 4, 9, 16, 25
```

Another functional construct is **lazy evaluation**, which delays computation until necessary. This is a key feature of Haskell, but it can also be implemented in Python using generators.

```
def infinite_numbers():
    num = 0
    while True:
        yield num
        num += 1

gen = infinite_numbers()
print(next(gen))  # Output: 0
print(next(gen))  # Output: 1
```

Understanding how functional programming is implemented across different languages allows developers to apply declarative techniques effectively. Whether using **map-reduce in Python**, **higher-order functions in JavaScript**, or **LINQ in C#**, embracing functional paradigms leads to more readable, predictable, and maintainable code.

Logic Programming Support in Multi-Paradigm Languages

Logic programming is a declarative paradigm where programs are expressed as a set of logical relations. Unlike imperative approaches, logic programming defines what is true rather than specifying the steps to achieve a result. While Prolog is the most well-known logic programming language, multi-paradigm languages like Python, JavaScript, and C# have incorporated logic programming techniques through libraries and extensions. Understanding how logic programming fits into multi-paradigm environments enables developers to leverage declarative reasoning alongside functional and imperative constructs.

One of the core concepts in logic programming is **rule-based inference**, where a system derives conclusions based on predefined facts and rules. Python provides logic programming capabilities through libraries like pyDatalog, which allows developers to express logical rules declaratively.

```
from pyDatalog import pyDatalog

pyDatalog.create_terms('X, Y, parent, ancestor')

# Defining parent relationships
+parent('John', 'Alice')
+parent('Alice', 'Bob')

# Defining the recursive ancestor relationship
ancestor(X, Y) <= parent(X, Y)
ancestor(X, Y) <= (parent(X, Z) & ancestor(Z, Y))

# Querying the ancestor relationship
print(ancestor('John', 'Bob'))  # Output: John is an ancestor of Bob.
```

JavaScript, though not designed for logic programming, supports declarative reasoning through pattern-matching libraries like json-logic. These libraries allow rule-based decision-making, a concept similar to Prolog's declarative execution.

```
const jsonLogic = require("json-logic-js");

let rules = { "and": [ { ">": [5, 3] }, { "==": [10, 10] } ] };

console.log(jsonLogic.apply(rules)); // Output: true
```

C# provides logic programming capabilities through LINQ queries combined with expression trees, allowing developers to model declarative reasoning. While it does not natively support Prolog-style inference, LINQ's declarative query execution offers powerful pattern-matching techniques.

```
using System;
using System.Linq;

class Program
{
    static void Main()
    {
        var numbers = new int[] { 1, 2, 3, 4, 5 };
        var evens = numbers.Where(n => n % 2 == 0);
        Console.WriteLine(string.Join(", ", evens)); // Output: 2, 4
    }
```

```
}
```

Another essential concept in logic programming is **constraint solving**, where solutions are derived by satisfying constraints rather than executing explicit procedural logic. Python's constraint library provides constraint satisfaction capabilities, enabling declarative problem-solving.

```
from constraint import Problem

problem = Problem()
problem.addVariable("x", range(10))
problem.addVariable("y", range(10))

# Adding constraint: x + y = 5
problem.addConstraint(lambda x, y: x + y == 5, ("x", "y"))

solutions = problem.getSolutions()
print(solutions)  # Output: [{'x': 0, 'y': 5}, {'x': 1, 'y': 4}, ...]
```

Logic programming in multi-paradigm languages enhances declarative capabilities, enabling developers to model complex relationships and solve problems with minimal imperative code. By integrating logic programming with functional and object-oriented constructs, developers can build more expressive and maintainable applications.

Declarative Interoperability across Systems

Interoperability in software systems is a crucial aspect of modern computing, allowing different programming languages, frameworks, and environments to communicate seamlessly. Declarative paradigms simplify interoperability by focusing on high-level specifications rather than procedural execution. Various languages provide declarative constructs that enable efficient cross-language communication, such as domain-specific languages (DSLs), data exchange formats, and rule-based logic engines. By leveraging these techniques, developers can integrate different systems while maintaining a declarative approach.

One common approach to declarative interoperability is the use of **data exchange formats** such as JSON, XML, and YAML. These formats serve as an intermediate representation between systems that use different programming languages. For example, a Python application can generate a JSON payload that a JavaScript frontend can interpret without requiring explicit step-by-step instructions.

```
import json

data = {"name": "Alice", "age": 30, "language": "Python"}
json_string = json.dumps(data)

# Simulating sending the JSON to another system
print(json_string)  # Output: {"name": "Alice", "age": 30, "language": "Python"}
```

On the JavaScript side, the same data can be processed declaratively using JSON.parse:

```
const jsonData = '{"name": "Alice", "age": 30, "language": "Python"}';
const parsedData = JSON.parse(jsonData);
```

```
console.log(parsedData.name); // Output: Alice
```

Another essential interoperability technique is **rule-based engines**, which enable different systems to evaluate conditions and derive conclusions declaratively. Drools, a rule engine for Java, allows declarative rule evaluation that can be integrated with external systems via APIs. Similarly, Python's pyDatalog enables logical reasoning across different components.

```
from pyDatalog import pyDatalog

pyDatalog.create_terms('X, Y, language, knows')

+knows('Alice', 'Python')
+knows('Bob', 'JavaScript')

print(knows(X, 'Python'))  # Output: Alice knows Python.
```

Cross-language interoperability is also achieved through **functional interfaces**. Functional programming constructs such as higher-order functions and currying enable declarative processing across languages. For example, Python's map function can be used to apply transformations to data that can be later processed in JavaScript.

```
numbers = [1, 2, 3, 4]
squared = list(map(lambda x: x ** 2, numbers))

print(squared)  # Output: [1, 4, 9, 16]
```

By exposing this transformation as an API, JavaScript can retrieve and process it further.

Another powerful interoperability technique is **SQL-based query execution across multiple environments**. SQL is inherently declarative and can be used within Python, Java, and JavaScript through ORM frameworks like SQLAlchemy (Python) and Sequelize (JavaScript).

```
from sqlalchemy import create_engine, Column, Integer, String, MetaData, Table

engine = create_engine("sqlite:///:memory:")
metadata = MetaData()

users = Table("users", metadata,
    Column("id", Integer, primary_key=True),
    Column("name", String),
)

metadata.create_all(engine)
```

Declarative interoperability ensures seamless integration across different programming paradigms and platforms. By utilizing data exchange formats, rule-based engines, functional interfaces, and SQL-based interactions, developers can build interconnected systems that leverage declarative programming principles for maintainability, flexibility, and efficiency.

Future Trends in Declarative Language Development

The evolution of declarative programming continues to shape modern software development, influencing languages, frameworks, and system architectures. As developers seek higher levels of abstraction and automation, declarative paradigms are expected to grow in prominence. The future of declarative language development is driven by advancements in artificial intelligence (AI), distributed computing, and domain-specific languages (DSLs), all of which contribute to making software development more efficient and expressive.

One major trend in declarative programming is the increasing role of **AI-driven code generation**. With tools like OpenAI's Codex and GitHub Copilot, developers can describe their intentions in natural language, and AI models generate corresponding declarative code. For instance, SQL queries, data transformations, and API specifications can be automatically inferred and generated with minimal manual intervention. This trend is pushing declarative programming beyond traditional language boundaries, allowing for seamless interactions between humans and machines.

Another transformative area is **serverless and edge computing**, where declarative infrastructure definitions such as AWS CloudFormation and Terraform allow developers to specify system configurations without managing underlying resources. Declarative Infrastructure as Code (IaC) is becoming essential for deploying scalable applications. Tools like Kubernetes manifest files describe containerized environments, ensuring automated, reproducible deployments.

```
apiVersion: apps/v1
kind: Deployment
metadata:
  name: my-app
spec:
  replicas: 3
  selector:
    matchLabels:
      app: my-app
  template:
    metadata:
      labels:
        app: my-app
    spec:
      containers:
        - name: my-app-container
          image: my-app-image
          ports:
            - containerPort: 80
```

The continued rise of **functional and logic-based paradigms** is shaping the future of declarative languages. Languages like Haskell, F#, and Scala are influencing mainstream languages such as Python, JavaScript, and C#. Functional reactive programming (FRP) is gaining traction in UI development, with frameworks like React, SwiftUI, and Jetpack Compose relying heavily on declarative state management and reactive data flows.

Another emerging area is **declarative machine learning and automation**, where frameworks like TensorFlow and PyTorch allow users to specify computational graphs declaratively rather than imperatively coding each operation.

```
import tensorflow as tf

# Define a simple computation declaratively
x = tf.Variable(3.0)
y = tf.Variable(4.0)
result = x * y + 2

print(result.numpy())  # Output: 14.0
```

Declarative programming is also influencing **low-code and no-code development**, enabling users to build complex workflows without writing traditional code. Platforms like Zapier and Power Automate use declarative models to define event-driven workflows, making automation accessible to non-developers.

The future of declarative programming is shaped by AI-driven code generation, serverless and edge computing, functional and reactive paradigms, declarative machine learning, and low-code automation. As abstraction levels continue to rise, declarative languages will become even more crucial in simplifying development and enhancing productivity across various domains.

Part 4:

Algorithm and Data Structure Support for Declarative Programming

Declarative programming relies on sophisticated algorithms and data structures that facilitate high-level problem-solving without requiring imperative control flow. This part explores **Boolean satisfiability, logic resolution, query optimization, syntax trees, declarative performance optimization, and pattern matching**, demonstrating how these fundamental techniques contribute to the efficiency and expressiveness of declarative programming. By examining the mathematical and computational foundations behind these mechanisms, developers will gain a deeper understanding of how declarative languages leverage formal structures to improve execution

SAT (Boolean Satisfiability) Algorithms

Boolean satisfiability (SAT) is a fundamental problem in computer science that determines whether a given Boolean formula can be satisfied by some assignment of truth values. SAT solvers use **backtracking, conflict-driven clause learning (CDCL), and heuristics** to efficiently explore the solution space. Constraint satisfaction problems (CSPs) extend SAT to a broader range of problems, making these algorithms widely applicable in **AI, formal verification, and automated theorem proving**, where declarative paradigms play a crucial role.

Logic Resolution Algorithms

Logic resolution is a key mechanism in **automated reasoning and logic programming**, particularly in declarative languages like Prolog. This module explores **Horn clauses**, a foundational structure in logic-based deduction. Unification enables **symbolic reasoning** through **forward and backward chaining**, allowing declarative programs to infer new knowledge from given rules. Resolution strategies enhance efficiency, reducing the search space in proof systems. By understanding logic resolution, developers can **build expert systems and implement rule-based AI models** using declarative principles.

Query Optimization Algorithms

Declarative database systems rely on sophisticated query optimization to improve performance. **Cost-based and heuristic optimization techniques** help determine the most efficient execution strategy for SQL and NoSQL queries. **Indexing, execution plan selection, and distributed query processing** further enhance query performance, ensuring that declarative queries scale efficiently. This module explores how **declarative languages express queries at a high level**, while underlying algorithms transform them into optimized execution plans, enabling efficient data retrieval and manipulation in large-scale systems.

Abstract Syntax Trees

Abstract Syntax Trees (ASTs) serve as the **intermediate representation** of code in declarative languages, capturing the hierarchical structure of expressions and statements. Parsing techniques construct ASTs, enabling **tree traversal and manipulation** in compilers and interpreters. Optimizations such as **constant folding, inlining, and dead code elimination** leverage ASTs to refine declarative code execution. This module explores **how ASTs facilitate declarative transformations**, ensuring that functional, logic, and dataflow programs are efficiently executed while preserving their high-level abstraction.

Optimization Techniques for Declarative Processing

Declarative processing benefits from **memoization, caching, and lazy evaluation**, which reduce redundant computations and improve efficiency. **Parallelism and dataflow optimization** enhance execution in distributed environments, while state management techniques ensure **referential transparency and immutability**. This module examines strategies for handling declarative execution efficiently, including **graph reduction in functional programming and dependency tracking in logic programming**. By understanding these optimizations, developers can build highly performant declarative systems that scale across **multi-core architectures and distributed computing platforms**.

Pattern Matching and Rule-Based Execution

Pattern matching simplifies **data manipulation and transformation** in declarative languages. **Rule-based execution** allows declarative systems to infer new facts using **decision trees, constraint logic, and expert systems**. These techniques are widely used in **machine learning, AI, and automated reasoning**, where declarative paradigms define knowledge-driven computations. This module explores how **functional languages like Haskell and logic languages like Prolog** utilize pattern matching to simplify complex computations, enabling concise and expressive declarative programming.

This part equips learners with the foundational algorithms and data structures behind declarative programming, enabling them to **write optimized, scalable, and logically sound declarative applications**.

Module 19:

SAT (Boolean Satisfiability) Algorithms

Boolean satisfiability (SAT) is a fundamental problem in computational logic that determines whether a given Boolean formula can be satisfied by some assignment of truth values. SAT algorithms form the foundation of many modern applications, including artificial intelligence, formal verification, and constraint-solving. This module explores the principles of Boolean satisfiability, the design of SAT solvers, constraint satisfaction problems (CSPs), and real-world applications in AI and verification. By understanding these topics, developers can leverage SAT-based techniques to solve complex logical and combinatorial problems more efficiently.

Introduction to Boolean Satisfiability

Boolean satisfiability, often abbreviated as SAT, is the problem of determining whether a Boolean formula can be satisfied by some assignment of truth values to its variables. The classic form of this problem is the **Conjunctive Normal Form (CNF)** representation, where a formula is expressed as a conjunction (AND) of disjunctions (OR) of literals. The **Boolean SAT problem** was the first problem proven to be NP-complete, meaning that solving it efficiently for all cases remains an open challenge in computer science. Various techniques such as brute-force evaluation, heuristic-based searching, and intelligent pruning strategies have been developed to optimize SAT solving. These methods play a critical role in solving complex real-world problems across multiple domains.

SAT Solvers and Optimization Techniques

Modern SAT solvers use a combination of algorithmic strategies to efficiently explore large solution spaces. **DPLL (Davis-Putnam-Logemann-Loveland)** is a classic recursive algorithm that systematically searches for satisfiability using unit propagation, pure literal elimination, and backtracking. More advanced solvers, such as **CDCL (Conflict-Driven Clause Learning)**, enhance DPLL by learning from conflicts and pruning the search space more effectively. Additionally, **heuristic-based approaches** like VSIDS (Variable State Independent Decaying Sum) improve efficiency by guiding the search toward promising paths. SAT solvers have become powerful tools for combinatorial optimization, model checking, and automated reasoning, making them integral to fields such as cryptography, scheduling, and electronic design automation.

Constraint Satisfaction Problems (CSPs)

Constraint Satisfaction Problems (CSPs) extend the principles of SAT to problems where multiple constraints must be simultaneously satisfied. A CSP consists of a set of variables, a domain of possible values for each variable, and a set of constraints that define valid

178

assignments. Unlike pure SAT problems, CSPs allow for a broader range of constraints, such as arithmetic relationships and logical dependencies. Techniques like **constraint propagation, backtracking search, and local consistency enforcement** are commonly used in solving CSPs. Applications of CSPs include Sudoku solvers, timetabling, and planning problems, where declarative methods enable efficient problem representation and solution generation.

Applications in AI and Verification

SAT solvers and CSP techniques are widely applied in artificial intelligence and formal verification. In AI, SAT-based reasoning is used in automated planning, natural language processing, and machine learning. In formal verification, SAT solvers ensure the correctness of hardware and software systems by checking whether logical properties hold under all possible conditions. Model checking, a technique used in verifying circuit designs and software programs, relies heavily on SAT solvers to detect potential errors or inconsistencies. The scalability and efficiency of modern SAT solvers make them essential tools in critical applications requiring high levels of reliability and correctness.

Boolean satisfiability and SAT algorithms provide a fundamental approach to solving logical and combinatorial problems. From theoretical foundations to practical implementations in AI and verification, the techniques explored in this module highlight the power of SAT solvers and CSP methods. As computational logic continues to evolve, SAT-based solutions will remain crucial in optimizing and automating decision-making processes across diverse fields.

Introduction to Boolean Satisfiability

Boolean satisfiability (SAT) is a fundamental problem in logic and computer science that determines whether a Boolean formula can be satisfied by some assignment of truth values to its variables. A Boolean formula consists of variables that take values of True or False, connected by logical operators such as AND ($\land$), OR ($\lor$), and NOT ($\neg$). The SAT problem is of particular importance because it was the first problem proven to be **NP-complete**, meaning that while solutions can be verified quickly, finding a solution efficiently for all cases remains an open challenge in computational complexity.

A common way to represent SAT problems is **Conjunctive Normal Form (CNF)**, where a Boolean formula is expressed as a conjunction of disjunctions. For example, the formula $(A \lor B) \land (\neg A \lor C) \land (B \lor \neg C)$ is in CNF, meaning that all clauses must be satisfied for the entire formula to be true. The goal of a SAT solver is to determine whether such a formula has a valid assignment of values that makes it true.

The brute-force approach to solving SAT involves evaluating all possible combinations of variable assignments. However, this method becomes impractical for large formulas due to exponential growth in complexity. To address this, modern SAT solvers employ optimization techniques such as **backtracking, heuristics, and clause learning** to prune the search space and find solutions efficiently.

Example: Checking SAT in Python

One of the simplest ways to check SAT in Python is by using brute-force evaluation for small cases:

```
from itertools import product

def is_satisfiable(clauses, variables):
    for assignment in product([True, False], repeat=len(variables)):
        env = dict(zip(variables, assignment))
        if all(any(env.get(lit, not env.get(lit[1:], True)) for lit in clause)
            for clause in clauses):
                return True, env
    return False, {}

clauses = [('A', 'B'), ('¬A', 'C'), ('B', '¬C')]
variables = {'A', 'B', 'C'}

result, assignment = is_satisfiable(clauses, variables)
print("Satisfiable:", result, "Assignment:", assignment)
```

This function generates all possible truth assignments and checks whether at least one assignment satisfies all clauses. While impractical for large problems, it illustrates the basic idea behind SAT solving.

Complexity and Importance of SAT

The Boolean SAT problem has significant implications in fields such as artificial intelligence, cryptography, circuit design, and automated theorem proving. Many problems in these areas can be translated into SAT and solved using efficient SAT solvers. The fact that SAT is **NP-complete** also means that if an efficient algorithm for SAT is found, it could theoretically be adapted to solve a wide range of other computationally hard problems.

Thus, Boolean satisfiability represents both a fundamental theoretical challenge and a practical tool in computer science, forming the basis for various real-world applications that require logical reasoning and constraint satisfaction.

SAT Solvers and Optimization Techniques

SAT solvers are algorithms that determine whether a given Boolean formula is satisfiable, meaning there exists a set of variable assignments that make the formula true. Modern SAT solvers use a combination of optimization techniques to tackle the exponential complexity of the problem. Below, we will explore some of these techniques, alongside code examples that illustrate their application.

The **Davis-Putnam-Logemann-Loveland (DPLL)** algorithm is a backtracking-based approach used in SAT solvers. It systematically tries different variable assignments and backtracks when contradictions arise. Key optimizations like **unit propagation** and **pure literal elimination** can significantly reduce the search space.

Unit Propagation Example

In unit propagation, whenever a clause has only one unassigned literal, that literal must be assigned a truth value to satisfy the clause. For example:

```
def unit_propagation(formula):
    changed = True
    while changed:
        changed = False
        for clause in formula:
            unassigned_literals = [lit for lit in clause if lit not in assigned]
            if len(unassigned_literals) == 1:
                literal = unassigned_literals[0]
                assigned.add(literal)
                changed = True
    return assigned
```

Here, formula represents the CNF formula, and assigned is a set that tracks assigned literals. The function continuously performs unit propagation until no more unit clauses are found.

Pure Literal Elimination Example

Pure literal elimination optimizes the SAT solving process by identifying literals that appear with only one polarity (either all positive or all negative) in all clauses. These literals can be safely assigned the truth value that satisfies all clauses.

```
def pure_literal_elimination(formula, assigned):
    pure_literals = set()
    for clause in formula:
        for literal in clause:
            if -literal not in pure_literals:
                pure_literals.add(literal)
    for lit in pure_literals:
        assigned.add(lit)
    return assigned
```

This function identifies pure literals in the formula and assigns them truth values that make all their clauses true.

Backtracking and Conflict-Driven Clause Learning (CDCL)

Modern solvers also implement **conflict-driven clause learning (CDCL),** which enhances backtracking by learning from conflicts encountered during the search. When a conflict is found, the solver learns a new clause that prevents similar conflicts in the future. Below is a simplified representation of backtracking with CDCL:

```
def backtrack_with_cdcl(formula, assigned):
    conflicts = []
    while not formula_is_satisfied(formula, assigned):
        conflict = detect_conflict(formula, assigned)
        if conflict:
            learned_clause = learn_clause(conflict)
            formula.append(learned_clause)
        else:
```

```
        assigned = backtrack(assigned)
    return assigned
```

The function detect_conflict identifies conflicts, and learn_clause adds a new clause to the formula to avoid similar conflicts during future iterations. The backtracking function restores previous assignments.

Heuristic Variable Selection Example

Efficient variable selection can dramatically speed up SAT solving. A heuristic like **VSIDS (Variable State Independent Decaying Sum)** prioritizes variables based on their occurrence in conflicts. In the example below, we track the frequency of variable occurrences and use this information to make variable selection decisions:

```
def vsids_heuristic(formula, conflict_history):
    scores = {}
    for clause in formula:
        for literal in clause:
            scores[literal] = scores.get(literal, 0) +
            conflict_history.get(literal, 0)
    sorted_literals = sorted(scores, key=scores.get, reverse=True)
    return sorted_literals
```

This function scores each literal based on how often it appears in conflicts, and selects the most frequent literals for assignment, potentially reducing the search space.

Parallelization for Large SAT Instances

When dealing with large SAT problems, solvers can be parallelized to explore multiple parts of the search space simultaneously. Here's a simple representation of parallelized SAT solving:

```
from concurrent.futures import ThreadPoolExecutor

def parallel_sat_solver(formula, num_threads):
    with ThreadPoolExecutor(max_workers=num_threads) as executor:
        futures = [executor.submit(solve_subproblem, formula, i) for i in
            range(num_threads)]
        results = [future.result() for future in futures]
    return results
```

This code divides the formula into subproblems and processes them concurrently using multiple threads, improving scalability and efficiency for large SAT instances.

Efficiency and Scalability

With the techniques mentioned, SAT solvers like **MiniSat**, **CryptoMiniSat**, and **Glucose** are able to handle large-scale industrial problems in areas such as hardware verification, artificial intelligence, and cryptography. As these solvers continue to evolve with improved heuristics, CDCL, and parallelization techniques, they remain essential tools in solving complex Boolean satisfiability problems.

SAT solvers utilize a range of optimization techniques, such as unit propagation, pure literal elimination, CDCL, and heuristic variable selection, to handle complex Boolean satisfiability problems. These methods enable efficient and scalable SAT solving, which is crucial for real-world applications.

Constraint Satisfaction Problems (CSPs)

Constraint Satisfaction Problems (CSPs) involve finding a solution to a set of constraints, where the variables involved must satisfy all given constraints. SAT solvers are often used to solve CSPs, as the constraints can be converted into a Boolean formula in Conjunctive Normal Form (CNF), making them suitable for Boolean satisfiability. This section will explore how SAT solvers can be applied to CSPs and illustrate this with code examples.

CSPs and Their Representation

In a CSP, we have variables, domains (possible values for each variable), and constraints. The goal is to find an assignment of values to the variables such that all constraints are satisfied. For example, a common CSP is the **N-Queens problem**, where the task is to place N queens on an N×N chessboard so that no two queens threaten each other.

A CSP can be represented in Boolean logic by converting the constraints into CNF formulas. For example, in the N-Queens problem, each queen can be represented by a Boolean variable, and constraints on the position of the queens can be converted into clauses.

Transforming CSPs into SAT Problems

The first step in using a SAT solver to solve a CSP is to translate the problem into a Boolean formula. For the N-Queens problem, each queen's position on the board can be represented by a Boolean variable, and constraints on rows, columns, and diagonals can be encoded as Boolean clauses.

For example, consider the following simplified constraint for the N-Queens problem: No two queens can be in the same row or column. This can be represented as a series of clauses where each clause ensures that at least one of the possible positions for a queen is true, and no two queens are placed in the same position.

Here's a Python code snippet to represent the N-Queens problem as a CNF formula:

```
def generate_n_queens_cnf(n):
    cnf = []
    # Row constraints: one queen per row
    for i in range(n):
        row_clause = [f"Q{i}{j}" for j in range(n)]
        cnf.append(row_clause)

    # Column constraints: no two queens in the same column
    for j in range(n):
        col_clause = [f"Q{i}{j}" for i in range(n)]
```

```
        cnf.append(col_clause)
    return cnf
```

This function generates a CNF formula for the N-Queens problem, where Qij represents a queen placed at position (i, j). The formula ensures that there is exactly one queen per row and column.

Solving CSPs with SAT Solvers

Once we have the CNF representation of the CSP, we can pass the formula to a SAT solver. The solver will attempt to find an assignment of truth values to the Boolean variables that satisfies all the constraints. The solver returns a solution, which can be interpreted as the values of the variables that satisfy the problem.

Using the previous example, we can now solve the N-Queens problem using a SAT solver like **PySAT**:

```
from pysat.solvers import Glucose3

def solve_csp_with_sat(cnf):
    solver = Glucose3()
    for clause in cnf:
        solver.add_clause(clause)

    if solver.solve():
        return solver.get_model()
    else:
        return None
```

Here, solve_csp_with_sat uses a SAT solver to check if the CNF formula has a satisfying assignment. If it does, the solver will return a solution (an assignment to the variables), which corresponds to a valid placement of queens on the board.

Constraint Propagation and Heuristics in SAT Solvers

To further improve the efficiency of SAT solvers when solving CSPs, techniques like **constraint propagation** can be employed. Constraint propagation works by simplifying the problem before running the solver, eliminating values that are impossible given the constraints. This can reduce the search space and make the SAT solver more efficient.

Additionally, heuristics such as **Most Constrained Variable (MCV)** and **Degree Heuristic** can be used to select the next variable to assign a value to, further optimizing the solving process. These heuristics guide the solver to make the most promising choices first, reducing the likelihood of hitting dead ends.

Applications of SAT Solvers in CSPs

SAT solvers can be applied to various CSPs, including scheduling problems, resource allocation, and puzzles like Sudoku or the N-Queens problem. They are powerful tools for solving real-world optimization problems and are used in fields such as artificial intelligence, operations research, and verification.

Using SAT solvers to solve Constraint Satisfaction Problems offers a robust method for finding solutions to complex combinatorial problems. By transforming the CSPs into Boolean formulas, we can leverage the power of SAT solvers and optimization techniques to efficiently find solutions. With the aid of constraint propagation and heuristics, SAT solvers can handle large and complex problems in various domains, providing a valuable tool for researchers and practitioners.

Applications in AI and Verification

SAT solvers have found significant applications in various fields, particularly in Artificial Intelligence (AI) and system verification. These areas benefit from SAT solvers' ability to efficiently handle Boolean satisfiability problems, which are crucial in tasks like automated reasoning, planning, model checking, and formal verification. This section explores these applications with examples to illustrate how SAT solvers are employed in AI and verification tasks.

SAT Solvers in AI Planning

AI planning involves finding a sequence of actions that transition a system from an initial state to a goal state, adhering to constraints. This problem can often be reduced to Boolean satisfiability, where the planning problem is represented as a series of logical clauses, and the SAT solver is tasked with finding a solution that satisfies all constraints.

For example, in a robotic planning problem where a robot needs to move between rooms, we can represent the movement of the robot and its actions as Boolean variables. A SAT solver can then be used to find the sequence of actions that satisfies the goal state.

Consider a simplified planning problem where the goal is to find a series of moves that gets a robot from room A to room D. The clauses representing the robot's movements (in a two-room scenario) might look like:

```
def generate_planning_cnf():
    # Representing the robot's initial position and goal position
    cnf = [
        ['R_A'],   # Robot starts in room A
        ['R_D'],   # Robot should end in room D
        ['not R_A or not R_D']  # Robot cannot be in both rooms simultaneously
    ]
    return cnf
```

This small example shows how a SAT solver can be used in planning problems by transforming them into logical constraints that the solver can process. Once the CNF is generated, the SAT solver attempts to find a solution that meets the constraints and produces a sequence of moves that transition the robot from room A to room D.

185

SAT Solvers in Model Checking and Formal Verification

Model checking is a method used in formal verification to check whether a given system satisfies certain properties, such as safety or liveness. Systems are modeled as finite-state machines, and the properties of interest are expressed as logical formulas. SAT solvers are used to check if a system's model satisfies the desired properties by solving a Boolean satisfiability problem.

For instance, consider a system with several states, and we need to verify if the system will always eventually reach a safe state (a liveness property). The state transitions and safety constraints can be encoded as a Boolean formula, and the SAT solver checks if the formula is satisfiable. If satisfiable, the solver finds a state transition sequence that fulfills the properties.

Here's a simple example of how a verification process might be set up:

```python
from pysat.solvers import Glucose3

def verify_system_properties(system_model, safety_conditions):
    solver = Glucose3()

    # Add clauses for the system model and safety conditions
    for clause in system_model:
        solver.add_clause(clause)

    for condition in safety_conditions:
        solver.add_clause(condition)

    # Check if the system satisfies all safety conditions
    return solver.solve()
```

In this case, verify_system_properties checks whether the given system model satisfies the provided safety conditions. The SAT solver will either find a satisfying assignment (showing the system satisfies the property) or prove that the system cannot satisfy the property.

Applications in AI Search and Constraint Optimization

SAT solvers are also widely used in AI search problems, where they are applied to constraint satisfaction and optimization problems. These problems often involve finding the best configuration of variables subject to certain constraints. SAT solvers help by finding feasible solutions to complex problems, such as scheduling or resource allocation, where the goal is to maximize or minimize certain values while adhering to constraints.

For instance, in a job scheduling problem, the goal is to allocate jobs to workers such that no worker is assigned conflicting tasks while minimizing the total completion time. SAT solvers can be used to represent the scheduling constraints and find an optimal solution.

Here is an example of a simple constraint optimization problem:

186

```
def schedule_jobs(job_constraints):
    solver = Glucose3()

    # Add job constraints
    for constraint in job_constraints:
        solver.add_clause(constraint)

    # Check if a feasible schedule exists
    if solver.solve():
        return solver.get_model()
    else:
        return None
```

This example demonstrates how SAT solvers can help in finding a feasible job schedule by representing the problem as a series of logical constraints.

AI and Verification with SAT Solvers

In both AI and system verification, SAT solvers provide a powerful tool for solving complex problems that involve logical constraints. Their ability to efficiently handle large sets of constraints and search for solutions makes them valuable in fields like automated reasoning, model checking, formal verification, and constraint optimization. By transforming these problems into Boolean satisfiability problems, SAT solvers help ensure that systems function correctly, meet desired properties, and optimize performance.

SAT solvers are indispensable tools in the fields of AI and verification, offering efficient solutions to a wide array of problems. From planning and model checking to search and optimization, these solvers help transform complex tasks into solvable Boolean satisfiability problems. As AI and system verification continue to evolve, SAT solvers will remain crucial for solving increasingly complex and large-scale challenges.

Module 20:
Logic Resolution Algorithms

Module 20 explores the foundations of logic resolution algorithms, essential for automated reasoning and decision-making in computer science. It covers the principles of logic resolution, the role of Horn clauses in automated deduction, and key strategies such as unification and chaining. Finally, it discusses resolution strategies used in Prolog and other programming languages for logic-based problem-solving.

Principles of Logic Resolution

Logic resolution is a fundamental method used to derive conclusions from a set of logical statements or axioms. The process involves applying inference rules to combine or eliminate clauses, progressively narrowing down possible solutions. Resolution is central to fields like artificial intelligence, automated theorem proving, and logic programming. It forms the basis of reasoning systems that need to derive new information from known facts. The key idea behind resolution is to manipulate logical statements in such a way that the desired conclusion can be drawn from the given premises.

Horn Clauses and Automated Deduction

Horn clauses are a specific type of logical formula often used in logic programming and automated deduction. A Horn clause consists of at most one positive literal and any number of negative literals. These clauses are particularly useful because they can be effectively handled by resolution-based algorithms. Automated deduction systems often rely on Horn clauses to simplify reasoning tasks by converting complex formulas into a series of simpler, more manageable logical conditions. This leads to more efficient inference systems and is especially relevant in areas like logic programming, where Prolog-based systems extensively use Horn clauses.

Unification and Forward/Backward Chaining

Unification is a central concept in logic programming and resolution. It involves finding a substitution of variables that makes two logical expressions identical. This process is key to resolving goals and facts in a logic system, particularly in Prolog and other declarative languages. Forward chaining and backward chaining are two strategies used to apply rules in reasoning systems. Forward chaining starts with known facts and applies inference rules to deduce new facts, while backward chaining works backward from a goal, seeking the necessary facts or premises to prove that the goal is achievable. These techniques are central to building efficient, logic-based systems.

Resolution Strategies in Prolog and Beyond

Prolog, a widely used logic programming language, is built around the concept of resolution. The language uses a form of resolution known as SLD (Selective Linear Definite clause) resolution, which combines unification and backward chaining to derive conclusions. Prolog systems often employ various optimization techniques to improve resolution efficiency, such as indexing and recursion elimination. Beyond Prolog, other systems, such as constraint logic programming (CLP) languages, adapt resolution strategies for more complex problem domains. These approaches extend the power of resolution to handle constraint satisfaction problems, further enhancing the capability of logic-based programming languages.

Logic resolution algorithms are essential for automated reasoning, providing powerful methods for drawing conclusions from sets of logical statements. From Horn clauses and unification to resolution strategies in languages like Prolog, these techniques form the backbone of modern declarative programming. As logic-based systems evolve, resolution will remain central to advancements in AI, automated reasoning, and constraint solving.

Principles of Logic Resolution

Logic resolution is a foundational technique in automated reasoning, enabling systems to derive conclusions from a set of logical statements or premises. The primary goal of resolution is to combine clauses by systematically applying inference rules, allowing the system to deduce new facts or prove the validity of a given claim. Resolution is typically used in conjunction with other methods, such as unification and backward/forward chaining, to simplify and combine logical formulas until either a contradiction is found or the desired conclusion is reached.

For example, in Python, logic resolution can be represented using a simple function that resolves two logical clauses:

```
def resolve(clause1, clause2):
    # Identifying complementary literals
    resolved_clause = set(clause1) ∧ set(clause2)
    return resolved_clause
```

In this code, clause1 and clause2 are two logical expressions, represented as sets. The resolve() function identifies the complementary literals (those that cancel each other out) and returns a new clause formed by applying the resolution rule.

Unification and Resolution

The resolution process often involves **unification**, which is the process of finding substitutions that make two terms identical. In the context of logic resolution, unification is essential for determining whether two literals can be combined. For example, consider two clauses:

- P(X) and P(a)

We can unify these terms by substituting X with a. This unification process is demonstrated in the following code:

```python
def unify(term1, term2):
    if term1 == term2:
        return {}
    elif isinstance(term1, str) and term1.isupper():
        return {term1: term2}
    elif isinstance(term2, str) and term2.isupper():
        return {term2: term1}
    else:
        return None

# Example of unification
unification_result = unify('X', 'a')
print(unification_result)  # {'X': 'a'}
```

Here, the unify() function takes two terms, and if they can be unified (i.e., made equal through substitution), it returns a substitution mapping. If they cannot be unified, it returns None. In this case, X is unified with a.

Forward and Backward Chaining

Logic resolution can be applied in both **forward chaining** and **backward chaining**. Forward chaining involves starting with known facts and applying inference rules to derive new facts. Backward chaining, on the other hand, starts with a goal and works backward, looking for facts that could prove or support the goal.

In Python, forward chaining can be simulated by iteratively applying resolution to a set of known facts. For instance, if we have the fact that P(a) and Q(b) are true, and we know the rule that $P(X) \land Q(X) \rightarrow R(X)$, we can derive R(a):

```python
def forward_chaining(facts, rules):
    inferred_facts = set(facts)
    new_facts = set(facts)

    while new_facts:
        current_fact = new_facts.pop()
        for rule in rules:
            if current_fact in rule:
                inferred_facts.add(rule[1])
                new_facts.add(rule[1])

    return inferred_facts

# Example facts and rules
facts = {'P(a)', 'Q(b)'}
rules = [('P(X)', 'Q(X)', 'R(X)')]

# Applying forward chaining
inferred_facts = forward_chaining(facts, rules)
print(inferred_facts)  # {'P(a)', 'Q(b)', 'R(a)'}
```

This code uses forward chaining to apply the rule and infer R(a) from the facts P(a) and Q(b).

Logic resolution and its associated techniques—unification, forward chaining, and backward chaining—are vital tools in automated reasoning. With their ability to combine and simplify logical clauses, these techniques form the backbone of systems like Prolog and other logic programming environments. Through the use of unification, forward and backward chaining, and the resolution principle, machines can simulate human-like reasoning and problem-solving in a declarative programming context.

Horn Clauses and Automated Deduction

Horn clauses are a special type of logical formula that plays a pivotal role in logic resolution, particularly in automated deduction and logic programming. They are a subset of propositional logic, characterized by having at most one positive literal in their disjunction. Horn clauses are especially useful in automated reasoning and are a key feature of languages like Prolog, where they enable efficient inference mechanisms.

A **Horn clause** is typically written as:

$$\neg A \lor \neg B \lor \ldots \lor \neg Z \to C$$

Which means, if all the literals in the clause are true, then the literal C must also be true. These clauses are useful because they simplify the process of inference, allowing for more efficient deduction in automated reasoning tasks.

For example, consider the following Horn clause:

$$\neg P(X) \lor Q(X) \to R(X)$$

This states that if P(X) is false and Q(X) is true, then R(X) must also be true. Horn clauses are often used in a **forward chaining** mechanism, where new facts are inferred by applying rules.

In Python, this mechanism can be simulated by creating a function that evaluates and applies Horn clauses based on current facts. Here's an example:

```python
def horn_clause_inference(facts, horn_clause):
    if all(literal in facts for literal in horn_clause[:-1]):
        facts.add(horn_clause[-1])
    return facts

# Example facts and Horn clause
facts = {'¬P(a)', 'Q(a)'}
horn_clause = {'¬P(a)', 'Q(a)', 'R(a)'}  # Horn clause in the form of a set

# Applying Horn clause inference
updated_facts = horn_clause_inference(facts, horn_clause)
print(updated_facts)  # {'¬P(a)', 'Q(a)', 'R(a)'}
```

In this code, horn_clause_inference() checks if all the required literals are present in the facts and, if so, adds the consequent (R(a)) to the facts.

Automated Deduction Using Horn Clauses

Automated deduction based on Horn clauses relies on **forward chaining**—starting with a set of known facts and continuously applying Horn clauses to deduce new facts. This approach can be applied iteratively until no new facts can be derived. The key benefit of Horn clauses is that they allow for efficient reasoning, as the inference is based on a limited set of rules, which makes the reasoning process scalable even for complex systems.

In a more generalized Python example, where multiple Horn clauses are applied to a set of facts:

```python
def apply_horn_clauses(facts, horn_clauses):
    new_facts = set(facts)
    while True:
        added_fact = False
        for clause in horn_clauses:
            if all(literal in new_facts for literal in clause[:-1]):
                if clause[-1] not in new_facts:
                    new_facts.add(clause[-1])
                    added_fact = True
        if not added_fact:
            break
    return new_facts

# Example Horn clauses
horn_clauses = [
    {'¬P(a)', 'Q(a)', 'R(a)'},
    {'¬R(a)', 'S(a)', 'T(a)'}
]
facts = {'¬P(a)', 'Q(a)'}

# Applying Horn clause inference
inferred_facts = apply_horn_clauses(facts, horn_clauses)
print(inferred_facts)  # {'¬P(a)', 'Q(a)', 'R(a)', 'S(a)', 'T(a)'}
```

In this code, the function apply_horn_clauses() iteratively applies each Horn clause to the facts until no more new facts can be inferred, simulating an automated reasoning system based on Horn logic.

Horn Clauses in Automated Theorem Proving

Horn clauses are widely used in automated theorem proving, where the goal is to prove that a given statement is logically valid based on a set of axioms. Because of their structure, Horn clauses are highly suitable for automated deduction techniques like **resolution** and **unification**.

In Prolog, a well-known logic programming language, Horn clauses form the basis of both the syntax and inference mechanisms. Prolog employs a resolution strategy to perform automated reasoning and find conclusions that satisfy the given Horn clauses.

Horn clauses play a crucial role in automated deduction and logic programming. They simplify logical reasoning by limiting the number of positive literals in a clause, making them particularly suitable for efficient inference mechanisms like forward chaining. By utilizing Horn clauses in automated theorem proving and reasoning systems, we can deduce new facts and perform logical deductions, enhancing the automation of logical tasks.

Unification and Forward/Backward Chaining

Unification and chaining (both forward and backward) are critical techniques used in logic resolution algorithms. These methods are essential for reasoning in logic programming, including in languages such as Prolog. Unification allows the matching of terms or expressions, while chaining helps derive new facts from known information, both of which are foundational to logic resolution.

Unification

Unification is a process that makes two logical expressions identical by finding a suitable substitution for their variables. It is a fundamental operation in many automated reasoning systems. In the context of logic programming, unification helps to determine whether two logical statements or terms can be made equivalent by substituting terms or values for variables.

For example, if we want to unify the terms $P(a, X)$ and $P(b, Y)$, unification will try to find a substitution where the variables X and Y are replaced with appropriate values so that both terms are identical. In this case, X must be replaced with b, and Y must be replaced with a for the two terms to unify.

In Python, we can implement unification by comparing the structure of terms and recursively matching variables. Here's a simple example:

```python
def unify(term1, term2):
    # Base case: both terms are identical
    if term1 == term2:
        return {}

    # Case where a term is a variable
    if isinstance(term1, str) and term1.islower():
        return {term1: term2}
    if isinstance(term2, str) and term2.islower():
        return {term2: term1}

    # Case for compound terms (e.g., P(a, X))
    if isinstance(term1, tuple) and isinstance(term2, tuple):
        if len(term1) != len(term2):
            return None
        substitutions = {}
        for subterm1, subterm2 in zip(term1, term2):
            result = unify(subterm1, subterm2)
            if result is None:
                return None
            substitutions.update(result)
        return substitutions
    return None

# Example usage
term1 = ('P', 'a', 'X')
term2 = ('P', 'b', 'Y')
```

```
substitutions = unify(term1, term2)
print(substitutions)  # {'X': 'b', 'Y': 'a'}
```

In this example, the unify() function recursively checks whether two terms can be unified, returning a dictionary of substitutions (or None if unification is not possible).

Forward and Backward Chaining

Chaining is a mechanism used to apply rules to known facts and derive new facts. It can be performed in two ways: forward chaining and backward chaining.

- **Forward Chaining**: This process starts with a set of known facts and uses rules to infer new facts. It's a data-driven approach, often used in expert systems. The system continually applies rules until no more new facts can be derived.

In forward chaining, if a rule's conditions (or premises) are satisfied, the conclusion (or consequent) is inferred and added to the set of facts. This process continues until no new facts can be derived.

```
def forward_chaining(facts, rules):
    new_facts = set(facts)
    while True:
        added_fact = False
        for rule in rules:
            if all(antecedent in new_facts for antecedent in rule[:-1]):
                if rule[-1] not in new_facts:
                    new_facts.add(rule[-1])
                    added_fact = True
        if not added_fact:
            break
    return new_facts

# Example facts and rules
facts = {'P(a)', 'Q(a)'}
rules = [
    {'P(a)', 'Q(a)', 'R(a)'},  # Rule: if P(a) and Q(a), then R(a)
]

# Apply forward chaining
result = forward_chaining(facts, rules)
print(result)  # {'P(a)', 'Q(a)', 'R(a)'}
```

In this example, the system starts with known facts (P(a) and Q(a)) and applies a rule to infer new facts (R(a)).

- **Backward Chaining**: This process starts with a goal (or hypothesis) and works backward, trying to determine which facts or rules are required to prove the goal. It's a goal-driven approach, often used in Prolog.

```
def backward_chaining(goal, facts, rules):
    if goal in facts:
        return True
    for rule in rules:
        if rule[-1] == goal:
            if all(backward_chaining(antecedent, facts, rules) for antecedent
            in rule[:-1]):
```

```
                    return True
        return False

    # Example facts and rules
    facts = {'P(a)', 'Q(a)'}
    rules = [
        {'P(a)', 'Q(a)', 'R(a)'},  # Rule: if P(a) and Q(a), then R(a)
    ]

    # Apply backward chaining
    goal = 'R(a)'
    result = backward_chaining(goal, facts, rules)
    print(result)  # True
```

In this example, we use backward chaining to check whether we can prove the goal R(a) starting from the known facts (P(a) and Q(a)), using the rules provided.

Unification and chaining are crucial components of logic resolution algorithms. Unification provides a way to match terms and infer substitutions, while forward and backward chaining allow for data-driven and goal-driven reasoning, respectively. These techniques are foundational in logic programming and automated reasoning systems, particularly in languages like Prolog.

Resolution Strategies in Prolog and Beyond

Resolution is a fundamental concept in logic programming, particularly in languages like Prolog, where it plays a crucial role in deriving new facts and answering queries based on a set of rules and facts. Resolution involves systematically searching for a way to satisfy a query by applying logical inference rules, with Prolog using this strategy to find solutions through backward chaining. The resolution process works by attempting to match the query to the database of facts and rules and systematically deducing new information through logical inference.

Resolution in Prolog

In Prolog, the resolution strategy starts with a query and works backward, trying to find the conditions under which the query can be satisfied. The Prolog engine takes the query and attempts to unify it with the facts and rules in the knowledge base. If a match is found, it continues recursively, searching for further facts that satisfy the query. The process is recursive and continues until all goals are resolved or no more matches are found.

The basic structure of resolution in Prolog involves:

1. **Unification**: Checking if a goal can be unified with a fact or rule.

2. **Backtracking**: If a goal does not unify, Prolog backtracks to try a different rule or fact.

3. **Recursive Rule Application**: Prolog applies rules recursively to solve subgoals until the original goal is satisfied or a contradiction is found.

195

For example, a Prolog program might contain rules such as:

```
father(john, mary).
father(john, tom).
parent(X, Y) :- father(X, Y).
```

When asked the query parent(john, Who), Prolog will try to find facts or rules that satisfy the goal. It first looks for father(john, Who), which unifies with the fact father(john, mary) and father(john, tom), hence producing the results Who = mary and Who = tom.

```
?- parent(john, who).
who = mary ;
who = tom.
```

Beyond Prolog: Other Resolution Strategies

While Prolog is one of the most famous examples of using resolution strategies, the concept extends beyond Prolog into other logic-based programming languages and systems. Different resolution strategies might be used based on the domain or type of logic problem being solved.

For instance, in automated theorem proving, resolution is used to prove the validity of logical statements. The technique uses a form of logical reasoning where statements are broken down into simpler parts and combined to prove the truth of a conclusion. The resolution process typically involves:

1. **Clause Normal Form**: Converting all statements into a standardized form (clauses).

2. **Refutation**: Trying to refute the negation of the statement being proved by applying resolution.

In **Prolog-like systems** such as **Mercury**, deterministic resolution is used, which provides more predictable execution by reducing ambiguity in the logic. Here's an example of Mercury code using deterministic logic:

```
:- module example.
:- interface.
:- pred father(string, string).
:- pred parent(string, string).

:- implementation.
father("john", "mary").
father("john", "tom").

parent(X, Y) :- father(X, Y).
```

In **Answer Set Programming (ASP)**, the resolution strategy involves solving problems by creating "answer sets" that satisfy a set of rules and constraints. Here's an example of a simple ASP program:

```
person(john).
person(mary).
```

```
person(tom).

father(john, mary).
father(john, tom).

parent(X, Y) :- father(X, Y).
```

The solver will attempt to find the set of facts (answer sets) that satisfy all constraints. For instance, it will derive that parent(john, mary) and parent(john, tom) are true.

Resolution strategies, central to logic programming languages like Prolog, are foundational to solving queries and deriving new information from a set of facts and rules. Whether in Prolog or more advanced systems like ASP or Mercury, resolution enables logic-based programming languages to perform automated reasoning effectively. The application of these strategies across different languages highlights their versatility in logical and constraint-solving domains.

Module 21:
Query Optimization Algorithms

Module Overview: Module 21 delves into the critical area of query optimization, focusing on the various techniques used to enhance the performance of SQL queries. It explores SQL query optimization methods, including cost-based and heuristic approaches, indexing strategies, and execution plan selection. The module also addresses the complexities of distributed query optimization in modern database systems.

SQL Query Optimization Techniques

SQL query optimization is the process of improving the efficiency of SQL queries to minimize their execution time and resource usage. Query optimization techniques aim to reduce the cost of executing queries by analyzing various execution strategies and choosing the most efficient one. Several factors are considered in query optimization, including data size, indexes, and query structure. The goal is to produce an optimal or near-optimal execution plan that minimizes the resources required to retrieve the desired results.

Optimization begins with the analysis of the query itself, followed by rewriting or transforming the query into a more efficient form. For example, queries that involve joins can be rewritten to reduce unnecessary operations. Optimization techniques also include eliminating redundant joins or using efficient operators. These methods are often implemented by query optimizers that are part of relational database management systems (RDBMS).

Cost-Based and Heuristic Optimization

Cost-based optimization is a mathematical approach to query optimization, where the system evaluates different execution plans and selects the one with the least estimated cost. The cost of an execution plan is typically determined by factors such as I/O operations, CPU usage, and memory consumption. This approach requires the optimizer to estimate the cost of various operations and then compare them to choose the most efficient path.

In contrast, heuristic optimization uses predefined rules or heuristics to guide the optimization process. These rules are typically based on general knowledge about how certain types of queries are usually executed efficiently. Heuristic optimization may involve decisions such as the order in which operations are performed or which indexes should be used. While cost-based optimization is more comprehensive, heuristic optimization is faster and can be used for simpler queries where precise cost estimation is not required.

Indexing and Execution Plan Selection

Indexing is a crucial aspect of query optimization, as it allows the database to retrieve data more efficiently. An index is a data structure that enables fast lookups of data without having to scan entire tables. Proper index design is essential for improving query performance, especially when dealing with large datasets.

The choice of indexes depends on the query patterns and the columns used in the WHERE, JOIN, and ORDER BY clauses. An efficient indexing strategy can dramatically reduce the execution time of queries by allowing the database engine to access the data with minimal scanning. Additionally, query optimizers use indexes to help select the most efficient execution plan. The optimizer evaluates different query execution plans that utilize available indexes and selects the one with the lowest cost.

Distributed Query Optimization

Distributed query optimization refers to the techniques used to optimize queries that are executed across multiple databases or servers in a distributed database system. In distributed environments, data may be stored on different nodes or locations, and queries must be optimized to minimize data transfer and ensure efficient processing.

Distributed query optimization is more complex than traditional query optimization because it requires consideration of network latency, data location, and distributed indexes. The optimizer must decide where to execute each part of the query to minimize communication overhead and optimize performance across the entire distributed system. Advanced algorithms and strategies are employed to determine the most efficient query plan that takes into account both local and remote data sources, data partitioning, and query execution across multiple nodes.

Query optimization is an essential aspect of database management, ensuring that queries are executed in the most efficient manner possible. By understanding SQL query optimization techniques, cost-based and heuristic optimization, indexing strategies, and distributed query optimization, developers and database administrators can improve the performance of complex queries in various database systems.

SQL Query Optimization Techniques

SQL query optimization is a crucial process for improving database query performance by minimizing execution time and resource consumption. The process involves transforming inefficient queries into optimized forms, ensuring faster response times and reduced load on databases. Below, we'll explore common optimization techniques, illustrated with practical examples.

Query Rewriting and Join Reordering

Query rewriting involves transforming a query into a more efficient form without changing its output. For instance, subqueries can often be rewritten as joins to improve performance. Consider the following query:

```sql
SELECT EmployeeID, Name
FROM Employees
WHERE DepartmentID IN (SELECT DepartmentID FROM Departments WHERE DepartmentName
    = 'HR');
```

This query can be rewritten using a JOIN:

```sql
SELECT e.EmployeeID, e.Name
FROM Employees e
JOIN Departments d ON e.DepartmentID = d.DepartmentID
WHERE d.DepartmentName = 'HR';
```

By converting the subquery into a join, we eliminate the need for a nested query, potentially improving performance.

Using Indexes for Faster Querying

Indexes significantly improve query performance by allowing faster data retrieval. Let's assume you often query the Employees table by DepartmentID:

```sql
SELECT EmployeeID, Name
FROM Employees
WHERE DepartmentID = 3;
```

Without an index on DepartmentID, the database would perform a full table scan, which is inefficient for large datasets. You can create an index on the DepartmentID column to speed up the query:

```sql
CREATE INDEX idx_department ON Employees(DepartmentID);
```

With the index in place, the query performance will improve significantly, as the database can quickly locate relevant rows using the index rather than scanning the entire table.

Choosing the Right Join Method

Join methods such as **nested loop joins**, **merge joins**, and **hash joins** are selected by the query optimizer based on the cost of execution. Here's an example using a simple nested loop join:

```sql
SELECT e.EmployeeID, e.Name, d.DepartmentName
FROM Employees e
JOIN Departments d ON e.DepartmentID = d.DepartmentID;
```

For large tables, a hash join might be more efficient. The optimizer evaluates the sizes of the tables involved and chooses the optimal join strategy based on available system resources. While this is handled automatically by the SQL engine, understanding these joins is vital for query optimization.

Execution Plan Selection

SQL query optimizers generate multiple execution plans and evaluate their performance using cost-based models. Here's how you can check the execution plan of a query:

```
EXPLAIN ANALYZE
SELECT e.EmployeeID, e.Name
FROM Employees e
WHERE DepartmentID = 3;
```

The EXPLAIN ANALYZE statement provides detailed information about how the query is executed, including which indexes are used and the estimated cost of each operation. Based on this information, you can fine-tune queries or indexes to improve performance.

Parallel Execution

For complex queries or large datasets, optimizers can use parallel execution. For example, if a query involves joining large tables, the database engine might divide the work into smaller tasks and process them simultaneously:

```
SELECT e.EmployeeID, e.Name, d.DepartmentName
FROM Employees e
JOIN Departments d ON e.DepartmentID = d.DepartmentID;
```

The optimizer could break this join into multiple operations that are executed concurrently across multiple CPU cores, improving overall performance, especially in high-load environments.

By leveraging these optimization techniques, you can significantly improve the performance of SQL queries, particularly when dealing with large datasets or complex operations.

Cost-Based and Heuristic Optimization

Cost-based optimization and heuristic-based optimization are two key strategies used by SQL query optimizers to determine the most efficient way to execute queries. In this section, we will explore both approaches, illustrating how they are used to optimize queries for better performance.

Cost-Based Optimization

Cost-based optimization relies on a model where the optimizer evaluates different execution plans based on the estimated cost of each plan. The "cost" is generally calculated using factors such as CPU time, disk I/O, and memory usage. The optimizer chooses the plan with the lowest cost.

For example, consider the following query that involves two tables, Employees and Departments:

```
SELECT e.EmployeeID, e.Name, d.DepartmentName
FROM Employees e
JOIN Departments d ON e.DepartmentID = d.DepartmentID;
```

The SQL engine may generate multiple execution plans for this query:

1. **Nested Loop Join:** The optimizer may decide to use a nested loop join if one of the tables is small and the other is large.

2. **Hash Join:** If the tables are both large, a hash join might be more efficient.

3. **Merge Join:** If both tables are sorted by DepartmentID, a merge join may be the optimal choice.

Each plan is assigned a cost estimate based on the expected number of operations required to execute the query. The optimizer then selects the plan with the lowest cost. You can view the execution plan with the following query:

```
EXPLAIN ANALYZE
SELECT e.EmployeeID, e.Name, d.DepartmentName
FROM Employees e
JOIN Departments d ON e.DepartmentID = d.DepartmentID;
```

The output will show the chosen plan and its associated cost, helping you understand the optimizer's decision-making process.

Heuristic Optimization

Heuristic optimization, in contrast, uses a set of predefined rules to optimize queries. These rules are based on commonly observed patterns that are known to improve performance in certain cases. For example, heuristic rules might favor specific join types or recommend filtering data early in the query execution process.

Consider the query:

```
SELECT e.EmployeeID, e.Name
FROM Employees e
WHERE e.DepartmentID IN (SELECT d.DepartmentID FROM Departments d WHERE
            d.DepartmentName = 'Sales');
```

Heuristic optimization might rewrite this query to use a JOIN instead of a subquery. It may also decide to apply the filter on DepartmentName early to reduce the number of rows involved in the join operation. The rewritten query would be:

```
SELECT e.EmployeeID, e.Name
FROM Employees e
JOIN Departments d ON e.DepartmentID = d.DepartmentID
WHERE d.DepartmentName = 'Sales';
```

While heuristic optimization can be faster than cost-based optimization in some scenarios, it is less flexible and may not always produce the best execution plan. However, in many cases, heuristic optimization is still a valuable tool for simplifying queries and improving performance without deep analysis.

Combining Cost-Based and Heuristic Optimization

Many modern query optimizers use a combination of cost-based and heuristic approaches. Initially, heuristic rules are applied to simplify and reformat the query. Then, the optimizer uses a cost-based model to evaluate the best execution plan. By combining both methods, SQL optimizers can leverage the strengths of each approach.

For example, an optimizer may use heuristic optimization to replace a subquery with a JOIN, and then apply cost-based optimization to determine the most efficient join algorithm (nested loop, hash, or merge).

Practical Implications for Query Tuning

Understanding both cost-based and heuristic optimization allows developers to write more efficient SQL queries. By avoiding common pitfalls, such as unnecessary subqueries or inefficient joins, and by understanding how the optimizer will evaluate different plans, you can improve the performance of your queries.

SQL query optimization tools, such as the EXPLAIN statement, allow you to examine the optimizer's choices and make informed decisions about how to rewrite or index queries to achieve optimal performance.

Indexing and Execution Plan Selection

Indexing and execution plan selection are crucial aspects of SQL query optimization that significantly impact the performance of database queries. By using appropriate indexes and understanding how the database selects execution plans, developers can ensure that queries run efficiently, especially with large datasets. In this section, we will explore how indexing and execution plans work together to optimize SQL query execution.

Indexing for Query Optimization

Indexes are structures that improve the speed of data retrieval operations on a database table. They are used to quickly locate data without having to search every row in a table. SQL optimizers automatically decide when to use an index based on the query's structure, but developers can also create custom indexes to optimize specific queries.

Consider a query on the Employees table:

```sql
SELECT e.EmployeeID, e.Name
FROM Employees e
WHERE e.DepartmentID = 101;
```

If the Employees table is large, a full table scan would be inefficient. Instead, creating an index on the DepartmentID column would allow the database engine to quickly find rows where DepartmentID = 101, reducing the time it takes to retrieve the results.

```sql
CREATE INDEX idx_department_id ON Employees (DepartmentID);
```

This index speeds up queries filtering by DepartmentID, as the database can now use the index to perform a more efficient lookup.

Indexes can also be composite, meaning they cover multiple columns. For example, if a query frequently filters on both DepartmentID and EmployeeID, creating a composite index on both columns would further optimize performance.

```
CREATE INDEX idx_dept_emp_id ON Employees (DepartmentID, EmployeeID);
```

While indexes speed up read operations, they can slow down write operations (inserts, updates, and deletes), as the index must be maintained whenever data changes. Therefore, indexes should be used judiciously, focusing on the queries that need optimization.

Execution Plan Selection

An execution plan is a detailed map of how SQL queries are executed by the database engine. The optimizer generates an execution plan for each query, selecting the most efficient approach based on factors like table size, available indexes, and query complexity.

You can view the execution plan of a query using the EXPLAIN statement. For example:

```
EXPLAIN
SELECT e.EmployeeID, e.Name
FROM Employees e
WHERE e.DepartmentID = 101;
```

This statement will show the database's selected execution plan, which could involve using the index idx_department_id, performing a full table scan, or applying a different strategy based on the optimizer's analysis.

Common Execution Plan Elements

1. **Table Scan:** If no suitable index exists, the optimizer may choose a full table scan, where the entire table is examined row by row. While simple, this is typically slower than an indexed lookup.

2. **Index Scan:** If an index is available, the optimizer may use an index scan, which allows the engine to quickly find rows matching the query condition.

3. **Join Operations:** For queries involving joins, the optimizer may choose between different types of joins (nested loop, hash, or merge joins) based on the available indexes and data distribution.

4. **Sort Operations:** If the query involves sorting, the optimizer may choose to perform sorting either in memory or on disk, depending on the size of the dataset.

5. **Aggregation and Grouping:** Queries involving aggregation (such as SUM, COUNT, or AVG) may lead the optimizer to use specific algorithms to group and aggregate data efficiently.

Analyzing and Improving Execution Plans

When optimizing queries, it's crucial to analyze the execution plan provided by the EXPLAIN statement. If the plan shows a full table scan or inefficient joins, indexing the relevant columns or rewriting the query may improve performance.

For example, suppose the query involves a JOIN between Employees and Departments. The optimizer might choose a nested loop join if one of the tables is small, or a hash join if both tables are large. You can influence the optimizer's choice by adding indexes on the join columns.

```
CREATE INDEX idx_employee_dept_id ON Employees (DepartmentID);
```

This index could make the query faster by allowing the database to quickly locate matching rows in the Employees table before joining them with the Departments table.

Balancing Indexing and Execution Plan Selection

The key to effective query optimization is balancing indexing and execution plan selection. Indexes can dramatically speed up data retrieval, but excessive indexing can increase the overhead of maintaining the indexes during write operations. Analyzing execution plans with tools like EXPLAIN enables you to see how the database engine uses indexes and to adjust your indexing strategy accordingly.

In addition, understanding how the optimizer selects execution plans allows you to rewrite queries in ways that make it easier for the optimizer to choose efficient plans. By combining the right indexes with a well-structured query, you can significantly improve the performance of your SQL queries.

Distributed Query Optimization

Distributed query optimization is an essential aspect of handling large-scale data systems where queries span multiple servers or databases. In such systems, the database engine needs to determine the most efficient way to execute a query across distributed resources. This optimization is particularly important when dealing with large datasets that are distributed across different nodes or locations, such as in cloud-based or big data applications.

Distributed Query Planning

In a distributed database system, data is spread across multiple machines, often to improve performance or support horizontal scalability. When a query is executed, the database system needs to plan how to retrieve data from various sources and combine the results efficiently. This involves partitioning the data, selecting the most optimal nodes, and deciding how to join data across different nodes.

Consider a scenario where two datasets, Employees and Departments, are stored on separate database servers. The query needs to fetch the names of employees along with their department names.

```
SELECT e.EmployeeName, d.DepartmentName
FROM Employees e
JOIN Departments d
ON e.DepartmentID = d.DepartmentID;
```

In a traditional system, this might be a straightforward join. However, in a distributed system, the optimizer needs to decide whether to pull all the data from the Employees table to one node and join it with the Departments data or to push part of the computation to the node that holds the Departments table.

Cost-Based Optimization for Distributed Queries

The database optimizer evaluates various strategies for distributed queries, calculating the cost of different execution plans based on factors like data locality, communication overhead, and resource utilization. The goal is to minimize the total cost of query execution, which includes both the computational cost and the network communication cost between nodes.

For instance, if the Departments table is small and resides on a node with less computational load, the optimizer may decide to send the join condition to that node and perform the join locally. Alternatively, if the Employees table is small and frequently queried, the optimizer may choose to pull that data to a central node and join it with the data from the Departments node.

One approach to reducing communication overhead is **data localization**, where the optimizer tries to limit data movement across nodes. This is achieved by partitioning the data in such a way that related data is stored together on the same node.

Query Routing and Execution

Once the optimizer selects a plan, the query is routed to the appropriate nodes for execution. Each node performs its local part of the query and returns intermediate results. The results are then combined at a central node or returned to the user. The execution of distributed queries involves considerations such as **data shuffling**, **partitioning**, and **parallel execution**.

In distributed systems like Apache Hadoop or Google BigQuery, query execution may involve data shuffling, where intermediate results are sorted and redistributed across nodes to facilitate joins or aggregations. The system may also parallelize the computation to increase speed, performing operations like filtering, aggregation, or sorting in parallel on different subsets of the data.

Distributed Indexing for Optimized Query Execution

For large distributed systems, indexing plays a critical role in speeding up query performance. Distributed systems often use specialized indexing strategies such as **range-based partitioning** or **hash-based partitioning**. These types of indexes allow the database to quickly locate the relevant partition or node where the data resides, reducing the time spent on query routing and retrieval.

For example, if the Employees table is partitioned based on DepartmentID and an index is built on DepartmentID, the optimizer can directly query the relevant partition that holds the employee data for the requested department.

```
CREATE INDEX idx_employee_deptid ON Employees (DepartmentID);
```

This index enables faster retrieval of employee data from the specific partition corresponding to a department, reducing the need to scan all partitions in the distributed system.

Handling Failures and Load Balancing

In a distributed system, handling failures and ensuring load balancing are also crucial aspects of query optimization. The optimizer must consider the current load on each node and distribute query execution accordingly. If a node is down or heavily loaded, the query can be rerouted to another available node, ensuring that the system remains responsive.

Moreover, advanced distributed query optimizers incorporate mechanisms to handle network latency, replication, and consistency between nodes to ensure fault tolerance and high availability of the data.

Distributed query optimization is a vital component of large-scale database systems, ensuring that queries are executed efficiently across multiple nodes. By carefully planning data partitioning, query routing, and execution strategies, databases can minimize communication overhead and maximize performance. In complex systems, such as cloud-based platforms or big data applications, distributed query optimization remains a key factor in delivering fast and reliable data retrieval for end-users.

Module 22:
Abstract Syntax Trees

Module 22 focuses on Abstract Syntax Trees (ASTs), an essential concept in programming language design and compiler construction. It covers the abstract representation of code structures, parsing techniques, tree traversal methods, and AST manipulation, highlighting their role in optimizing the execution of declarative code. The module provides insight into how ASTs improve code readability and execution efficiency.

Abstract Representation of Code Structures

An Abstract Syntax Tree (AST) is a tree-like data structure that represents the syntactic structure of code. Each node in the tree represents a construct in the programming language, such as variables, operators, or function calls, while the edges define the relationships between these constructs. Unlike parse trees, which are based on grammar rules and can be cumbersome, ASTs abstract away unnecessary details, presenting a simplified view of the code's logical structure.

ASTs are crucial in understanding the meaning of a program beyond its textual representation. In declarative programming, this abstraction allows for easier manipulation of code structures, enabling optimizations and transformations that enhance performance. The nodes in an AST are typically designed to reflect the key components of the language, such as expressions, declarations, and statements, while omitting non-essential information like punctuation marks.

Parsing and Tree Traversal Techniques

Parsing is the process of analyzing code to generate an AST, which involves reading and interpreting the structure of the source code based on the language's grammar. The parser converts the linear sequence of tokens into a tree structure, where each node represents a language construct. This process is critical in building the internal representation of a program for further analysis or execution.

Tree traversal is the process of visiting each node in the AST. There are different traversal techniques, including **pre-order**, **in-order**, and **post-order** traversals, each useful for different types of analysis. For example, in pre-order traversal, the root node is processed before its children, which is useful for tasks like expression evaluation. Post-order traversal, on the other hand, processes the children before the root, making it ideal for tasks like code generation.

Traversal techniques are essential for efficiently extracting information or modifying the AST. In declarative programming, where code readability and transformations are key, traversal allows for the manipulation of ASTs to optimize and refine the declarative statements that the code represents.

AST Manipulation in Compilers

In compiler design, ASTs are used to represent the intermediate form of a program after it has been parsed but before it is optimized or compiled into machine code. AST manipulation involves transforming the tree to improve performance or correctness. These transformations include simplifying expressions, eliminating redundant computations, and applying optimization strategies such as constant folding and inlining.

AST manipulation can also be applied to improve declarative code execution. For example, a declarative statement like a filter operation can be transformed into a more efficient loop or query based on the underlying structure of the AST. By analyzing the tree and applying transformations, the compiler can optimize code execution without altering the high-level declarative meaning.

In declarative programming languages, AST manipulation allows the underlying system to optimize the code while maintaining the high-level abstraction. It enables various optimization techniques that focus on enhancing the efficiency of the resulting code, making it more suitable for execution without compromising the clarity and expressiveness of the declarative statements.

Optimizing Declarative Code Execution

One of the primary uses of ASTs in declarative programming is optimizing the execution of declarative code. Since declarative programming focuses on expressing logic and relationships rather than explicit control flow, optimizing execution involves finding the most efficient way to interpret and execute the high-level expressions.

ASTs can help in this process by enabling transformations that simplify code without changing its intended meaning. For instance, repeated subexpressions in declarative code can be identified and simplified through AST analysis. Additionally, the structure of the AST can reveal opportunities for parallel execution or other performance enhancements.

Another key aspect of optimizing declarative code execution involves reordering operations in a way that minimizes resource usage or execution time. By traversing and manipulating the AST, the compiler or interpreter can apply advanced optimization techniques like lazy evaluation or just-in-time compilation, ultimately improving runtime performance.

Abstract Syntax Trees play a central role in the optimization of declarative code execution. Through parsing, tree traversal, and manipulation, ASTs allow for the abstraction and transformation of code structures, leading to enhanced performance and efficiency. By optimizing the execution of declarative code, ASTs help balance readability with high-performance execution.

Abstract Representation of Code Structures

Abstract Syntax Trees (ASTs) are a fundamental concept in representing the hierarchical structure of source code, capturing the program's logical constructs in a simplified manner. In an AST, each node represents a syntactic construct, such as operators, variables, and expressions, while edges define the relationships between these elements. The tree abstraction helps in focusing on the semantic structure rather than low-level syntactic details, making it particularly useful in declarative programming.

For example, consider the following Python code:

```
x = 2 + 3 * 4
```

The AST for this expression would abstract the arithmetic operations while omitting unnecessary syntax like parentheses or operators. It could look like this:

```
Assign
├── Name (x)
└── BinOp
    ├── Num (2)
    └── BinOp
        ├── Num (3)
        └── Mult
            └── Num (4)
```

Here, the root node (Assign) represents the assignment statement. The left child (Name x) represents the variable assignment, and the right child (BinOp) captures the arithmetic operation. The AST makes it clear that multiplication (Mult) has higher precedence than addition (Add), which is a key benefit of abstract representation—allowing compilers or interpreters to focus on the logic rather than parsing syntax.

In declarative programming, ASTs offer a high-level representation that helps automate various tasks like optimizations and transformations without altering the program's intended output. For example, in SQL, an AST can represent a query's logical flow, making it easier to optimize how the query is executed without altering its structure. Consider this SQL query:

```
SELECT name FROM employees WHERE age > 30
```

The AST for this query might look something like:

```
Select
├── Columns
│   └── Column (name)
├── From
│   └── Table (employees)
└── Where
    └── Comparison
        ├── Column (age)
        └── Number (30)
```

In this AST, the SQL query is represented as a tree, with the Select node indicating what data to retrieve (name from employees) and a condition (age > 30) attached to the Where clause. The declarative nature of the query remains intact, while the AST allows for easier query optimization, such as reordering operations or applying indexes.

In declarative programming frameworks, ASTs are also helpful for optimizing code execution. For example, in a declarative UI framework, manipulating an AST can lead to more efficient updates by determining the minimal set of changes needed in the user interface, rather than re-rendering the entire UI from scratch.

The abstraction of ASTs also facilitates the creation of Domain-Specific Languages (DSLs), which are often used in declarative programming. A DSL can be designed to target a specific problem domain, and the AST provides a unified representation that can be optimized for that domain. For example, a DSL for financial calculations can utilize ASTs to evaluate expressions in a highly efficient manner.

Abstract Syntax Trees offer a powerful abstraction for representing code in declarative programming. By focusing on the program's logical structure and relationships, ASTs enable optimizations and manipulations that simplify both code readability and execution performance. Their use is fundamental in declarative paradigms where logic is prioritized over syntax.

Parsing and Tree Traversal Techniques

Parsing is the process of converting a sequence of tokens, typically generated by a lexer or tokenizer, into an Abstract Syntax Tree (AST). The parser analyzes the syntax of the code to produce this hierarchical structure, ensuring that the code conforms to the rules of the language. Tree traversal techniques are used to navigate and manipulate the AST for various purposes, such as evaluation, optimization, or transformation.

To illustrate the parsing and traversal process, consider the Python expression $x = 2 + 3 * 4$. The parser takes this expression and generates an AST representation, as discussed earlier. A typical parser for arithmetic expressions would use techniques like recursive descent parsing or a pushdown automaton to handle the various operators and precedence rules.

Let's break down how parsing works in this case. The parser will first identify the operators (+ and *) and the operands (2, 3, 4). It then constructs an AST that reflects the order of operations, with the multiplication operation (*) taking precedence over addition (+).

For example, a simple recursive descent parser for arithmetic expressions might follow these steps:

1. **Tokenization**: The input string $x = 2 + 3 * 4$ is tokenized into a list of tokens: [Assign, Name, 2, Plus, 3, Multiply, 4].

2. **Parsing**: The parser processes this token list. It first handles the assignment (Assign), then parses the right-hand side of the equation. It identifies the addition and multiplication operators, ensuring correct precedence.

3. **AST Creation**: The parser constructs an AST, ensuring that the multiplication is represented as a higher-level operation in the tree.

The resulting AST structure might look like this:

```
Assign
├── Name (x)
└── BinOp
     ├── Num (2)
     └── BinOp
          ├── Num (3)
          └── Mult
               └── Num (4)
```

Tree Traversal Techniques

Once the AST is built, tree traversal techniques are used to process or manipulate it. Tree traversal refers to the method used to visit all nodes in the tree, usually in a specific order. The two most common traversal techniques are **depth-first traversal (DFS)** and **breadth-first traversal (BFS)**. In DFS, the traversal starts at the root node and explores as far as possible along each branch before backtracking. In BFS, the tree is explored level by level, starting from the root.

In a depth-first traversal, we may start at the root of the AST and recursively visit each subtree. For example, consider an evaluator that walks through the AST to compute the value of the expression:

1. Start at the root (Assign), then visit the right-hand side.

2. Traverse the binary operator (BinOp), and visit its left child (Num 2).

3. Move to the right subtree, where another BinOp node is encountered.

4. Continue traversing the tree, visiting the operands (Num 3, Mult, and Num 4).

5. Compute the result from the leaf nodes upwards, following the operation hierarchy.

This depth-first traversal approach ensures that all subexpressions are evaluated in the correct order. The result of 3 * 4 is computed first, followed by adding 2 to the result.

```
def evaluate(ast):
    if isinstance(ast, Num):
        return ast.value
    if isinstance(ast, BinOp):
        left = evaluate(ast.left)
        right = evaluate(ast.right)
```

```
        if isinstance(ast.op, Add):
            return left + right
        elif isinstance(ast.op, Mult):
            return left * right
```

In this example, the evaluate function performs a depth-first traversal to compute the result of an arithmetic expression stored in the AST.

Another common operation is **AST manipulation**, where traversal techniques are applied to modify the AST structure for optimization or transformation purposes. For example, a tree traversal can be used to simplify expressions or apply algebraic transformations.

Parsing and tree traversal are essential for working with Abstract Syntax Trees in declarative programming. Parsing transforms code into a structured representation, while traversal techniques are used to process, evaluate, and optimize the code. By understanding how these processes work, developers can manipulate ASTs effectively to optimize and transform declarative code.

AST Manipulation in Compilers

Abstract Syntax Tree (AST) manipulation plays a crucial role in compilers. After parsing source code into an AST, compilers use AST manipulation to optimize, transform, and generate intermediate code that will eventually be converted into machine code. AST manipulation can range from simplifying expressions to reordering code for performance gains or translating high-level language constructs into lower-level representations.

In this section, we will explore how AST manipulation occurs within compilers, highlighting how transformations are applied to enhance performance or functionality.

Code Simplification

One of the primary goals of AST manipulation is simplifying code. A compiler might take a complex or redundant expression and reduce it to a simpler equivalent. For instance, the expression x + 0 could be optimized to just x. Similarly, x * 1 can be simplified to x.

In a compiler, such transformations often require traversing the AST, identifying subexpressions that can be simplified, and replacing them with simpler nodes.

For example, consider an expression such as:

```
x + 0
```

The AST might initially look like this:

```
BinOp
├── x
└── Num(0)
```

The compiler would then manipulate the AST to simplify this to:

X

Here is an example of how a simplification function might be implemented for AST nodes representing binary operations:

```python
class BinOp:
    def __init__(self, left, right, op):
        self.left = left
        self.right = right
        self.op = op

class Num:
    def __init__(self, value):
        self.value = value

def simplify(ast):
    if isinstance(ast, BinOp):
        if isinstance(ast.right, Num) and ast.right.value == 0 and ast.op == '+':
            return ast.left
        if isinstance(ast.right, Num) and ast.right.value == 1 and ast.op == '*':
            return ast.left
        # Add other simplifications as needed
    return ast
```

This function recursively traverses the AST, checking for cases that can be simplified. For x + 0, it returns x, simplifying the AST structure.

Loop Unrolling and Code Reordering

Another significant manipulation in compilers is loop unrolling, which can improve performance by reducing the number of iterations in a loop. Compilers may analyze loop structures in the AST and convert them into a more efficient form.

For example, consider a loop in high-level code:

```python
for i in range(0, 10):
    sum += i
```

The AST for this might initially represent a loop structure. The compiler could manipulate this AST to unroll the loop, creating a series of repeated operations to avoid the overhead of a loop control mechanism.

For example, after loop unrolling, the AST might look like:

```python
sum += 0
sum += 1
sum += 2
...
sum += 9
```

This kind of optimization eliminates the need for loop control at runtime, making the code more efficient.

Expression Reordering

Compilers also manipulate the AST to reorder expressions for better performance. This might involve applying mathematical transformations, such as reordering addition or multiplication to minimize computation. For example, in the case of floating-point arithmetic, some operations are more expensive than others, and reordering the AST to prioritize less costly operations can help optimize the execution time.

Consider the expression:

```
(x * y) + (z * w)
```

In some cases, the compiler may decide that factoring out common subexpressions or reordering terms in a different order would yield better performance. The AST might be transformed into a new structure like this:

```
(x + z) * (y + w)
```

This transformation could lead to fewer computational steps depending on the situation.

Intermediate Code Generation

Once the AST is optimized and manipulated, compilers typically generate intermediate code, often represented as three-address code or intermediate representations (IR). These representations are closer to machine code but still abstract enough to allow for optimization and machine-independent transformations. This intermediate code is easier to manipulate than the high-level source code, and the compiler can further optimize it before generating the final machine code.

For example, the code x + y might be translated into an intermediate representation as:

```
t1 = x + y
```

This allows subsequent optimizations like register allocation and instruction selection to be performed efficiently.

AST manipulation is a key process in compiler design, enabling code optimization, transformation, and the generation of efficient intermediate representations. Through techniques such as code simplification, loop unrolling, expression reordering, and intermediate code generation, compilers are able to produce highly optimized machine code. Understanding AST manipulation is crucial for improving the performance and efficiency of software.

Optimizing Declarative Code Execution

Optimizing declarative code execution involves improving the efficiency of code while preserving the declarative nature of the logic. In declarative programming, developers describe *what* they want the program to do, rather than focusing on *how* to do it. While this leads to cleaner, more readable code, it may not always be the most efficient for performance. Optimizations are crucial in ensuring that the declarative code executes in an optimal manner, balancing readability with performance.

In this section, we will explore how declarative code can be optimized, especially in the context of Abstract Syntax Trees (ASTs), and provide examples of how to enhance performance.

Optimizing Database Queries

In many declarative applications, especially those dealing with databases, queries must be optimized to reduce time and resources. A common scenario is using SQL in a declarative way to express data retrieval tasks. To optimize such declarative code, we can rely on AST manipulation to rewrite queries for better performance.

Consider a SQL query:

```
SELECT * FROM employees WHERE department = 'Sales' AND age > 30
```

While this query might be declarative and simple, it's not necessarily optimized. The declarative approach allows for optimizations like indexing or filtering in the query execution plan, which are typically handled by the database's query planner. However, at a higher level, we can manually optimize certain aspects before passing the query to the database.

In Python, a higher-level approach might involve automatically translating an AST representing such a query into a more efficient form by selecting appropriate indices or breaking down the query into smaller, more manageable subqueries. This could be done programmatically by using libraries such as SQLAlchemy for SQL generation and optimization.

```
from sqlalchemy import select, Table, MetaData

metadata = MetaData()
employees = Table('employees', metadata, autoload_with=engine)

query = select([employees]).where(employees.c.department ==
        'Sales').where(employees.c.age > 30)
```

In this Python example, the ORM (Object Relational Mapping) framework automatically handles some optimizations, but manual adjustments may still be necessary to further optimize database queries.

Loop Optimization in Functional Programming

Another way to optimize declarative code is by improving how loops and iterations are handled, especially in functional programming. A key feature of functional programming is the use of higher-order functions like map, filter, and reduce, which allow data to be transformed declaratively. However, these functions often involve repeated processing that could be optimized.

Consider a declarative function that sums a list of numbers in a functional programming style:

```
numbers = [1, 2, 3, 4, 5]
result = sum(map(lambda x: x**2, numbers))
```

In this case, the map function applies a lambda to each number in the list, and sum calculates the total. While this is a simple and declarative approach, it may be inefficient for large datasets because it applies the lambda and sum separately.

To optimize, we could combine the operations into one traversal of the list. By combining the power of map and sum into a single loop, we avoid multiple iterations over the dataset.

```
result = sum(x**2 for x in numbers)
```

Here, we use a generator expression to square each number and calculate the sum in one pass. This minimizes the overhead of creating an additional list, improving performance.

Memoization for Declarative Functions

In declarative code, certain calculations may be repeated multiple times, which can lead to inefficiency. A simple optimization technique to handle this is memoization—storing the results of expensive function calls and reusing the results when the same inputs occur again.

In Python, we can implement memoization using a decorator:

```
from functools import lru_cache

@lru_cache(maxsize=None)
def expensive_function(n):
    # Simulating an expensive computation
    return n * n
```

Here, the @lru_cache decorator ensures that results of expensive_function are cached, which speeds up subsequent calls with the same argument. Memoization reduces the number of redundant calculations, making the code more efficient without altering the declarative nature of the logic.

Lazy Evaluation for Optimization

Another optimization technique is lazy evaluation, which delays computation until the result is actually needed. This technique can be particularly useful when working with large datasets, as it prevents the program from unnecessarily evaluating all values at once.

In Python, lazy evaluation can be achieved using generators. For instance, instead of evaluating all elements of a list immediately, you can create a generator that computes values only when they are requested:

```python
def lazy_sum(numbers):
    for number in numbers:
        yield number * 2

lazy_result = lazy_sum(range(1, 1000))
```

In this case, lazy_sum only calculates values when they are needed, allowing for the optimization of memory and processing time.

Optimizing declarative code execution is essential for improving performance without sacrificing the clarity and expressiveness of declarative logic. Techniques such as query optimization, loop optimization, memoization, and lazy evaluation can significantly improve the efficiency of declarative programs. By manipulating the AST and applying these optimization strategies, we ensure that declarative code runs as efficiently as possible while preserving its readability and high-level abstraction.

Module 23:
Optimization Techniques for Declarative Processing

Module 23, "Optimization Techniques for Declarative Processing," delves into various methods to enhance the performance of declarative programming. By focusing on techniques such as memoization, lazy evaluation, parallelism, and handling state in a declarative manner, this module highlights how declarative programs can be optimized while maintaining readability and clarity. These optimization techniques are essential for improving the efficiency and scalability of declarative systems, especially in the context of functional programming and data-driven applications.

Memoization and Caching Strategies

Memoization is a powerful optimization technique used to speed up programs by storing the results of expensive function calls and reusing the cached results when the same inputs occur again. In declarative programming, where functions are treated as first-class citizens, memoization helps prevent redundant computations, which can significantly enhance performance. It is particularly useful when dealing with recursive functions or functions that are repeatedly called with the same arguments. Caching strategies, such as least-recently-used (LRU) caches, can further enhance the efficiency of memoization by limiting the size of the cache and ensuring that only the most recently accessed results are stored. By employing memoization and caching, developers can reduce the overhead of function calls and improve the execution speed of declarative programs.

Lazy Evaluation in Functional Programming

Lazy evaluation is a technique in which expressions are not evaluated until their results are required. In functional programming, lazy evaluation enables the creation of efficient, memory-conscious programs by delaying computations and avoiding unnecessary evaluations. This is particularly useful when working with large datasets, streams, or infinite sequences, as it prevents the program from evaluating values that will not be used. Lazy evaluation allows for the construction of efficient data pipelines that compute values only when needed, reducing both memory consumption and processing time. When implemented effectively, lazy evaluation enhances the declarative nature of functional programming by allowing the program to focus on expressing logic rather than managing execution details.

Parallelism and Dataflow Optimization

Parallelism and dataflow optimization are critical for improving the performance of declarative systems, especially when dealing with large-scale data processing. Parallelism allows for the concurrent execution of tasks, which can dramatically speed up the processing of data-intensive operations. In declarative programming, parallelism can be achieved by dividing the computation into independent tasks that can run concurrently. Dataflow optimization, on the other hand, involves improving the flow of data between different components of a program, ensuring that data is processed in the most efficient manner possible. In functional programming, this often involves ensuring that data transformations are applied in parallel, taking advantage of multi-core processors. By optimizing parallelism and dataflow, declarative programs can process large volumes of data more efficiently and scale better under heavy workloads.

Handling State in a Declarative Manner

In declarative programming, managing state can be challenging since the paradigm focuses on expressing *what* should happen, rather than detailing the steps to achieve it. However, many real-world applications require the management of state, such as tracking the values of variables or maintaining data persistence across function calls. The challenge lies in managing state while preserving the declarative nature of the program. One common approach is using immutable data structures, which prevent direct modification of state and encourage the use of pure functions. Another approach is employing concepts like functional reactive programming (FRP) and the use of state monads, which allow for state handling in a declarative way. These approaches ensure that state transitions are explicit and predictable, maintaining the declarative nature of the code while enabling efficient state management.

Module 23 highlights essential optimization techniques for improving the performance and scalability of declarative programs. Memoization, lazy evaluation, parallelism, and state management are all vital strategies for making declarative code more efficient while preserving its clarity and simplicity. By understanding and applying these techniques, developers can ensure their declarative programs are both high-level and performant.

Memoization and Caching Strategies

Memoization is a technique used to optimize the performance of functions by storing the results of expensive function calls and reusing them when the same inputs occur again. In declarative programming, where functions are first-class citizens, memoization can prevent redundant computations, leading to efficiency gains. In Python, we can implement memoization using a decorator or by using built-in caching mechanisms like functools.lru_cache.

Here's a Python example of memoization using the functools.lru_cache decorator:

```python
import functools

@functools.lru_cache(maxsize=None)   # Cache all results without limit
def fibonacci(n):
    if n < 2:
        return n
```

```
    return fibonacci(n-1) + fibonacci(n-2)

print(fibonacci(35))  # This will be much faster after the first computation
```

In the example above, the fibonacci function uses memoization to avoid recalculating the same Fibonacci numbers repeatedly. The @functools.lru_cache decorator stores previously computed values, significantly reducing the time complexity.

Additionally, developers can implement their caching strategies, especially when custom behavior is needed. Here's an example of a simple caching mechanism without the functools module:

```
def memoize(func):
    cache = {}
    def wrapper(*args):
        if args in cache:
            return cache[args]
        result = func(*args)
        cache[args] = result
        return result
    return wrapper

@memoize
def expensive_function(x, y):
    print("Computing...")
    return x * y

print(expensive_function(5, 10))  # Computes the result
print(expensive_function(5, 10))  # Returns cached result, no computation
```

In this example, the memoize function defines a simple cache to store the results of the expensive_function. When the function is called with the same arguments, the result is returned from the cache, saving computational resources.

Caching, when used properly, helps reduce redundant computations, making programs more efficient. However, developers need to consider the trade-offs in terms of memory usage. If a function has many different input values and doesn't benefit from caching (i.e., inputs rarely repeat), the cache may consume more memory than the performance gains it provides. It's important to analyze the use case and decide on the appropriate cache size or strategy.

When memoization is used in functional programming, especially with immutable data and pure functions, it ensures that the declarative nature of the program is maintained. This approach allows for optimizations without introducing side effects, keeping the code clean and predictable.

Memoization and caching are essential optimization techniques in declarative programming, especially when handling costly recursive computations or large datasets. Properly applying these strategies can significantly improve performance without compromising code clarity or purity.

Lazy Evaluation in Functional Programming

221

Lazy evaluation is an optimization technique used primarily in functional programming, where expressions are not evaluated until their values are actually needed. This strategy allows for the deferral of computation, which can be useful for handling potentially expensive operations in a more efficient manner. In declarative programming, lazy evaluation promotes efficiency by avoiding unnecessary computations, particularly when working with large data structures or infinite sequences.

In Python, lazy evaluation can be achieved using generators. A generator allows the function to yield values one by one, pausing between each yield and only resuming when the next value is requested. This ensures that values are produced only as needed, making it an excellent tool for working with potentially infinite or large data streams.

Here's an example of lazy evaluation using a Python generator:

```
def generate_numbers():
    n = 0
    while True:
        yield n
        n += 1

gen = generate_numbers()
print(next(gen))  # Prints 0
print(next(gen))  # Prints 1
print(next(gen))  # Prints 2
```

In this example, the generate_numbers function produces an infinite sequence of numbers. The values are computed lazily: the next number is not generated until the next() function is called. This allows the program to handle large or infinite data sequences efficiently, as only the required values are generated at any given time.

Lazy evaluation also allows the composition of computations that may not be fully evaluated unless necessary. A common use case is working with large data sets or computations that could be expensive if fully evaluated upfront. The following is an example of chaining lazy computations:

```
def even_numbers(start):
    while True:
        if start % 2 == 0:
            yield start
        start += 1

def square_numbers(start):
    while True:
        yield start * start
        start += 1

even_gen = even_numbers(2)
squared_gen = square_numbers(1)

for _ in range(5):
    print(next(even_gen), next(squared_gen))
```

In this case, two sequences are generated lazily: even numbers and their squares. The generator functions yield values one at a time, with the sequence only progressing when the next value is requested. This allows for chaining complex operations without generating the entire sequence upfront, saving both memory and processing power.

Lazy evaluation is particularly useful when working with large-scale data processing, such as data pipelines, where not all of the data is needed at once. It can also be an excellent tool for optimizing recursive functions that deal with potentially infinite data structures, such as streams or trees, where calculations can be deferred and executed only when necessary.

Lazy evaluation is a powerful technique that promotes efficiency in functional programming. By deferring computation until values are required, lazy evaluation reduces unnecessary work and can handle large datasets or infinite structures with ease. In declarative programming, it helps maintain a clean, functional approach while optimizing performance.

Parallelism and Dataflow Optimization

Parallelism and dataflow optimization are crucial techniques in declarative programming for improving performance, particularly when handling large datasets or computationally intensive tasks. These techniques allow a program to divide work into smaller independent units that can be processed concurrently, reducing execution time and enhancing efficiency. In declarative programming, where the focus is often on expressing the logic of a computation rather than its control flow, parallelism and dataflow optimization can provide significant performance improvements without complicating the program's structure.

Parallelism in declarative programming involves executing different parts of a computation simultaneously. This is particularly effective for tasks that can be broken down into independent sub-tasks, such as data processing, mathematical computations, or simulations. Modern programming languages, including Python, provide libraries and frameworks for implementing parallelism, such as concurrent.futures, multiprocessing, and parallel libraries like joblib.

For example, the concurrent.futures library in Python allows for parallel execution of functions across multiple threads or processes, making it easy to distribute tasks in a declarative manner. The following code demonstrates how you can use parallelism to apply a function across multiple elements in a list:

```python
import concurrent.futures

def square(x):
    return x * x

nums = [1, 2, 3, 4, 5]

with concurrent.futures.ThreadPoolExecutor() as executor:
    results = list(executor.map(square, nums))

print(results)  # Output: [1, 4, 9, 16, 25]
```

223

In this example, the ThreadPoolExecutor is used to execute the square function concurrently for each element in the list nums. The executor.map method maps the function to each element in the list and handles the parallel execution behind the scenes, ensuring that each task is processed simultaneously.

Dataflow optimization takes this concept further by focusing on how data is passed through a system. In declarative programming, dataflow optimization aims to reduce redundant data processing and ensure that computations are only performed when necessary. By analyzing how data flows between components, unnecessary dependencies can be removed, and tasks can be restructured to minimize bottlenecks.

In Python, libraries like Dask provide advanced dataflow optimization techniques, allowing for the parallel and distributed execution of complex data transformations. These libraries enable users to define a computation graph, which can be optimized by the framework to minimize redundant computation and efficiently distribute tasks across multiple processes or machines.

Here's an example of a simple dataflow optimization using Dask:

```
import dask.array as da

x = da.from_array([1, 2, 3, 4, 5], chunks=2)
y = x + 1  # Deferred operation
result = y.compute()

print(result)  # Output: [2 3 4 5 6]
```

In this example, the computation x + 1 is deferred until y.compute() is called. Dask optimizes the dataflow by scheduling and executing the operation in parallel, without performing redundant calculations. This optimization allows the code to handle larger-than-memory datasets efficiently and can be extended to more complex computations, such as matrix operations or machine learning algorithms.

Parallelism and dataflow optimization are essential techniques in declarative programming to improve performance. By distributing tasks across multiple threads or processes and optimizing how data flows through the system, these techniques allow for efficient computation and resource utilization, making them ideal for large-scale data processing and computationally intensive tasks.

Handling State in a Declarative Manner

In declarative programming, handling state is a challenge because of the paradigm's focus on expressing computations without explicit control flow or mutable state. Declarative programming models, such as functional programming, emphasize immutability and pure functions, which do not change state or have side effects. However, certain tasks—especially those involving complex systems or user interfaces—often require some form of state management. The key is to handle state in a way that aligns with the principles of declarative programming, such as immutability and transparency.

224

One of the primary techniques for handling state in declarative systems is the use of immutable data structures. These structures cannot be altered once they are created, which means that any "modification" results in the creation of a new data structure with the updated values. This approach avoids side effects, which are typically associated with mutable state, and ensures that the state is explicit and predictable. Languages like Haskell and functional libraries in Python, such as Pyrsistent and Immutable, provide tools to work with immutable data structures.

For example, consider how you would represent a simple counter in an immutable manner:

```python
from pyrsistent import v

# Original immutable state
state = v(1, 2, 3)

# "Modifying" state: create a new version
new_state = state.append(4)

print(state)        # Output: v(1, 2, 3)
print(new_state)    # Output: v(1, 2, 3, 4)
```

In this example, the state is represented as an immutable list. When we attempt to add a new element, it doesn't modify the original list but instead creates a new version with the updated value. This ensures that the state transitions are transparent and traceable, a critical feature in declarative programming.

Another approach to handling state in a declarative manner is through state monads or similar abstractions. A monad encapsulates a value and allows for computation with that value while ensuring that state changes are managed in a controlled, predictable way. In functional programming languages like Haskell, monads are frequently used to handle side effects, including state.

In Python, while there are no built-in monads, similar abstractions can be created to manage state transitions in a controlled manner. For example, a simple state monad might encapsulate a function that carries state through a series of transformations:

```python
class StateMonad:
    def __init__(self, state):
        self.state = state

    def bind(self, func):
        new_state = func(self.state)
        return StateMonad(new_state)

    def get_state(self):
        return self.state

# Example usage: incrementing a state
def increment(state):
    return state + 1

state_monad = StateMonad(0)
new_state = state_monad.bind(increment).bind(increment)
print(new_state.get_state())  # Output: 2
```

225

In this example, the StateMonad allows the encapsulation of state changes, and the bind method chains transformations in a declarative manner. This approach keeps the state handling abstracted away from the logic of the program and ensures that state transitions are explicit and clean.

Another technique is the use of functional reactive programming (FRP) or state-driven UI frameworks, where state changes are modeled as streams of data or signals that can be observed and reacted to declaratively. In frameworks like RxPy for Python or React for JavaScript, components automatically update when the state changes, offering a clear way to handle state in a declarative programming style.

Handling state in a declarative manner can be accomplished by using immutable data structures, monads, and reactive programming paradigms. These techniques ensure that state transitions are explicit, predictable, and transparent, aligning with the core principles of declarative programming and allowing for clean, manageable code even in complex systems.

Module 24:

Pattern Matching and Rule-Based Execution

Module 24 delves into the principles of declarative pattern matching and rule-based execution, emphasizing their application in programming languages, expert systems, and machine learning. The module provides an exploration of how declarative approaches to pattern matching simplify logic and decision-making. We will also explore the role of rule-based systems, decision trees, and constraints in AI and machine learning.

Declarative Pattern Matching in Programming

Declarative pattern matching allows developers to express logic concisely and clearly by describing patterns that data structures or expressions must match. Unlike traditional imperative approaches, which focus on explicit instructions, declarative pattern matching defines the desired outcomes based on structural or value matches. In programming languages like Python, pattern matching has gained traction with its introduction in Python 3.10, offering a clean and powerful syntax for matching complex data structures. This style promotes readability and helps prevent errors by abstracting intricate control flow logic. Pattern matching supports the notion of conditionally matching values based on specific patterns or properties, making programs more concise and declarative.

Rule-Based Systems and Expert Systems

A rule-based system operates on predefined "rules" to make decisions based on input. These systems use a set of "if-then" statements or rules, which are evaluated and applied to derive conclusions or take actions. Expert systems, a subclass of rule-based systems, replicate the decision-making abilities of a human expert by using a vast knowledge base of rules. The declarative nature of rule-based systems allows users to define the rules independently of the underlying implementation, making these systems easy to modify and extend. The advantage of rule-based systems lies in their ability to separate business logic from the application code, enabling flexible and maintainable systems.

Constraint Logic and Decision Trees

Constraint logic programming integrates rules with constraints that define the relationships between variables, ensuring that solutions meet certain criteria. By utilizing logical relationships, constraint logic can narrow down the search space for solutions, leading to efficient decision-making. This method is particularly useful in solving problems like scheduling, resource allocation, and optimization. Decision trees, another form of declarative logic, represent a hierarchical model of decisions where each node represents a test or decision. The branches represent the possible outcomes, and the leaves represent the decisions or classifications. These trees are crucial in decision-making processes, particularly in machine learning applications like classification and regression tasks.

Applications in Machine Learning and AI

In the fields of machine learning and AI, declarative pattern matching, rule-based systems, and constraint logic play critical roles in enabling intelligent systems. Rule-based reasoning allows AI to make decisions by applying learned or predefined rules to a given problem space. Constraint-based systems help optimize machine learning algorithms by narrowing down feasible solution sets. In machine learning, decision trees are widely used for classification tasks, where the structure of the tree defines decision boundaries and classification rules. Furthermore, pattern matching is integral to natural language processing (NLP) and image recognition, where the system identifies and acts upon specific patterns in the data.

Module 24 provides a deep dive into how declarative programming paradigms such as pattern matching, rule-based systems, and decision trees improve the expressiveness and efficiency of problem-solving in AI and machine learning. The integration of these techniques enables simpler, more readable logic in complex applications, leading to improved system performance and decision-making capabilities.

Declarative Pattern Matching in Programming

Declarative pattern matching simplifies code logic by allowing developers to express rules and conditions in a clear, high-level manner. This feature, which is now available in several programming languages such as Python, offers a powerful way to inspect and manipulate data structures without resorting to lengthy conditionals or loops. Instead of explicitly stating how to manipulate data, developers define patterns that the language runtime matches against the data. Pattern matching enables cleaner and more maintainable code, especially when dealing with complex data structures like lists, tuples, or dictionaries. Python's pattern matching (introduced in version 3.10) allows for matching specific values, structures, or properties of data, making the code more expressive and less error-prone.

The beauty of declarative pattern matching lies in its readability and conciseness. For instance, instead of manually checking conditions using if-else statements, you can declaratively match values to a pattern. This reduces boilerplate code and enhances the clarity of the developer's intentions. Pattern matching is a natural fit for handling data structures that can have multiple variations or cases, such as working with tree-like structures or handling different formats in APIs. In addition, pattern matching supports more advanced use cases, such as guard clauses or combining multiple conditions into a single match.

One key advantage of declarative pattern matching is its potential for exhaustive checking. By defining all the possible cases for a structure, developers can ensure that no case is left unhandled. This increases the robustness of the code and reduces the likelihood of missing edge cases. Furthermore, because patterns are evaluated declaratively, they offer a more logical structure for problem-solving, rather than focusing on the implementation details.

Here is an example of declarative pattern matching in Python, introduced in version 3.10:

```python
def shape_area(shape):
    match shape:
        case {"type": "circle", "radius": r}:
            return 3.14 * r * r
        case {"type": "square", "side": s}:
            return s * s
        case {"type": "triangle", "base": b, "height": h}:
            return 0.5 * b * h
        case _:
            raise ValueError("Unknown shape")

# Testing the function
print(shape_area({"type": "circle", "radius": 5}))  # Output: 78.5
print(shape_area({"type": "square", "side": 4}))    # Output: 16
print(shape_area({"type": "triangle", "base": 4, "height": 6}))  # Output: 12
```

In this example, the match statement is used to declaratively match a dictionary structure containing information about different shapes. Instead of multiple if-elif conditions, each shape is matched to a specific pattern. The case blocks correspond to specific patterns for a circle, square, or triangle, and the area calculation is performed accordingly. If an unrecognized shape is passed, the _ wildcard is used to catch all unmatched cases and raise an error.

Overall, declarative pattern matching encourages the use of higher-level abstractions and improves code clarity. It also supports easier maintenance and debugging by reducing the complexity of branching logic and enhancing the natural flow of control through the program. As programming languages continue to adopt more declarative features, pattern matching will likely remain a key tool in simplifying complex decision-making logic.

Rule-Based Systems and Expert Systems

Rule-based systems and expert systems represent a significant aspect of declarative programming, focusing on decision-making through a set of rules. These systems are structured around the **if-then** rule format, which allows for automatic inference based on predefined facts and rules. Rule-based systems consist of two primary components: facts and rules. The facts are the data or knowledge that the system operates on, while the rules define relationships or actions that apply when certain conditions are met. In expert systems, rules are crafted by domain experts, enabling the system to mimic expert decision-making.

Expert systems differ from basic rule-based systems in their scope and complexity. While both use rules for decision-making, expert systems are more focused on emulating the reasoning of a human expert in a specific domain. The rules in an expert system represent the knowledge of domain professionals, and the system applies these rules to interpret new facts and make decisions. A key strength of expert systems is their ability to handle complex scenarios, providing decisions that are transparent and based on documented rules.

A simple example of a rule-based system can be a medical diagnostic system. The system can be set up with rules that assess patient symptoms and suggest potential diagnoses. Below is a basic implementation using Python's rule-based approach for decision-making:

```python
class RuleBasedSystem:
    def __init__(self):
        self.facts = []

    def add_fact(self, fact):
        self.facts.append(fact)

    def evaluate(self):
        if "fever" in self.facts and "cough" in self.facts:
            return "Possible Flu"
        elif "shortness of breath" in self.facts and "chest pain" in self.facts:
            return "Possible Heart Attack"
        else:
            return "No Diagnosis"

# Example usage
patient = RuleBasedSystem()
patient.add_fact("fever")
patient.add_fact("cough")

diagnosis = patient.evaluate()
print(f"Diagnosis: {diagnosis}")
```

In this example, the system checks the presence of certain facts (like "fever" and "cough") to determine the diagnosis. The rules are hardcoded as simple conditions that map to possible diagnoses. This structure mimics the process of expert reasoning, where facts (the symptoms) are matched to known diagnoses (the rules). The inference engine evaluates these conditions to draw conclusions based on the provided facts.

Expert systems, on the other hand, involve a more sophisticated approach to handle complex problem-solving. The rules are typically structured using a more robust rule engine. Here's an extended example to show forward chaining (deductive reasoning) and backward chaining (goal-driven reasoning) approaches in rule-based systems:

```python
class ExpertSystem:
    def __init__(self):
        self.rules = {
            "flu": ["fever", "cough"],
            "heart_attack": ["shortness of breath", "chest pain"]
        }
        self.facts = []

    def add_fact(self, fact):
        self.facts.append(fact)

    def forward_chaining(self):
```

```
    for disease, symptoms in self.rules.items():
        if all(symptom in self.facts for symptom in symptoms):
            return f"Diagnosis: {disease}"
    return "Diagnosis: Unknown"

# Example usage
patient = ExpertSystem()
patient.add_fact("fever")
patient.add_fact("cough")

diagnosis = patient.forward_chaining()
print(f"Diagnosis: {diagnosis}")
```

In this code, the ExpertSystem class evaluates a patient's symptoms using a forward chaining mechanism. The system checks the facts against predefined rules to deduce a possible diagnosis. If all required symptoms for a disease are found in the facts, it triggers a diagnosis.

These systems offer transparency and flexibility in decision-making, enabling easy updates to rules without changing the underlying system logic. By mimicking human expertise, rule-based systems provide efficient solutions in a wide range of applications, from diagnostics to financial planning and automated customer service. As rule-based systems continue to evolve, they will increasingly play a critical role in AI and machine learning, offering insights through clear and interpretable decision-making processes.

Constraint Logic and Decision Trees

Constraint logic and decision trees are two powerful concepts within declarative programming that facilitate decision-making and problem-solving through constraints and hierarchical decision structures. Both approaches aim to reduce the complexity of computational models by providing a clear, systematic method of reasoning based on a set of conditions or constraints.

Constraint Logic

Constraint logic is a declarative paradigm where solutions to problems are defined by a set of constraints that must be satisfied. Rather than explicitly defining how to solve the problem, the system simply specifies the conditions that must hold true. The process of finding a solution involves determining values for variables that meet all the specified constraints. This paradigm is used extensively in fields like optimization, scheduling, and resource allocation, where constraints define permissible solutions.

For example, consider a constraint satisfaction problem (CSP) where a set of variables (e.g., hours of work, tasks to be completed) needs to be assigned values that satisfy a set of constraints (e.g., no task can overlap with another, total hours cannot exceed a limit). Constraint solvers utilize algorithms such as backtracking or constraint propagation to find solutions that satisfy all constraints.

Here's an example of using constraint logic in Python to solve a simple problem, such as assigning time slots to tasks:

```python
from constraint import Problem, AllDifferentConstraint

# Create a problem instance
problem = Problem()

# Add variables (task names) with possible time slot values
problem.addVariable('Task1', [1, 2, 3])
problem.addVariable('Task2', [1, 2, 3])
problem.addVariable('Task3', [1, 2, 3])

# Add constraint that no two tasks can share the same time slot
problem.addConstraint(AllDifferentConstraint)

# Get solutions
solutions = problem.getSolutions()

# Print solutions
print(f"Possible Assignments: {solutions}")
```

In this example, the tasks are assigned to different time slots with the constraint that no two tasks can share the same time slot. The constraint solver will find all valid assignments that satisfy the conditions. Constraint logic, as demonstrated, makes it possible to express the problem in a highly declarative manner.

Decision Trees

Decision trees are a hierarchical model used for classification and regression tasks, where decisions are made based on a sequence of conditions. Each node in a decision tree represents a decision based on a particular attribute, and each branch represents the outcome of that decision, leading to further conditions or final classifications. Decision trees are intuitive, interpretable, and often used in machine learning for tasks like decision analysis, classification, and predictive modeling.

The basic idea behind a decision tree is that it splits data into subsets based on attributes, creating a tree-like structure where each branch represents a decision or test. The tree is built recursively by choosing the attribute that best splits the data at each node, and the tree terminates when it reaches a leaf node, which provides a classification or decision.

Here is a simple example in Python that demonstrates how a decision tree can be used to classify animals based on features:

```python
class DecisionTree:
    def __init__(self):
        self.tree = {}

    def fit(self, data):
        for sample in data:
            if sample["has_wings"]:
                self.tree["classification"] = "Bird"
            else:
                self.tree["classification"] = "Mammal"
```

```
    def predict(self, sample):
        if sample["has_wings"]:
            return "Bird"
        else:
            return "Mammal"

# Sample data
data = [
    {"has_wings": True, "classification": "Bird"},
    {"has_wings": False, "classification": "Mammal"}
]

# Create and train the decision tree
tree = DecisionTree()
tree.fit(data)

# Test prediction
sample = {"has_wings": True}
prediction = tree.predict(sample)
print(f"Prediction: {prediction}")
```

In this simple decision tree, we classify animals as either birds or mammals based on whether they have wings. The decision tree makes predictions by testing a condition (has_wings) and classifying the sample accordingly.

Applications in AI and Machine Learning

Both constraint logic and decision trees have significant applications in AI and machine learning. In AI, constraint logic is used in planning, scheduling, and solving optimization problems. Decision trees, on the other hand, are widely used in supervised machine learning algorithms, such as in the construction of classifiers and regression models. For example, decision trees form the basis of more complex algorithms like random forests and gradient boosting machines, which are widely used for their accuracy and interpretability.

Together, constraint logic and decision trees provide powerful declarative tools for decision-making and problem-solving. These paradigms help simplify complex tasks, such as optimization, classification, and scheduling, by focusing on constraints or hierarchical decision structures, making them integral to many real-world AI applications.

Applications in Machine Learning and AI

Pattern matching, rule-based systems, and decision trees are extensively applied in Machine Learning (ML) and Artificial Intelligence (AI), providing robust solutions for decision-making, automation, and pattern recognition. These techniques offer structured ways to simplify reasoning, data extraction, and model interpretation in AI tasks such as classification, inference, and optimization.

Pattern Matching in AI

Pattern matching in AI enables systems to detect and process patterns in data. It's widely used in natural language processing (NLP), image recognition, and symbolic reasoning. AI systems utilize pattern matching to match predefined patterns with incoming data, making problem-solving more efficient.

Consider an example in NLP, where pattern matching is used for tasks like part-of-speech tagging. Here, predefined patterns are used to identify words or phrases in a sentence. The system matches these patterns to identify syntactic structures, like identifying a verb or noun in a sentence.

Example:

```
import re

def tag_parts_of_speech(sentence):
    patterns = [
        (r'\b(is|am|are)\b', 'Verb'),
        (r'\b(I|you|he|she|they)\b', 'Pronoun'),
        (r'\b([A-Za-z]+)\b', 'Noun')
    ]

    tags = []
    for pattern, tag in patterns:
        matches = re.findall(pattern, sentence)
        tags.extend([(match, tag) for match in matches])

    return tags

sentence = "I am a student"
print(tag_parts_of_speech(sentence))
```

Rule-Based Systems in AI

Rule-based systems form the foundation of expert systems in AI. They use "if-then" logic to simulate expert knowledge and provide solutions for decision-making tasks. By matching input conditions against a set of predefined rules, these systems deduce conclusions or recommend actions.

Example: A basic rule-based medical diagnosis system could be built using predefined symptoms and diagnostic rules. If a set of symptoms matches a rule, the system outputs a diagnosis.

```
def diagnose(symptoms):
    rules = {
        'Cold': ['cough', 'sore throat', 'runny nose'],
        'Flu': ['fever', 'muscle aches', 'fatigue'],
        'COVID-19': ['fever', 'cough', 'shortness of breath']
    }

    diagnosis = []
    for condition, symptoms_set in rules.items():
        if all(symptom in symptoms for symptom in symptoms_set):
            diagnosis.append(condition)

    return diagnosis

symptoms = ['fever', 'cough', 'shortness of breath']
print(diagnose(symptoms))  # Outputs: ['COVID-19']
```

Decision Trees in AI and ML

Decision trees are one of the most common tools in both AI and machine learning. These trees break down data into decision nodes based on specific features, aiding in classification or regression. The simplicity and interpretability of decision trees make them a popular choice for building decision-making models.

In machine learning, decision trees are particularly useful for classification tasks. For example, a decision tree can predict whether a customer will buy a product based on various features such as age, income, and previous purchasing behavior.

Example: Using scikit-learn, a popular machine learning library, we can create a simple decision tree model to classify data.

```
from sklearn.tree import DecisionTreeClassifier
from sklearn.datasets import load_iris
from sklearn.model_selection import train_test_split

# Load iris dataset
iris = load_iris()
X = iris.data
y = iris.target

# Split into training and testing sets
X_train, X_test, y_train, y_test = train_test_split(X, y, test_size=0.3)

# Initialize and train a decision tree classifier
clf = DecisionTreeClassifier()
clf.fit(X_train, y_train)

# Predict on the test set
y_pred = clf.predict(X_test)

# Accuracy of the model
accuracy = (y_pred == y_test).mean()
print(f"Accuracy: {accuracy:.2f}")
```

Integration in Machine Learning and AI Workflows

Pattern matching, rule-based systems, and decision trees are often integrated into larger AI models to create intelligent systems capable of handling complex tasks. In practice, a system like a chatbot can use pattern matching to understand user queries, apply rule-based systems for response generation, and use decision trees to recommend the best actions.

For example, a recommendation system might use a decision tree to analyze past user behaviors and predict which products a customer is likely to purchase next, or an autonomous driving system may use pattern matching to identify pedestrians and rule-based systems to make driving decisions.

The combination of pattern matching, rule-based systems, and decision trees plays a significant role in the development of AI and machine learning systems. These declarative techniques help build interpretable, efficient, and powerful models for a wide range of AI applications, from NLP to computer vision and autonomous systems.

Part 5:

Design Patterns and Real-World Case Studies in Declarative Programming

Declarative programming extends beyond theoretical constructs into practical design patterns and industry applications. This part explores **reusable patterns, machine learning pipelines, large-scale systems, business applications, and real-world case studies** demonstrating how declarative techniques streamline complex problem-solving. By focusing on structured methodologies and best practices, developers will gain a deeper appreciation of declarative programming's ability to enhance maintainability, scalability, and expressiveness. Through case studies and challenges, this section provides insight into applying declarative paradigms effectively in diverse domains, reinforcing their significance in **software engineering, cloud computing, AI, and business applications**.

Common Design Patterns in Declarative Programming

Declarative programming employs well-defined patterns that enhance code structure and reusability. **Monads and functors** simplify state management and encapsulate side effects in functional programming. **Pipes and streams** facilitate efficient dataflow processing, allowing composition of transformations. **Higher-order functions** enable powerful abstraction mechanisms for functional composition. **Declarative state management** patterns provide immutability and predictable updates, ensuring consistency in complex systems. Understanding these design patterns helps developers write modular, composable, and maintainable declarative code.

Declarative Machine Learning Pipelines

Machine learning benefits from declarative paradigms by **defining models, data transformations, and hyperparameter tuning declaratively**. Frameworks like TensorFlow and scikit-learn leverage declarative approaches for feature engineering and pipeline construction. **Hyperparameter tuning** relies on search spaces defined in a declarative manner, reducing manual effort. Deployment strategies incorporate **declarative model versioning and reproducibility**, ensuring consistent results across environments. This module covers how declarative principles streamline machine learning workflows, making AI systems more structured, scalable, and maintainable.

Declarative Programming in Large-Scale Systems

Large-scale systems utilize declarative programming to manage complexity efficiently. **Infrastructure as Code (IaC)** enables cloud automation with tools like Terraform and Kubernetes. **Declarative configuration management** ensures consistent software environments, reducing manual configuration drift. **Data pipelines** in distributed systems use declarative paradigms to process streaming data efficiently. **Event sourcing** in functional architectures tracks system state as immutable event logs, enabling auditability and resilience. Understanding these declarative approaches helps architects build robust, fault-tolerant, and scalable cloud and enterprise solutions.

Declarative Programming in Business Applications

Business applications leverage declarative techniques to enhance automation and decision-making. **Business rule engines** use declarative logic to drive enterprise automation in financial and operational processes. **Declarative financial modeling** simplifies risk assessment and forecasting through structured formulas and rule-based computations. **Decision support systems** rely on declarative reasoning to analyze and infer insights from structured data. **Knowledge representation** in AI-driven business applications enables intelligent automation. This module explores the role of declarative programming in improving efficiency, compliance, and decision-making in business environments.

Real-World Industry Case Studies

Real-world applications showcase the power of declarative programming across industries. **Declarative web development** enhances UI design and state management using frameworks like React and Vue.js. **Enterprise data processing** leverages SQL and XSLT for structured queries and transformations. **AI systems** implement declarative logic through expert systems and symbolic reasoning. **Blockchain smart contracts** utilize functional programming principles to enforce contract logic immutably. These case studies provide practical insights into how declarative paradigms solve complex problems, ensuring code maintainability, correctness, and scalability in diverse technological landscapes.

Challenges and Best Practices

Despite its advantages, declarative programming presents unique challenges. **Debugging and testing declarative code** require specialized approaches such as **property-based testing** and **logic-based verification**. **Performance optimization** in declarative systems focuses on **lazy evaluation, memoization, and parallelism** to enhance execution speed. **Hybrid approaches** integrate declarative and imperative paradigms to tackle real-world constraints. **Future-proofing declarative codebases** involves adhering to best practices for **readability, maintainability, and performance scalability**. Understanding these challenges and strategies helps developers navigate practical considerations when implementing declarative programming at scale.

This part equips learners with **design patterns, real-world applications, and best practices**, helping them build efficient, scalable, and maintainable declarative systems across **AI, business, web, and cloud computing**.

Module 25:
Common Design Patterns in Declarative Programming

This module explores the various design patterns employed in declarative programming. It covers essential concepts such as Monads, Functors, Pipes and Streams for dataflow, declarative state management, and higher-order functions. These patterns facilitate easier handling of side effects, control flow, and composition in functional and declarative paradigms.

Monads and Functors in Functional Programming

Monads and Functors are crucial abstractions in functional programming that help manage side effects and maintain compositional integrity in declarative code. A Functor allows for the mapping of functions over values in a context, like lists or Option types. A Monad, on the other hand, extends this concept by adding the ability to chain operations while encapsulating side effects such as I/O or state. Monads simplify the management of these side effects and maintain immutability by providing a clean way to sequence operations. These patterns allow for safe, reusable, and composable functional programming in complex systems.

Pipes and Streams for Dataflow

In declarative programming, the concept of Pipes and Streams is pivotal for modeling dataflow. Pipes allow data to flow through a series of processing stages, with each stage applying transformations to the data. Streams represent sequences of data that can be lazily evaluated, enabling efficient handling of large datasets or continuous data sources. This pattern is widely used in reactive programming and real-time data processing systems. The ability to compose different stages of transformation into a pipeline allows for clean, modular, and maintainable code, making it easier to reason about and scale.

Declarative State Management Patterns

State management is a critical concern in many declarative applications, particularly in functional programming, where immutability is often emphasized. Declarative state management patterns allow systems to model and track changes in state without resorting to imperative constructs. One common pattern is the use of immutable data structures that ensure that any state change results in the creation of a new state. Another key pattern involves event sourcing, where all state transitions are captured as a sequence of events, which can then be replayed or queried. These patterns help maintain consistency, predictability, and scalability in systems managing state in a declarative fashion.

Higher-Order Functions and Composition

Higher-order functions and function composition are foundational patterns in declarative programming, particularly in functional languages. A higher-order function is one that takes another function as an argument or returns a function as a result. Function composition allows developers to build complex operations by combining simpler functions into larger ones. These patterns enable cleaner, more modular code, making it easier to compose new functionality from existing code. They also promote reusability and abstraction, essential qualities for declarative systems that aim for readability and expressiveness. By composing smaller, focused functions, developers can create complex behavior without introducing unnecessary side effects.

The design patterns discussed in this module—Monads, Functors, Pipes, Streams, declarative state management, and higher-order functions—are essential tools for declarative programming. They help manage complexity, enhance composability, and maintain clean, maintainable, and predictable code. By mastering these patterns, developers can write more efficient, understandable, and modular declarative code.

Monads and Functors in Functional Programming

Monads and Functors are essential design patterns in functional programming, especially within declarative programming paradigms. They simplify managing side effects, maintain immutability, and promote functional composition. Here's an in-depth look at both patterns with code examples, particularly in Python.

Functors

A Functor is a design pattern that allows for mapping a function over a value wrapped in a container (context). It enables transformations without modifying the container structure. Functors are particularly useful when dealing with lists, Optionals, or other container types.

In Python, the concept of a Functor can be implemented using a custom class that mimics the map operation. Here's a simple implementation using lists:

```python
class Functor:
    def __init__(self, value):
        self.value = value

    def fmap(self, func):
        """Map a function over the contained value."""
        return Functor(func(self.value))

# Example usage:
f = Functor(5)
result = f.fmap(lambda x: x + 1)
print(result.value)  # Output: 6
```

In this example, Functor wraps a value, and the fmap method applies a transformation to that value while maintaining the context (the Functor).

A list is also a common example of a Functor:

```
# Using list as a Functor:
numbers = [1, 2, 3]
result = list(map(lambda x: x + 1, numbers))
print(result)  # Output: [2, 3, 4]
```

Here, the map function acts as fmap, applying the function to each element inside the list (the container).

Monads

Monads extend the concept of Functors by adding the ability to chain computations while maintaining context. In addition to fmap, Monads provide bind (often called flatMap in some languages), which is used to chain operations that return Monads.

Let's implement the Maybe Monad, a common Monad type that encapsulates computations that might fail:

```
class Maybe:
    def __init__(self, value):
        self.value = value

    def is_nothing(self):
        return self.value is None

    def bind(self, func):
        """Chain operations on the value if it's not None."""
        if self.is_nothing():
            return self
        return func(self.value)

    def __str__(self):
        return f"Maybe({self.value})"
# Example usage:
def safe_divide(x):
    """Perform division, return Maybe with result or None if error."""
    return Maybe(x / 2) if x != 0 else Maybe(None)

m = Maybe(4)
result = m.bind(safe_divide).bind(safe_divide)
print(result)  # Output: Maybe(1.0)
```

In this example, Maybe is a Monad that either contains a value (Maybe(value)) or represents a failure (Maybe(None)). The bind method chains operations, and if any operation results in None, the computation chain stops without throwing an error.

Practical Example Using Monads and Functors

Monads and Functors are useful for handling side effects or computations that may fail, like working with optional values, asynchronous calls, or handling errors. For example, combining both concepts allows for clean chaining of computations that manage state or error handling without needing explicit checks.

```
# Using both Functor and Monad
def safe_add(x):
    """Safe addition function that returns a Maybe."""
```
241

```
      return Maybe(x + 5) if x is not None else Maybe(None)

f = Functor(10)
result = f.fmap(lambda x: x * 2).fmap(safe_add).fmap(lambda x: x + 3)
print(result.value)  # Output: Maybe(23) -> result of fmap chaining
```

In this case, fmap is used to apply transformations on the value inside the Functor, while the Maybe Monad ensures any failure is gracefully handled, and computation continues only when valid.

Monads and Functors are crucial tools for declarative programming, enabling better handling of side effects, state, and error management. By using these patterns, code can be more modular, predictable, and easier to maintain. In Python, these concepts can be implemented to achieve clean, declarative, and functional programming styles.

Pipes and Streams for Dataflow

Pipes and Streams are powerful design patterns used in declarative programming to manage data flow efficiently and in a composable manner. These patterns enable a clean and functional approach to processing sequences of data without modifying the original data. They are particularly useful in scenarios where large data sets need to be processed step by step in a controlled manner, such as in data transformation pipelines.

The Pipe Pattern

The Pipe pattern allows functions to be chained together, where the output of one function becomes the input of the next. This enables a fluent and declarative approach to transforming data. In Python, this can be achieved by defining functions that accept data and return the modified data, using composition to chain them.

Consider a simple example of using pipes to transform a sequence of data:

```
def add_five(x):
    return x + 5

def multiply_by_three(x):
    return x * 3

def subtract_two(x):
    return x - 2

# Pipe composition
def pipe(data, *functions):
    for function in functions:
        data = function(data)
    return data

result = pipe(5, add_five, multiply_by_three, subtract_two)
print(result)  # Output: 28 (5 + 5 -> 10 * 3 -> 30 - 2 -> 28)
```

In this example, we define several transformation functions (add_five, multiply_by_three, subtract_two), then compose them using the pipe function. The pipe function takes an initial value and applies the transformations step by step, passing the result from one

242

function to the next. This approach is declarative, as it focuses on describing the sequence of transformations without needing to explicitly manage the flow.

Streams for Dataflow

Streams extend the idea of pipes by representing sequences of data as an ongoing flow, often with asynchronous processing. Streams can handle infinite or large data sources efficiently without loading all data into memory at once. They enable reactive or event-driven systems, such as reading from a file, handling web requests, or processing real-time data.

In Python, streams can be implemented using generators, which allow for lazy evaluation of data. Here's a simple example of using streams to process a large dataset:

```python
def stream_data():
    """A generator function simulating streaming data."""
    for i in range(1, 11):
        yield i

def transform_data(data):
    return data * 2

# Using stream and pipe pattern
stream = stream_data()
transformed_stream = map(transform_data, stream)

for item in transformed_stream:
    print(item)  # Output: 2, 4, 6, 8, 10, 12, 14, 16, 18, 20
```

In this example, stream_data is a generator function that yields data one item at a time. The map function is used to apply the transform_data function to each item of the stream as it is generated. This setup allows for efficient processing without holding all data in memory, demonstrating the power of streams for data flow.

Data Flow with Reactive Streams

For more complex data flow, such as handling events or asynchronous streams, Python's asyncio library and reactive programming patterns can be employed. Reactive streams allow for real-time data processing where computations react to data as it becomes available, often used in applications like real-time analytics or live data feeds.

```python
import asyncio

async def async_stream():
    for i in range(1, 6):
        await asyncio.sleep(1)  # Simulate delay
        yield i

async def process_stream():
    async for number in async_stream():
        print(number * 2)

# Run asynchronous stream processing
asyncio.run(process_stream())
```

Here, async_stream is an asynchronous generator that yields values with a delay. The process_stream function asynchronously processes the data, doubling each value and printing it. Using asynchronous streams helps manage real-time data and control flow efficiently.

Pipes and Streams are essential tools in declarative programming that help manage data flow with a clean, functional approach. They allow for composition, lazy evaluation, and efficient processing of sequences, which are especially useful in large-scale data transformations, reactive programming, and real-time data processing. These patterns help create more maintainable and efficient programs by focusing on what to compute rather than how to compute it.

Declarative State Management Patterns

State management is a crucial aspect of programming, particularly when dealing with complex applications. In declarative programming, state management focuses on expressing the logic of how data should be transformed or updated, rather than explicitly controlling the state change through imperative commands. Declarative state management patterns aim to reduce side effects, enhance maintainability, and make code easier to reason about.

Immutable State

One of the primary principles in declarative state management is immutability. When state is immutable, once a value is set, it cannot be changed. This prevents accidental modifications to data and ensures that the state remains consistent throughout the program. In declarative programming, the focus is on producing new state based on the current state, rather than modifying the existing one. This can be seen in functional programming, where functions return new versions of the data rather than altering the original data structure.

In Python, you can use immutable data structures like tuples and frozensets, and functions that return new instances of objects rather than changing them in place:

```
def update_state(state, value):
    return state + [value]

# Immutable state
state = [1, 2, 3]
new_state = update_state(state, 4)

print(state)       # Output: [1, 2, 3]
print(new_state)   # Output: [1, 2, 3, 4]
```

In this example, the original state list is left unchanged. Instead, the update_state function returns a new list with the added value, adhering to the principle of immutability.

State as a Function

Another common pattern in declarative state management is treating state as a function. In this approach, the state is defined as a function of its inputs, which makes it easier to predict and trace the evolution of state over time. State transitions can be modeled as functions that accept the current state as input and return the new state. This functional approach is key in declarative programming because it eliminates side effects and provides clear, predictable behavior.

For example, consider a simple state transition model that updates the state of a user's account:

```python
def account_state(current_balance, transaction_amount):
    return current_balance + transaction_amount

# Applying state transitions
initial_balance = 100
new_balance = account_state(initial_balance, -30)  # Withdraw 30

print(new_balance)  # Output: 70
```

Here, the function account_state takes the current balance and transaction amount as arguments and returns the new balance, reflecting the state transition. The state is represented declaratively through a pure function, making it easy to reason about and test.

Declarative UI State Management

State management is also a fundamental concept in building user interfaces (UIs), particularly in frameworks that emphasize declarative programming like React or Vue. In declarative UI programming, the state is not directly modified by the user interface, but instead, the UI is re-rendered based on changes to the state. This allows the UI to always reflect the current state without requiring manual manipulation of the DOM.

In Python, you can achieve a similar declarative approach in UI frameworks like Tkinter or Dash, where state changes automatically trigger UI updates. For example, in Dash, the layout is defined declaratively, and changes in the state are automatically reflected in the UI:

```python
import dash
from dash import dcc, html
from dash.dependencies import Input, Output

app = dash.Dash(__name__)

app.layout = html.Div([
    dcc.Slider(id='slider', min=0, max=100, step=1, value=50),
    html.Div(id='output')
])

@app.callback(
    Output('output', 'children'),
    [Input('slider', 'value')]
)
def update_output(value):
    return f'Slider Value: {value}'
```

```
if __name__ == '__main__':
    app.run_server(debug=True)
```

In this Dash application, the state is managed declaratively. The slider's value is automatically bound to the output, and when the slider value changes, the UI updates without needing to manually manage state transitions.

Declarative state management patterns provide a structured way to handle data and state transitions while avoiding the complexity and unpredictability of mutable state. By focusing on immutability, treating state as a function, and using frameworks that support declarative UI patterns, developers can write cleaner, more maintainable code. This approach not only simplifies state management but also enhances the predictability and testability of programs.

Higher-Order Functions and Composition

In declarative programming, higher-order functions and composition are powerful tools for creating flexible, reusable, and maintainable code. Higher-order functions are functions that can take other functions as arguments or return functions as their results. Composition, on the other hand, refers to combining functions to create new functionality in a modular and declarative manner. These concepts help in building more abstract and flexible solutions, and they align with the principles of declarative programming by emphasizing what should be done, rather than how it should be done.

Higher-Order Functions

A higher-order function is a function that either accepts one or more functions as arguments or returns a function as its result. This concept is central to functional programming and enables the creation of more abstract, reusable, and modular code. Higher-order functions allow for greater flexibility by enabling the combination and transformation of behavior at a high level.

For instance, Python's built-in map and filter functions are examples of higher-order functions. These functions take another function as input to operate on elements of a sequence:

```
# Using map as a higher-order function
def square(x):
    return x ** 2

numbers = [1, 2, 3, 4]
squared_numbers = list(map(square, numbers))
print(squared_numbers)  # Output: [1, 4, 9, 16]
```

Here, the map function is a higher-order function because it takes the square function as an argument and applies it to each element of the numbers list.

246

Higher-order functions are useful in declarative programming because they allow for behavior to be abstracted and passed around as first-class objects, enabling better reuse and modularity.

Function Composition

Function composition is the process of combining two or more functions to produce a new function. The resulting function applies the functions in a sequence, with the output of one function becoming the input for the next. This concept is foundational in declarative programming because it allows developers to build complex operations by composing simpler ones, making the code more modular and expressive.

In Python, function composition can be implemented using a variety of approaches. One simple method is to define a function that takes two other functions and returns a new function that applies them in sequence:

```python
# Function composition
def compose(f, g):
    return lambda x: f(g(x))

# Example functions
def add_one(x):
    return x + 1

def multiply_by_two(x):
    return x * 2

# Composing functions
composed = compose(add_one, multiply_by_two)
result = composed(3)
print(result)  # Output: 7 (multiply_by_two(3) = 6, add_one(6) = 7)
```

In this example, compose is a higher-order function that takes two functions, add_one and multiply_by_two, and returns a new function that applies multiply_by_two followed by add_one. This approach enables flexible and declarative function composition, making complex operations simpler to understand and maintain.

Benefits of Higher-Order Functions and Composition

The combination of higher-order functions and function composition provides several key advantages in declarative programming:

1. **Abstraction**: By passing functions as arguments or returning them from other functions, developers can abstract away specific implementation details and focus on what the program should do rather than how.

2. **Reusability**: Functions can be combined in different ways to build new functionality, making code more modular and reusable.

3. **Declarative Style**: Function composition allows you to express operations declaratively, focusing on the sequence of transformations to be applied to data without needing to describe the step-by-step execution.

4. **Readability**: Code becomes more readable as complex operations are broken down into smaller, more understandable functions. Composing small, simple functions can often lead to clearer and more concise code.

Higher-order functions and composition are integral to declarative programming, enabling modular, reusable, and flexible code. These concepts allow developers to abstract operations and transform them declaratively, fostering better code organization and maintainability. By combining functions, complex behavior can be achieved through simple, understandable steps, leading to cleaner and more efficient programs.

Module 26:
Declarative Machine Learning Pipelines

This module introduces the concept of declarative programming in the context of machine learning pipelines. It focuses on how declarative approaches can simplify model definition, feature engineering, hyperparameter tuning, and model deployment. By using higher-level abstractions, declarative methods improve readability and maintainability of machine learning code while promoting reusability and flexibility in the workflow.

Model Definition Using Declarative Approaches

In machine learning, model definition is typically one of the most complex tasks, as it involves creating algorithms that accurately represent data patterns. Declarative programming offers a way to express models at a high level without worrying about low-level implementation details. This involves describing the desired behavior of the model rather than focusing on the specific steps needed to achieve it.

Declarative approaches often use a pipeline-style framework where each component or transformation is abstracted as a step in the pipeline. For instance, defining a machine learning model declaratively might focus on specifying the type of model, such as decision trees or support vector machines, along with the features and target variable, rather than writing out the exact code for training and evaluation. This high-level approach allows for faster experimentation and better separation of concerns in the code.

Feature Engineering and Transformation Pipelines

Feature engineering is one of the most critical steps in the machine learning workflow, as the quality of the features directly impacts model performance. Declarative approaches to feature engineering focus on specifying how data should be transformed without specifying the low-level implementation details. This is particularly useful when dealing with complex datasets where preprocessing steps are required to extract meaningful features.

Declarative pipelines allow data transformations such as scaling, normalization, encoding, and feature selection to be defined as a series of high-level operations. By describing the transformations as stages in a pipeline, the process becomes more modular, easier to understand, and maintain. As a result, feature engineering can be done in a flexible and reusable way, ensuring that changes to the pipeline are easy to implement without affecting the overall workflow.

Hyperparameter Tuning with Declarative Methods

Hyperparameter tuning is another key aspect of the machine learning process, but it can be time-consuming and complex. Declarative approaches to hyperparameter tuning focus on specifying the range or values for the hyperparameters to be optimized, rather than explicitly writing optimization code. This allows machine learning practitioners to define the search space and tuning strategy without needing to worry about the underlying mechanics.

Declarative frameworks for hyperparameter tuning enable the user to specify search grids or distributions of hyperparameters to be explored by optimization algorithms like grid search or random search. These high-level descriptions allow users to focus on the parameters that matter for their model's performance, and the framework handles the complexities of the search process. Such methods improve scalability and reduce the likelihood of errors in manually implementing the search.

Deployment and Model Management

The deployment and management of machine learning models are crucial for operationalizing machine learning pipelines. Declarative approaches extend to deployment by focusing on defining how models should be deployed and monitored, rather than manually writing scripts for deployment. This approach ensures that models are consistent, reliable, and easy to manage in production environments.

With declarative deployment, machine learning pipelines can be automatically packaged and deployed as services or containers, simplifying model management tasks. Additionally, declarative pipelines can be used to monitor models in production, track their performance, and trigger re-training when necessary. By abstracting deployment details, these frameworks ensure that models are easily maintained and updated over time, promoting a seamless transition from development to production.

Declarative machine learning pipelines significantly enhance the efficiency and maintainability of the machine learning workflow. By abstracting key steps such as model definition, feature engineering, hyperparameter tuning, and deployment, declarative methods allow machine learning practitioners to focus on high-level problem-solving. This results in cleaner code, faster development cycles, and more scalable solutions.

Model Definition Using Declarative Approaches

In machine learning, model definition typically involves specifying the architecture, training process, and evaluation method. Declarative programming allows you to focus on defining *what* the model should do rather than *how* it should do it. With this approach, users describe the model at a high level, leaving the details to be handled by the underlying framework.

For example, when building a machine learning model using a declarative approach, you can specify the model architecture, such as the type of algorithm, the number of layers, the activation functions, and other hyperparameters, while the underlying system will take care of the implementation details. This can be much simpler than manually writing the training loop and backpropagation for each model.

Example with Scikit-Learn

Here's an example using scikit-learn, which allows for a declarative approach to defining models:

```python
from sklearn.ensemble import RandomForestClassifier
from sklearn.model_selection import train_test_split
from sklearn.datasets import load_iris

# Load dataset
data = load_iris()
X = data.data
y = data.target

# Define model declaratively
model = RandomForestClassifier(n_estimators=100, max_depth=3)

# Split data into training and testing sets
X_train, X_test, y_train, y_test = train_test_split(X, y, test_size=0.2)

# Train the model
model.fit(X_train, y_train)

# Evaluate the model
accuracy = model.score(X_test, y_test)
print(f'Model Accuracy: {accuracy}')
```

In this example, the RandomForestClassifier is defined in a declarative way, specifying the number of estimators and maximum depth without needing to write out the details of the training process. The library handles the underlying training process, and all you need to do is specify the high-level parameters.

Example with TensorFlow/Keras

For neural networks, frameworks like TensorFlow and Keras provide an even more declarative approach. Here's an example using Keras to define a simple neural network:

```python
import tensorflow as tf
from tensorflow.keras.models import Sequential
from tensorflow.keras.layers import Dense
from tensorflow.keras.optimizers import Adam

# Define model declaratively using Keras API
model = Sequential([
    Dense(64, activation='relu', input_shape=(4,)),
    Dense(32, activation='relu'),
    Dense(3, activation='softmax')
])

# Compile the model
model.compile(optimizer=Adam(), loss='sparse_categorical_crossentropy',
            metrics=['accuracy'])

# Load data
(X_train, y_train), (X_test, y_test) = tf.keras.datasets.iris.load_data()
```

```
# Train the model
model.fit(X_train, y_train, epochs=10, batch_size=32)

# Evaluate the model
accuracy = model.evaluate(X_test, y_test)
print(f'Model Accuracy: {accuracy[1]}')
```

In this case, Keras allows you to declaratively define the layers and their activation functions. You don't need to worry about how the optimizer, backpropagation, or training loop works—those details are abstracted away. The focus is on describing the structure of the model, making the code concise and easier to maintain.

Benefits of Declarative Model Definition

The declarative approach to model definition offers several advantages:

- **Simplicity**: You specify *what* you want the model to do without worrying about implementation details.

- **Modularity**: It's easier to replace or modify individual components like layers or hyperparameters.

- **Readability**: The code is easier to understand, especially for non-experts.

- **Flexibility**: You can easily switch between different model architectures by changing high-level parameters.

Using declarative programming for model definition improves both code readability and maintainability by focusing on the high-level specification of the machine learning problem, while the implementation details are handled by the underlying framework.

Feature Engineering and Transformation Pipelines

Feature engineering is a critical step in the machine learning pipeline, involving the transformation of raw data into a format suitable for training models. In a declarative machine learning pipeline, feature engineering can be described as a sequence of transformations, enabling more readable and modular code. By adopting declarative approaches, you can focus on specifying *what* transformations should be applied, without worrying about the implementation details.

The declarative approach simplifies the chaining of multiple transformations in a pipeline. Instead of manually handling each transformation and applying them to the data, you define the transformations at a higher level, and the system takes care of executing them in the correct sequence.

Example with Scikit-Learn

One of the most common tools for implementing declarative data transformations is scikit-learn's Pipeline class. It allows for creating a series of data preprocessing steps and machine learning models in a single flow.

```python
from sklearn.compose import ColumnTransformer
from sklearn.preprocessing import StandardScaler, OneHotEncoder
from sklearn.pipeline import Pipeline
from sklearn.ensemble import RandomForestClassifier
from sklearn.model_selection import train_test_split
from sklearn.datasets import load_iris

# Load dataset
data = load_iris()
X = data.data
y = data.target

# Define feature transformations
numeric_features = [0, 1, 2, 3]
numeric_transformer = StandardScaler()

# Combine transformations into a pipeline
preprocessor = ColumnTransformer(
    transformers=[
        ('num', numeric_transformer, numeric_features)
    ])

# Define the overall model pipeline
model_pipeline = Pipeline(steps=[
    ('preprocessor', preprocessor),
    ('classifier', RandomForestClassifier(n_estimators=100))
])

# Split the data
X_train, X_test, y_train, y_test = train_test_split(X, y, test_size=0.2)

# Train the model
model_pipeline.fit(X_train, y_train)

# Evaluate the model
accuracy = model_pipeline.score(X_test, y_test)
print(f'Model Accuracy: {accuracy}')
```

In this example, the feature transformations are specified declaratively with ColumnTransformer, which scales the numeric features. The overall pipeline, which includes preprocessing and classification, is created with Pipeline. This approach abstracts away the manual application of transformations, leading to cleaner and more maintainable code.

Example with TensorFlow (Keras)

In deep learning workflows, declarative feature engineering typically involves defining custom layers or preprocessing pipelines. TensorFlow's tf.data API allows for building declarative data processing pipelines, which can be used to load and transform datasets before feeding them into a model.

```python
import tensorflow as tf
from tensorflow.keras.models import Sequential
from tensorflow.keras.layers import Dense
```

```python
# Define feature transformation pipeline using tf.data
def preprocess_data(file_path):
    dataset = tf.data.TextLineDataset(file_path)
    dataset = dataset.map(lambda x: tf.strings.split(x, ','))
    dataset = dataset.map(lambda x: (tf.strings.to_number(x[1:], tf.float32),
            x[0]))  # Convert features to floats
    return dataset

# Define model
model = Sequential([
    Dense(64, activation='relu', input_shape=(4,)),
    Dense(32, activation='relu'),
    Dense(3, activation='softmax')
])

# Create a training pipeline
train_data = preprocess_data('train.csv')
train_data = train_data.batch(32)

# Compile and train the model
model.compile(optimizer='adam', loss='sparse_categorical_crossentropy',
            metrics=['accuracy'])
model.fit(train_data, epochs=10)
```

Here, tf.data allows for the creation of a declarative data pipeline that reads a CSV file, splits the data, and transforms it into the appropriate format for training. The pipeline is easily modifiable, allowing for complex preprocessing tasks to be added simply by chaining operations.

Benefits of Declarative Feature Engineering Pipelines

Using declarative pipelines for feature engineering offers multiple advantages:

- **Modularity**: It's easy to modify individual transformations without affecting the rest of the pipeline.

- **Reusability**: Once defined, feature engineering pipelines can be reused for multiple models or experiments.

- **Consistency**: Ensures that the same transformations are applied consistently across training and evaluation datasets.

- **Maintainability**: Higher-level abstraction makes the code easier to understand and maintain, especially as the complexity of data transformations grows.

By abstracting away the implementation details, declarative feature engineering enables developers to focus on the "what" of data processing while the system handles the "how." This approach streamlines the creation of robust data pipelines, resulting in cleaner, more efficient code for machine learning projects.

Hyperparameter Tuning with Declarative Methods

Hyperparameter tuning is a crucial part of developing a machine learning model. It involves finding the optimal values for model parameters that cannot be directly learned from the data. Declarative methods simplify this process by allowing users to define the search space and the optimization process without focusing on the implementation details of the search algorithms themselves.

In traditional approaches, hyperparameter tuning often requires manually specifying the ranges or values for each parameter, followed by a trial-and-error process or grid search. Declarative frameworks, on the other hand, enable defining the hyperparameter optimization problem at a higher level, focusing on "what" parameters should be optimized and "how" to search for the best values.

Hyperparameter Optimization Frameworks

There are several declarative frameworks available for hyperparameter optimization, such as **Optuna** and **Hyperopt**, which allow users to specify optimization goals declaratively, without needing to manually implement search algorithms like grid search or random search.

Example with Optuna

In Optuna, hyperparameter tuning is defined as an optimization objective, and the system automatically handles the optimization process. The following example demonstrates how a hyperparameter tuning task can be set up declaratively for a machine learning model.

```python
import optuna
from sklearn.ensemble import RandomForestClassifier
from sklearn.datasets import load_iris
from sklearn.model_selection import train_test_split
from sklearn.metrics import accuracy_score

# Define objective function
def objective(trial):
    # Define search space for hyperparameters
    n_estimators = trial.suggest_int('n_estimators', 10, 200)
    max_depth = trial.suggest_int('max_depth', 1, 10)

    # Load dataset and split
    data = load_iris()
    X_train, X_test, y_train, y_test = train_test_split(data.data, data.target,
            test_size=0.2)

    # Define and train the model
    model = RandomForestClassifier(n_estimators=n_estimators,
            max_depth=max_depth)
    model.fit(X_train, y_train)

    # Evaluate the model
    y_pred = model.predict(X_test)
    return accuracy_score(y_test, y_pred)

# Create study and optimize
study = optuna.create_study(direction='maximize')
study.optimize(objective, n_trials=50)
```

```
# Print the best parameters and the best score
print(f"Best hyperparameters: {study.best_params}")
print(f"Best accuracy: {study.best_value}")
```

In this code, the objective function defines the search space for n_estimators and max_depth using the trial.suggest_int method, which allows the system to sample values from within the specified range. The optimization process is declarative, specifying the parameters to tune and the objective metric (accuracy) to optimize. Optuna handles the search process, making it simple to explore hyperparameter combinations.

Example with Hyperopt

Hyperopt is another powerful framework that supports declarative hyperparameter tuning through optimization algorithms such as Random Search, TPE (Tree-structured Parzen Estimator), and more. Here's a simplified example:

```python
from hyperopt import fmin, tpe, hp, Trials
from sklearn.ensemble import RandomForestClassifier
from sklearn.datasets import load_iris
from sklearn.model_selection import train_test_split
from sklearn.metrics import accuracy_score

# Define search space for hyperparameters
space = {
    'n_estimators': hp.quniform('n_estimators', 10, 200, 10),
    'max_depth': hp.quniform('max_depth', 1, 10, 1)
}

# Define objective function
def objective(params):
    # Load data and split
    data = load_iris()
    X_train, X_test, y_train, y_test = train_test_split(data.data, data.target,
            test_size=0.2)

    # Train the model with given parameters
    model = RandomForestClassifier(n_estimators=int(params['n_estimators']),
            max_depth=int(params['max_depth']))
    model.fit(X_train, y_train)

    # Evaluate the model
    y_pred = model.predict(X_test)
    return -accuracy_score(y_test, y_pred)  # Minimize negative accuracy for
            Hyperopt

# Run the optimization process
trials = Trials()
best = fmin(fn=objective, space=space, algo=tpe.suggest, max_evals=50,
        trials=trials)

print(f"Best hyperparameters: {best}")
```

In this code, Hyperopt's fmin function is used to perform the optimization. The search space is defined declaratively using hp.quniform, which allows for sampling integers from a specified range. The function is then optimized using the Tree-structured Parzen Estimator (TPE) algorithm.

Benefits of Declarative Hyperparameter Tuning

1. **Automated Optimization**: Declarative approaches abstract away the details of the optimization algorithm, automatically selecting the best hyperparameters based on the defined objective.

2. **Flexibility**: You can easily specify different types of optimization algorithms, such as grid search, random search, or more advanced methods like TPE, without manually coding each method.

3. **Better Performance**: By automating the search process, declarative frameworks help find optimal hyperparameter combinations that might be overlooked in manual search processes.

4. **Efficiency**: Declarative methods allow for parallel execution of optimization tasks, speeding up the process.

Declarative hyperparameter tuning frameworks like Optuna and Hyperopt provide a higher-level abstraction, making it easier to focus on the search space and the optimization goal while leaving the details of the optimization process to the system. This results in cleaner, more efficient, and more manageable code.

Deployment and Model Management

Once a machine learning model has been trained and optimized, the next crucial step is deploying it into a production environment and managing its lifecycle. Declarative approaches offer a high-level, efficient way to define, deploy, and manage machine learning models without the complexities of dealing with low-level infrastructure or deployment configurations. These approaches ensure that models can be consistently deployed across various platforms and monitored effectively.

Declarative Model Deployment

Declarative deployment focuses on specifying *what* needs to be deployed, rather than *how*. Instead of manually setting up server configurations, resource allocations, or orchestrating deployments, declarative systems allow users to define the desired state of the model in terms of resources, environment, and dependencies. Tools like **Kubernetes**, **Docker**, and **TensorFlow Serving** offer declarative interfaces for managing the deployment of machine learning models.

For instance, in Kubernetes, you can declaratively define the deployment of a machine learning model by creating configuration files (YAML or JSON) that specify the containerized environment in which the model should run, including resource limits, replicas, and networking. The declarative nature of these tools ensures that the system will automatically manage any changes required to maintain the desired state, such as scaling up or down based on demand.

Example: Kubernetes Deployment

A declarative Kubernetes deployment of a machine learning model would look something like this:

```yaml
apiVersion: apps/v1
kind: Deployment
metadata:
  name: ml-model
spec:
  replicas: 3
  selector:
    matchLabels:
      app: ml-model
  template:
    metadata:
      labels:
        app: ml-model
    spec:
      containers:
      - name: ml-model-container
        image: my_ml_model_image:v1
        ports:
        - containerPort: 8080
```

In this YAML file, you declare the deployment of a machine learning model container. Kubernetes then takes care of ensuring that the container is running with the specified replicas and exposed ports. Any changes, like updating the model image or scaling the number of replicas, can be handled declaratively.

Model Management and Versioning

Model management and versioning are essential for ensuring that the correct version of the model is in production at any given time. Declarative methods in model management focus on tracking and versioning models in a systematic way. Tools like **MLflow** and **DVC (Data Version Control)** allow users to declaratively manage model versions, store metadata, and track experiment results.

These tools provide functionality to store and retrieve models, track parameters, and log experiment results in a version-controlled environment, all through a declarative API. For example, with MLflow, you can log a model and its parameters with simple, high-level commands, keeping a record of every version of the model.

Example: Model Versioning with MLflow

```python
import mlflow
from sklearn.ensemble import RandomForestClassifier
from sklearn.model_selection import train_test_split
from sklearn.datasets import load_iris
```

```
# Load dataset and split
data = load_iris()
X_train, X_test, y_train, y_test = train_test_split(data.data, data.target,
            test_size=0.2)

# Train model
model = RandomForestClassifier(n_estimators=100)
model.fit(X_train, y_train)

# Log model with MLflow
with mlflow.start_run():
    mlflow.sklearn.log_model(model, "rf_model")
    mlflow.log_params({'n_estimators': 100})

# Retrieve the model
model_uri = "runs:/<run_id>/rf_model"
loaded_model = mlflow.sklearn.load_model(model_uri)
```

In this example, you use MLflow's declarative API to log the model and its parameters. Later, you can load the model version from the tracking system and deploy it as needed.

Continuous Model Monitoring

Once deployed, continuous monitoring of machine learning models is essential to ensure their accuracy and efficiency. Declarative monitoring systems allow users to define the monitoring metrics and thresholds for model performance. Tools like **Prometheus** or **Grafana** provide declarative configurations to monitor model health, resource usage, and prediction accuracy over time.

Declarative monitoring helps detect issues like model drift (where the model's performance degrades over time) or data distribution changes, which may require retraining. It also ensures that alerts are set up automatically when specific conditions are met, such as when a model's accuracy falls below a predefined threshold.

Benefits of Declarative Deployment and Model Management

1. **Consistency**: Declarative approaches ensure that the deployment environment remains consistent, regardless of how many times it is applied or how it is updated.

2. **Scalability**: Declarative tools like Kubernetes automatically scale resources based on demand, ensuring that the model can handle increasing loads without requiring manual intervention.

3. **Efficiency**: By using declarative interfaces for deployment and management, you minimize the need for manual configuration and orchestration, allowing more focus on model development.

4. **Version Control**: Declarative tools ensure that different versions of models are tracked, stored, and easy to retrieve, enhancing reproducibility.

Declarative model deployment and management approaches ensure that machine learning models can be easily deployed, monitored, and maintained with minimal manual intervention. By focusing on defining the desired outcomes rather than the details of the process, these methods improve scalability, consistency, and efficiency in the machine learning pipeline.

Module 27:
Declarative Programming in Large-Scale Systems

Module 27 of the book, *Declarative Programming in Large-Scale Systems*, explores how declarative programming techniques are applied in large-scale systems. It covers the integration of declarative principles with cloud infrastructure, configuration management, data pipelines, and event sourcing. Each section demonstrates how declarative approaches improve scalability, maintainability, and system efficiency.

Cloud Infrastructure as Code

Cloud infrastructure has become a pivotal component in the development of modern systems. Declarative programming shines when it comes to defining infrastructure using tools such as **Terraform** or **AWS CloudFormation**, where users specify the desired state of the infrastructure without worrying about the low-level details of implementation. By leveraging declarative approaches, developers can describe what resources they need (like virtual machines, networking components, or databases), and the system automatically manages the creation, updates, and deletion of these resources to match the desired state. This reduces complexity, enhances repeatability, and ensures consistency in cloud infrastructure.

In declarative cloud infrastructure management, developers can express the "what" of the infrastructure without having to manually handle every step of resource provisioning. This contrasts with imperative approaches, where every step of the process would need to be explicitly defined. The declarative method promotes a higher-level way of thinking about cloud deployments and fosters easier collaboration, as teams can focus on specifying desired outcomes instead of the procedural steps to achieve them.

Configuration Management with Declarative Tools

Configuration management refers to the process of managing and maintaining computer systems in a consistent state. In the context of large-scale systems, declarative tools like **Ansible**, **Chef**, and **Puppet** have revolutionized how configuration management is performed. These tools allow administrators to define the desired state of systems in configuration files, and the system itself ensures that the current state matches the desired configuration.

Unlike imperative configuration management, which involves defining step-by-step processes to configure systems, declarative configuration management focuses on stating the end state, leaving the system to determine how to reach it. This paradigm is particularly useful in large systems, where managing thousands of machines manually would be time-consuming and error-

261

prone. It ensures consistency, reduces manual intervention, and provides a means to easily replicate configurations across different environments.

Data Pipelines in Distributed Systems

Data pipelines are integral to processing and transforming large datasets in distributed systems. Declarative programming plays a crucial role in the design and management of these pipelines, particularly when it comes to specifying transformations and workflows. Frameworks like **Apache Spark** and **Apache Flink** use declarative paradigms to define the flow of data processing tasks, allowing users to specify what needs to be done without having to manually control the low-level details of data distribution or parallel execution.

In declarative data pipelines, the system determines the most efficient way to process and transform data based on the high-level descriptions provided. By abstracting away the intricacies of parallelism, fault tolerance, and distributed execution, declarative systems make building and scaling data pipelines easier, more efficient, and less prone to human error. Furthermore, such approaches are well-suited for complex, dynamic data processing tasks that require scalability and flexibility across large datasets.

Event Sourcing in Functional Architectures

Event sourcing is a technique used in modern architectures where state changes are captured as a series of events rather than storing the current state of the system. This approach works particularly well in functional programming paradigms, where immutability and statelessness are key concepts. Declarative programming can greatly enhance the design and implementation of event-driven systems, where events are processed and stored in an ordered, immutable log, often leading to more efficient and scalable architectures.

In a declarative approach to event sourcing, the logic for handling events is described in terms of what needs to be achieved, rather than the specific procedural steps required. This enables better management of system state, auditability of changes, and a more straightforward method of building reactive systems that can scale dynamically. It also simplifies debugging and recovering from errors, as each event can be traced back through the system to understand how the current state was derived.

Module 27 demonstrates how declarative programming is applied in large-scale systems, offering substantial benefits in terms of scalability, maintainability, and automation. By integrating declarative principles with cloud infrastructure, configuration management, data pipelines, and event sourcing, systems can be designed to be more efficient and less error-prone, while also being easier to manage and scale.

Cloud Infrastructure as Code

Cloud infrastructure management has seen a significant shift with the introduction of declarative programming, enabling developers to define infrastructure in a more high-level, human-readable way. With **Terraform** and **AWS CloudFormation**, you can define your cloud resources and configurations as code, focusing on "what" the infrastructure should look like rather than "how" to achieve it.

For example, in **Terraform**, you define the desired state of cloud resources using HashiCorp Configuration Language (HCL), a declarative configuration language. Here's an example of how you might define an AWS EC2 instance in Terraform:

```
provider "aws" {
  region = "us-east-1"
}

resource "aws_instance" "example" {
  ami           = "ami-12345678"
  instance_type = "t2.micro"
}
```

In this example, you specify the **desired state** of the infrastructure—an AWS EC2 instance with a specific AMI and instance type. Terraform takes care of the low-level steps needed to provision this instance on AWS. Once applied, Terraform ensures that the infrastructure matches the desired state, whether it's the initial setup or the result of an update.

AWS CloudFormation is another tool that enables declarative infrastructure management but works with JSON or YAML templates. Here's an example of defining an EC2 instance in CloudFormation:

```
AWSTemplateFormatVersion: '2010-09-09'
Resources:
  MyEC2Instance:
    Type: AWS::EC2::Instance
    Properties:
      ImageId: "ami-12345678"
      InstanceType: t2.micro
```

In CloudFormation, you use YAML or JSON to describe the infrastructure, where Resources define the types and properties of the AWS resources to be created, just like in Terraform. Both tools enable you to define and manage your infrastructure in a consistent, version-controlled way.

In both cases, the declarative nature of the language allows developers to describe the "end state" of the system, while the tool figures out how to reconcile the current state with the desired state. If there are any discrepancies (for instance, if the EC2 instance is missing), Terraform or CloudFormation will create or modify resources to bring the infrastructure into the desired state.

Declarative cloud infrastructure as code ensures consistency and repeatability in deployments. For example, if you need to replicate the environment in another region or update the version of the instance, you simply modify the configuration file and apply the changes. The cloud platform takes care of the details, automatically managing resource creation, deletion, and updates.

Moreover, this approach allows for greater flexibility across different cloud providers. Since you define your infrastructure in a declarative language, it can be easily ported to different providers like **Google Cloud** or **Microsoft Azure** by switching the configuration or using cross-platform tools like Terraform.

Overall, declarative infrastructure as code streamlines cloud management, enhances consistency, and ensures that large-scale systems are easier to manage, scale, and maintain.

Configuration Management with Declarative Tools

Configuration management is an essential aspect of managing large-scale systems, particularly when dealing with multiple servers, services, or applications. Declarative configuration management tools, such as **Ansible**, **Puppet**, and **Chef**, have simplified this process by enabling users to describe the end state of the system rather than specifying step-by-step instructions for achieving that state.

Ansible, for example, uses YAML to define configurations in a way that declares what the system should look like once it's configured, rather than how to configure it. Here's an example of an Ansible playbook that installs a package on a server:

```
---
- name: Ensure NGINX is installed
  hosts: webservers
  become: yes
  tasks:
    - name: Install NGINX package
      apt:
        name: nginx
        state: present
```

In this example, the playbook defines that the nginx package should be present on all machines listed under webservers. The state: present directive ensures that the package is installed, and Ansible handles the steps necessary to achieve that state. If NGINX is already installed, the playbook does nothing. If it's not installed, Ansible will install it. The system's configuration is declarative, stating only the desired final state.

In **Puppet**, the configuration is defined in a similar declarative manner, using Puppet's domain-specific language (DSL) to specify the end state. A Puppet manifest that ensures NGINX is installed looks like this:

```
package { 'nginx':
  ensure => installed,
}
```

This Puppet manifest declares that the NGINX package should be installed. The system configuration is focused on the final state—whether NGINX is installed or not—and Puppet takes care of the steps to achieve that state.

Similarly, **Chef** uses Ruby-based DSL to declare the desired state of the system. A Chef recipe to install NGINX might look like this:

264

```
package 'nginx' do
  action :install
end
```

Again, the declarative approach is to specify that the system should have the NGINX package installed. Chef will determine the necessary actions to achieve this state and execute them.

One of the key benefits of declarative configuration management is the ability to maintain consistency across large-scale systems. By describing the desired state of a system in a configuration file or script, administrators can ensure that all systems are set up in a uniform way, regardless of the underlying infrastructure. This makes managing complex environments with multiple machines or services much more efficient.

Additionally, declarative configuration management allows for idempotency. If the desired state is already in place (for example, NGINX is already installed), running the configuration tool again will not cause any unnecessary changes or disruptions. This ensures that the system can be consistently and predictably managed over time.

Declarative tools like Ansible, Puppet, and Chef also offer scalability. They can be used to manage a few machines or scale up to thousands, providing a unified way to define and maintain system configurations, improving reliability and reducing the likelihood of human error.

Declarative configuration management tools simplify the complexity of managing large-scale systems by focusing on describing the desired end state of the system, rather than how to achieve it. These tools enhance consistency, idempotency, and scalability, making them vital in the modern infrastructure landscape.

Data Pipelines in Distributed Systems

Data pipelines are essential in modern distributed systems, especially when handling large volumes of data across multiple sources and destinations. Declarative programming plays a key role in simplifying the design, implementation, and maintenance of these pipelines, allowing developers to focus on high-level objectives and ensure consistent data flow and transformation.

A declarative approach to data pipelines enables the definition of the desired sequence of data transformations without specifying how the pipeline should execute them. Instead of writing step-by-step instructions for data processing, developers declare what the end result should look like, and the system takes care of the implementation details.

For example, **Apache Kafka** and **Apache Flink** are widely used in distributed systems for stream processing and managing data pipelines. These tools allow for declarative configuration of data flows that are distributed across clusters of machines, providing high scalability and fault tolerance.

In **Apache Kafka**, a producer can be defined to send messages to topics, and consumers can read those messages to process them. Kafka's API allows developers to declare topics and messages, with an underlying guarantee that data will be handled efficiently across systems. Here's a simple Python example using Kafka's confluent_kafka library:

```python
from confluent_kafka import Producer

def delivery_report(err, msg):
    if err is not None:
        print('Message delivery failed: {}'.format(err))
    else:
        print('Message delivered to {} [{}]'.format(msg.topic(),
            msg.partition()))

producer = Producer({'bootstrap.servers': 'localhost:9092'})

# Produce a message
producer.produce('my_topic', key='key', value='value', callback=delivery_report)
producer.flush()
```

In this example, we declare the topic ('my_topic') and send a message to Kafka. The Kafka producer takes care of how to actually send and distribute the message across servers in the Kafka cluster. The declarative nature of Kafka abstracts away the lower-level details of message distribution.

Similarly, **Apache Flink** supports declarative data stream processing. It allows developers to declare the transformations they want to perform on streams of data without specifying how the processing should be executed on distributed machines. The declarative nature of Flink ensures that high-level operations such as filtering, aggregating, and windowing are executed efficiently on large data streams.

In **Flink**, one can define data transformations as a chain of operations using its high-level API. The Flink job is designed in a declarative manner by focusing on what transformations should occur, rather than managing the underlying execution of those operations across a cluster of machines.

Here's a simplified Python code snippet using Flink's Python API:

```python
from pyflink.datastream import StreamExecutionEnvironment

env = StreamExecutionEnvironment.get_execution_environment()

# Define a stream source and transformation
stream = env.from_collection(['data1', 'data2', 'data3'])
stream = stream.map(lambda x: x.upper())

# Print the result to stdout
stream.print()

env.execute('Flink Declarative Pipeline')
```

In this example, we define a stream (stream) and apply a declarative transformation (map(lambda x: x.upper())) to convert the data to uppercase. The Flink engine handles how this operation is distributed and executed across the system's infrastructure.

By using declarative data pipeline frameworks like Kafka and Flink, developers can simplify the design of complex data workflows in distributed environments. The declarative approach abstracts away the complexities of managing concurrency, fault tolerance, and resource allocation. This makes it easier to scale data pipelines across multiple nodes, handle large volumes of data, and maintain high availability.

Moreover, declarative data pipelines also support versioning, reusability, and traceability, as the transformation steps are clearly defined. If the pipeline needs to be modified or extended, developers can simply update the transformations or the flow without worrying about how to change the underlying execution.

Declarative programming enhances the design and management of data pipelines in distributed systems by allowing developers to focus on the desired transformations and outcomes. By abstracting the complexities of execution, declarative approaches help manage scalability, fault tolerance, and consistency in distributed data processing systems.

Event Sourcing in Functional Architectures

Event sourcing is an architectural pattern that stores the state of an application as a sequence of events rather than directly storing the current state. In functional programming, event sourcing aligns well with declarative approaches as it focuses on the immutability of state and the transformation of data through a series of functional, stateless operations.

In event sourcing, the system captures all changes to the application state as discrete events, which are persisted in an event store. These events represent actions or state transitions, and they can be replayed at any time to reconstruct the current state of the system. The key advantage of event sourcing is that it offers a complete and auditable history of all state changes, making it ideal for applications that require traceability and recovery capabilities.

A declarative approach in functional architectures focuses on the idea of "what" needs to be achieved rather than "how" the system performs it. By relying on functions that transform events into state changes, developers can define the desired transformations declaratively, leaving the system to manage how the events are processed and stored.

For example, in **Akka**, an actor-based concurrency model used in distributed systems, event sourcing is often implemented in a functional style. Akka allows developers to define state transitions by specifying the handling of events declaratively, where the events themselves are immutable and processed as functions of previous state.

A simple event-sourcing system in a functional architecture would involve a sequence of immutable events that represent changes in an entity's state. These events could be handled through functions that transform the previous state into the next state based on the event received. For instance, consider an event-driven architecture in which each event represents an action on an account, such as a deposit or withdrawal. Each event can be processed through a function that updates the account balance accordingly.

Here's an example of event sourcing with a functional style in Python, focusing on a simple bank account scenario:

```python
class Account:
    def __init__(self, balance=0):
        self.balance = balance

    def apply_event(self, event):
        if isinstance(event, Deposit):
            self.balance += event.amount
        elif isinstance(event, Withdrawal):
            self.balance -= event.amount

class Deposit:
    def __init__(self, amount):
        self.amount = amount

class Withdrawal:
    def __init__(self, amount):
        self.amount = amount

# Example usage
events = [Deposit(100), Withdrawal(50), Deposit(200)]
account = Account()

# Applying events to modify account state
for event in events:
    account.apply_event(event)

print(account.balance)  # Output: 250
```

In this example, the Account class uses an apply_event function to modify the balance based on events such as Deposit and Withdrawal. Each event represents an action that modifies the state of the account, and the functional approach treats these events as immutable values. The declarative style is embodied in how the events define state changes without specifying the underlying mechanics of how they're handled—these are abstracted away.

Event sourcing is particularly powerful in distributed systems where consistency and recoverability are critical. By storing events rather than the current state, systems can easily rebuild state by replaying events, making the system fault-tolerant and resilient. Additionally, the declarative approach to event processing allows developers to focus on defining the behavior of events and state transitions, rather than managing the complexities of state persistence.

Event sourcing in functional architectures offers a powerful way to manage state through a sequence of immutable events. By embracing declarative principles, developers can focus on defining how the system should behave in response to events, while the system itself handles the complexities of event processing, persistence, and state reconstruction. This pattern ensures traceability, recoverability, and consistency, making it a key technique in modern distributed systems.

Module 28:
Declarative Programming in Business Applications

Module 28 focuses on the integration of declarative programming into business applications. It covers areas such as business rule engines, declarative financial modeling, decision support systems, and knowledge representation and reasoning. These topics highlight how declarative approaches streamline decision-making, improve automation, and support complex business logic in real-world scenarios.

Business Rule Engines and Declarative Automation

Business rule engines (BREs) are designed to manage and automate business logic within applications. By using a declarative approach, business rules can be written in a high-level, human-readable form, making them easier to understand and maintain. This separation of business logic from application code improves scalability and flexibility. In a BRE, rules are defined declaratively to specify "what" needs to happen, rather than "how" it should be done. This allows for more rapid adjustments to business rules and easier adaptation to changing business requirements. Declarative automation in this context allows companies to focus on defining business logic, while the underlying engine handles the execution details.

Declarative Financial Modeling

In the field of finance, declarative approaches can simplify the modeling of complex financial systems. Financial models often involve intricate calculations and dependencies, which can be expressed more effectively using a declarative approach. With declarative financial modeling, financial professionals can specify the relationships between different financial variables and define the desired outcomes without needing to worry about the underlying computational steps. This can improve the accuracy, transparency, and efficiency of financial modeling processes. For instance, cash flow analysis or risk assessment models can be represented declaratively, making them easier to modify and scale as business conditions change.

Decision Support Systems

Decision support systems (DSS) assist business executives and managers in making informed decisions based on data and analysis. A declarative approach in DSS focuses on the presentation of decision rules and the logic behind the decisions rather than the implementation details. Declarative programming enables decision support systems to be more adaptive and intuitive, allowing end-users to adjust decision-making criteria without needing deep technical expertise. By using declarative constructs, DSS can more easily incorporate new data sources, models, and evaluation metrics, thereby enhancing the system's ability to provide relevant, data-driven insights for decision-making.

Knowledge Representation and Reasoning

Knowledge representation and reasoning (KR&R) is concerned with how knowledge can be symbolically represented and manipulated within a computer system to facilitate logical reasoning. Declarative programming plays a key role in KR&R by allowing the representation of knowledge in a way that is closer to human understanding. For example, in expert systems, knowledge can be modeled declaratively through facts, rules, and logic that closely resemble the way human experts reason. Declarative approaches in KR&R systems enable automated inference, allowing systems to deduce new facts from existing ones. This capability is crucial for applications such as natural language processing, AI-driven decision-making, and problem-solving in various business domains.

Declarative programming offers significant advantages in business applications, from automating complex rule-based systems to simplifying financial modeling and decision-making processes. By emphasizing the "what" over the "how," declarative approaches streamline the management of business logic, improve adaptability, and enhance the scalability of business applications. This module underscores the transformative impact of declarative programming on modern business practices.

Business Rule Engines and Declarative Automation

Business Rule Engines (BREs) are essential in automating decision-making processes within business applications. They allow the definition, management, and execution of business rules separately from the application code. By leveraging declarative programming, BREs provide a way to express business logic in human-readable terms, focusing on *what* needs to be done rather than *how* it is done. The rules are typically written using simple logical constructs such as if-then conditions or constraints.

For example, in Python, we can define a basic rule-based system using dictionaries and functions. Suppose we have a rule that states, "If a customer's order total exceeds $1000, apply a 10% discount." This could be represented declaratively as follows:

```
def apply_discount(order_total):
    rules = {
        'discount_threshold': 1000,
        'discount_percentage': 0.1
    }
    if order_total > rules['discount_threshold']:
        return order_total * (1 - rules['discount_percentage'])
    return order_total
```

Here, the rule is defined in terms of *conditions* (if the order total exceeds $1000) and *actions* (apply a 10% discount). The rule is abstracted from the rest of the application, making it easy to adjust the logic without changing the rest of the system.

In a more complex system, we might use a class-based approach to encapsulate business rules and manage their execution. For instance:

```python
class BusinessRuleEngine:
    def __init__(self):
        self.rules = []

    def add_rule(self, rule):
        self.rules.append(rule)

    def execute(self, data):
        for rule in self.rules:
            if rule['condition'](data):
                data = rule['action'](data)
        return data

# Define rules
discount_rule = {
    'condition': lambda order: order['total'] > 1000,
    'action': lambda order: {**order, 'total': order['total'] * 0.9}  # Apply
            10% discount
}

# Create engine and add rule
engine = BusinessRuleEngine()
engine.add_rule(discount_rule)

# Apply rules to an order
order = {'total': 1200}
order = engine.execute(order)
print(order)  # Output: {'total': 1080.0}
```

In this example, the BusinessRuleEngine class manages multiple rules, with each rule having a condition and an action. This approach makes the BRE highly modular and adaptable to changes. New rules can be easily added, modified, or removed without impacting the existing business logic, fulfilling the declarative principle of abstraction.

The declarative nature of this engine allows business users to focus on specifying the conditions and actions of business rules without needing to understand the underlying implementation details. For instance, rules like "Apply a discount if the total exceeds $1000" can be directly translated into business logic with minimal code changes.

Additionally, declarative rule engines enable better maintainability and scalability. Rules are typically stored in a centralized repository, allowing for quick updates when business requirements change. The engine automatically applies these changes, ensuring consistency across all parts of the system.

Using declarative programming within Business Rule Engines allows for highly flexible, scalable, and maintainable systems. The abstracted nature of rule definition in BREs ensures that business rules can be updated and managed easily, without requiring deep technical knowledge from business users.

Declarative Financial Modeling

Declarative financial modeling focuses on describing the relationships between financial entities and their behavior without specifying the procedural steps to compute outcomes. This high-level approach simplifies the representation of complex financial structures, such as portfolios, risk management, and asset valuation. Using declarative programming in financial models makes it easier to maintain, adapt, and extend models without delving into implementation details.

A key advantage of declarative financial modeling is that the logic is expressed as formulas or constraints rather than step-by-step algorithms. For example, in a financial model for portfolio management, we may need to calculate the total value of a portfolio given the prices and quantities of various assets.

In Python, we can create a declarative approach to modeling portfolio value:

```python
class Portfolio:
    def __init__(self):
        self.assets = []

    def add_asset(self, asset):
        self.assets.append(asset)

    def calculate_value(self):
        return sum(asset['quantity'] * asset['price'] for asset in self.assets)
# Example: Define assets and portfolio
portfolio = Portfolio()
portfolio.add_asset({'symbol': 'AAPL', 'quantity': 10, 'price': 150})
portfolio.add_asset({'symbol': 'GOOG', 'quantity': 5, 'price': 2800})

# Calculate portfolio value
portfolio_value = portfolio.calculate_value()
print(portfolio_value)  # Output: 14650
```

In this example, the Portfolio class manages a collection of assets. Each asset is represented as a dictionary containing the symbol, quantity, and price. The calculate_value method uses a declarative approach to sum the value of all assets in the portfolio by applying a simple formula: quantity * price.

The declarative nature of this model allows for easy extension. For instance, to account for dividends, we can add a new attribute for each asset and modify the calculation to incorporate dividends:

```python
def calculate_value_with_dividends(self):
    return sum((asset['quantity'] * asset['price']) + asset.get('dividends', 0)
            for asset in self.assets)
```

This simple change in the model does not require reworking the entire portfolio calculation process, making it easy to adapt as new financial requirements arise.

In more complex financial modeling, constraints and risk factors are often used. For instance, risk management models may define a constraint that the portfolio's risk exposure must not exceed a certain threshold. This can be expressed declaratively using rules or formulas:

```python
class RiskManagement:
    def __init__(self, risk_threshold):
        self.risk_threshold = risk_threshold

    def check_risk(self, portfolio):
        risk_exposure = sum(asset['quantity'] * asset['price'] *
            asset.get('risk_factor', 0) for asset in portfolio.assets)
        return risk_exposure <= self.risk_threshold

# Example: Define a risk management check
risk_manager = RiskManagement(risk_threshold=5000)
print(risk_manager.check_risk(portfolio))  # Output: True/False depending on
            risk calculation
```

Here, the RiskManagement class represents a declarative rule that checks if the portfolio's risk exposure is within the allowed threshold. The use of risk_factor and the formula quantity * price * risk_factor allows for a high-level description of risk, abstracting away the underlying implementation.

Declarative financial models make it easier to simulate different financial scenarios, manage risk, and apply changes to financial rules or constraints. They also support easy interpretation by financial analysts or decision-makers, as the logic is presented in a way that aligns with business understanding rather than technical implementation.

Declarative financial modeling provides a powerful way to describe complex financial relationships while remaining flexible and easily adjustable. The high-level abstraction makes it simple to update and adapt the model, ensuring that it remains relevant in dynamic financial environments.

Decision Support Systems

A Decision Support System (DSS) is a computer-based system designed to support decision-making activities. It helps analyze data, present information, and assist decision-makers in making informed choices. In a declarative programming context, DSS can leverage high-level programming constructs to model decision-making rules and simplify the logic required to generate actionable insights.

A declarative approach to decision support focuses on defining what the system should achieve, rather than how it should achieve it. This approach allows for easier adaptation and management of decision-making logic, especially in complex systems like business analysis, resource allocation, or customer support.

In Python, we can create a simple DSS that determines the best course of action based on predefined business rules. For example, consider a scenario where a company needs to decide whether to approve a loan application based on credit score and income. The declarative nature of the system can be expressed in the following way:

273

```python
class LoanApproval:
    def __init__(self, credit_score, income):
        self.credit_score = credit_score
        self.income = income

    def approve(self):
        return self.decision_rules()

    def decision_rules(self):
        if self.credit_score >= 700 and self.income > 50000:
            return "Approved"
        elif self.credit_score >= 650 and self.income > 40000:
            return "Conditional Approval"
        else:
            return "Rejected"

# Example: Create a LoanApproval instance
loan = LoanApproval(credit_score=720, income=55000)
print(loan.approve())  # Output: Approved
```

In this example, the LoanApproval class encapsulates the decision-making logic in a declarative form, where the decision_rules method clearly outlines the conditions for loan approval. By separating the business logic (rules) from the procedural implementation, we maintain a flexible system that can easily accommodate changes to the decision criteria.

A key advantage of declarative decision-making systems is that they allow decision logic to be expressed as rules or formulas, rather than requiring programmers to implement complex algorithms. This makes it easier to modify or extend the system to meet new requirements, such as incorporating new factors into the decision-making process.

For instance, if we need to include a rule where applicants with a good history of repaying past loans should be given priority, we can modify the rules declaratively:

```python
class LoanApprovalWithHistory:
    def __init__(self, credit_score, income, repayment_history):
        self.credit_score = credit_score
        self.income = income
        self.repayment_history = repayment_history

    def approve(self):
        return self.decision_rules()

    def decision_rules(self):
        if self.credit_score >= 700 and self.income > 50000 and \
            self.repayment_history == 'Excellent':
            return "Approved"
        elif self.credit_score >= 650 and self.income > 40000:
            return "Conditional Approval"
        else:
            return "Rejected"

# Example: Create a LoanApproval instance with repayment history
loan = LoanApprovalWithHistory(credit_score=680, income=45000,
        repayment_history="Excellent")
print(loan.approve())  # Output: Approved
```

In this enhanced version of the system, the decision rule incorporates a repayment history check, offering further flexibility in the decision-making process. The declarative nature allows for easy rule extensions without altering the underlying logic structure, making the system more scalable and adaptable to business needs.

Declarative decision support systems can also benefit from the use of more sophisticated decision trees, decision tables, or rule engines to handle larger and more complex decision scenarios. These systems can be further optimized by integrating them with machine learning models that can predict outcomes based on historical data and changing conditions.

Declarative programming in Decision Support Systems offers an efficient and flexible way to model decision-making processes. By focusing on defining the desired outcomes and rules, businesses can easily adjust their decision-making criteria to meet evolving needs while maintaining clarity and reducing implementation complexity.

Knowledge Representation and Reasoning

Knowledge Representation and Reasoning (KRR) is a crucial aspect of artificial intelligence (AI) and business applications. It involves formalizing information in a way that allows systems to reason, draw inferences, and make decisions based on that knowledge. Declarative programming is particularly effective for KRR as it allows knowledge to be expressed in a high-level, readable manner, focusing on *what* should be done rather than *how* it should be done.

In declarative KRR, knowledge is typically represented using facts, rules, and constraints. These elements help the system infer new facts or make decisions. For instance, business rules that govern the conditions under which certain actions should be taken can be encoded as logical statements or predicates. The system then uses a reasoning engine to evaluate these rules and generate appropriate conclusions.

In Python, we can implement a simple KRR system using predicates and rules. For example, consider a knowledge base about employee performance:

```python
class EmployeeKnowledgeBase:
    def __init__(self, employee_name, sales_performance, attendance):
        self.employee_name = employee_name
        self.sales_performance = sales_performance
        self.attendance = attendance

    def evaluate_performance(self):
        return self.reasoning()

    def reasoning(self):
        if self.sales_performance > 100000 and self.attendance > 90:
            return f"{self.employee_name} is a top performer."
        elif self.sales_performance > 50000:
            return f"{self.employee_name} has a good performance."
        else:
            return f"{self.employee_name} needs improvement."

# Example: Create an EmployeeKnowledgeBase instance
employee = EmployeeKnowledgeBase("John Doe", sales_performance=120000,
        attendance=95)
```

```
print(employee.evaluate_performance())  # Output: John Doe is a top performer.
```

In this example, the EmployeeKnowledgeBase class encapsulates knowledge about an employee's performance. The reasoning method evaluates this knowledge according to predefined business rules. This allows the system to determine the performance level of the employee based on their sales performance and attendance.

A key benefit of declarative KRR systems is their ability to separate knowledge from the reasoning process. By expressing knowledge as declarative facts and rules, the system becomes more maintainable and flexible. For example, if new performance criteria need to be added or changed, it can be done simply by modifying the rules or adding new facts, without affecting the underlying reasoning process.

As KRR systems grow in complexity, they can use more sophisticated techniques, such as ontologies, logic programming, or rule-based engines, to represent and reason over large amounts of information. In Python, libraries such as PyKnow or Rete can be used to implement advanced rule engines that allow for more complex rule matching and reasoning capabilities.

For example, consider a more complex scenario where we incorporate multiple business rules regarding employee performance, job roles, and eligibility for promotions:

```python
class AdvancedEmployeeKnowledgeBase:
    def __init__(self, employee_name, sales_performance, attendance, job_role):
        self.employee_name = employee_name
        self.sales_performance = sales_performance
        self.attendance = attendance
        self.job_role = job_role

    def evaluate_performance(self):
        return self.reasoning()

    def reasoning(self):
        if self.sales_performance > 100000 and self.attendance > 90:
            if self.job_role == "Sales":
                return f"{self.employee_name} is eligible for promotion."
            else:
                return f"{self.employee_name} is a top performer."
        elif self.sales_performance > 50000:
            return f"{self.employee_name} has a good performance."
        else:
            return f"{self.employee_name} needs improvement."

# Example: Create an AdvancedEmployeeKnowledgeBase instance
employee = AdvancedEmployeeKnowledgeBase("Jane Doe", sales_performance=110000,
        attendance=92, job_role="Sales")
print(employee.evaluate_performance())  # Output: Jane Doe is eligible for
        promotion.
```

In this enhanced version, the system now considers the employee's job role when determining promotion eligibility, making the reasoning more nuanced and business-specific. The declarative approach ensures that knowledge representation remains clear and easily modifiable, promoting scalability and maintainability.

Declarative knowledge representation in business applications supports efficient, logic-driven reasoning. By focusing on expressing knowledge and relationships declaratively, systems can easily evolve and adapt to new requirements. This leads to improved decision-making and a more agile approach to business operations.

Declarative KRR in business applications provides a powerful framework for managing and reasoning over knowledge. By leveraging simple rules and facts, companies can build flexible and scalable systems for decision support, automation, and knowledge-based reasoning, helping them make better, more informed decisions.

Module 29:
Real-World Industry Case Studies

This module explores real-world applications of declarative programming in various industries. By analyzing case studies across different domains, we illustrate how declarative paradigms provide simplicity, scalability, and maintainability in complex systems. Each case study highlights the power of declarative programming in solving industry-specific challenges.

Declarative Web Development Case Study

Declarative web development focuses on defining what a web page or application should do, rather than how to implement the solution step-by-step. This approach emphasizes readability, modularity, and separation of concerns. The case study will explore the use of declarative frameworks like React.js and Vue.js, where components are described declaratively. These libraries abstract away much of the procedural complexity, allowing developers to focus on the user interface and logic. The benefits of this approach are clear in modern web development, where responsiveness, dynamic updates, and maintainability are critical. This section will show how declarative principles improve web app scalability and developer productivity.

Enterprise Data Processing with SQL & XSLT

In enterprise systems, handling large-scale data transformation is essential. SQL, particularly with declarative queries, enables efficient retrieval, manipulation, and updating of data. Through SQL-based approaches, businesses can write complex queries without worrying about the procedural steps needed to fetch or process data. Coupled with XSLT (Extensible Stylesheet Language Transformations), enterprises can declaratively transform XML data into various formats like HTML or CSV. This case study explores how declarative data processing with SQL and XSLT streamlines data operations and reduces the need for imperative scripting. It demonstrates how organizations leverage these tools to manage vast datasets with minimal effort, improving both performance and accuracy.

AI Systems Using Declarative Logic

Artificial Intelligence (AI) systems benefit from declarative programming because of its ability to model knowledge and decision-making rules clearly and logically. In AI, declarative logic helps in tasks such as expert systems, rule-based reasoning, and constraint satisfaction problems. This case study will highlight how declarative approaches, such as Prolog, are used in AI systems to describe complex relationships and enable automated reasoning. By abstracting the "how" of computation, AI systems can focus on higher-level goals, leading to more maintainable and extensible applications. The case study will also explore the integration of declarative logic in machine learning, where it aids in knowledge representation and rule generation.

Blockchain Smart Contracts with Functional Approaches

Smart contracts, which are self-executing contracts with the terms of the agreement directly written into code, represent a practical use case of declarative programming within the blockchain ecosystem. This case study will investigate how functional programming approaches, such as Haskell or Solidity, are used to write smart contracts declaratively. These contracts are highly secure and automate various processes within the blockchain network, such as asset transfer and execution of agreements. Declarative programming paradigms make smart contracts more reliable by ensuring that the logic behind these contracts is simple, transparent, and auditable. By removing the complexity of manual contract execution, blockchain developers can focus on defining the high-level objectives of the contract.

Module 29 provides concrete examples of declarative programming in action across multiple industries, from web development to blockchain. The case studies demonstrate the power of declarative approaches in simplifying complex processes, enhancing productivity, and ensuring system scalability. These real-world examples show how declarative programming can revolutionize industry practices, providing both efficiency and clarity.

Declarative Web Development Case Study

Declarative web development, through modern frameworks like React, Vue, and Angular, has simplified building dynamic user interfaces. This approach focuses on describing the desired outcome rather than the exact steps to achieve it, making code more readable, maintainable, and scalable. In this case study, we explore how declarative programming enhances web development by allowing developers to declare "what" the UI should do, while frameworks take care of the "how."

In React.js, for example, developers build UI components that describe what the UI should look like based on the application state. The framework then efficiently handles the process of updating the DOM when the state changes, ensuring that only the necessary parts of the UI are re-rendered. Consider the following example:

```
import React, { useState } from 'react';

function Counter() {
    const [count, setCount] = useState(0);

    return (
        <div>
            <p>You clicked {count} times</p>
            <button onClick={() => setCount(count + 1)}>Click me</button>
        </div>
    );
}

export default Counter;
```

In this example, the Counter component declares what should be rendered: a paragraph displaying the current count and a button that increments the count when clicked. The state (count) is managed internally using React's useState hook. When the button is clicked,

React automatically handles the DOM update, reflecting the new value of count. The developer only needs to describe the UI and its behavior, and React takes care of the underlying logic.

This approach avoids direct manipulation of the DOM, which is common in imperative programming. In imperative approaches, developers need to manually update the DOM by specifying exactly how elements should change in response to events. With declarative programming, the framework optimizes this for you, focusing on the desired outcome (the updated UI) rather than the steps needed to achieve it.

Another important feature of declarative web development is the concept of component reusability. Components like Counter can be reused in different parts of the application, with each instance maintaining its own state. React ensures that each component's state is independent and is automatically updated when the state changes. This modularity promotes clean code and reduces redundancy, improving maintainability.

Declarative programming in web development also promotes faster development cycles. For instance, React's virtual DOM minimizes direct interactions with the actual DOM, resulting in better performance. When a state change occurs, React first updates the virtual DOM and then calculates the most efficient way to apply the changes to the actual DOM, reducing unnecessary re-renders. This approach can significantly improve the responsiveness of web applications, especially in large-scale apps with complex UIs.

In addition to performance and maintainability, declarative frameworks provide a straightforward approach to creating responsive web applications. In a declarative framework, you can define what should be displayed at different screen sizes without manually writing media queries or handling window resizing events. This allows for faster development of cross-platform applications with minimal effort.

Declarative web development, exemplified by React and other modern frameworks, simplifies the process of building dynamic, responsive, and maintainable web applications. By focusing on declaring the desired outcome, developers can create more efficient, reusable, and scalable user interfaces, enhancing both development speed and software quality.

Enterprise Data Processing with SQL & XSLT

Enterprise data processing often involves handling large volumes of data, transforming it, and making it accessible for business operations. Declarative programming techniques such as SQL and XSLT offer robust solutions for managing and transforming data in enterprise systems. These technologies enable developers to focus on defining what data is needed or how it should be transformed, rather than specifying the step-by-step procedures to achieve it.

SQL (Structured Query Language) is the backbone of many enterprise data management systems, enabling users to interact with databases. It is declarative in nature because it allows developers to specify *what* data they need without detailing *how* the database should retrieve that data. Consider a simple SQL query:

```sql
SELECT name, department FROM employees WHERE age > 30;
```

This query describes what data should be fetched: the names and departments of employees older than 30. The underlying SQL engine handles the complexity of retrieving the data from various tables, applying the necessary filters, and optimizing the query for performance. Developers don't need to manually specify how the database should scan or join tables, as SQL engines perform these tasks automatically.

The power of declarative programming in SQL lies in its optimization capabilities. The database management system (DBMS) takes the declarative query and analyzes it for the best execution plan. This may involve deciding on the most efficient indexes to use, determining the best way to join tables, and applying filters in an optimal order. Developers can trust the DBMS to optimize these processes, enabling faster data retrieval.

On the other hand, XSLT (Extensible Stylesheet Language Transformations) is used for transforming XML data into different formats, such as HTML, plain text, or other XML structures. XSLT allows developers to declaratively specify how the content of an XML document should be transformed, without manually handling the procedural logic. An XSLT template could look like this:

```xml
<xsl:template match="/employees/employee">
  <p>Name: <xsl:value-of select="name" /></p>
  <p>Department: <xsl:value-of select="department" /></p>
</xsl:template>
```

In this example, XSLT defines a template for transforming an XML structure. It specifies what to extract (employee names and departments) and how to output it (as HTML paragraphs). The XSLT processor takes care of applying these transformations to the XML data, making it an excellent tool for web services and integration tasks in enterprise systems.

Together, SQL and XSLT offer a powerful combination for enterprise data processing. SQL handles data retrieval and manipulation within relational databases, while XSLT excels in transforming and presenting that data. The declarative nature of both technologies ensures that developers can focus on the logic and structure of the data, rather than the implementation details of processing it.

In large-scale enterprise systems, declarative approaches streamline data processing by reducing complexity. Developers can define the required data and transformations, while the underlying systems handle the intricacies of optimization, query execution, and transformation. This leads to more maintainable code and improves the scalability and performance of enterprise applications.

Using declarative approaches like SQL and XSLT for enterprise data processing simplifies complex operations, reduces the risk of errors, and allows developers to focus on business logic. The declarative nature of these tools enhances both the performance and maintainability of large-scale data-driven applications.

AI Systems Using Declarative Logic

Artificial Intelligence (AI) systems often require sophisticated logic to simulate intelligent behavior, but the complexity of AI systems can be significantly reduced using declarative programming approaches. Declarative logic enables AI systems to focus on describing *what* the solution should look like, rather than detailing the steps to solve a problem. This shift in perspective simplifies the design, maintenance, and scalability of AI models.

One of the core areas in AI where declarative logic proves powerful is in knowledge representation. Declarative programming can be employed to model knowledge in a way that is both interpretable and extensible. For example, in expert systems, declarative logic is used to represent rules and facts that form the basis for decision-making. In Prolog, a declarative programming language, facts and rules can be written to model knowledge bases, and the system can infer answers based on the facts provided.

A basic example in Prolog might look like this:

```
parent(john, mary).
parent(mary, susan).

grandparent(X, Y) :- parent(X, Z), parent(Z, Y).
```

Here, the facts parent(john, mary) and parent(mary, susan) define the relationships between individuals, while the rule grandparent(X, Y) defines a relationship based on the facts. The declarative nature of Prolog allows the system to automatically infer that john is a grandparent to susan without explicitly programming the procedural steps of such an inference.

Declarative logic also excels in the area of constraint satisfaction problems (CSPs), which are common in AI applications such as scheduling, resource allocation, and puzzle-solving. In CSPs, the goal is to find values for variables that satisfy a set of constraints. These problems are typically modeled in a declarative manner by describing the constraints, and the solver then handles the procedure of finding solutions.

For example, in AI-based scheduling, one might declare constraints such as "Event A must occur before Event B" or "Resource X is required for Task Y". A declarative solver then determines a schedule that meets these constraints, freeing developers from the need to manually define the algorithms for conflict resolution and optimization.

Moreover, declarative logic can be used in AI systems that focus on learning from data. In machine learning, a declarative approach might involve specifying the features or relationships to model, leaving the underlying learning algorithms to handle the details of fitting a model. For example, frameworks like TensorFlow or PyTorch enable developers to declaratively define neural network architectures, specifying the layers and their connections, while the framework handles the optimization and training process.

Declarative programming also plays a crucial role in AI reasoning tasks. In tasks like automated theorem proving or logic programming, declarative approaches enable the system to reason about the relationships between concepts and derive conclusions. The system focuses on defining logical relationships and inferring results, rather than following an explicit sequence of instructions.

Declarative programming has a significant impact on AI systems by simplifying the design of intelligent behavior, allowing the AI to focus on the "what" rather than the "how". This leads to more efficient, maintainable, and scalable AI systems, particularly in knowledge representation, constraint satisfaction, and reasoning tasks. The use of declarative logic empowers AI systems to autonomously solve problems with less effort from developers.

Blockchain Smart Contracts with Functional Approaches

Blockchain technology has revolutionized industries by enabling decentralized, trustless systems for transactions and contract execution. One of the most powerful features of blockchain is the ability to implement *smart contracts*, which are self-executing contracts with the terms of the agreement directly written into code. While blockchain platforms such as Ethereum have enabled widespread adoption of smart contracts, functional programming techniques, especially those derived from declarative approaches, provide a natural fit for creating these contracts in a clear, predictable, and secure way.

Smart contracts are typically written in Solidity on Ethereum, but functional programming languages like Haskell and F# also offer robust ways to define contracts with declarative constructs. Functional approaches allow the developer to focus on the high-level description of the contract's behavior rather than the procedural steps, enabling better reasoning about the contract's logic. In particular, functional programming's focus on immutability, first-class functions, and higher-order abstractions enhances the predictability and security of smart contracts.

Functional programming encourages immutability, which is a crucial aspect of smart contracts in the blockchain space. Immutability ensures that once a smart contract is deployed, its logic cannot be altered. This feature is inherently declarative since developers specify the desired behavior without worrying about side effects or state changes after deployment. By using immutable data structures, the contract remains consistent throughout its execution, reducing the risk of errors or malicious tampering.

A notable feature of smart contracts is their ability to enforce business logic automatically once predefined conditions are met. A typical smart contract might specify rules for transferring tokens, executing payments, or releasing assets when certain conditions are satisfied. For instance, a smart contract might contain a clause like "if Party A transfers tokens to Party B, then Party B is allowed to release the payment." With declarative programming, the contract's logic is expressed in terms of *what* should happen (e.g., tokens are transferred or payments are released) rather than *how* the system should process those events.

The declarative nature of functional programming lends itself well to the creation of such conditions. Take, for example, a functional approach to modeling a smart contract in Haskell for an escrow service. The contract could be written declaratively to specify conditions like:

```
data Contract = Escrow Party Party Amount

releasePayment :: Contract -> Bool
releasePayment (Escrow partyA partyB amount)
    | partyA_paid partyA amount = True
    | otherwise = False
```

In this example, the Escrow contract specifies that Party A must pay a certain amount for the payment to be released. The declarative nature allows the developer to focus on the relationships and conditions that must hold true without worrying about the underlying mechanics of how payments are handled.

Declarative programming is also invaluable in the context of contract verification. Functional programming's emphasis on purity and mathematical correctness lends itself to formal verification of smart contracts. By expressing the contract in a declarative, functional form, developers can more easily reason about its correctness and prove properties such as safety, liveness, and fairness. This capability is critical for ensuring that smart contracts behave as expected and that they are free from vulnerabilities or exploits.

Using declarative programming, especially within functional programming paradigms, enhances the design and deployment of blockchain-based smart contracts. Through immutability, clear expression of business rules, and formal verification, functional approaches improve both the security and reliability of smart contracts. Declarative programming offers a powerful way to reason about and implement blockchain systems that are efficient, secure, and easy to understand.

Module 30:
Challenges and Best Practices

Module 30 focuses on addressing the challenges developers face when working with declarative programming and provides best practices for overcoming them. It covers essential topics such as debugging and testing declarative code, optimizing performance in declarative systems, leveraging hybrid approaches for complex applications, and ensuring that declarative codebases remain future-proof in evolving technology landscapes.

Debugging and Testing Declarative Code

Debugging declarative code presents unique challenges compared to imperative programming. In declarative programming, the programmer specifies the desired outcome rather than the step-by-step procedure to achieve it, which can make tracking down the cause of an issue less straightforward. Traditional debugging tools, such as breakpoints or step-through debugging, may not be as effective because they rely on a procedural flow of execution that declarative code does not follow.

To address these challenges, developers need to rely on tools and techniques tailored for declarative paradigms. Logging and tracing mechanisms can be helpful for understanding the flow of data through the system. Additionally, automated testing frameworks, including property-based testing, are vital for ensuring that the code behaves as expected under a variety of conditions. Declarative programming benefits from a strong focus on ensuring correctness, which is best achieved through comprehensive unit tests that verify the output for given inputs, leaving less room for side-effects to introduce unexpected behaviors.

Performance Optimization in Declarative Systems

Performance optimization in declarative systems can be difficult because declarative languages tend to focus on what should be done, not how. While declarative programming simplifies logic, it can lead to inefficiencies, especially when systems are dealing with large-scale data processing or complex computation. Optimizing these systems requires careful analysis of the underlying execution models and the trade-offs inherent in declarative abstractions.

One common approach to optimizing declarative systems is to use lazy evaluation, which delays computation until necessary, thus avoiding unnecessary work. Memoization and caching strategies can also help optimize performance by storing intermediate results for reuse. Additionally, techniques such as parallelism or distributing the computation can improve performance when applied judiciously to declarative frameworks. Developers must ensure that optimization strategies align with the declarative philosophy to maintain readability and simplicity.

Hybrid Approaches for Complex Applications

While declarative programming offers many benefits, it is not always suitable for all parts of an application, especially in highly complex systems. In such cases, a hybrid approach, combining declarative and imperative programming styles, may be necessary to achieve the desired balance of simplicity and control. Hybrid approaches allow developers to harness the strengths of both paradigms, applying declarative programming where it excels—such as in domain-specific languages, business rules, or querying—and using imperative code where more control is needed for performance, resource management, or system-level interactions.

For example, a web application might leverage declarative code for its UI layout and business logic but resort to imperative code for handling specific, low-level interactions like data access or complex algorithms. Striking the right balance between declarative and imperative code helps address the challenges posed by the complexity of real-world applications, without losing the benefits of declarative approaches.

Future-Proofing Declarative Codebases

Declarative codebases must be designed with longevity in mind, as they can face challenges with evolving frameworks, libraries, and standards. Future-proofing declarative codebases requires an emphasis on flexibility and adaptability. Code should be modular, with a clear separation of concerns that allows for easy updates and integrations as new technologies emerge. Additionally, it's essential to stay updated on language and framework evolution and adopt practices like version control, automated tests, and continuous integration to maintain code quality.

Refactoring is also an important practice in keeping declarative systems relevant over time. As requirements change and technologies evolve, regularly revisiting and optimizing the codebase ensures its robustness and adaptability to new challenges. By future-proofing declarative systems, developers can ensure that their code remains effective and maintainable long into the future.

Module 30 covers critical aspects of declarative programming that developers must navigate to ensure their systems are efficient, reliable, and maintainable. By addressing the challenges of debugging, optimizing performance, using hybrid approaches, and future-proofing codebases, developers can build declarative systems that remain robust and scalable in the long term.

Debugging and Testing Declarative Code

Debugging and testing declarative code can be challenging because the focus of declarative programming is on *what* the program should accomplish, rather than specifying the *how*. Unlike imperative programming, which provides a clear step-by-step process, declarative code abstracts the logic and flow, often leaving the execution details hidden. This can make it difficult to identify errors, especially when dealing with complex data transformations or systems with high-level specifications.

To address this challenge, tools like logging, tracing, and profiling can help. Here's an example of how we might use Python's logging module to trace the flow of data through a declarative function:

```python
import logging

# Set up logging
logging.basicConfig(level=logging.DEBUG)

def process_data(data):
    logging.debug(f"Input data: {data}")
    result = [x * 2 for x in data if x % 2 == 0]
    logging.debug(f"Filtered and processed data: {result}")
    return result

# Test the function
data = [1, 2, 3, 4, 5, 6]
processed_data = process_data(data)
```

In this example, logging is used to trace how data is transformed at each step. By enabling the logging module, we can easily track the input and output values of the process_data function to verify its correctness. These logs provide valuable insights into how the data is processed without needing to step through the code manually.

Automated testing is another key tool for debugging declarative code. Python's unittest module makes it easy to write tests for declarative functions. Here's an example of unit testing a declarative function:

```python
import unittest

def process_data(data):
    return [x * 2 for x in data if x % 2 == 0]

class TestProcessData(unittest.TestCase):
    def test_process_data(self):
        self.assertEqual(process_data([1, 2, 3, 4, 5, 6]), [4, 8, 12])

if __name__ == "__main__":
    unittest.main()
```

In this case, we use unit tests to verify that the process_data function behaves as expected. The test checks that even numbers are doubled and returned correctly, providing a way to automate the verification of declarative behavior.

For more complex systems, where declarative code may include higher-order functions or composition, property-based testing can help ensure that the logic holds up across a range of inputs. Libraries like hypothesis allow for such tests in Python:

```python
from hypothesis import given
from hypothesis.strategies import lists, integers

def process_data(data):
    return [x * 2 for x in data if x % 2 == 0]

@given(lists(integers()))
def test_process_data_property(data):
```

```
result = process_data(data)
assert all(x % 2 == 0 for x in result)  # Only even numbers should remain
assert len(result) <= len(data)  # No more elements than input
```

Here, hypothesis generates random input data, and the property-based test verifies that all numbers in the output are even and that the output contains no more elements than the input.

Additionally, immutability and referential transparency are key concepts in declarative programming, ensuring that functions always return the same output for the same input. This predictability makes it easier to reason about the behavior of the code and write tests that focus purely on input-output correctness. In declarative programming, since the program's state doesn't change, you can focus on ensuring that the logic always holds true by comparing inputs with outputs.

Finally, for declarative languages or environments with specialized debugging needs, using tools designed for those environments can provide more advanced insights. For example, Prolog and other logic programming languages often have built-in debuggers that step through logical inferences and help visualize how conclusions are reached based on the rules.

Debugging and testing declarative code require a shift from traditional step-by-step debugging. By using logging, automated testing, and property-based testing, developers can ensure that declarative systems are correct and maintainable. Tools like unittest and hypothesis make it easier to automate these processes and validate logic.

Performance Optimization in Declarative Systems

Performance optimization in declarative systems can be a challenge due to the inherent abstraction and lack of explicit control over execution flow. In declarative programming, you define *what* needs to be done, rather than specifying the exact steps to accomplish it. While this provides clarity and readability, it can sometimes result in inefficiencies that need to be addressed, especially when working with large datasets or complex computations.

One key strategy for performance optimization is **lazy evaluation**, where expressions are evaluated only when they are needed, rather than all at once. In Python, libraries like itertools and functools allow for lazy evaluation of data structures, avoiding unnecessary computations.

For instance, the map() function in Python returns a generator instead of a list, meaning it will only compute values as they are requested:

```
import itertools

data = [1, 2, 3, 4, 5]

# Lazy evaluation with itertools
```

```
lazy_data = itertools.filterfalse(lambda x: x % 2 == 0, data)
# Values are computed only when iterated
for value in lazy_data:
    print(value)
```

In this example, the filterfalse function from itertools lazily filters the data, ensuring that elements are processed only when needed, instead of generating a full intermediate list in memory. This can drastically reduce memory usage and improve performance when handling large data sets.

Another optimization approach in declarative programming is **memoization**. Memoization stores the results of expensive function calls and reuses the cached result when the same inputs occur again. Python's functools.lru_cache is an excellent tool for this purpose:

```
from functools import lru_cache

@lru_cache(maxsize=128)
def expensive_computation(n):
    # Simulate a time-consuming computation
    if n <= 1:
        return n
    return expensive_computation(n - 1) + expensive_computation(n - 2)

# Test memoization
print(expensive_computation(30))
```

In this example, the function expensive_computation calculates Fibonacci numbers. With memoization enabled through lru_cache, previous results are stored, and the function avoids redundant calculations. This drastically reduces computation time for repeated function calls with the same arguments, improving overall performance.

However, in more complex systems, simply applying caching or lazy evaluation may not be enough. You need to consider **parallelism** and **concurrency**. Many declarative systems can be parallelized by breaking down computations into independent units that can be processed simultaneously. In Python, the concurrent.futures module can help parallelize tasks by executing them concurrently across multiple threads or processes.

```
from concurrent.futures import ThreadPoolExecutor

def compute_square(n):
    return n * n

numbers = [1, 2, 3, 4, 5]

with ThreadPoolExecutor() as executor:
    results = list(executor.map(compute_square, numbers))

print(results)
```

Here, the ThreadPoolExecutor runs multiple tasks concurrently, calculating the square of each number in parallel. This reduces the total execution time, especially for I/O-bound tasks.

For **data-intensive operations**, leveraging **distributed computing frameworks** such as Apache Spark or Dask allows declarative code to scale across multiple machines. These tools handle data processing in parallel across large clusters, enabling faster execution even with massive datasets.

Performance optimization in declarative systems requires careful consideration of techniques such as lazy evaluation, memoization, and parallelism. By utilizing tools and libraries like itertools, functools.lru_cache, and concurrent.futures, Python developers can enhance the performance of declarative code and scale systems effectively.

Hybrid Approaches for Complex Applications

Hybrid approaches combine different programming paradigms to take advantage of the strengths of each, especially when building complex applications. In declarative programming, this typically involves mixing declarative logic with more imperative or object-oriented approaches to handle complex scenarios that may be difficult to model declaratively alone. Hybrid models are essential when working with large, performance-sensitive applications that also require flexibility in data manipulation, state management, or procedural logic.

For instance, declarative programming is highly suitable for defining high-level logic and rules, while imperative programming can be used to optimize lower-level operations or to control detailed flow of execution. In web development, combining declarative UI frameworks like React (which emphasizes a declarative approach to UI state management) with imperative logic for handling events and more complex user interactions is a common practice.

In Python, hybrid approaches are often used when managing databases and web servers. Declarative frameworks such as SQLAlchemy allow developers to define database models declaratively, while the actual database operations (e.g., data manipulation, transactions) can still be written in imperative code. SQLAlchemy's ORM (Object Relational Mapping) enables developers to write database queries declaratively, abstracting the SQL logic, while still providing an imperative API to execute complex queries or manage sessions. Here's an example of a hybrid approach with SQLAlchemy:

```
from sqlalchemy import create_engine, Column, Integer, String
from sqlalchemy.ext.declarative import declarative_base
from sqlalchemy.orm import sessionmaker

Base = declarative_base()

class User(Base):
    __tablename__ = 'users'
    id = Column(Integer, primary_key=True)
    name = Column(String)

# Declare database connection
engine = create_engine('sqlite:///:memory:')
Base.metadata.create_all(engine)
```

```
# Hybrid: Imperative session management with declarative model
Session = sessionmaker(bind=engine)
session = Session()

# Imperative approach to adding a new user
new_user = User(name='John Doe')
session.add(new_user)
session.commit()

# Query using the declarative ORM system
user = session.query(User).filter_by(name='John Doe').first()
print(user.name)
```

In this example, the declarative User class defines the structure of the database, while the imperative session.add() and session.commit() commands perform the actual database operations. This hybrid approach allows for both flexible high-level modeling and detailed control over data persistence.

In machine learning, hybrid approaches also play a key role. Declarative programming can be used to define data transformations and model pipelines, but imperative programming is often needed for tasks such as model training, error handling, and tuning. Libraries like TensorFlow and PyTorch provide declarative abstractions for model construction (e.g., defining neural network layers) while requiring imperative code for training loops, optimizer steps, and evaluation.

In the case of data pipelines, declarative programming shines when defining transformations and the flow of data. However, when it comes to handling exceptions, managing retries, or controlling execution sequences for complex workflows, imperative logic may be necessary to ensure the reliability and robustness of the application. A hybrid approach can use frameworks like Apache Kafka or Apache Airflow to model the data flow declaratively, while allowing for imperative logic to handle edge cases or apply custom transformations.

Hybrid approaches in declarative programming integrate multiple paradigms to handle complex scenarios that cannot be easily modeled by a single paradigm alone. By combining declarative and imperative styles, developers can leverage the benefits of both flexibility and performance, making complex applications easier to develop, optimize, and maintain.

Future-Proofing Declarative Codebases

Future-proofing declarative codebases involves preparing the code for scalability, flexibility, and ease of maintenance as technologies and requirements evolve over time. Declarative programming, while focusing on high-level logic rather than implementation details, requires attention to modularity, extensibility, and compatibility with changing dependencies. In this section, we explore strategies that help future-proof declarative codebases using code examples.

Modularity and Separation of Concerns

291

One of the most important strategies for future-proofing declarative code is modularity. Code should be divided into reusable components or functions that handle specific concerns. This makes it easier to maintain and update the system over time. For instance, when working with a declarative data transformation pipeline, you can separate each transformation step into independent functions.

```
# Example of a modular declarative pipeline for data transformation
def clean_data(data):
    return [item.strip().lower() for item in data if item]

def filter_data(data):
    return [item for item in data if len(item) > 5]

def process_data(data):
    data = clean_data(data)
    data = filter_data(data)
    return data

raw_data = ["  Hello ", "world", "   ", "Python ", "programming"]
processed_data = process_data(raw_data)
print(processed_data)
```

In this example, each function handles a specific transformation step. By breaking down the logic into smaller, focused functions, the code becomes easier to maintain and extend in the future.

Abstracting Dependencies

Declarative code often relies on external libraries or services, but these dependencies can change over time. By abstracting the use of external libraries, you can future-proof your code against breaking changes. For example, when working with a declarative query language like SQL, you can use an abstraction layer to handle changes in the database system or query syntax.

```
# Abstracting a database query
class QueryBuilder:
    def __init__(self, db):
        self.db = db

    def fetch_users(self):
        return self.db.query("SELECT * FROM users WHERE active = 1")

# Using the query builder
class MySQLDatabase:
    def query(self, sql):
        # Logic to execute the SQL query on a MySQL database
        pass

db = MySQLDatabase()
query_builder = QueryBuilder(db)
users = query_builder.fetch_users()
```

In this example, the QueryBuilder class abstracts the specifics of the database query, making it easier to switch to a different database or query language in the future.

Extensibility with Plugins

Future-proofing declarative systems also means allowing for easy extension of functionality. A plugin architecture enables developers to add new features without modifying the core system. For example, in a declarative rule engine, you can use a plugin system to add new rules.

```python
# Simple plugin-based system for adding new rules
class RuleEngine:
    def __init__(self):
        self.rules = []

    def add_rule(self, rule):
        self.rules.append(rule)

    def execute_rules(self, data):
        for rule in self.rules:
            data = rule.apply(data)
        return data

# A new rule can be added dynamically
class AddTaxRule:
    def apply(self, data):
        return data + (data * 0.15)

rule_engine = RuleEngine()
rule_engine.add_rule(AddTaxRule())
total = rule_engine.execute_rules(100)
print(total)
```

In this example, the RuleEngine class allows for new rules to be added dynamically, making the system more extensible and adaptable to future requirements.

Automated Testing for Maintainability

Testing is essential for future-proofing declarative code, as it ensures that changes and additions do not introduce bugs. By writing unit tests for each component, you can guarantee that your system continues to function correctly as it evolves. Here is an example of testing a declarative function:

```python
import unittest

class TestDataProcessing(unittest.TestCase):
    def test_process_data(self):
        raw_data = ["  Hello ", "world", "  ", "Python ", "programming"]
        processed_data = process_data(raw_data)
        self.assertEqual(processed_data, ["hello", "world", "python",
            "programming"])

if __name__ == "__main__":
    unittest.main()
```

This unit test checks that the process_data function works as expected. Having such tests in place will help you avoid regressions when making changes to the code in the future.

Clear Documentation

While declarative code tends to be more readable than imperative code, it still requires clear documentation to ensure maintainability. By documenting the purpose of each module or function and providing examples of how to use them, you make it easier for future developers to understand and extend the system.

```
# Documentation for the `process_data` function
def process_data(data):
    """
    Cleans and filters the given data.

    Parameters:
    data (list): A list of strings to process.

    Returns:
    list: A list of processed strings.
    """
    data = clean_data(data)
    data = filter_data(data)
    return data
```

Clear documentation not only helps maintain the system but also provides a reference for future developers who may need to modify or extend the code.

Future-proofing declarative codebases requires a combination of strategies: modularity, abstraction of dependencies, extensibility, automated testing, and clear documentation. By designing systems that are easy to extend and maintain, developers can ensure that their declarative code remains flexible and adaptable to future changes.

Part 6:

Research Directions in Declarative Programming

Declarative programming continues to evolve as researchers explore new applications and theoretical advancements. This final installment part examines cutting-edge developments in **functional and logic programming, quantum computing, artificial intelligence, cybersecurity, and theoretical foundations**. It also provides a forward-looking perspective on **industry adoption trends, emerging technologies, and future research opportunities**. By understanding these research directions, developers and academics can stay ahead of the curve, contributing to innovative solutions that leverage declarative paradigms for **efficiency, correctness, and scalability** in complex computational environments.

Advances in Functional and Logic Programming

Recent innovations in **functional and logic programming** push the boundaries of declarative computing. Functional languages such as **Haskell, Scala, and F#** continue to introduce advanced type systems and performance optimizations. **Logic programming's role in AI** has expanded with automated reasoning and symbolic learning. **Declarative parallel computing** enables scalable concurrency models, reducing complexity in multi-threaded execution. This module explores **new theoretical models** driving these advancements, emphasizing the growing impact of declarative paradigms in computational research.

Declarative Programming in Quantum Computing

Quantum computing introduces new computational paradigms that align well with declarative methodologies. **Quantum declarative programming** defines computations without explicit state manipulation, leveraging quantum superposition and entanglement. **Functional representations in quantum algorithms** optimize quantum logic gates using lambda calculus and higher-order functions. **Constraint-based quantum computation** formalizes problem-solving for quantum optimization and cryptographic protocols. As quantum hardware matures, declarative programming plays a crucial role in defining **high-level abstractions** for quantum programming, opening new research frontiers.

Declarative Programming for AI and Machine Learning

Declarative programming enhances AI and machine learning by improving model transparency and expressiveness. **Explainable AI (XAI)** benefits from declarative rule-based inference, enabling human-readable decision processes. **Declarative data processing frameworks** streamline large-scale feature engineering and transformation. **Logic-based AI systems** incorporate reasoning mechanisms that enhance knowledge representation and inference accuracy. As machine learning evolves, declarative approaches offer **scalable, interpretable, and reusable** methodologies, shaping future research into intelligent automation, ethical AI, and AI-driven decision-making models.

Declarative Cybersecurity and Cryptography

Security systems increasingly rely on declarative programming for policy enforcement and formal verification. **Policy-based security management** uses declarative rules to define access controls and compliance policies. **Logic-based intrusion detection systems (IDS)** analyze system behavior through declarative event processing. **Cryptographic protocols** leverage functional languages like Haskell to express encryption schemes with mathematical precision. **Formal verification techniques** ensure provable security in software systems. This module explores how declarative paradigms advance **cybersecurity, cryptographic systems, and secure computing architectures** in modern software development.

Theoretical Advances in Declarative Computing

Declarative computing continues to inspire new theoretical models and language constructs. **Domain-specific languages (DSLs)** improve declarative expressiveness for niche applications. **Category theory in programming languages** refines mathematical abstractions for **type theory and functional composition**. Research in **declarative software engineering** explores methodologies for improving **scalability, maintainability, and correctness**. Compiler optimizations leverage **lazy evaluation and program synthesis** to enhance performance. This module delves into ongoing research that pushes declarative paradigms forward, shaping how developers and researchers design efficient and expressive computational models.

The Future of Declarative Programming

The future of declarative programming lies in its growing adoption and emerging challenges. **Industry trends** indicate increasing reliance on declarative paradigms in **cloud infrastructure, AI automation, and data processing**. However, **challenges in debugging, performance, and hybrid integration** persist, requiring novel research solutions. **Emerging technologies**, including **serverless computing, AI-driven programming assistants, and quantum declarative computing**, shape the next wave of declarative applications. This module provides a **forward-thinking perspective**, helping developers and researchers anticipate **new paradigms, best practices, and interdisciplinary applications** in declarative computing.

This part offers insights into **cutting-edge research, emerging technologies, and future applications** of declarative programming, equipping learners to **contribute to theoretical advancements and practical innovations** in computational paradigms.

Module 31:
Advances in Functional and Logic Programming

Functional and logic programming have continuously evolved, introducing innovations that enhance their expressiveness, efficiency, and applicability in modern computing. This module explores recent advances in functional programming languages, their impact on artificial intelligence through logic programming, their role in parallel computing, and the theoretical advancements shaping the future of declarative paradigms. As functional and logic programming become increasingly relevant in high-performance and AI-driven applications, understanding these advances enables developers to build more robust and scalable solutions. By examining these topics, we gain insight into the expanding capabilities of declarative programming in contemporary and emerging computational challenges.

Innovations in Functional Languages

Functional programming has witnessed significant innovations, particularly in language design, type systems, and compiler optimizations. Modern functional languages such as Haskell, Scala, and F# introduce powerful type inference mechanisms, algebraic data types, and higher-order abstractions that simplify complex computations. Additionally, innovations like effect systems manage side effects without compromising purity, leading to safer and more predictable code execution. The rise of functional-reactive programming (FRP) further exemplifies functional programming's evolution, allowing for seamless handling of asynchronous data flows. As functional paradigms integrate with mainstream languages like Python and JavaScript, these innovations are becoming accessible to a broader audience of developers.

Applications of Logic Programming in AI

Logic programming has long been associated with artificial intelligence due to its declarative nature and suitability for knowledge representation and reasoning. Prolog, Datalog, and Answer Set Programming (ASP) are extensively used in expert systems, constraint satisfaction problems, and automated theorem proving. With the advent of machine learning and symbolic AI integration, logic programming is regaining prominence in explainable AI (XAI) systems, where logical inference enhances transparency in decision-making. Furthermore, rule-based systems and knowledge graphs leverage logic programming to extract insights from structured and semi-structured data, reinforcing its role in AI-driven applications across various industries.

Declarative Approaches in Parallel Computing

Parallel computing presents challenges that traditional imperative paradigms struggle to address efficiently. Declarative approaches in functional and logic programming offer solutions by abstracting low-level concurrency concerns while ensuring correctness and determinism. Functional languages with immutable data structures facilitate parallel execution without race conditions, while declarative dataflow programming optimizes task scheduling in distributed environments. Innovations such as parallel monads, asynchronous combinators, and constraint-based parallelism enable fine-grained control over computational workflows. These techniques are increasingly applied in cloud computing, big data processing, and high-performance computing, where scalable and fault-tolerant solutions are critical.

Advanced Theoretical Models

Theoretical advancements in declarative programming continue to refine computational models and reasoning frameworks. Category theory, lambda calculus extensions, and type theory innovations provide formal underpinnings that enhance the expressiveness and correctness of functional and logic programming languages. Research in dependent types and proof assistants, such as Coq and Agda, pushes the boundaries of verified programming, ensuring mathematical correctness in software development. Meanwhile, logic programming benefits from advances in constraint logic programming (CLP) and probabilistic logic, which expand its applicability to fields such as bioinformatics, optimization, and automated reasoning. These theoretical models drive both academic research and practical applications, shaping the future of declarative programming.

The advances in functional and logic programming are reshaping how developers approach software design, AI, and parallel computing. By leveraging innovations in language design, integrating logic programming in AI, utilizing declarative parallelism, and exploring advanced theoretical models, developers can build more efficient, scalable, and reliable systems. This module highlights these key developments, ensuring that programmers remain at the forefront of declarative programming's evolution.

Innovations in Functional Languages

Functional programming has evolved significantly, incorporating innovations that improve expressiveness, performance, and ease of use. Modern functional languages such as Haskell, Scala, and F# have introduced powerful type systems, optimized compiler designs, and enhanced abstraction mechanisms. One of the most notable advancements is **type inference**, which reduces boilerplate code by allowing the compiler to infer types without explicit annotations. This feature, common in languages like OCaml and Haskell, helps developers focus on logic rather than low-level type management.

Another key innovation is **algebraic data types (ADTs)**, which provide structured ways to define complex data. ADTs combine **sum types** (variants of a type) and **product types** (combinations of values), enabling expressive and robust data modeling. Pattern matching, often used with ADTs, simplifies control flow and reduces the need for imperative conditionals. Additionally, many functional languages now support **effect systems**, which manage side effects like I/O and state changes in a controlled manner.

The rise of **functional-reactive programming (FRP)** has further expanded the applicability of functional languages. FRP allows programmers to handle asynchronous events and data streams declaratively, avoiding complex callback-based logic. This is particularly useful in UI development and real-time systems.

Functional programming has also influenced mainstream languages. Python, JavaScript, and even Java have integrated functional constructs such as **higher-order functions**, **immutability**, and **monads**, making functional paradigms more accessible.

Type Inference in Action

Consider the following example of type inference in Haskell:

```
doubleValue x = x * 2  -- No explicit type declaration needed
```

The compiler automatically infers that x is a numeric type, improving code readability and maintainability.

Algebraic Data Types Example

In Haskell, an algebraic data type representing a binary tree can be defined as:

```
data Tree a = Empty | Node a (Tree a) (Tree a)
```

Pattern matching simplifies recursive operations:

```
treeSum :: Num a => Tree a -> a
treeSum Empty = 0
treeSum (Node value left right) = value + treeSum left + treeSum right
```

Functional-Reactive Programming

In JavaScript, FRP libraries like RxJS implement declarative event handling:

```
const { fromEvent } = require('rxjs');
const { map } = require('rxjs/operators');

fromEvent(document, 'click')
  .pipe(map(event => `Clicked at ${event.clientX}, ${event.clientY}`))
  .subscribe(console.log);
```

This approach abstracts event handling, making it more readable and manageable.

Innovations in functional languages continue to improve software development by simplifying type management, enforcing structured data definitions, and introducing powerful abstractions for handling complexity. As functional paradigms become more integrated into mainstream languages, these advancements shape the future of declarative programming, ensuring greater expressiveness, reliability, and maintainability in software applications.

Applications of Logic Programming in AI

Logic programming has played a foundational role in artificial intelligence (AI) by providing a declarative approach to knowledge representation, reasoning, and problem-solving. Unlike imperative paradigms, logic programming describes relationships and rules rather than step-by-step procedures, making it well-suited for AI applications like expert systems, natural language processing, and automated reasoning.

One of the most prominent logic programming languages is **Prolog (Programming in Logic)**, which is used for symbolic reasoning and knowledge-based systems. Prolog operates by defining **facts**, **rules**, and **queries**, allowing developers to describe problems in terms of logical constraints. The **inference engine** uses a process called **unification and backtracking** to deduce answers, making Prolog an ideal choice for AI applications that require rule-based decision-making.

Another key area where logic programming is used in AI is **constraint logic programming (CLP)**, which extends Prolog to handle constraints over different domains such as integers, real numbers, and finite sets. CLP is widely applied in scheduling, planning, and optimization problems. Additionally, **answer set programming (ASP)** provides an alternative approach to logic programming, particularly for non-monotonic reasoning, where knowledge can change dynamically.

Beyond Prolog, logic programming concepts have influenced AI frameworks in other languages. For instance, **Datalog**, a declarative subset of Prolog, is used in database query optimization, graph analysis, and security policy enforcement. In modern AI, logic programming principles are integrated into machine learning and neural-symbolic systems, where symbolic reasoning complements data-driven learning models.

Prolog Example: Rule-Based Expert System

The following Prolog example demonstrates a simple expert system for diagnosing flu:

```
% Facts
symptom(john, fever).
symptom(john, cough).
symptom(john, fatigue).

% Rules
has_flu(Person) :- symptom(Person, fever), symptom(Person, cough),
          symptom(Person, fatigue).

% Query
?- has_flu(john).
```

When executed, this query returns true, indicating that John has flu based on the defined rules.

Constraint Logic Programming Example

CLP can solve scheduling problems declaratively:

```
:- use_module(library(clpfd)).

schedule(Start1, Start2) :-
    Start1 + 3 #=< Start2,  % Task 1 must finish before Task 2 starts
    labeling([], [Start1, Start2]).
```

This program ensures that Task 2 does not start before Task 1 completes, enforcing constraints without imperative control structures.

Logic programming continues to be a powerful tool in AI, providing robust frameworks for knowledge representation, expert systems, and constraint solving. With its declarative nature, it enables complex reasoning and decision-making processes, making it invaluable in AI-driven applications like automated planning, rule-based systems, and hybrid AI models that integrate symbolic and neural learning techniques.

Declarative Approaches in Parallel Computing

Parallel computing has become essential for optimizing performance in modern applications, particularly in data-intensive and high-performance computing environments. Declarative programming offers a unique approach to parallelism by abstracting away low-level thread management and synchronization details, allowing developers to focus on describing **what** needs to be computed rather than **how** to execute it concurrently.

In declarative paradigms, parallelism is often achieved through **functional programming** constructs such as **pure functions**, **monads**, and **lazy evaluation**, which eliminate side effects and make it easier to run computations in parallel. Additionally, **logic programming** supports parallel execution through **independent rule evaluation**, enabling concurrent inference in AI systems.

One of the most widely used declarative models for parallel computing is **dataflow programming**, where execution is driven by the availability of data rather than a predefined sequence of instructions. This model is especially effective for distributed systems, **big data processing**, and **stream-based computing frameworks** like Apache Spark and TensorFlow.

Another powerful approach is **parallel functional programming**, which leverages **higher-order functions** such as map, reduce, and filter to distribute computations across multiple processors. These functions operate on immutable data structures, ensuring thread safety without the need for explicit locks or synchronization.

Moreover, declarative languages like **Haskell** and **Elixir** provide built-in support for **implicit parallelism**, where the runtime system automatically determines the best way to execute computations concurrently. Prolog also supports **or-parallelism** and **and-parallelism**, enabling different branches of a computation to execute simultaneously.

Parallel Computing in Python

Python, although not inherently declarative, offers functional programming constructs and frameworks that support parallelism in a declarative manner. The multiprocessing and concurrent.futures modules allow developers to express parallel computation at a high level without manually managing threads.

Functional Parallelism with map

The map function enables parallel computation over a dataset:

```python
from concurrent.futures import ProcessPoolExecutor

def square(n):
    return n * n

numbers = [1, 2, 3, 4, 5]

with ProcessPoolExecutor() as executor:
    results = list(executor.map(square, numbers))

print(results)  # [1, 4, 9, 16, 25]
```

Here, map distributes the square function across multiple processes, computing results concurrently.

Declarative Dataflow with Dask

Dask provides a declarative interface for parallel computing:

```python
import dask.array as da

arr = da.arange(1, 1000000, chunks=100000)
result = (arr * 2).sum().compute()

print(result)  # Efficient parallel computation
```

Dask automatically parallelizes computations across CPU cores while keeping the code readable and high-level.

Declarative approaches simplify parallel computing by focusing on defining computations rather than managing execution. Functional programming, dataflow paradigms, and high-level frameworks enable efficient parallelism while maintaining readability and correctness. As multi-core and distributed systems become more prevalent, declarative parallelism will continue to play a crucial role in scalable software development.

Advanced Theoretical Models

Declarative programming is grounded in strong theoretical foundations that enable abstraction, composability, and correctness in software development. Over the years, advanced theoretical models have shaped the evolution of **functional** and **logic programming**, driving innovations in **parallel computing**, **type theory**, and **formal verification**. These models provide mathematical rigor to programming paradigms, ensuring predictability and maintainability in complex systems.

One of the most influential theoretical models in declarative programming is the **Lambda Calculus**, a formal system for function definition, application, and recursion. As the foundation of functional programming, Lambda Calculus abstracts computation into **pure mathematical functions**, eliminating state mutations and side effects. This model enables optimizations like **lazy evaluation**, **referential transparency**, and **function composition**, making functional programming ideal for parallelism and mathematical reasoning.

In logic programming, **Horn Clauses** and **Resolution** form the basis of languages like **Prolog** and **Datalog**. These models allow programmers to define rules and constraints declaratively, letting the inference engine deduce solutions rather than following procedural steps. **Answer Set Programming (ASP)** extends these concepts, allowing the modeling of **non-monotonic reasoning**, crucial in artificial intelligence and decision-making systems.

Another theoretical framework is **Category Theory**, which provides a high-level mathematical structure for reasoning about functions, types, and transformations. **Monads**, a concept from category theory, are widely used in functional languages like Haskell to model side effects while preserving purity. **Functor** and **Applicative** abstractions further enhance code modularity and reusability in declarative programming.

Additionally, **Dependent Types** and **Homotopy Type Theory (HoTT)** push the boundaries of declarative verification by embedding proofs within types. Languages like **Coq** and **Idris** leverage these models to allow developers to **prove program correctness** at compile-time, reducing runtime errors and improving reliability in critical software systems.

Practical Implementation of Lambda Calculus in Python

Though Python is not purely functional, it can model **Lambda Calculus** using anonymous functions (lambda):

```
# Church encoding: Representing True and False using Lambda Calculus
true = lambda x: lambda y: x
false = lambda x: lambda y: y

# Implementing logical operations
AND = lambda p: lambda q: p(q)(p)
OR = lambda p: lambda q: p(p)(q)
NOT = lambda p: p(false)(true)

# Evaluating logical expressions
```

```
print(AND(true)(false)("Yes")("No"))   # Output: No
print(OR(false)(true)("Yes")("No"))    # Output: Yes
print(NOT(false)("Yes")("No"))         # Output: Yes
```

This example showcases **pure functional computation** using **higher-order functions**, a concept derived directly from Lambda Calculus.

Category Theory: Functors in Python

Using **functors**, we can apply transformations over wrapped values:

```
class Functor:
    def __init__(self, value):
        self.value = value

    def map(self, func):
        return Functor(func(self.value))

# Applying transformations
f = Functor(10).map(lambda x: x * 2).map(lambda x: x + 3)
print(f.value)  # Output: 23
```

Here, **functors** allow transformations to be **composable**, maintaining immutability and purity.

Advanced theoretical models in declarative programming provide the **mathematical backbone** for safe, predictable, and composable software. From **Lambda Calculus** and **Logic Programming** to **Category Theory** and **Dependent Types**, these models enhance code correctness and scalability. Their influence continues to shape modern **functional**, **logic**, and **AI-driven** declarative paradigms.

Module 32:
Declarative Programming in Quantum Computing

Declarative programming has traditionally been associated with functional and logic paradigms, but its principles are also applicable in quantum computing. As quantum systems evolve, declarative approaches provide an effective way to express computations without explicitly defining the sequence of state changes. This module explores how declarative paradigms align with quantum computing through functional representations, constraint-based models, and future innovations.

Introduction to Quantum Declarative Programming

Quantum computing introduces a new paradigm of computation based on **quantum mechanics principles**, such as superposition, entanglement, and interference. Unlike classical computing, where data exists in a deterministic state, quantum data can exist in multiple states simultaneously, enabling new computational models. Declarative programming in quantum computing focuses on **high-level abstractions** that describe the desired computation rather than detailing how to achieve it.

Languages like **Qiskit, Quipper, and Silq** offer functional and declarative constructs that allow quantum programmers to **express transformations on quantum states** without managing low-level gate operations. Declarative quantum programming relies on **immutable state transformations**, enabling optimizations such as **automatic circuit simplifications** and **resource-efficient computations**. Functional programming paradigms, particularly **higher-order functions** and **category theory**, provide a natural fit for quantum computations, ensuring composability and correctness.

Functional Representations in Quantum Algorithms

Functional programming concepts are fundamental in quantum computing, as quantum computations are naturally **reversible** and **stateless**. Functional quantum programming defines computations as **pure functions** that map input quantum states to output quantum states. Higher-order functions, lambda calculus, and monads play a crucial role in expressing quantum transformations **compositionally**.

One major advantage of functional representations in quantum algorithms is the **concise and expressive nature** of defining quantum operations, such as the **Hadamard transform, Grover's search, and quantum Fourier transform (QFT)**. Functional languages like **Quipper** allow quantum circuits to be defined declaratively, ensuring correctness through type safety and immutability. Additionally, **category theory** offers powerful abstractions for reasoning about quantum programs, making it possible to **compose quantum gates and transformations algebraically**.

Constraint-Based Quantum Computation

Constraint programming, a declarative paradigm commonly used in logic programming and optimization problems, can be extended to quantum computation. In **constraint-based quantum programming**, computations are expressed as a set of constraints that define valid quantum states and transformations. This approach is particularly useful in **quantum annealing** and **variational quantum algorithms**, where solutions to optimization problems are encoded as quantum states that satisfy predefined constraints.

Quantum programming languages like **D-Wave's Ocean SDK** leverage declarative constraints to define energy minimization problems. Constraint-based models allow quantum programmers to express computations **abstractly**, relying on quantum solvers to determine optimal states. This model aligns with **constraint logic programming (CLP)** in classical computing, but in a quantum context, it enables solving NP-hard problems such as **combinatorial optimization** and **machine learning**.

Future Prospects

The future of declarative quantum programming is promising, with advances in **high-level quantum languages, formal verification, and quantum cloud computing**. As quantum hardware matures, declarative models will play a crucial role in making quantum programming more **accessible, scalable, and efficient**. The integration of **functional, logic, and constraint-based paradigms** will continue to shape quantum computing, allowing developers to **leverage powerful abstractions** while ensuring correctness and performance in quantum algorithms.

Introduction to Quantum Declarative Programming

Quantum computing represents a fundamental shift from classical computing by leveraging the principles of **superposition, entanglement, and quantum interference**. Declarative programming in quantum computing focuses on specifying **what** needs to be computed rather than **how** to perform computations at the gate level. This abstraction is crucial for working with complex quantum algorithms, as it allows developers to define **quantum transformations** without worrying about the underlying hardware implementation.

Declarative quantum programming is enabled by **functional and logic-based paradigms**, where computations are expressed as **pure functions** mapping quantum states. Quantum languages such as **Qiskit (Python), Quipper (Haskell), and Silq** provide declarative constructs that simplify defining and composing quantum operations. Functional principles like **immutability and referential transparency** align well with quantum mechanics, making functional programming an ideal foundation for quantum algorithms.

A simple example in Python using **Qiskit** illustrates the declarative approach to quantum programming:

```python
from qiskit import QuantumCircuit, transpile, Aer, execute

# Define a quantum circuit with two qubits
qc = QuantumCircuit(2)

# Apply a Hadamard gate to qubit 0
qc.h(0)

# Apply a CNOT gate (controlled-X) to create entanglement
qc.cx(0, 1)

# Measure both qubits
qc.measure_all()

# Execute on a quantum simulator
simulator = Aer.get_backend('qasm_simulator')
result = execute(qc, simulator).result()

# Display results
print(result.get_counts())
```

In this example, **entanglement** is declared using high-level transformations (Hadamard and CNOT), rather than manually managing quantum state transitions. This approach ensures **readability, correctness, and scalability**, making declarative programming a powerful model for quantum computations.

Declarative models also simplify **quantum circuit optimization**, as compilers can automatically **reduce redundant operations** or **rearrange gates** for improved performance. This abstraction is essential as quantum computing moves towards large-scale implementations where low-level control is impractical.

Future advancements in declarative quantum programming will integrate **constraint-solving, category theory, and functional composition** to develop more efficient and expressive quantum languages. By leveraging declarative paradigms, quantum developers can focus on defining **computational goals**, leaving the execution details to quantum compilers and solvers.

Functional Representations in Quantum Algorithms

Functional programming plays a crucial role in quantum computing by providing a **declarative approach** to defining quantum transformations. In functional representations, quantum states and operations are expressed as **pure functions** that map inputs to outputs without side effects. This approach aligns well with the **linear algebraic nature of quantum mechanics**, where quantum gates are unitary transformations applied to qubit states.

Functional representations allow quantum algorithms to be defined in a **compositional manner**, enabling **higher-order functions** that combine basic quantum operations into complex transformations. Languages like **Quipper (Haskell), Qiskit (Python), and Silq** support functional paradigms by enabling the **immutable transformation of quantum states** through declarative constructs.

In Python, **Qiskit** can be used to define quantum functions that compose multiple operations declaratively:

```python
from qiskit import QuantumCircuit, Aer, execute

# Define a function for a quantum Hadamard transformation
def hadamard_transform(n):
    qc = QuantumCircuit(n)
    for qubit in range(n):
        qc.h(qubit)   # Apply Hadamard gate to each qubit
    return qc

# Define a function to apply a quantum oracle
def oracle(qc, qubits):
    qc.cz(qubits[0], qubits[1])   # Apply controlled-Z gate
    return qc

# Define Grover's algorithm functionally
def grover_algorithm(n):
    qc = hadamard_transform(n)    # Apply Hadamard transform
    qc = oracle(qc, [0, 1])       # Apply oracle function
    qc.measure_all()              # Measure all qubits
    return qc

# Execute the quantum circuit
backend = Aer.get_backend('qasm_simulator')
qc = grover_algorithm(2)
result = execute(qc, backend).result()
print(result.get_counts())
```

In this example, **functional composition** enables the construction of **Grover's search algorithm** by modularly defining the **Hadamard transform**, an **oracle function**, and an **algorithmic pipeline** that applies them in sequence. This approach simplifies reasoning about quantum logic by abstracting **individual transformations** into **high-level function calls**.

Functional representations also facilitate **higher-order transformations**, allowing quantum programs to be **parametric** and **reusable**. This is particularly useful for defining **quantum Fourier transforms (QFT), quantum walks, and error correction protocols**.

The declarative nature of functional programming allows **compiler optimizations**, such as **gate cancellation and circuit compression**, leading to **efficient quantum execution**. Moreover, the functional paradigm makes **parallel execution** easier, as functional purity ensures that **quantum transformations do not interfere with one another**, a crucial property in noisy quantum environments.

By adopting functional representations, quantum computing can move towards **high-level, composable, and maintainable** programs, making it accessible to a broader audience of programmers while leveraging the full power of quantum mechanics.

Constraint-Based Quantum Computation

Constraint-based programming is a declarative paradigm that expresses problems as a set of **constraints** that a solution must satisfy. In quantum computing, constraint-based approaches define quantum states and operations by **restricting valid solutions through mathematical conditions**, aligning well with **quantum optimization, error correction, and constraint satisfaction problems (CSPs)**.

Quantum constraint solvers use **superposition, entanglement, and interference** to explore solution spaces efficiently. A notable example is **Quantum Approximate Optimization Algorithm (QAOA)**, which solves combinatorial problems by **encoding constraints into quantum circuits** and iteratively refining solutions. **Variational Quantum Eigensolver (VQE)** also applies constraints to optimize molecular structures in quantum chemistry.

In **Qiskit**, constraint-based quantum computation can be implemented using **quadratic unconstrained binary optimization (QUBO)**, where constraints are encoded as **Hamiltonians**. The following example demonstrates solving a **binary optimization problem** using a **quantum constraint-based approach**:

```
from qiskit.optimization import QuadraticProgram
from qiskit.optimization.algorithms import MinimumEigenOptimizer
from qiskit.aqua.algorithms import QAOA
from qiskit import Aer

# Define a constraint optimization problem
problem = QuadraticProgram()
problem.binary_var('x')
problem.binary_var('y')

# Objective function: Minimize (x XOR y)
problem.minimize(linear={'x': 1, 'y': 1}, quadratic={('x', 'y'): -2})

# Solve using Quantum Approximate Optimization Algorithm (QAOA)
backend = Aer.get_backend('qasm_simulator')
qaoa = QAOA(optimizer=None, quantum_instance=backend)
solver = MinimumEigenOptimizer(qaoa)

result = solver.solve(problem)
print(result)
```

Here, we define a **binary constraint optimization problem**, where the **XOR relation between two variables is minimized**. The **QAOA algorithm** is used to solve the problem by applying a **quantum circuit to encode the constraints** and iteratively refining the solution. This demonstrates how quantum systems efficiently **explore constrained solution spaces**.

Constraint-based quantum approaches also apply to **quantum error correction (QEC)**, where constraints define valid quantum states that mitigate decoherence. **Stabilizer codes**, such as **Shor's and Steane's codes**, enforce constraints on qubits to preserve quantum information.

Another critical application is in **constraint-based quantum scheduling**, where resources (such as qubits and gate operations) must satisfy timing and connectivity constraints. **Quantum annealers**, like those in **D-Wave systems**, solve constraint problems by evolving qubits towards an optimal solution.

The advantage of constraint-based quantum computation is its ability to **natively express combinatorial problems in a quantum framework**, leading to potential **exponential speedups** for problems like **graph coloring, SAT-solving, and route optimization**.

By leveraging declarative constraints, quantum computing can **formalize and optimize problem-solving strategies** in domains ranging from **logistics and finance to cryptography and artificial intelligence**, pushing the boundaries of quantum-enhanced computation.

Future Prospects

Declarative programming in quantum computing represents a promising direction for high-level, abstract reasoning over quantum systems. As quantum hardware and software continue to advance, declarative paradigms will play a crucial role in simplifying **quantum algorithm design, optimization, and execution**. Future prospects include the development of **quantum-specific declarative languages**, improved quantum **constraint solvers**, and integration with **classical declarative systems**.

One of the most exciting areas of development is the **creation of high-level declarative quantum languages** that abstract away low-level quantum gate operations. **Silq**, a quantum language with built-in reversibility and uncomputation, is an example of an early step in this direction. Future languages could extend concepts from **Prolog (logic programming)** or **Haskell (functional programming)** to **express quantum computations in a purely declarative manner**.

Another crucial area is **quantum-enhanced constraint solving**. Future quantum solvers could leverage **Grover's search algorithm** to efficiently explore large search spaces for **optimization problems, decision-making, and scheduling**. In machine learning, **Quantum Boltzmann Machines (QBMs)** and **Quantum Variational Circuits** could provide **declarative frameworks for feature selection and generative modeling**.

Quantum computing will also integrate **seamlessly with classical declarative frameworks**. Hybrid systems will enable declarative languages like **Datalog** or **SQL** to execute quantum-enhanced queries. For instance, a **quantum-enhanced SQL engine** could declaratively optimize **database search queries using Grover's algorithm**, drastically reducing retrieval times for large datasets.

Below is an example of how a **hybrid quantum-classical system** might work, using Python's Qiskit to accelerate a search query:

```python
from qiskit import QuantumCircuit, Aer, transpile
from qiskit.circuit.library import GroverOperator
from qiskit.algorithms import AmplificationProblem, Grover
from qiskit.visualization import plot_histogram

# Define a simple quantum database search problem
oracle = QuantumCircuit(2)
oracle.cz(0, 1)  # Example constraint for a search condition

# Define the Grover operator
grover_op = GroverOperator(oracle)

# Run Grover's algorithm to find the solution
backend = Aer.get_backend('qasm_simulator')
problem = AmplificationProblem(oracle)
grover = Grover()
result = grover.amplify(problem)

# Display results
print(result.circuit_results)
plot_histogram(result.circuit_results).show()
```

This program defines a **simple declarative constraint (an oracle function)**, applies **Grover's algorithm** to search for a valid solution, and simulates the quantum execution. Future declarative quantum systems will seamlessly integrate with **big data processing**, enabling optimizations in **logistics, cryptography, and AI**.

With ongoing advancements in **quantum cloud services (IBM Q, Google Quantum AI, AWS Braket)**, we can expect **declarative quantum platforms** to become more accessible. These platforms will allow developers to **write high-level quantum logic** without deep knowledge of quantum hardware.

Declarative quantum programming is poised to **redefine how we express, optimize, and execute quantum computations**, bridging the gap between **classical declarative reasoning and quantum advantage**. As research progresses, we can anticipate **more expressive, efficient, and scalable declarative quantum paradigms**, unlocking the full potential of quantum computing.

Module 33:
Declarative Programming for AI and Machine Learning

Declarative programming is becoming an essential paradigm in artificial intelligence (AI) and machine learning (ML) due to its ability to express logic clearly, enforce constraints, and promote explainability. This module explores the role of declarative programming in AI, covering explainable AI models, declarative data processing, the evolution of logic-based AI systems, and future research directions. By emphasizing high-level specifications over imperative control flow, declarative techniques enable AI models that are **interpretable, scalable, and efficient**. As AI continues to grow, declarative methodologies offer solutions to address the challenges of transparency, bias, and reliability in machine learning systems.

Explainable AI Through Declarative Models

Explainability in AI is crucial for trust, compliance, and debugging. Declarative models, such as those based on **logic programming, constraints, and symbolic reasoning**, provide **inherently interpretable** solutions by making **decision rules explicit**. Unlike black-box deep learning models, declarative AI systems specify **what needs to be achieved rather than how**. For example, **Prolog-based expert systems** can **logically derive decisions**, ensuring that AI models remain interpretable. Declarative rule-based systems are particularly useful in domains like **finance, healthcare, and legal AI**, where transparency is necessary. The combination of **probabilistic logic, knowledge graphs, and symbolic AI** allows declarative systems to enhance explainability while maintaining flexibility in reasoning.

Declarative Data Processing for Machine Learning

Machine learning pipelines involve extensive data transformations, feature engineering, and preprocessing, all of which can be declaratively specified. Declarative data processing frameworks, such as **SQL-based feature selection** and **functional dataflows**, enable efficient and readable transformations. Tools like **Apache Spark's SQL API, Dask, and TensorFlow's data pipelines** leverage declarative paradigms to **optimize data workflows automatically**. This approach allows **lazy evaluation, query optimization, and parallel execution**, reducing computational costs while improving maintainability. Declarative feature engineering techniques, such as **domain-specific languages (DSLs) for feature selection**, further streamline ML development. By **separating data manipulation logic from execution details**, declarative approaches enhance **scalability and modularity** in ML pipelines.

Evolution of Logic-Based AI Systems

Logic-based AI systems have evolved from **early expert systems and symbolic reasoning models** to **modern neuro-symbolic AI** approaches. Declarative AI was initially driven by **Prolog, Datalog, and constraint satisfaction systems**, which allowed knowledge representation and inference. However, traditional rule-based AI struggled with **scalability and uncertainty**. Recent advancements integrate **probabilistic reasoning, statistical learning, and deep learning** into declarative logic systems. **Probabilistic programming languages (PPLs)** like **Pyro and Turing.jl** now enable declarative specification of Bayesian models, bridging the gap between symbolic AI and statistical inference. This hybrid evolution allows modern AI systems to **combine reasoning with learning**, enhancing robustness and adaptability.

Future Research Directions

The future of declarative programming in AI and ML lies in the convergence of **symbolic reasoning, statistical learning, and automated decision-making**. Key research areas include **declarative fairness constraints**, ensuring AI models adhere to **ethical principles** without requiring manual interventions. Advances in **explainable neuro-symbolic AI** seek to combine **deep learning's pattern recognition** with **logic-based inference**. Declarative reinforcement learning (RL) is another emerging direction, where high-level rules guide **autonomous decision-making systems**. Additionally, **quantum declarative AI models** may revolutionize **optimization and search problems**. As AI moves towards **self-explaining and interpretable systems**, declarative programming will continue to play a pivotal role in shaping the next generation of AI-driven solutions.

Explainable AI through Declarative Models

Explainability is a crucial aspect of AI, ensuring transparency, fairness, and trust in decision-making processes. Declarative programming provides an effective approach to explainable AI (XAI) by structuring models around **explicit rules, constraints, and logical inference**. Unlike black-box neural networks, declarative AI models define decisions **in terms of symbolic rules**, making them easier to interpret. **Logic programming languages like Prolog** allow for reasoning with facts and rules, making AI systems more interpretable. Probabilistic logic programming (PLP) extends this by **handling uncertainty** in decision-making, making declarative approaches suitable for real-world AI applications like medical diagnosis, fraud detection, and recommendation systems.

A core advantage of declarative AI is that its reasoning process can be directly queried and understood. For example, if an AI system denies a loan application, a declarative system can explicitly state which rules were triggered to reach that decision. In contrast, deep learning models typically function as opaque mathematical functions, requiring external tools for interpretability. Declarative programming integrates **symbolic reasoning with machine learning models**, allowing AI systems to **justify decisions, detect biases, and adjust rules dynamically**.

Example: Explainable AI with Prolog

The following Prolog example illustrates how declarative AI can be used to **explain loan eligibility** based on defined rules:

```
% Facts about customers
income(john, high).
credit_score(john, good).
has_debt(john, no).

% Rules defining loan eligibility
eligible_for_loan(X) :- income(X, high), credit_score(X, good), has_debt(X, no).

% Query example
?- eligible_for_loan(john).
```

When queried, the system **explains the decision explicitly**, showing that John qualifies because all conditions were met. This contrasts with machine learning models, which typically require post-hoc explanation tools like SHAP or LIME to interpret their predictions.

Declarative Explainability in Machine Learning

Declarative programming also enhances explainability in **ML model decisions** by enforcing structured logic within AI pipelines. **Constraint-based rule engines**, such as Drools and TensorFlow Decision Forests, allow AI models to be **interpretable by design**. Consider the following Python example using **rule-based classification** in sklearn:

```
from sklearn.tree import DecisionTreeClassifier
from sklearn import tree

# Sample data (features: income, credit_score, debt_status)
X = [[1, 1, 0], [1, 0, 1], [0, 1, 1], [0, 0, 0]]
y = ["Eligible", "Not Eligible", "Not Eligible", "Eligible"]

# Create and train a decision tree classifier
clf = DecisionTreeClassifier()
clf.fit(X, y)

# Visualizing decision rules
tree.plot_tree(clf, feature_names=["Income", "Credit Score", "Debt"],
          class_names=["Eligible", "Not Eligible"], filled=True)
```

This decision tree represents a **declarative model** where eligibility rules are **explicitly learned** and **visualized**. The explainability is derived from the model's structure, which outlines **clear decision paths**. Unlike deep learning, where model decisions remain complex, declarative techniques enable **interpretable AI models** that justify decisions with structured logic.

As AI progresses, the **integration of declarative paradigms with statistical learning** will play a significant role in **ensuring transparency and accountability in AI-driven systems**.

Declarative Data Processing for Machine Learning

Machine learning (ML) relies on efficient data processing techniques to prepare raw data for training and inference. Declarative programming simplifies this process by expressing **what should be done** rather than **how it should be executed**. **SQL-based data transformations, functional pipelines, and declarative frameworks** like Apache Spark provide a structured, readable, and efficient way to manage ML data workflows. These declarative approaches enable scalability and **optimized execution plans**, making them essential for handling large-scale datasets in ML applications.

Declarative programming allows for **composable data transformations**, meaning operations like **filtering, aggregation, and feature extraction** can be expressed as high-level logic rather than imperative loops. This simplifies debugging and ensures efficient execution by leveraging **query optimizations**. SQL, for instance, is inherently declarative and widely used for ML data pipelines, allowing feature selection and transformation through simple queries instead of complex scripts. Frameworks like **Pandas, Dask, and PySpark** bring declarative data processing to Python, enabling ML workflows that scale seamlessly across distributed systems.

Example: Data Processing with SQL for ML

Consider a dataset stored in a SQL database where we need to extract and normalize features for an ML model:

```sql
SELECT
    customer_id,
    (income - AVG(income) OVER()) / STDDEV(income) OVER() AS normalized_income,
    (credit_score - AVG(credit_score) OVER()) / STDDEV(credit_score) OVER() AS
            normalized_credit_score
FROM customers;
```

This declarative SQL query **normalizes features** for ML training without requiring explicit looping or manual calculations, leveraging database optimizations for fast execution.

Declarative Data Pipelines with Pandas

Pandas provides a declarative approach to processing ML data. Instead of using explicit loops, **operations are performed in a functional manner**, applying transformations directly to entire datasets.

```python
import pandas as pd

# Sample dataset
data = pd.DataFrame({
    "income": [50000, 70000, 55000, 80000],
    "credit_score": [650, 700, 620, 750]
})

# Declarative feature normalization
data["normalized_income"] = (data["income"] - data["income"].mean()) /
            data["income"].std()
```

```
data["normalized_credit_score"] = (data["credit_score"] -
        data["credit_score"].mean()) / data["credit_score"].std()
print(data)
```

This approach ensures **readability and maintainability**, allowing feature engineering to be performed with concise, **declarative transformations** instead of iterative loops.

Declarative Data Pipelines with PySpark

For large-scale ML applications, declarative frameworks like PySpark enable **distributed data processing** without explicit iteration:

```
from pyspark.sql import SparkSession
from pyspark.sql.functions import col, mean, stddev

# Initialize Spark session
spark = SparkSession.builder.appName("MLPipeline").getOrCreate()

# Sample dataset
data = spark.createDataFrame([
    (1, 50000, 650),
    (2, 70000, 700),
    (3, 55000, 620),
    (4, 80000, 750)
], ["id", "income", "credit_score"])

# Normalize features declaratively
mean_income, std_income = data.select(mean(col("income")),
        stddev(col("income"))).first()
data = data.withColumn("normalized_income", (col("income") - mean_income) /
        std_income)

data.show()
```

By using **declarative transformations**, PySpark eliminates the need for manual iteration and distributes computations efficiently across multiple nodes.

Declarative data processing is **crucial for ML workflows**, enabling **efficient, scalable, and readable** transformations that seamlessly integrate with training and inference pipelines. By leveraging SQL, Pandas, and PySpark, ML practitioners can build robust feature engineering workflows **without imperative complexity**.

Evolution of Logic-Based AI Systems

Logic-based AI systems have played a crucial role in artificial intelligence research, providing a foundation for reasoning, knowledge representation, and automated decision-making. Unlike statistical machine learning models, logic-based AI relies on **symbolic reasoning**, allowing systems to derive conclusions from a structured set of rules and facts. Declarative programming, especially in **Prolog, Datalog, and Answer Set Programming (ASP)**, has significantly influenced the development of these AI systems. Over time, these methods have evolved to integrate with **modern AI techniques, including hybrid models that combine symbolic reasoning with machine learning**.

Early AI systems were built using **first-order logic (FOL) and rule-based inference engines**, which allowed them to **encode human knowledge explicitly**. For example, **expert systems** like MYCIN (used in medical diagnosis) relied on declarative rules to infer diagnoses based on patient symptoms. However, traditional logic-based AI faced challenges in **handling uncertainty, scalability, and adaptability**, leading to the emergence of **probabilistic logic models and neural-symbolic AI**. Today, declarative programming continues to be an essential tool for building **explainable AI systems** that can justify their reasoning processes.

Declarative Knowledge Representation in Prolog

Prolog, a logic-based declarative language, allows AI systems to **represent knowledge and derive conclusions through logical inference**. Consider a simple AI system that identifies animals based on their characteristics:

```
% Facts
mammal(dog).
mammal(cat).
bird(eagle).
bird(sparrow).

% Rules
has_feathers(X) :- bird(X).
has_fur(X) :- mammal(X).

% Query
?- has_fur(dog).
```

This Prolog program **declaratively encodes knowledge** about animals and allows inference through simple queries, demonstrating the power of logic programming for AI applications.

Hybrid AI: Combining Symbolic Logic with Machine Learning

To overcome the limitations of purely logic-based AI, modern systems integrate symbolic reasoning with machine learning. **Neural-symbolic AI** combines **deep learning models with logic-based reasoning**, allowing AI to learn from data while maintaining **human-interpretable decision-making**.

For example, **probabilistic logic programming** (PLP) extends traditional logic programming by incorporating probabilistic reasoning, enabling AI to handle **uncertainty in decision-making**. A Python-based example using **PyProbLog**, a probabilistic logic programming library, is shown below:

```
from problog.program import PrologString
from problog import get_evaluatable

# Probabilistic rules
model = """
0.7::rain.
0.8::umbrella :- rain.
```

317

```
query(umbrella).
"""

# Evaluate probability of carrying an umbrella
result = get_evaluatable().create_from(PrologString(model)).evaluate()
print(result)
```

This **probabilistic logic program** represents uncertainty about rain and the likelihood of carrying an umbrella, demonstrating how declarative AI systems can handle **real-world ambiguity**.

Declarative Reasoning in AI Systems

Modern logic-based AI systems benefit from declarative approaches that support **explainability, modularity, and composability**. **Knowledge graphs**, for instance, rely on declarative rule-based reasoning to infer new relationships between entities. AI models like **Google's Knowledge Graph** and **IBM Watson** use declarative logic to extract insights from structured knowledge bases.

Declarative programming continues to shape **AI research and applications**, from **automated reasoning and expert systems to explainable AI and hybrid neural-symbolic approaches**. By combining **logic-based declarative models with modern AI techniques**, the evolution of AI is moving towards **more interpretable, scalable, and knowledge-driven intelligent systems**.

Future Research Directions

The future of declarative programming in AI and machine learning lies in the convergence of **logic-based reasoning, neural networks, probabilistic models, and quantum computing**. As AI systems become more complex, researchers seek **more interpretable, explainable, and generalizable approaches**, where declarative programming plays a vital role. This evolution involves the development of **hybrid AI models, advanced declarative frameworks, and scalable reasoning engines** that can handle real-world uncertainties and dynamic environments.

One key research direction is **explainable AI (XAI)**, where declarative programming can **encode explicit reasoning rules** for machine learning models. Current deep learning models often function as **black boxes**, making it difficult to understand their decision-making processes. Declarative rule-based models, however, **allow AI systems to provide step-by-step justifications** for their conclusions. Research in **neural-symbolic integration** focuses on developing **hybrid AI systems** that combine **logical inference with deep learning** to enhance transparency and reliability.

Enhancing Declarative AI with Probabilistic Logic

Another major area of exploration is **probabilistic declarative programming**, which enhances traditional logic programming by incorporating **uncertainty and probabilistic**

318

reasoning. Probabilistic logic frameworks, such as **ProbLog and Bayesian Logic Networks (BLNs)**, enable AI systems to handle **noisy and uncertain data**, which is crucial for real-world applications. Consider a **declarative probabilistic AI model** that predicts whether a patient has a disease based on symptoms:

```
from problog.program import PrologString
from problog import get_evaluatable

# Probabilistic logic program
model = """
0.6::fever.
0.4::cough.
0.9::flu :- fever, cough.
query(flu).
"""

result = get_evaluatable().create_from(PrologString(model)).evaluate()
print(result)
```

This **probabilistic reasoning model** assigns likelihoods to symptoms and infers the probability of flu, demonstrating how **uncertainty can be modeled declaratively** in AI. Future research aims to improve the efficiency of such **probabilistic logic frameworks** for large-scale applications.

Scalable Declarative AI for Large-Scale Systems

Another promising research area is **scaling declarative AI to handle big data and distributed environments**. **Declarative knowledge representation techniques**, such as **Datalog-based query systems and semantic web reasoning**, enable AI to **process massive knowledge graphs efficiently**. Distributed reasoning engines, like **Apache Flink's declarative processing framework**, facilitate large-scale data-driven AI applications. Research in **distributed declarative AI** seeks to improve the **scalability, parallelization, and real-time reasoning capabilities** of logic-based AI models.

In addition, **quantum declarative AI** is an emerging field that explores the potential of **quantum computing for logic-based AI reasoning**. Quantum logic programming languages, such as **QuLog**, are being developed to leverage **quantum parallelism** for advanced reasoning tasks. Future research focuses on how **quantum logic and classical declarative programming can be integrated** to solve complex AI problems more efficiently.

The future of declarative programming in AI is defined by **hybrid reasoning models, probabilistic declarative AI, scalable distributed logic systems, and quantum logic programming**. Research continues to enhance **interpretability, efficiency, and adaptability** in AI applications, ensuring that **declarative paradigms remain central to AI's evolution**. By combining **logic-based declarative approaches with machine learning, probabilistic reasoning, and quantum computing**, the next generation of AI will be **more explainable, reliable, and capable of handling complex real-world problems**.

Module 34:
Declarative Cybersecurity and Cryptography

Declarative programming plays a crucial role in cybersecurity and cryptography, offering **high-level, policy-driven approaches** for managing security rules, detecting intrusions, implementing cryptographic protocols, and formally verifying security systems. By defining **security policies, logical intrusion detection mechanisms, and functional cryptographic algorithms**, declarative methods enhance **readability, correctness, and automation** in security applications. This module explores how declarative paradigms **simplify security management, strengthen intrusion detection, support cryptographic implementations, and ensure provable security guarantees** through formal verification.

Policy-Based Security Management

Policy-based security management enables organizations to define **high-level security policies declaratively** rather than relying on **imperative, rule-based configurations**. Declarative security policies specify **access controls, authentication mechanisms, and system behavior constraints** in a clear and structured manner. Security frameworks such as **XACML (eXtensible Access Control Markup Language)** and **SELinux (Security-Enhanced Linux)** leverage declarative specifications to enforce **fine-grained access control rules**. By defining security constraints independently of enforcement mechanisms, declarative security policies improve **maintainability, consistency, and adaptability** in large-scale systems.

Modern cloud platforms also adopt **policy-as-code approaches**, where security policies are **written in declarative languages** like **Rego (used in Open Policy Agent, OPA)**. These policies govern **network access, user permissions, and compliance enforcement** across distributed environments. Declarative security policies **reduce misconfigurations, improve auditability, and enable automated enforcement** in enterprise security management.

Logic-Based Intrusion Detection

Intrusion detection systems (IDS) benefit significantly from declarative programming, particularly through **logic-based reasoning models**. Instead of relying on **static rule-based detection mechanisms**, declarative IDS define security threats using **logical inference and pattern-matching techniques**. Languages like **Datalog** and **Prolog** facilitate the specification of **network traffic rules, behavioral patterns, and anomaly detection heuristics** in a concise and expressive manner.

Logic-based intrusion detection allows security teams to **analyze network logs, detect suspicious activity, and correlate security events declaratively**. This approach enhances **scalability, modularity, and adaptability** in detecting sophisticated cyber threats. By leveraging **machine learning and probabilistic reasoning**, logic-based IDS can **dynamically update threat models** and identify new attack patterns in real time.

Cryptographic Protocols in Functional Languages

Cryptographic algorithms and security protocols benefit from **functional programming paradigms** due to their **immutability, referential transparency, and high-level abstraction capabilities**. Functional languages like *Haskell, OCaml, and F (F-Star)** are widely used to implement **secure cryptographic primitives, encryption schemes, and secure multi-party computation protocols**. The declarative nature of functional languages **reduces side-channel vulnerabilities, simplifies reasoning about security properties, and ensures correctness-by-construction**.

For example, **purely functional implementations of AES encryption, RSA key exchange, and zero-knowledge proofs** leverage **strong type systems and mathematical proofs** to enforce security guarantees. The use of **monadic constructs and composable functions** allows developers to write **provably secure cryptographic protocols** that adhere to formal security specifications.

Formal Verification in Security Systems

Formal verification ensures that security systems **conform to mathematical correctness proofs and logical specifications**. Declarative methods, particularly in **theorem proving and model checking**, help verify cryptographic protocols, authentication schemes, and access control mechanisms with **rigorous formal guarantees**. Tools like **Coq, Isabelle/HOL, and TLA+** enable security researchers to **define security models declaratively and prove their correctness** against adversarial threats.

By applying **formal logic and type theory**, security engineers can **eliminate vulnerabilities, ensure compliance with security standards, and enhance software assurance** in critical applications. Formal verification techniques are essential for securing **smart contracts, blockchain protocols, and secure communication systems**, making declarative programming a foundational approach in cybersecurity research and practice.

Declarative programming provides **a robust foundation for cybersecurity and cryptography**, offering **policy-driven security management, logic-based intrusion detection, functional cryptographic implementations, and formal verification techniques**. By leveraging declarative paradigms, security professionals can **design more reliable, scalable, and provably secure systems** that resist cyber threats effectively. This module highlights how declarative methods **enhance security automation, reduce vulnerabilities, and improve system integrity** in modern cybersecurity applications.

Policy-Based Security Management

Security management in modern systems requires **structured, rule-based policies** to control access, authentication, and enforcement mechanisms. Declarative programming enables a **high-level approach** where security policies are defined as **explicit rules**, separate from implementation logic. Policy-based security management frameworks such as **XACML (eXtensible Access Control Markup Language)** and **Open Policy Agent (OPA)** allow organizations to specify security constraints in a **readable, maintainable, and verifiable** manner.

Declarative security policies follow a **policy-as-code** approach, where access control rules are stored as **structured definitions** in configuration files rather than imperative scripts. These rules dictate **who can access which resources, under what conditions, and with what level of permissions**. The advantage of this method is its ability to **simplify security administration, reduce human error, and enable automated enforcement** across complex systems.

A practical example of a declarative security policy can be implemented using **OPA with Rego**, a policy language that allows administrators to define access rules in **a logic-based, readable format**. Consider a policy that restricts API access based on user roles:

```
package example.auth

default allow = false

allow {
    input.user.role == "admin"
}
```

This policy ensures that only users with an **"admin"** role are granted access. The declarative nature allows security policies to be **easily modified, audited, and deployed** across distributed systems without altering core application logic.

Access Control with XACML

XACML is an XML-based language that enables organizations to define **fine-grained access control policies** declaratively. It separates security decision-making from enforcement, ensuring **consistency and scalability**. Below is an example of an XACML policy defining access rules for employees based on roles:

```
<Policy RuleCombiningAlgId="permit-overrides">
    <Rule Effect="Permit">
        <Condition>
            <Apply FunctionId="string-equal">
                <AttributeValue>Manager</AttributeValue>
                <AttributeDesignator AttributeId="role"/>
            </Apply>
        </Condition>
    </Rule>
</Policy>
```

This policy grants access **only to users assigned a "Manager" role**. Declarative security definitions like these **reduce implementation complexity and ensure centralized access control management**.

Cloud Security and Policy Enforcement

Cloud platforms such as **AWS, Azure, and Google Cloud** implement policy-based security using declarative configurations. **Infrastructure-as-Code (IaC)** tools like **Terraform and AWS IAM policies** enable defining security constraints declaratively.

Example of an AWS IAM policy allowing read-only access to S3 buckets:

```
{
    "Version": "2012-10-17",
    "Statement": [
        {
            "Effect": "Allow",
            "Action": "s3:GetObject",
            "Resource": "arn:aws:s3:::example-bucket/*"
        }
    ]
}
```

Such policies ensure **consistency, auditability, and compliance** across cloud environments, preventing misconfigurations that could lead to security vulnerabilities.

Declarative security management simplifies **policy enforcement, reduces operational risks, and enhances security governance**. By defining security constraints as **high-level rules**, organizations can ensure **scalability, flexibility, and compliance** in security management. Whether through **OPA, XACML, or cloud-based policies**, declarative programming strengthens **access control, authentication, and system security** in modern applications.

Logic-Based Intrusion Detection

Intrusion Detection Systems (IDS) play a crucial role in cybersecurity by monitoring network traffic, detecting anomalies, and identifying security breaches. Traditional IDS implementations rely on **imperative programming** with predefined signatures and heuristics, making them rigid and difficult to scale. **Declarative approaches**, on the other hand, utilize **logic programming** to define detection rules in a more expressive, maintainable, and adaptable way.

Logic-based intrusion detection leverages **rules, constraints, and inference mechanisms** to analyze network behavior. Instead of manually coding detection logic, declarative IDS define security threats **using high-level logical statements**. Languages such as **Prolog, Datalog, and Rego** allow cybersecurity analysts to express intrusion detection rules in a structured manner. These rules describe attack patterns, unauthorized access attempts, and policy violations in a format that the IDS can evaluate against live network data.

Intrusion Detection with Prolog

Prolog is a **logic programming language** well-suited for defining **security rules declaratively**. A simple intrusion detection rule in Prolog can identify repeated failed login attempts, a common sign of brute-force attacks:

```
failed_login(john, 2025-03-14, 12:01).
failed_login(john, 2025-03-14, 12:02).
failed_login(john, 2025-03-14, 12:03).

brute_force_attack(User) :-
    failed_login(User, _, T1),
    failed_login(User, _, T2),
    failed_login(User, _, T3),
    T1 < T2, T2 < T3.
```

This rule states that if a user has three failed login attempts within a short time, the system should flag it as a **potential brute-force attack**. Unlike traditional IDS implementations that rely on **hardcoded scripts**, this declarative approach makes intrusion detection **more adaptable and easier to update**.

Real-Time Intrusion Detection with Rego

Rego, the policy language used by **Open Policy Agent (OPA)**, enables intrusion detection in **cloud environments** and microservices. The following Rego policy detects multiple failed API login attempts within a short timeframe:

```
package security.ids

default alert = false

alert {
    count([x | x = input.failed_logins[_]]) > 3
}
```

Here, the IDS raises an alert if there are more than three failed login attempts within a given period. The declarative nature of Rego allows **scalability** across distributed cloud applications, providing **centralized security policies** without modifying application logic.

Network Traffic Analysis with Datalog

Datalog, a logic programming language similar to Prolog, is often used in **network traffic analysis and security monitoring**. It enables declarative querying of logs to identify suspicious behavior. Consider the following Datalog rule detecting unauthorized SSH access attempts:

```
attack(X) :-
    connection(X, "SSH", "failed"),
    count([Y | connection(Y, "SSH", "failed")]) > 5.
```

This rule detects repeated failed SSH login attempts, flagging them as a potential attack. Since Datalog **queries structured event logs**, it is well-suited for large-scale intrusion detection across **enterprise networks and cloud security systems**.

Logic-based intrusion detection leverages **declarative rules and logical inference** to enhance cybersecurity monitoring. By expressing detection logic in **Prolog, Datalog, or Rego**, security teams can **define attack patterns declaratively**, making detection **more scalable, adaptable, and maintainable**. This approach significantly improves the efficiency of **modern IDS systems** in combating cyber threats.

Cryptographic Protocols in Functional Languages

Cryptography is a cornerstone of modern cybersecurity, ensuring data confidentiality, integrity, and authenticity. Traditional cryptographic implementations rely on imperative programming, where developers manually orchestrate encryption and decryption processes. However, **functional programming languages** offer a more declarative approach to cryptography by emphasizing **immutability, higher-order functions, and pure computations**, which enhance security and reduce implementation errors.

Functional languages like **Haskell, OCaml, and F#** provide robust cryptographic libraries and **algebraic abstractions** that enable secure computations with minimal side effects. These languages facilitate cryptographic operations such as **hashing, symmetric and asymmetric encryption, key exchange protocols, and digital signatures**, offering a structured and more mathematically sound approach to security.

Hashing with Haskell

Hashing is a fundamental cryptographic operation used for **password storage, integrity verification, and digital signatures**. Functional languages provide **pure functions** that ensure deterministic and side-effect-free hash computations. The following Haskell example demonstrates SHA-256 hashing using the cryptonite library:

```
import Crypto.Hash (SHA256, hashWith)
import Data.ByteString.Char8 (pack)
import Data.ByteArray.Encoding (convertToBase, Base(Base16))

hashPassword :: String -> String
hashPassword password =
    let hashed = hashWith SHA256 (pack password)
    in show (convertToBase Base16 hashed)

main :: IO ()
main = putStrLn (hashPassword "securepassword")
```

Here, hashWith SHA256 applies a cryptographic hash function to the input, ensuring that password storage follows **secure, one-way encryption principles**. Unlike imperative approaches, Haskell's purity guarantees that no hidden state manipulations occur, reducing vulnerabilities such as **side-channel attacks**.

Functional Encryption in OCaml

Functional encryption ensures data confidentiality by encoding messages securely using **public-key cryptography (RSA, ECC)**. The following OCaml example demonstrates RSA encryption and decryption using the mirage-crypto library:

```
open Mirage_crypto_pk
open Mirage_crypto_rng

let generate_keys () =
  let priv, pub = Rsa.generate ~bits:2048 () in
  (priv, pub)

let encrypt_decrypt () =
  let priv, pub = generate_keys () in
  let message = Cstruct.of_string "Confidential Data" in
  let encrypted = Rsa.encrypt ~key:pub message |> Option.get in
  let decrypted = Rsa.decrypt ~key:priv encrypted |> Option.get in
  Printf.printf "Decrypted message: %s\n" (Cstruct.to_string decrypted)

let () = encrypt_decrypt ()
```

This **purely functional approach** to encryption ensures that cryptographic keys remain **immutable and reusable**, reducing risks of unintended state modifications. **OCaml's type safety and functional purity** make it an excellent choice for cryptographic applications.

Secure Key Exchange with Haskell

Key exchange protocols like **Diffie-Hellman (DH)** allow two parties to establish a shared secret over an insecure channel. The following Haskell example demonstrates a basic **Diffie-Hellman key exchange** using the cryptonite library:

```
import Crypto.PubKey.DH
import Crypto.Random (getRandomBytes)
import Data.ByteString (ByteString)

generateKeyPair :: IO (PrivateNumber, PublicNumber)
generateKeyPair = do
    let params = dhParams (1024, 2)
    priv <- getRandomBytes 128
    let pub = calculatePublic params priv
    return (priv, pub)

main :: IO ()
main = do
    (privA, pubA) <- generateKeyPair
    (privB, pubB) <- generateKeyPair
    let sharedSecretA = getShared params privA pubB
    let sharedSecretB = getShared params privB pubA
    print (sharedSecretA == sharedSecretB)
```

This **declarative approach** abstracts cryptographic complexity while ensuring correctness through **type safety and immutability**. The **functional paradigm eliminates state-related vulnerabilities**, making it highly suitable for **secure communications**.

Cryptographic protocols implemented in functional languages **enhance security, correctness, and maintainability**. By leveraging **pure functions, immutability, and strong typing**, declarative cryptography minimizes attack vectors and ensures reliable encryption mechanisms. Functional programming offers a structured, **mathematically rigorous approach** to cryptographic security, making it a powerful tool in cybersecurity applications.

Formal Verification in Security Systems

Formal verification is a crucial approach in cybersecurity, ensuring that cryptographic algorithms, authentication protocols, and access control mechanisms adhere to strict security guarantees. Unlike traditional testing, which only validates specific inputs, **formal methods mathematically prove that a system meets its security specifications**. This approach is particularly useful for **cryptographic implementations, secure protocols, and access control mechanisms**, where errors can lead to catastrophic vulnerabilities.

Functional and declarative languages, such as **Haskell, Coq, and Prolog**, offer strong support for formal verification by allowing developers to express security policies and cryptographic proofs in a **mathematically rigorous** way. These languages enable **static analysis, theorem proving, and model checking**, ensuring that security properties hold under all conditions.

Theorem Proving for Cryptographic Algorithms in Coq

Coq is a dependently typed functional programming language and proof assistant that enables the **formal verification of cryptographic protocols**. The following example demonstrates how to formally verify that XOR encryption is **self-inverting** (i.e., decrypting an encrypted message with the same key restores the original message).

```
Require Import Coq.Bool.Bool.

Theorem xor_involution : forall b k : bool, xorb (xorb b k) k = b.
Proof.
  intros b k.
  destruct b, k; simpl; reflexivity.
Qed.
```

This proof guarantees that the XOR operation, when applied twice with the same key, **correctly recovers the original bit**. By extending this logic to byte sequences, **Coq can verify larger cryptographic protocols**, such as block ciphers and hash functions.

Model Checking for Authentication Protocols

Model checking is another formal method used to **validate security protocols** by systematically exploring all possible states. A common use case is verifying authentication mechanisms, ensuring that an attacker cannot **bypass authentication or gain unauthorized access**. The **Tamarin Prover**, a tool for formal security analysis, allows defining security properties and checking whether protocols satisfy them.

Below is an example of defining a **simple authentication protocol** in Tamarin:

```
rule Initiator_Send:
  [ Fr(~Na), Fr(~K) ]
  --[ Start(A, B) ]->
  [ Sent(A, B, ~Na, ~K) ]

rule Responder_Receive:
  [ Sent(A, B, Na, K) ]
  --[ Accept(A, B, Na, K) ]->
  [ Established(A, B, Na, K) ]
```

Here, we formally specify that a protocol participant (A) generates a **fresh nonce (Na)** and sends it securely to participant (B). The Responder_Receive rule ensures that B correctly establishes a session only if the nonce and key are authentic. **Tamarin verifies that an attacker cannot inject or modify messages**, proving the protocol's security.

Prolog for Logic-Based Security Verification

Prolog, a declarative logic programming language, is well-suited for verifying access control policies and security rules. The following **Prolog example ensures that users can only access files based on predefined rules**:

```
access(admin, _).
access(user, read).
access(guest, read) :- not(admin).

can_access(User, Action) :- access(User, Action).
```

A query such as can_access(user, write). would return false, enforcing security constraints automatically. **Prolog's declarative nature ensures that security policies are consistently applied** without imperative control structures.

Formal verification strengthens cybersecurity by **mathematically proving system security** rather than relying on empirical testing. Tools like **Coq, Tamarin, and Prolog** enable developers to verify cryptographic protocols, authentication mechanisms, and access control rules with **mathematical precision**. This declarative approach ensures that security guarantees hold across all possible execution scenarios, making it a **critical tool in cybersecurity applications**.

Module 35:
Theoretical Advances in Declarative Computing

Declarative computing has evolved significantly with contributions from theoretical computer science, particularly in areas such as language design, software engineering, and compiler optimization. This module explores the theoretical advancements that drive modern declarative programming, focusing on **domain-specific languages, category theory, software engineering research, and compiler optimization techniques**. Understanding these foundational theories enhances the practical application of declarative programming in various computing domains, ensuring better abstraction, modularity, and efficiency. By analyzing these theoretical advancements, developers and researchers can **design better declarative languages, optimize performance, and push the boundaries of modern computing paradigms**.

Domain-Specific Languages for Declarative Programming

Domain-Specific Languages (DSLs) play a crucial role in declarative programming by **abstracting complex operations into expressive, problem-focused syntax**. Unlike general-purpose languages, DSLs are tailored for specific tasks, such as database queries (SQL), build automation (Makefiles), and infrastructure management (Terraform). The rise of **embedded DSLs (EDSLs) in functional languages** has further enhanced the power of declarative paradigms by allowing users to create problem-specific abstractions within existing languages. These advancements enable developers to **express complex logic succinctly while ensuring correctness and efficiency**. Theoretical research in **denotational semantics, type systems, and program synthesis** continues to refine the expressiveness and usability of DSLs.

Category Theory in Modern Programming Languages

Category theory provides a **mathematical framework for reasoning about functions, transformations, and composability** in programming languages. Concepts such as **functors, monads, and adjunctions** are widely used in declarative and functional programming paradigms to ensure composability and correctness. Category theory has influenced the development of modern languages such as **Haskell, Scala, and Idris**, where higher-order abstractions simplify the manipulation of data structures and effects. By treating **programs as mathematical objects**, category theory enables more **predictable, modular, and reusable code**, offering a structured approach to software design. The ongoing research into **categorical logic, dependent types, and algebraic effects** continues to expand the theoretical foundation of declarative programming.

Research in Declarative Software Engineering

Declarative software engineering explores how high-level abstractions can improve **software correctness, maintainability, and scalability**. The field has seen advancements in **contract-based programming, constraint solving, and automated reasoning**, where declarative paradigms ensure that programs are provably correct before execution. Techniques such as **specification-driven development, SAT solvers, and SMT (Satisfiability Modulo Theories) reasoning** enable developers to **define system behavior without explicitly stating control flow**. This shift reduces **imperative complexity** and enhances **reliability** in mission-critical software applications, such as formal verification, embedded systems, and automated theorem proving. Research continues to refine **verification techniques, proof assistants, and automated synthesis tools** to improve declarative software engineering methodologies.

Trends in Declarative Compiler Optimization

Compiler optimization techniques have advanced significantly with declarative computing, allowing programs to be **automatically optimized for performance, parallelization, and memory efficiency**. Modern compilers leverage **graph-based optimization, lazy evaluation, and partial evaluation** to improve program execution. Techniques such as **supercompilation, deforestation, and rewrite rules** help eliminate unnecessary computations, making declarative programs as efficient as imperative counterparts. Research in **abstract interpretation, symbolic execution, and automatic differentiation** continues to push the boundaries of **compiler optimizations for declarative languages**, enabling them to scale to **high-performance computing, distributed systems, and AI applications**.

Theoretical advances in declarative computing provide a **solid foundation for language design, software engineering, and compiler optimization**. By understanding **domain-specific abstractions, category-theoretic foundations, formal verification techniques, and compiler optimizations**, developers and researchers can build **more expressive, efficient, and reliable declarative systems**. These ongoing theoretical contributions ensure that declarative programming remains at the **forefront of modern computing paradigms**, shaping the future of software development.

Domain-Specific Languages for Declarative Programming

Domain-Specific Languages (DSLs) are a key component of declarative programming, offering high-level abstractions tailored to specific problem domains. Unlike general-purpose programming languages, DSLs are designed to be **concise, expressive, and optimized for a particular task**. Examples include **SQL for databases, Terraform for infrastructure as code, and Regex for pattern matching**. The primary advantage of DSLs is their ability to **simplify complex operations, reduce boilerplate code, and enhance maintainability**. With the rise of embedded DSLs (EDSLs), developers can define specialized languages within host programming languages, allowing seamless integration and better performance. Research in DSLs focuses on **improving expressiveness, type safety, and compilation techniques to enhance efficiency and correctness**.

330

Implementing a Simple DSL in Python

A DSL can be implemented in Python using **parsing techniques or embedded DSL approaches**. Consider a simple **DSL for defining mathematical expressions declaratively**:

```python
class Expression:
    def evaluate(self):
        raise NotImplementedError()

class Number(Expression):
    def __init__(self, value):
        self.value = value

    def evaluate(self):
        return self.value

class Add(Expression):
    def __init__(self, left, right):
        self.left = left
        self.right = right

    def evaluate(self):
        return self.left.evaluate() + self.right.evaluate()

# Example usage
expr = Add(Number(10), Number(5))
print(expr.evaluate())  # Output: 15
```

Here, expressions are **constructed declaratively** using object composition, rather than writing imperative calculations. This is a foundational principle in DSLs—**defining what should be done rather than how to do it**.

Embedded DSLs and Functional Programming

Functional languages like **Haskell and Lisp** are widely used for DSL development due to their **strong type systems and abstraction capabilities**. Embedded DSLs (EDSLs) allow programmers to **build domain-specific constructs within existing languages** rather than creating a new syntax from scratch. Python provides tools like **decorators, operator overloading, and metaprogramming** to achieve similar expressiveness.

```python
class Variable:
    def __init__(self, name):
        self.name = name

    def __add__(self, other):
        return f"({self.name} + {other.name})"

x = Variable("x")
y = Variable("y")
expr = x + y  # Outputs "(x + y)"
print(expr)
```

This approach allows **declarative composition of expressions** using natural language constructs, making the code more intuitive and readable.

Optimizing DSL Execution

One major challenge in DSL development is **efficient execution and compilation**. DSLs can be **interpreted or compiled into lower-level representations** for better performance. Python frameworks like **PLY (Python Lex-Yacc) and ANTLR** help build parsers and interpreters for custom DSLs.

```python
from lark import Lark, Transformer

grammar = """
    start: expr
    expr: expr "+" term  -> add
        | term
    term: NUMBER         -> number
    %import common.NUMBER
    %import common.WS
    %ignore WS
"""

class EvalTransformer(Transformer):
    def number(self, n):
        return int(n[0])

    def add(self, args):
        return args[0] + args[1]

parser = Lark(grammar, parser="lalr", transformer=EvalTransformer())
print(parser.parse("3 + 5"))  # Output: 8
```

This example **parses arithmetic expressions using a declarative grammar** and evaluates them dynamically. Such techniques are widely used in **DSL compilers, rule engines, and expression evaluators**.

DSLs provide a powerful **abstraction mechanism** in declarative programming, enabling concise and readable code for specific problem domains. By **leveraging functional programming concepts, embedded DSLs, and efficient parsing techniques**, developers can create highly expressive languages that improve software reliability and maintainability. The evolution of **type systems, syntax transformations, and JIT compilation** continues to shape the future of DSLs in declarative programming.

Category Theory in Modern Programming Languages

Category theory provides a mathematical foundation for **abstraction, composition, and transformation**, making it an essential tool in modern programming languages. It plays a significant role in **functional programming**, influencing concepts such as **functors, monads, and morphisms**. By defining computations in terms of **objects and morphisms**, category theory helps developers reason about **data transformations, program correctness, and composability**. Languages like **Haskell and Scala** integrate category-theoretic principles directly, while Python and JavaScript adopt them through libraries. The growing adoption of **category-theoretic constructs** enables developers to write **safer, more predictable, and reusable** code.

332

Functors and Mapping Structures

One fundamental concept in category theory is the **functor**, which maps values inside a structure while preserving composition. In programming, a **functor is often represented as a container or a computational context that supports mapping**. Python's map function, list comprehensions, and the functools module illustrate functorial behavior.

```
class Functor:
    def __init__(self, value):
        self.value = value

    def fmap(self, func):
        return Functor(func(self.value))

# Example usage
num = Functor(10)
result = num.fmap(lambda x: x * 2)
print(result.value)  # Output: 20
```

This example encapsulates a value inside a **functor** and allows functions to be applied declaratively without modifying the structure. Functors appear in **data processing pipelines, functional reactive programming (FRP), and monadic computations**.

Monads: Handling Side Effects Declaratively

A monad extends the concept of **functors** by enabling **chained computations while managing side effects**. A monad consists of three key components:

1. **A wrapper (Monad type) to encapsulate values**

2. **A unit (or return) function to lift a value into the monad**

3. **A bind function (>>=) to chain operations while preserving structure**

```
class Monad:
    def __init__(self, value):
        self.value = value

    def bind(self, func):
        return func(self.value)

# Example usage
monad = Monad(5)
result = monad.bind(lambda x: Monad(x + 10)).bind(lambda x: Monad(x * 2))
print(result.value)  # Output: 30
```

This **monadic structure** helps model **state, exceptions, and I/O operations** declaratively, as seen in **Haskell's IO monad, Scala's Option monad, and Python's context managers**.

Category Theory in Type Systems

Category theory influences **type systems in functional programming**, leading to concepts such as:

- **Algebraic Data Types (ADTs)**, including **sum types (variants) and product types (tuples, records)**

- **Higher-Kinded Types (HKT)**, allowing generic types to accept type constructors

- **Compositional design**, where functions can be expressed using **pure transformations**

Python's **dataclasses, pattern matching, and typing module** facilitate category-theoretic approaches:

```python
from dataclasses import dataclass
from typing import Generic, TypeVar

T = TypeVar("T")

@dataclass
class Container(Generic[T]):
    value: T

    def map(self, func):
        return Container(func(self.value))

# Example usage
c = Container(4)
print(c.map(lambda x: x * x).value)  # Output: 16
```

This demonstrates **mapping over a generic structure**, similar to **functors and applicatives in functional languages**.

Category theory provides **a mathematical framework for structuring programs declaratively**, making it vital for **functional programming, type theory, and compositional design**. Concepts like **functors, monads, and morphisms** enhance **code safety, predictability, and modularity**. As modern programming languages **incorporate more category-theoretic principles**, developers can build more **robust, scalable, and maintainable** applications.

Research in Declarative Software Engineering

Declarative programming has transformed software engineering by emphasizing **what** needs to be done rather than **how** to do it. Research in **declarative software engineering** explores its applications in **software development methodologies, specification languages, verification techniques, and domain-specific optimizations**. By abstracting away imperative control structures, declarative paradigms allow engineers to focus on logic, correctness, and high-level specifications, improving **maintainability, scalability, and verification** of complex software systems.

Declarative Specification Languages

One area of research focuses on **declarative specification languages**, which describe **software behavior and constraints** instead of procedural implementations. Languages like **Z Notation, Alloy, and TLA+** enable **formal specification, model checking, and correctness verification**. In Python, z3-solver provides a constraint-solving approach to declarative specifications:

```
from z3 import Int, Solver

x, y = Int('x'), Int('y')
solver = Solver()
solver.add(x + y == 10, x > 2, y < 8)

if solver.check() == 'sat':
    print(solver.model())  # Example output: [x = 3, y = 7]
```

This example **encodes logical constraints declaratively** and finds a solution satisfying all conditions, mirroring real-world **software verification tasks**.

Automated Reasoning in Software Engineering

Another research area in declarative software engineering is **automated reasoning**, which applies logical inference to **debugging, correctness proofs, and code synthesis**. Declarative approaches allow programs to **prove correctness properties** instead of relying on **runtime tests alone**. The **Coq proof assistant, Dafny, and Lean theorem prover** demonstrate how declarative reasoning enhances software **reliability and correctness**.

Python offers **constraint solvers and theorem provers** for declarative reasoning:

```
from sympy import symbols, Eq, solve

a, b = symbols('a b')
equation = Eq(2 * a + b, 8)
solution = solve(equation, b)
print(solution)  # Output: {b: 8 - 2*a}
```

Here, **symbolic computation** expresses and solves mathematical constraints without imperative iteration. This approach is applicable in **AI, verification, and automated code generation**.

Declarative Debugging Techniques

Declarative debugging shifts the focus from stepwise execution to **logical inconsistencies and constraint violations. Research explores declarative techniques for debugging large-scale distributed systems, software verification, and constraint-based fault detection**. One example is **tracing dependency violations in reactive or rule-based systems**.

In Python, logging frameworks combined with **rule-based assertions** help implement declarative debugging:

335

```
def check_rules(fact):
    rules = [lambda x: x % 2 == 0, lambda x: x > 10]
    assert all(rule(fact) for rule in rules), "Rule violation detected!"

check_rules(12)  # Passes
check_rules(9)   # Fails assertion
```

This technique ensures that **code adheres to declarative constraints** without requiring step-by-step imperative debugging.

Research in declarative software engineering explores **specification languages, formal verification, automated reasoning, and declarative debugging**. These advances help **improve software correctness, maintainability, and efficiency** by shifting from **imperative stepwise execution** to **high-level logical specifications**. As research progresses, **declarative paradigms will continue influencing software reliability and AI-assisted programming tools**.

Trends in Declarative Compiler Optimization

Declarative compiler optimization is an emerging field that focuses on **leveraging high-level specifications, rule-based transformations, and automatic reasoning** to improve the performance of compiled programs. Unlike traditional imperative optimizations, which rely on step-by-step transformations, declarative compiler optimization **defines optimization rules declaratively** and applies them systematically. This approach enhances **performance, parallelism, and correctness guarantees** while reducing manual intervention.

Rule-Based Optimization in Compilers

Modern compilers increasingly use **rule-based optimization strategies** to transform and optimize code at the intermediate representation (IR) level. **Declarative optimization frameworks**, such as **MLIR (Multi-Level Intermediate Representation)** and **Halide**, allow developers to specify transformations in a high-level declarative form. In Python, a **basic rule-based optimizer** can be implemented using **pattern-matching and rewriting techniques**:

```
import re

def optimize_expression(expr):
    rules = {
        r'\b(x \* 1)\b': 'x',  # Multiplication by 1
        r'\b(x \+ 0)\b': 'x',  # Addition by 0
        r'\b(x \* 0)\b': '0',  # Multiplication by 0
    }

    for pattern, replacement in rules.items():
        expr = re.sub(pattern, replacement, expr)
    return expr

print(optimize_expression("x * 1 + 0"))  # Output: x
```

This example shows a **basic declarative compiler optimization rule set**, where expressions are rewritten based on predefined **mathematical simplifications**.

Declarative Parallelization Techniques

Another key trend in declarative compiler optimization is **automatic parallelization**, where the compiler detects opportunities to **execute computations in parallel** without explicit programmer intervention. Languages like **Halide and TensorFlow XLA (Accelerated Linear Algebra)** use declarative scheduling to optimize execution. In Python, the **Numba library** allows declarative parallelization:

```python
from numba import jit, prange
import numpy as np

@jit(nopython=True, parallel=True)
def parallel_sum(arr):
    total = 0
    for i in prange(len(arr)):
        total += arr[i]
    return total

arr = np.array([1, 2, 3, 4, 5])
print(parallel_sum(arr))  # Output: 15
```

Here, the @jit decorator **instructs the compiler to optimize the function for parallel execution**, reducing computation time.

Constraint-Based Register Allocation

Register allocation is a classic compiler optimization problem, where variables must be assigned to a limited number of CPU registers efficiently. **Constraint-based optimization techniques** can be applied declaratively using **constraint solvers**.

A Python example using z3-solver for register allocation might look like this:

```python
from z3 import Int, Solver

r1, r2, r3 = Int('r1'), Int('r2'), Int('r3')
solver = Solver()
solver.add(r1 != r2, r2 != r3, r1 != r3, r1 >= 0, r2 >= 0, r3 >= 0)

if solver.check() == 'sat':
    print(solver.model())  # Output: Valid register assignments
```

This approach ensures **optimal register assignment** while respecting architectural constraints, leading to efficient compiled code.

Declarative compiler optimization focuses on **rule-based transformations, parallelization, and constraint-solving techniques** to enhance program performance. As research advances, **compiler frameworks will increasingly rely on declarative methodologies**, reducing the need for manual tuning and making optimizations more **scalable, predictable, and efficient** in real-world applications.

Module 36:
The Future of Declarative Programming

Declarative programming continues to evolve, shaping how developers express logic in high-level, readable ways. As industries increasingly adopt declarative paradigms, they must also navigate associated challenges, such as debugging complexity and performance concerns. This module explores **industry trends, challenges, emerging technologies, and future research directions** that will define the next phase of declarative computing.

Industry Adoption Trends

Industries across diverse domains are recognizing the benefits of declarative programming. **Cloud infrastructure, artificial intelligence, and data analytics** have embraced declarative paradigms due to their high-level abstraction capabilities. In DevOps, **Infrastructure as Code (IaC)** solutions like Terraform and AWS CloudFormation allow teams to specify system states rather than imperative configurations. AI and machine learning frameworks, such as TensorFlow and PyTorch, integrate declarative constructs to define computation graphs efficiently. The increasing use of **functional programming languages** in large-scale data processing, including Haskell and Scala, demonstrates industry momentum toward declarative approaches. As enterprises prioritize automation and maintainability, declarative programming is expected to become **a cornerstone of modern software architecture**.

Challenges and Limitations

Despite its advantages, declarative programming presents notable challenges. **Debugging and error handling** remain complex, as declarative abstractions can obscure low-level execution details. Unlike imperative code, where step-by-step logic is explicit, declarative constructs rely on **underlying engines** to determine execution order, making performance tuning difficult. **Scalability concerns** also emerge in large-scale systems, where declarative optimization strategies may introduce unexpected overhead. Another limitation is the **learning curve**, as developers accustomed to imperative paradigms may struggle to transition to declarative models. Overcoming these challenges requires **advancements in debugging tools, compiler optimizations, and education initiatives** to ease adoption.

Emerging Technologies in Declarative Computing

Emerging technologies are shaping the next generation of declarative computing. **Quantum computing** is exploring functional and constraint-based paradigms to optimize quantum algorithms declaratively. The rise of **low-code and no-code platforms** leverages declarative principles to enable users to build applications with minimal programming effort. **Declarative AI frameworks** are integrating logic-based reasoning and constraint satisfaction techniques to

338

improve decision-making capabilities. In cybersecurity, **policy-based access control (PBAC)** and **declarative intrusion detection systems** are advancing security automation. These innovations highlight **the expanding influence of declarative programming**, as new computational models embrace its high-level approach to problem-solving.

Next Steps for Developers and Researchers

For developers and researchers, the future of declarative programming presents exciting opportunities. Engineers should focus on mastering **domain-specific declarative languages**, such as SQL for data processing or Prolog for logic programming. Research should prioritize **enhanced debugging techniques**, **compiler optimizations**, and **hybrid models** that blend declarative and imperative paradigms for performance improvements. As declarative computing intersects with AI, quantum computing, and distributed systems, exploring **multi-paradigm approaches** will be crucial. By staying informed on **new declarative tools and methodologies**, both practitioners and academics can contribute to the **next wave of innovation in declarative programming**.

Declarative programming is poised for continued growth, with increasing industry adoption and technological advancements driving its evolution. While challenges such as debugging and performance tuning persist, emerging solutions promise to enhance its practicality. Developers and researchers who invest in declarative methodologies will be at the forefront of **the next era of programming**, shaping more efficient and maintainable software systems.

Industry Adoption Trends

Declarative programming is seeing widespread adoption across industries due to its ability to simplify complex system management, improve maintainability, and reduce human error. In cloud computing, DevOps practices rely on declarative Infrastructure as Code (IaC) tools like Terraform and AWS CloudFormation, which enable engineers to define system states rather than writing imperative scripts. Similarly, in artificial intelligence and data analytics, frameworks such as TensorFlow and SQL-based query systems employ declarative paradigms to abstract away execution complexities. As organizations seek to improve automation, scalability, and reliability, declarative programming is becoming an essential part of modern software development.

A strong example of declarative adoption is **Terraform**, a widely used IaC tool. With Terraform, users define their desired cloud infrastructure in a declarative language, allowing the tool to compute the necessary operations to achieve that state. Consider a simple Terraform configuration for deploying an AWS S3 bucket:

```
resource "aws_s3_bucket" "example" {
  bucket = "my-declarative-bucket"
  acl    = "private"
}
```

This approach contrasts with imperative scripts, which require manually specifying each step. By focusing on **state rather than process**, declarative programming improves reproducibility and minimizes configuration drift, which is crucial for managing large-scale systems.

Another major area of adoption is **SQL-based data processing**, where users specify what data they need without defining the execution flow. A simple SQL query to fetch customer records illustrates the declarative nature of the language:

```
SELECT name, email FROM customers WHERE country = 'USA';
```

Instead of specifying how to iterate through records, developers **declare** the data they need, and the database optimizer determines the best execution plan. This pattern is widely used in enterprise data processing, showcasing the power of declarative programming in large-scale data-driven applications.

In machine learning, **TensorFlow** provides a declarative API for defining computation graphs. Instead of writing procedural code to execute mathematical operations in a sequence, users **declare** relationships between tensors, enabling the framework to optimize execution. The following example defines a simple TensorFlow computation declaratively:

```
import tensorflow as tf

x = tf.constant(3.0)
y = tf.constant(4.0)
z = x * y

print(z.numpy())  # Output: 12.0
```

Here, the multiplication is not performed immediately. Instead, a computation graph is built, allowing TensorFlow to optimize and execute the operation efficiently.

As declarative programming continues to gain traction, industries are expanding its applications beyond cloud infrastructure and data processing. **Policy-driven security models, low-code/no-code platforms, and blockchain smart contracts** are emerging areas where declarative paradigms are proving valuable. Despite challenges such as debugging and performance optimizations, the demand for declarative approaches is growing, indicating a shift toward **high-level, intent-driven programming** in enterprise and cloud-native environments.

The future of software development will likely see an increased emphasis on declarative programming, making it essential for engineers to understand its principles and best practices. By adopting declarative methodologies, industries can build **more scalable, maintainable, and resilient systems**, ensuring efficiency in large-scale software operations.

Challenges and Limitations

While declarative programming provides numerous advantages, it also presents significant challenges and limitations that must be addressed for effective adoption. One of the primary difficulties is **debugging and error tracing**. Unlike imperative programming, where each step is explicitly defined, declarative programming abstracts control flow, making it difficult to pinpoint the exact cause of an issue. In systems like SQL queries, infrastructure as code (IaC), or functional programming languages, errors may appear indirectly as unintended states rather than explicit failures. This complexity requires specialized debugging tools and techniques to trace back to the root cause.

For example, in SQL, a query might return unexpected results due to **implicit optimizations** performed by the database engine. Consider the following query:

```
SELECT name, age FROM users WHERE status = 'active' ORDER BY created_at;
```

If there is no proper index on created_at, this query could perform inefficiently on large datasets, leading to slow execution times. However, identifying such performance bottlenecks requires **query execution analysis tools** like EXPLAIN ANALYZE in PostgreSQL.

Another challenge is **performance tuning and optimization**. Declarative programming relies on execution engines to determine the best way to achieve the desired state. However, these engines do not always choose the most efficient approach, leading to **suboptimal performance** in large-scale applications. For instance, functional programming languages, which encourage immutability, can cause excessive memory usage due to frequent object allocations. Consider the following Python example using a functional approach:

```
from functools import reduce

numbers = [1, 2, 3, 4, 5]
result = reduce(lambda x, y: x + y, numbers)

print(result)  # Output: 15
```

While this approach is declarative, it may introduce overhead compared to a simple sum(numbers) function, which is internally optimized in Python.

Another major limitation is **learning curve and adoption resistance**. Developers accustomed to imperative programming may find declarative paradigms unintuitive, especially in domains like functional programming, logic programming, or Infrastructure as Code (IaC). Consider a Terraform example:

```
resource "aws_instance" "web" {
  ami           = "ami-0abcdef1234567890"
  instance_type = "t2.micro"
}
```

While this defines the desired infrastructure state, debugging issues such as incorrect instance configurations or dependency resolution requires a different mindset compared to traditional scripting approaches.

Moreover, **tooling and ecosystem maturity** can limit declarative programming adoption. While declarative frameworks like Terraform, Kubernetes, and Ansible are widely used, debugging, performance profiling, and **interoperability with imperative codebases** remain areas needing improvement. Many organizations struggle with transitioning from imperative to declarative models due to **existing system constraints and integration challenges**.

Despite these challenges, declarative programming continues to gain traction due to its scalability and maintainability. Overcoming these limitations requires improved debugging tools, optimized execution engines, and a gradual learning curve for developers. Organizations must **adopt hybrid approaches** to balance declarative efficiency with imperative control where necessary, ensuring smooth integration and maximizing the benefits of declarative methodologies.

Emerging Technologies in Declarative Computing

The landscape of declarative programming is rapidly evolving, driven by emerging technologies that seek to enhance automation, scalability, and abstraction in computing. Innovations in **domain-specific languages (DSLs), AI-driven optimizations, cloud-native declarative frameworks, and quantum programming paradigms** are reshaping how developers interact with complex systems. These technologies aim to further reduce manual configuration efforts while increasing efficiency, reliability, and maintainability.

One of the most significant trends is **AI-assisted declarative programming**, where machine learning models optimize query execution, code generation, and resource management. AI-powered tools such as **Microsoft's PROSE (Programming by Examples)** use declarative paradigms to enable automated data transformation, text processing, and spreadsheet manipulation. Consider a case where AI optimizes an SQL query dynamically based on workload patterns:

```
SELECT customer_id, SUM(purchase_amount)
FROM transactions
WHERE transaction_date >= '2023-01-01'
GROUP BY customer_id;
```

Using AI, the query execution engine can **predict indexing strategies**, **optimize joins**, and **adapt caching mechanisms** to improve performance based on historical query patterns. This approach enhances declarative query optimization beyond static rule-based techniques.

Another major innovation is **cloud-native declarative computing**, exemplified by Infrastructure as Code (IaC) frameworks like **Pulumi and AWS CloudFormation**, which provide declarative configurations for scalable cloud deployments. Kubernetes' **Custom Resource Definitions (CRDs)** extend this concept further by allowing developers to define new declarative abstractions for orchestration. A **Kubernetes deployment in YAML** showcases this principle:

342

```
apiVersion: apps/v1
kind: Deployment
metadata:
  name: web-app
spec:
  replicas: 3
  selector:
    matchLabels:
      app: web
  template:
    metadata:
      labels:
        app: web
    spec:
      containers:
      - name: web-container
        image: my-app:latest
        ports:
        - containerPort: 80
```

This approach eliminates the need for imperative scripting, enabling **automated scaling, self-healing, and resource optimization** in cloud environments.

Declarative programming is also advancing in **blockchain and smart contract development**, where functional programming languages such as **Haskell (for Cardano) and Michelson (for Tezos)** enforce strict mathematical correctness. These languages define contract behavior declaratively, minimizing the risk of security vulnerabilities. For instance, in Ethereum's Solidity, developers are moving towards **functional-like smart contract execution** to enhance readability and security:

```
mapping(address => uint) balances;

function transfer(address recipient, uint amount) public {
    require(balances[msg.sender] >= amount, "Insufficient funds");
    balances[msg.sender] -= amount;
    balances[recipient] += amount;
}
```

A new frontier in declarative computing is **quantum programming**, where languages like Qiskit (Python-based) and Silq (functional quantum language) introduce high-level abstractions for quantum state manipulation. **Quantum declarative models** simplify quantum circuit design by focusing on **what operations should achieve** rather than **how they should execute** at a hardware level.

These emerging technologies collectively demonstrate that declarative programming is at the forefront of computing evolution. The shift towards **AI-assisted programming, cloud-native orchestration, blockchain formal verification, and quantum computing** signifies that declarative paradigms will continue shaping next-generation software development, offering **higher efficiency, automation, and security** across diverse industries.

Next Steps for Developers and Researchers

As declarative programming continues to gain momentum, developers and researchers must navigate evolving paradigms, refine best practices, and contribute to the future of declarative computing. The next steps involve **expanding industry adoption, enhancing tooling, integrating AI-driven optimizations, and addressing the challenges of scalability, debugging, and formal verification**. These advancements will ensure that declarative programming remains a core methodology for building efficient, maintainable, and robust software systems.

For developers, the most immediate step is mastering **modern declarative frameworks** such as **Terraform for infrastructure automation, GraphQL for data querying, and functional programming languages like Haskell and Elixir** for business logic. Mastery of declarative paradigms allows engineers to build scalable, resilient systems with **minimal side effects and higher-level abstractions**. For instance, consider an automated **Terraform configuration** that declaratively provisions a cloud-based PostgreSQL database:

```
resource "aws_db_instance" "example" {
    engine          = "postgres"
    instance_class = "db.t3.micro"
    allocated_storage = 20
    username        = "admin"
    password        = "securepassword"
}
```

This approach eliminates manual infrastructure setup, enabling **repeatable, predictable deployments** across environments. Developers should also explore **reactive programming models** like **RxJS (for JavaScript) or Akka Streams (for Scala)** to handle **asynchronous data processing declaratively**.

Researchers, on the other hand, must focus on **optimizing declarative execution models**, improving query planning for large-scale data systems, and innovating in areas such as **formal verification of declarative code**. One promising area of research is **automated debugging for declarative languages**, where AI-driven analysis tools **detect logical inconsistencies** in SQL queries, functional programs, or Infrastructure as Code (IaC) configurations. Consider the case of an **SQL query planner using heuristics to optimize execution**:

```
EXPLAIN ANALYZE
SELECT customer_id, COUNT(*)
FROM orders
WHERE order_date >= '2024-01-01'
GROUP BY customer_id;
```

By analyzing the query execution plan, researchers can devise **automated optimizations**, dynamically reordering filters and aggregations to **minimize execution time**.

Another critical research direction is **AI-assisted declarative programming**, where machine learning models **generate, validate, and refine declarative code**. For instance, tools like **GitHub Copilot** can already suggest SQL queries or functional transformations

344

based on developer intent. The next frontier involves **explainable AI (XAI) techniques for declarative models**, ensuring that AI-driven code suggestions **remain interpretable, verifiable, and aligned with business logic**.

Furthermore, formal methods like **dependent types in Haskell or Isabelle/HOL theorem proving** offer robust verification for declarative software. A key goal is to **bridge formal logic and real-world engineering**, enabling mission-critical systems in **finance, healthcare, and cybersecurity** to leverage declarative correctness guarantees.

Developers should embrace **modern declarative tools and patterns**, while researchers should tackle challenges in **debugging, AI-assisted programming, and formal verification**. The next phase of declarative programming will be **defined by automation, scalability, and correctness**, ensuring that declarative paradigms continue to shape the future of software engineering.

Review Request

Thank you for reading "Declarative Programming: A High-Level Approach to Simplified Logic and Readability"

I truly hope you found this book valuable and insightful. Your feedback is incredibly important in helping other readers discover the CompreQuest series. If you enjoyed this book, here are a few ways you can support its success:

1. **Leave a Review:** Sharing your thoughts in a review on Amazon is a great way to help others learn about this book. Your honest opinion can guide fellow readers in making informed decisions.

2. **Share with Friends:** If you think this book could benefit your friends or colleagues, consider recommending it to them. Word of mouth is a powerful tool in helping books reach a wider audience.

3. **Stay Connected:** If you'd like to stay updated with future releases and special CompreQuest series offers, please visit my author ptofile on Amazon at https://www.amazon.com/stores/Theophilus-Edet/author/B0859K3294 or follow me on social media facebook.com/theoedet, twitter.com/TheophilusEdet, or Instagram.com/edettheophilus. Besides, you can mail me at theo.edet@comprequestseries.com, or visit us at https://www.comprequestseries.com/.

Thank you for your support and for being a part of our community. Your enthusiasm for learning and growing in the field of Declarative Programming is greatly appreciated.

Wishing you continued success on your programming journey!

Theophilus Edet

Embark on a Journey of ICT Mastery with CompreQuest Series

Discover a realm where learning becomes specialization, and let CompreQuest Series guide you toward ICT mastery and expertise

- **CompreQuest's Commitment**: We're dedicated to breaking barriers in ICT education, empowering individuals and communities with quality courses.

- **Tailored Pathways**: Each book offers personalized journeys with tailored courses to ignite your passion for ICT knowledge.

- **Comprehensive Resources**: Seamlessly blending online and offline materials, CompreQuest Series provide a holistic approach to learning. Dive into a world of knowledge spanning various formats.

- **Goal-Oriented Quests**: Clear pathways help you confidently pursue your career goals. Our curated reading guides unlock your potential in the ICT field.

- **Expertise Unveiled**: CompreQuest Series isn't just content; it's a transformative experience. Elevate your understanding and stand out as an ICT expert.

- **Low Word Collateral**: Our unique approach ensures concise, focused learning. Say goodbye to lengthy texts and dive straight into mastering ICT concepts.

- **Our Vision**: We aspire to reach learners everywhere, fostering social progress and enabling glamorous career opportunities through education.

Join our community of ICT excellence and embark on your journey with CompreQuest Series.